THE BLACK BUTTERFLY

MARCUS WOOD

The Black Butterfly

BRAZILIAN SLAVERY AND THE
LITERARY IMAGINATION

WEST VIRGINIA UNIVERSITY PRESS
MORGANTOWN 2019

Copyright © 2019 by West Virginia University Press
All rights reserved
First edition published 2019 by West Virginia University Press
Printed in the United States of America

ISBN
Cloth 978-1-949199-02-4
Paper 978-1-949199-03-1
Ebook 978-1-949199-04-8

Library of Congress Cataloging-in-Publication Data
Names: Wood, Marcus, author.
Title: The black butterfly : Brazilian slavery and the literary imagination / Marcus Wood.
Other titles: Brazilian slavery and the literary imagination
Description: Morgantown, West Virginia : West Virginia University Press, 2019. | Includes index.
Identifiers: LCCN 2019019869| ISBN 9781949199024 (cloth) | ISBN 9781949199031 (paperback) | ISBN 9781949199048 (Ebook)
Subjects: LCSH: Brazilian literature–19th century–History and criticism. | Brazilian literature–20th century–History and criticism. | Alves, Castro, 1847-1871–Criticism and interpretation. | Machado de Assis, 1839-1908–Criticism and interpretation. | Cunha, Euclides da, 1866-1909–Criticism and interpretation. | Slavery in literature. | Slavery–Brazil–History. | Abolitionists–Brazil–History. | Africans–Brazil–History. | Blacks–Brazil–History. | BISAC: LITERARY CRITICISM / Caribbean & Latin American. | SOCIAL SCIENCE / Slavery.
Classification: LCC PQ9550 .W66 2019 | DDC 869.09/35881–dc23
LC record available at https://lccn.loc.gov/2019019869

Book and cover design by Than Saffel / WVU Press

Contents

List of Illustrations vii

Introduction 1
1. Castro Alves, *O Navio Negreiro*,
   and a New Poetics of the Middle Passage 13
2. Castro Alves, *Voices of Africa*, and the
   Paulo Afonso Falls: From Afro-Brazilian Monologic
   Propopeia to Brazilian Plantation Anti-Pastoral 47
3. Obscure Agency: Machado de Assis Framing Black Servitudes 82
4. "The child is father to the man": Bad Big Daddy and the Dilemmas
   of Planter Patriarchy in *Memórias Póstumas de Brás Cubas* 135
5. Magnifying Signifying Silence: Afro-Brazilians
   and Slavery in Euclides da Cunha, *Os Sertões* 171
6. After-Words and After-Worlds: Freyre, Llosa,
   Slavery, and the Cultural Inheritance of *Os Sertões* 218
Conclusion 245

Notes 277
Index 307

Illustrations

1. Detail from Turner, *Slave Ship* 31
2. Stahl, *Paulo Afonso Falls* 64
3. Azevedo, *Polka-Lundu* 119
4. Agostini, *Law of the Sixty Year Olds* 121
5. Paff, "Slave Performing as Carrier for Child" 147
6. *Corpse of Antonio Conselheiro* 174
7. *Surviving Prisoners at Canudos* 175
8. Coutinho, "Bodarrada" 263

Introduction

The Black Butterfly: Brazilian Slavery and the Literary Imagination is first and foremost a tripartite study of one narrow but intensely fertile subject area, namely slavery, in the writing of three of Brazil's most important creative writers, Castro Alves, Machado de Assis, and Euclides da Cunha. The book, however, also incorporates an introduction and conclusion that set these key figures in wider literary contexts. The introduction thinks about Alves, Assis, and da Cunha against the backdrop of later populist Brazilian authors writing on race, and Gilberto Freyre in particular. There is also a brief consideration of Caribbean Negritude writing and its relevance for Alves and Assis in particular. The conclusion sets up a wider literary context for my core authors by introducing a comparative study of their great literary abolitionist predecessors Luís Gonzaga Pinto da Gama and Joaquim Nabuco. The conclusion also considers the dubious status of what has been claimed to be Brazil's only surviving slave narrative, written by Mahommah G. Baquaqua. Alves was writing in the latter half of the nineteenth century, but his major poems on slavery discussed in this book were all published after his death (1871) in the late 1870s and into the 1880s. *Memórias Póstumas de Brás Cubas* (*The Posthumous Memoirs of Brás Cubas*), technically Assis's most experimental work, and also the work containing his most subtle and devastating treatments of slavery, came out in 1880, eight years before the Lei Áurea, the Brazilian Abolition Law, was passed in May 1888. Assis died in 1908. Two other novels containing significant material on race and slavery were published: in 1904, *Esaú e Jacób* (*Esau and Jacob*), and in 1908, *Memorial de Ayres* (*Counselor Ayres' Memorial*). Da Cunha published his masterpiece *Os Sertões* (The Backlands) in 1902, although he worked on the manuscript for the previous five years. *The Black Butterfly* provides the first comparative extended study of how slavery and its cultural legacies have been creatively approached in very different intellectual, formal, and political ways by three exceptionally bold experimenters. The opening discussions of each key author in chapters 1, 3, and 6 provide detailed introductory considerations of why and how each author has been constructed around the aesthetics of Atlantic slavery. This short introduction serves a different function and provides a brief and more general consideration of the cultural gulf *The Black Butterfly* is designed to fill, globally.

One reason this book happened is because Brazilian literature, even the very greatest Brazilian literature, is still not very widely known outside Brazil, and it should be. Terry Caesar stated quite simply in 1999: "If the country of Brazil has an extremely marginal place in American literature, the literature of Brazil has none. Its greatest writer, Machado de Assis, remains virtually unknown (as he is in most of the rest of the world)."[1] This was even then a bit of an overstatement and in the first two decades of the new millennium things have improved a little, but not that much. It remains true that all three of the figures I consider here have been, and continue to be, largely marginalized and ignored outside Brazil. This study hopes to change that state of affairs.

Another reason I wanted to write the book relates to my obsession with slavery and cultural representation. Compared to North America, Brazilian slavery studies are still in their infancy. The most important literary responses to Afro-Brazilian culture and the inheritance of slavery remain almost unknown outside Brazil. Given the undeniable strength in imaginative and creative depth of Brazilian literature, it is odd that these writers have no global profile. Alves, as a Romantic poet with passionate liberationist politics, deserves to be as famous as William Blake or Lord Byron; Assis as an experimental modernist deserves to be as well known as Marcel Proust or James Joyce; da Cunha as cultural fantasist, mythographer, and narrator of revolutions deserves to be as celebrated as Thomas Carlyle or Victor Hugo.[2] Each of these Brazilian authors forged a quite distinctive creative space around slavery and its inheritance in Brazil, and yet the works in which they achieved this have not been integrated in any meaningful way into the Atlantic slavery archive, or indeed into the literary canon of Atlantic slavery studies, and the passionate and increasingly voluminous debates it has generated. *The Black Butterfly* was written in order to inaugurate a sea change in the form of a book that explains, from my inevitably European perspectives, the unique contribution of each of these Brazilian geniuses to our understanding of cultural and social life in Brazil under slavery. The book is also written in the knowledge that Brazilian cultural responses to slavery have insights that can teach Europe and America in profound ways about our inherited blindness and closure. There is reluctance within Europe's first Slave Power Nations (Portugal, Spain, Holland, Britain, and France) to see the memory of slavery as a bleeding wound. It is a wound that we have not begun to search, let alone staunch, a wound that remains open and toxic; the infection is only scabbed over. That the negative white energies that gave rise to slavery live on is evident in the precise forms of discrimination, racism, violence, denial, and sexual fetishizing of the black body that continue to thrive and to be sanctioned.

Brazilian Cultural Memory and Colonization: Jorge Amado as a Test Case

What does the rest of the world demand from Brazilian literature, and why does it seem to translate so badly to other cultures? Only one Brazilian author from any period has popular "Super Star" status outside Brazil, and that author is Jorge Leal Amado de Faria, commonly known as Jorge Amado. In terms of sales, number of novels translated, and film and television adaptations, Amado has no competitors inside or outside Brazil.[3] Since his death in 2001, this popularity has continued to rise. Without doubt Amado is the author who has traveled best without being completely lost in translation, yet the terms of his acceptance and "translation" are illuminating. The version of Amado that Europe and America embraces in many ways is the Amado they demanded and created.

Amado began his career as a serious political novelist with a passionate agenda directed at exposing the suffering of Brazil's poorest agricultural workers, and at sympathetically treating aspects of the Afro-Brazilian culture of the North East, and its Africanist elements in particular. Working as both novelist and journalist, Amado's early hard-hitting political work climaxed with *Terras do sem fim* (1942; translated as *The Violent Land*, the title means literally "lands without end"), a brutal treatment of Brazil's cacao laborers. Yet this work, and this opening phase of Amado's career, did not make him popular in Brazil, or internationally well known. The exception was his recognition by leftist intellectuals in Paris, and his novel *Jubaiabá* was favorably assessed in a short review by no less a figure than Albert Camus. Amado's early books were dangerous enough to be burned publicly in Brazil by the Vargas dictatorship in 1937. He was deemed too political, too extreme, and a little too difficult, and he ended up with several stints in prison and lived for various periods in exile in Argentina, Uruguay, Czechoslovakia, and Stalinist Russia from the 1930s through to the 1950s, as repayment for his pains. Amado then, for whatever reasons, changed direction during the period 1954 onwards and started writing politically less heavy, and culturally more playful, crowd pleasers. The work started to have an eye open for the exoticist fantasies of Brazil's North East that would go down well not only with Brazil's white elite readership (influenced by the proclivities of the "Regionalist" movement) but with the expectations and demands of liberal European and North American audiences. These were large novels, rather reassuringly old fashioned if not backward looking, and almost Dickensian or Hugo-esque in terms of plot and character construction.

It was the publication in 1958 of *Gabriela, Cravo e Canela* (1958, *Gabriella, Clove and Cinnamon*) that Amado hit the big time in Brazil, selling eight hundred thousand copies in six months in what remained a largely illiterate country. The television series based on this Romcom paean to the cult of the spicy *mulatta* had an audience in Brazil of over twenty-five million. The book became Brazil's first novelistic global hit, becoming a bestseller in translation in Europe and North America. Amado's international reputation was then cemented with a series of subsequent titles, none of which hit the sales and distribution heights of *Gabriella*. The most popular of these late works were *Dona Flor e seus dois maridos* (1966; *Dona Flor and Her Two Husbands*; film, 1978), *Tenda dos Milagres* (1969; *Tent of Miracles*; film 2011), *O Sumiço da Santa* (1988; *The War of the Saints*). In these books Amado had clearly abandoned the hard-line politics and style of the early work and turned himself into a sort of living fantasy of what the ideal Bahian, Brazilian author should look like and read like. Amado was a self-publicist of genius, who presented precisely the type of comforting patriarchal white North East Brazilian liberal whom Western liberal readers desired. He packaged black Brazil for an international clientele; indeed, Amado the man has a claim to be the ultimate Brazilian cultural export package. He was a self-described Communist who confessed or at least publicly claimed that he had never read a word of Marx, and who had no problem befriending extreme right-wing politicians in Salvador Bahia. He was an antiracist who saw the solution to Brazil's racial divisions to lie in unlimited miscegenetic free love, and who had a capacity to create mulatta heroines with a highly predictable, delectable, and mildly pornographic soft core. He was a celebrant of Bahia's Afro-Brazilian cultures, but he celebrated them in ways that could be easily absorbed and patronized by white elites in Brazil, America, or Europe. He was above all a reassuring cultural presence, a Bahian *vade mecum*, dishing up cultural stereotype after cultural stereotype, and operating hand in hand with Gilberto Freyre's homemade regionalist anthropology. Freyre hailed from just up the Slave Coast in Recife, and his sensualist take on mixed-race Brazil also traveled well in translation to Europe and North America. Amado and Freyre boiled Brazilian Africanity down to the stereotypes desired by international readerships—African cooking (*arroz com feijão* [black beans and rice], *bacalhau* [the salt cod dish of the slaves], the *feijoada* [which in traditional form involves cooking every part of the whole pig but which European celebrity chefs have now murdered with over-refinement]). They also prioritized African-evolved dance forms (Bossa Nova, Bahian carnival and samba queens, *batuque*), African art (miracle painting, the paraphernalia of *Candomblé* ceremonies, costumes of the gods, "ethnic" sculpture) and Afro-Brazilian religious intellectual gurus and *capoeira* masters (the libidinous, autodidact, intellectual Pedro Archanjo, hero of Amado's novel *Tent of Miracles*, is the *locus classicus*).[4]

Amado did not by any means go uncriticized for his chameleon cultural changes and ambivalence. In old age and after his death there was some coruscating criticism accusing him of being a cultural sellout. Yet to give him his due Amado had a much more biting critical presence than Freyre, and never completely lost his political teeth.[5] Indeed he remained something of an ideological wolf in sheep's clothing and actually smuggled in some rather radical satiric agendas in the later work, particularly the whacky *Tent of Miracles*. This is an attack on Brazil's increasing cultural subservience to the United States. It is also, however, an attack on the American imposition of its cultural fantasies *of* Brazil *onto* Brazil and of Brazil's absurd alacrity in embracing this parodic version of itself.[6]

What is finally educative about Amado's international celebrity, and the reason I have called him up as an introductory contextual backdrop for this book, lies in the way he is clearly split into the two halves of his literary life, before and after 1958. The difficult early work, with its committed hard-line Communist agenda, remains neglected even within Brazil. The comfy rehashing of Bahia as an all singing all dancing exotic, erotic, cultural melting pot in *Gabriella* and the novels that followed is what made Amado into the current cozy custodian of Bahian international identity. It seems then that it is only when Brazilians start to travesty and to parody their national culture in accordance with the demanded fictional expectations evolved in Europe and North America that they get noticed, accepted, and digested by Europe and North America. This is an old story, as applicable to Carmen Miranda, or the Euro-American cultural colonization of *capoeira*, as it is to Jorge Amado. This process, whereby the Western center kidnaps the cultural iconography of Black Brazil and then reinjects it into the country of origin in grotesquely simplified versions, is not a form of Creolization but of racist distortion. The most extreme forms of such misrepresentation are to be found in the novel *Brazil*, published in 1994 by the American novelist John Updike. Updike perverted the writings of da Cunha and Gilberto Freyre, and his novel was widely read in Brazil. None of the authors I analyze in *The Black Butterfly* produced texts open to such processes of possessive assimilation. Alves, Assis, and da Cunha remain, in their very different ways, true to their Brazilian cultural agendas and resistant to caricature. Ironically, it is their very "Brazilian-ness," together with the comparative obscurity of the

Portuguese language, and the difficulty of each author's uniquely complicated style, that explains why they have not as yet been embraced by mass readerships in Europe and North America.

One motive for writing *The Black Butterfly* is, then, didactic and educative, a desire to break the cultural mold still surrounding, delimiting, and conditioning how English and Americans want their Brazilian poetry and fiction served up, particularly in the areas of Afro-Brazilian culture and slavery. Yet there are several other reasons, beyond a commitment to familiarization, why I felt that it was necessary to write this book.

Brazil's Creative Resistance to the Myth of the Emancipation Moment

Brazil has consistently responded culturally to the memory of slavery in ways very different from those of Europe and North America. Outside Brazil these differences have not been thought about very much, and are indeed difficult to carry over cultural divides. Europeans and Americans have grown up with, and grown into, their own established fictions of slavery and post-slavery culture. As I have argued at great length elsewhere, these fictions are often predicated upon a sort of "Moral Big-Bang" theory of origination. In this narrative the foregrounding of emancipation as a beautiful gift from the slave power, to the slave populations, is of paramount importance. An explosive Emancipation Moment is foregrounded that emerges as both a legal and mystical instant of an-nihilistic cleansing, a process of closure and paradoxical rebirth.[7] The Emancipation Moment is overseen by a series of "Great Emancipators," white patriarchal moral colossae, the Wilberforces, Schoelchers, Lincolns, and Nabucos embedded within the nationalistic mythologies of each of the Atlantic slavery superpowers. The story goes that after an agonistic battle, the slave powers of Europe and the Americas travel through a moral "dark night of the soul" in which they confront their sin. They then emerge into a triumphant form of cultural apotheosis, often configured as a variant of the biblical *Jubilee*, in which they "give" the slaves their freedom and a new post-slavery age of enlightenment and universal freedom begins.[8] Brazil of course provided its own potent variations on this theme, and yet the work of Alves, Assis, and da Cunha ingeniously, committedly, and terrifyingly refuses such clean-cut fictional options.[9] *The Black Butterfly* is concerned to think about how these authors evolved a uniquely honest creative legacy that denied Anglo-American abolitionism's mythic norms. Alves, Assis, and da Cunha were each driven to confront the most unspeakable elements of slavery and memory. As a result, their work occupies a unique space within the cultural archive of Atlantic slavery. Each writer develops a personal vision and style in which slavery emerges as an ungainly, horrifying, and above all a living legacy. Slavery is conformed as a confused and confusing inheritance in which Brazil will always have to negotiate and reapproach how slavery's buried and obscured enormities can be uncovered and reinvented.

I have been working on Brazil's cultural responses to slavery for a long time, and much of my work in this area so far has focused on visual culture. I have now written at length about the popular woodcut and lithographic print culture of nineteenth-century Brazil, and what elements in this tradition stand for if compared with Europe and North America. I have done a similar comparative study of nineteenth-century photography in Brazil and what it is that separates this slavery archive from any other. I have also thought about Afro-Brazilian culture, and syncretic religion in particular, and again about what is unique here in terms of how slavery and Africanity are remembered. This work has taken me into museum studies and into thinking about which institutions remember slavery in Brazil and how they do this.[10] Yet I have not, up to this point, tackled Brazil's major writers of poetry and fiction in terms of what they have to say about slavery that is different from anyone else. Assis, Alves, and da Cunha, the *crème de la crème* of the Brazilian literary canon, emerge as the creations of an energized set of vital and combative literary experiments, reinventing the cultural memory of slavery in ways that we are still trying to come to grips with.

Over the last thirty years I have read and reread the three greatest writers working in Brazil during the latter stages of slavery and in the two decades immediately following the emancipation law of 1888. The more deeply I absorbed their work, the more it became evident that each of these authors poses unique problems when it comes to responding creatively to Atlantic slavery and its workings and inheritance in Brazil. They also pose a series of perhaps unsolvable problems in terms of making their work comprehensible to literary markets outside Brazil. I wanted to solve, or inaugurate the process of thinking through, aspects of these problems. The importance of such work lies in the fact that da Cunha and Assis have not, so far, been seen as centrally engaged with race and slavery in their work. I decided that the best way to do this was through immersion and propinquity, and good old-fashioned close reading. Alves, Assis, and da Cunha are each inimitable and untranslatable; they draw on Brazilian Portuguese as a language and as a space of cultural intermission in ways that cannot easily be moved into any other diction or idiom. In trying somehow to uncover the layers of meaning locked up in each author's words, I hope to pluck out at least a part of the heart of their mystery, and bring it into the English-speaking world.

Slavery, Memory, and Brazil's Intimate Ambiguity

I would argue that ambiguity, and profoundly humorous or seriously ludic ambiguity, is a key element in each author, but an element approached very differently by each of them. Slavery and laughter is one deeply disturbing lowest common denominator which these great writers share. With Castro Alves the ambiguity shades into a furious satiric black humor that evolves out of intense crafted word play, and is the result of working a poetic diction hard, fully aware of the complete range of etymological implications contained in each word. With Assis the ambiguity is of a more Borgesian type and comes from playing games with narrational dependability and with apparently stereotyped and stable plot structures and character set-ups, which are suddenly bent beyond recognition. With da Cunha the ambiguity comes out of terrific formal transplantations. He toys with form and formal expectations in ways that uproot, morph, ironize, and reconstitute whole genres and narrative typologies.

What all three authors also share is an ability to achieve an extraordinarily heightened intimacy around their artistic investigations of slavery. With Alves this intimacy comes out of the narrational persona of the poet himself. His passion, be it outrage, love, empathy, or hatred, could easily become absurdly self-indulgent melodrama. Alves as narrational entity constantly stands on the brink of catastrophe, both in terms of what he writes about and how he writes about it. It is the way in which this Alvesian hyperintensity destabilizes not only language but symbolic structures that takes the verse beyond conventional effects of hyperbole and into a new frighteningly unstable visionary linguistic world. The instability is generated around a single pressure, namely the intense psychological sorrows that saturate slave societies. Yeats, thinking about political commitment and the zeitgeist in Europe just after World War I, warned with a somewhat fatuous arrogance that "The best lack all conviction, while the worst / Are full of passionate intensity." Alves confounds such easy distinctions: he is all reasoned conviction yet full of passionate intensity.

What saves Alves's verse from sentimental self-indulgence is his insane emotional commitment to moral outrage. Alves puts wrath and high seriousness center stage; he not only claims but he constitutes the moral high ground. The destabilization of meaning within his poetic diction comes from the intensity of his feeling for the slave body, and his outrage puts language under such pressure that it sucks up contradiction and becomes capable of articulating opposing fictions simultaneously. His ecstatic fury over the question of slavery has a distilled intensity that is unique within the Romantic canon. His rhetoric takes us into a space of maniacal outrage and raw moral *agon* that remains distinctive. Alves can call upon the stripped-down diction of Greek tragedy at its moments of most extreme suffering, yet also often anticipates the necessary stylistic excesses of Negritude Surrealism. Alves's O *Navio Negreiro* moves into a territory of ironic bleak comic extremity that is close to René Depestre and Aimé Césaire. In many ways Alves also enabled the experimental symbolism of Cruz e Souza. Alves seems to share with the Césaire of *Notebook of a Return to My Native Land* the sense that in order to write through, and do justice to, something as mad, incomprehensible, and emotionally unprecedented as Atlantic slavery, a new, mad, unstable, unforeseen creative diction must be evolved. Whitman asked "Do I contradict myself" and happily concluded "Very well then I contradict myself": for Alves the unique horror of slavery demands that it be configured in a new horrible creative language where contradictions live together symbiotically.

With Assis the intimacy is very different, generated around the precise exploration of social conditions within the sophisticated center of what was then Brazil's capital, Rio de Janeiro. Assis gets into the banal affluent capitalist environment of mid- to late nineteenth-century Rio. He explores the uncomfortable tensions around how the superficially benign and civilized social sphere of Rio's emergent middle class relates to the extremes of suffering, disempowerment, and poverty in which slaves, and disempowered poor whites, are forced to exist. The sudden violence, and occasionally full-blown Gothic horrors, inflicted upon slaves by their owners are presented and announced by urbane white voices in affluent town houses, complete with gas lighting and good plumbing. In these apparently advanced social settings, the most horrible things happen but appear as reasonable, indeed inevitable, and often as all but invisible. It is the delicacy, urban sophistication, moral self-blinding, and astounding hypocrisy of his white characters that make Assis's anatomization of the Slave Power uniquely valuable. Assis's slave owners are terrible in their normality, morally outrageous in their snide contentedness. Slave owners appear as distinctively modern urban creatures— sophisticated, sympathetic, rich, rather bored, tired, feckless, sarcastic, and above all civilized gentlefolk. They whisper, rather seductively, the most terrible things into our ears. Assis creates a ghastly social and characterizational environment, as if Laurence Sterne, Jane Austen, and the Marquis de Sade could all be fused around the ownership and persecution of slaves, in a single suburban drawing room, in fin de siècle Rio, or come to that a modern Saudi household in a mews in South Kensington or Marble Arch.

Da Cunha is even harder to work out than the other two. On the face of it he seems to want to excise black bodies, miscegenation, plantation slavery, slave rebellion, and the torture of the slave body from his account of the Canudos Rebellion and the life of Antonio Conselheiro in the barren backlands of North East Brazil. Yet as his peculiar literary edifice progresses, it becomes apparent that his approach to slavery, and its dominance of the North East coast of Brazil, is at the center of his artistic vision. It is, however, through indirections, and through vast transformative, indeed genuinely epic metaphor, that his mystical meditation on slavery and Afro-Brazilianism emerges. At the climax of *Os Sertões* it is through chains of imagery growing out of precise, sensual, and extended landscape description that an intensely emotional engagement with slavery suddenly shoots up and comes into sharp focus. Da Cunha finally, ironically, almost it seems in spite of himself, fights through to some of the most uplifting rhetoric ever created to celebrate violent slave resistance. His tortured and suffering landscape descriptions emerge as terrific manifestations of the agony of the slave body, and of the social upheavals Brazil underwent in the immediate aftermath of the abolition of slavery and monarchy and the introduction of a tenuous republic. He uses the gorgeous minutiae of the natural world to take us into the darkest places of slavery.

The Black Butterfly—What Does It Mean?

"He uses the gorgeous minutiae of the natural world to take us into the darkest places of slavery." This sentence not only essentializes da Cunha's method but also takes me back to my title, "Black Butterfly" or "*Borboleta Preta.*" The metaphoric games Assis plays with the details of the natural world and its abuses under the shadow of slavery combine an observational precision and symbolic resonance reminiscent of the protosurreal intensity of Hieronymus Bosch's *Temptation of St. Anthony*. Early in Assis's *Posthumous Memoirs*, the recently deceased paradoxical narrator Brás Cubas casually destroys a large and lovely black butterfly. The creature has fluttered into his room, settled upon Brás Cubas's head, and then settled on a photograph of his father and obscured his father's face. The fate of the butterfly and the treatment of its corpse are central to my analysis of Assis's metaphoric explanations of the corruption generated by slavery. My consideration of this episode constitutes the climax of the discussion of Assis below, and needs no further elaboration here.[11] With regard, however, to justifying the use of the strange image of the *borboleta preta* for this book's title, I would stress that Assis's perfect black butterfly and its amoral physical obliteration is an open sign. It is a sign opening into a dark space that can then extend itself to embrace all white cruelty, both planned and arbitrary, and all black slave suffering. The gorgeous black butterfly is stupidly destroyed by Brás Cubas with the flick of a towel, its dying body left out for ants to devour. The creature, its death, and the disposal of its corpse form a little bleak parable that takes in all the black bodies randomly exploited and casually laid waste by slavery. The illogical cruelty of this death stands beside other profound creative examinations of spontaneous acts of white murder where the colonial victim is simply the wrong color or shape, or just in the wrong place at the wrong time. This killing might be another version, a very corrupt bourgeois version, of the "hellish thing," which the motiveless Mariner does to the pure white Albatross of Coleridge, or the outwardly inexplicable petulant shooting of the Arab by Meursault in Camus's *The Outsider*. In the end it seems that white people, once invested in a notion of power, will inexplicably and spontaneously kill beautiful things for no reason. Their motive seems to be an irrational fear and an instinctive violence, or perhaps nothing more complex than the fact that those with the power can do absolutely anything they want.

Camus and Coleridge do not let their white murderers get away with it, however; they hold them morally accountable for their actions at great, if not interminable, length. Assis, because he is dealing with slavery and slave owners, because he is dealing with a Brazilian capacity for complacent self-deception, and because he is never indulgently self-righteous, wants to explain that this is a world where there is no moral accountability and no aesthetic retribution. This is a world of complete moral depravity where nobody cares about good or evil, or about who is to blame for depraved actions. Here Brás Cubas, the slave owner, delights to meditate upon his crime, and explains away his actions in a bout of self-serving logic chopping which ends in a casual racist quip. Slavery is a world where the black butterfly has been, and will continue to be, tortured and murdered for no good reason, indeed for no reason at all. The butterfly's blackness bleeds into racial significations, disconcertingly referred to as both *a borboleta preta* and *a borboleta negra*, these two words bringing in a plethora of meanings submerged in slavery. Both words imply both the color black and also have racial significations for black slaves and emotional intimations of somberness, darkness, obscurity, much like the associations Edmund Burke attaches to blackness in his definition of the Sublime. The words also carry racist associations:

in slang, "negro" and the feminine form "negra" mean "nigger" or "darkey."[12] Slavery thrives on the fact that it is a world of absolute power, absolute hatred, and absolute racial divisions, where slave owners can do whatever they want to do to their black butterflies at any time and in any space. Brás Cubas's analysis ironically prefigures an insight that the great Martiniquean negritude poet Aimé Césaire would articulate with an angry black humor in *Notebook of a Return to My Native Land*:

> L'homme famine, l'homme-insulte, l'homme-torture
> On pouvait à n'importe quel moment le saisir le rouer
> De coups, le tuer—parfaitement le tuer—sans avoir
> De compte à rendre à personne sans avoir d'excuse à
> Présenter à personne[13]

> (The famine man, the insult man, the torture man, it is of no importance which moment you seize him, beat him up, kill him—absolutely, kill him—without having to pay account, without having to make excuses to anyone.)

The white operates outside reason in a mental space where a deep loathing of absolute blackness is the bottom line. This instinctive and finally murderous prejudice is slavery's darkest inheritance. As Brás Cubas curtly observes in his final evaluation of the blackness of this butterfly and its accompanying dark fate: "ela era melhor ter nascido azul" (it would have been better if it had been born blue). If it is born black, then too bad; in the eyes of white slaveholders and their descendants, it is "negra," "preta," a "nigger," and it is doomed. The mild-mannered Brás Cubas tosses his impenetrable bleak racist determinism in front of us; the only way to avoid the fate that awaits all black beings is to be born a different color. How we read the *borboleta negra* is a metaphoric conundrum that still needs investigation, and that is why I wrote this book.

CHAPTER 1

Castro Alves, *O Navio Negreiro*, and a New Poetics of the Middle Passage

Prologue

Castro Alves (1847–1871) is the most mythical, mythologized, and adored of all Brazilian literary figures. Hugely Romantic (with a very big R) he lived, loved, and died perhaps the ideal Latin American poetic life. He burst upon the Brazilian literary scene, a lovely boy, performing his works to elite literary coteries and to huge theatre audiences in the major cities of the North East coast. By the time he was in his early twenties he had also been in high-profile relationships with a series of glamorous and lovely actresses and singers. At the age of twenty, he was shot in the leg while hunting and had to have his foot amputated, thereafter limping spectacularly and walking with a cane. He never recovered his health, and like all those good Romantics in England (Alves, like Pushkin, adored Byron) he died young and tragically aged twenty-four from tuberculosis. In his short life he poured out white-hot lyric verse and one great drama, *Gonzaga*, which like all his best work is focused on Brazilian slavery and its abolition. From the moment of his death he became public property and the basis for a biographical industry. He generated an explosion of publications and iconography going into every detail of his loves and life, much of it ridiculous, and this is an inheritance that shows no sign of diminishing in Brazil.[1] By 1900 his birth town, Curralinho, was renamed "Castro Alves." By 1949 his life was up on the silver screen in *Vendaval Maravilhoso* (Most Marvellous Tempest), a spectacular biopic evolved out of Jorge Amado's popular guidebook to all things Alvesian, *The ABC of Castro Alves*, which remains a perennial best seller. In 1999 a big-budget docudrama, *Castro Alves Retrato Falado do Poeta* (Castro Alves Picturing the Fame of the Poet), came out to popular acclaim. The Alves publicity juggernaut roles on with another big biopic in the pipeline.

The following study has no interest in this side of Alves whatsoever. In robust sympathy with the wise dictate of François Lyotard that "La biographie c'est imbécillité," I have focused fiercely on the major texts that treat the subject of slavery. These poems are quite simply the most powerful poetical response to the colossal crime of the Atlantic slave trade ever created. Horrible and beautiful, crazily lyrical and yet as propaganda quite practical, these works are a quintessence of the Romantic sublime, and are consequently, like the best of Shelley, inimitable and for all practical purposes wonderfully untranslatable. It is this latter quality that explains why Alves remains very little known outside Brazil, Portugal, and Lusophone Africa. I have consequently tried to place his achievement as a grand cultural synthesizer of the abject sins of Atlantic slavery in comparative perspective wherever possible. I have looked to North American and European contexts and poets when I feel they highlight the unique aspects of Alves's art. When he shuns the cynicism of Heine on the "Middle Passage," it needs noting; when he outshines British and North American abolition literatures, it needs explaining.

Alves is one of the great formal, technical creative experimentalists within Brazilian Romantic verse. He devoted a major proportion of the most important poetry he wrote in his short life to the subject of Brazilian slavery. These poems were so deeply loved and full of impact that Alves was, and still is, quite simply known in Brazil under the sobriquet "O poeta dos Escravos" (the poet of the slaves). Although he assumes a highly rhetorical, indeed hyperbolical, emotionalism at points, he was no sentimental abolitionist. He wrote about slave consciousness with a peculiarly heightened emotionalism, and his fury at Brazilian moral corruption over the issue of slavery often took him close to hysteria and visionary incomprehensibility. At the same time his work maintains a constant gaze that never shifts from uncovering the corrupting myths generated by the white literatures of Atlantic slavery, myths justifying the slave power and misrepresenting Africa. His poetry also ironically sets about exposing how racist myths functioned and morphed. His uniquely inspiring and terrifying work remains alive in the main blood vessels of Brazil's creative circulation, much as William Blake operates in the cultural lifeblood of Great Britain, and Alves is as a moralist equally powerful, ambitious, and inimitable. Alves wrote three astonishing long lyric poems that transform key sites of memory in relation to Atlantic slavery. Those key sites are, first, the imagining of Africa by the slave power; second, the suffering of slaves because of the crime of the Atlantic slave trade and the nature of that crime's inheritance; and third, the intimate relations of slaves within plantation slavery and the impossibility of love within this depraved environment. The following analysis provides close readings of those three poems, namely *Vozes de Africa* (Voices from Africa), *O Navio Negreiro* (The Slave Ship), *A Cachoeira de Paulo Afonso* (The Paulo Afonso Waterfall). All quotations from these poems are from the text of Castro Alves, *The Major Abolitionist Poems*, and I explain the reason for using this edition in the textual note below. All English prose translations are my own.[2] The emphasis of my readings is primarily focused upon what defines the creative inimitability of Alves when it comes to addressing Atlantic slavery's inheritance.

O Navio Negreiro Tragédia do Mar, an Anathema on the *Lusíadas*

Castro Alves completed his great meditation on the maritime slave trade, *O Navio Negreiro Tragédia do Mar*, on April 18, 1868. He then went from Bahia to Rio in the autumn of that year with letters of introduction to literary celebrities. After two private readings, the second to Machado de Assis (what an astonishing scenario!), Alves performed the work publicly to general and often ecstatic acclaim in Rio theatres in September 1868.[3] Thereafter the poem remained lodged deep in the heart of Brazilian culture, reinterpreted by actors, artists, and musicians, up to the present day.

Before the moment of its first performance, there had been no great long poem to come out of the Atlantic diaspora devoted to the slave ships and the thousands of Africans who died at sea. There had of course been enormous and complicated epic works devoted to the rise of the great maritime empires of Portugal and Britain, one, Camões's *Lusíadas*, was the greatest verse epic to come out of the Portuguese Renaissance. Yet over the four hundred years of the existence of the Atlantic slave trade, for all the mountains of propaganda generated for and against the Guinea traders of Portugal, England, France, Spain, Holland, and their colonies, really only one aesthetically significant and groundbreaking poem had been produced on this subject from the sixteenth century until the late 1860s and the performance of *O Navio Negreiro*.[4] Ironically this exception was composed not by a member of one of the leading slavery nations but by the German Heinrich Heine, living self-exiled in Paris and crippled with a spinal condition, writing from what he termed his "matrazengruft" or "mattress-grave." *Das Sklavenschiff* (The Slave Ship) published in 1854 (assuming, as I do, that Coleridge's *Rime of the Ancient Mariner* is not directly a poem on the Atlantic slave trade) remains European Romanticism's only significant poetic treatment of the Middle Passage.[5] Heine's poem was written near the end of his life when he was thinking ironically about nascent capitalism and its effects on humanity, and when he wrote several poems that have been constructed as dark proto-Brechtian attacks on international big business. He was also deeply immersed in thinking about North America and the paradoxes surrounding liberty in the context of slavery and emergent capitalism. Heine had been deeply affected, as had so much of Europe, by Stowe's *Uncle Tom's Cabin*, and he had been impressed by its satiric method in particular. It was in this context that he created *Das Sklavenschiff*, which is above all consummate satire, indeed the greatest piece of ironic black humor ever to damn the slave trade out of the mouth of its imagined primary practitioners, a pragmatic Dutch slave captain and a pimple-nosed ship's doctor.[6] Outside this work, which was well known in Brazilian literary circles in a rather weak French translation entitled *Le Négriere*, which Alves may or may not have seen, there is no major poetry focused on the Middle Passage that might provide an immediate context for Alves.

After Castro Alves, or indeed before him, there is the question, where is Europe or America's great poetry of the slave trade, and where is North America's great slave-trade poem? It is not controversial to observe that from its beginning until now there is very little aesthetically distinguished poetry in American literature on the subject of slavery, while there is virtually none on the subject of the maritime slave trade. What verse there is on the Middle Passage, good and bad, is worth noting.

The thinness of this part of the slavery archive is important to foreground if the exceptionality of Alves's aesthetic choices is to be brought out in a larger comparative cultural context. In North America both Whittier and Longfellow had written shorter poems that do call in ironic ways on the memory of the slave trade and that, in their very different ways, called up the slave ship as a theme. Earlier, now forgotten American poets, the earliest of whom is the formally cumbrous Thomas Branagan, had attempted to mine the Middle Passage as a creative option.

Branagan, an Irish-American ex-slave-ship captain and religious enthusiast, was the first to write an extended poetic treatment of the subject, in book five of his 1805 abolitionist pseudo-Augustan epic *Avenia or a Tragical Lament on the Oppression of the Human Species*.[7] The poem is a stern reminder of the limitations of the propagandistic inheritance of the English-speaking anti-slave trade poets working in the Americas.[8] Reading this work is a harsh lesson in the imaginative and technical gulf separating the American late-Augustan poetic tradition from the late-flowering of Brazilian Romanticism, when it came to an artistic response to the Atlantic slave trade. The following description of the slave hold during a storm is a concise demonstration of both Branagan's technical inability to manipulate the Popean rhyming couplet and of the complete inappropriateness of this essentially satiric and circumlocutory verse form to describe the mass trauma of the Middle Passage:

> During the dire event each slave remains
> Seasick, oppress'd with grief and bound in chains,
> Twice twenty by the hand of death set free,
> And twelve, half starved, were launched into the sea.
> The rest promiscuously to heav'n complain;
> And strive to breathe the wholesome air in vain.
> Down in the stinking hold they vent their woe,
> And down each sable cheek the sorrows flow...[9]

The final couplet with its tastefully encoded reference to human excretion and incontinence, and with its euphemistic objectification of mental anguish, as manifested in the act of weeping, is an exhausted reiteration of a formula that appeared merely thirty lines before describing a female slave: "While down her cheeks the copious sorrows flow, / In loud laments thus deprecates her woe..." Indeed, the poor girl appears completely enchained within Branagan's compulsive rhyming of "woe" with "flow," and is forced to end her lament describing the rape of slave women with the words: "Thus those indulge their lusts, and these their woe, / And here the tears, and there the bumpers flow." It is hard to know if a dirty innuendo is implied in the phallic/vaginal "flowing bumpers" of ship's crew and "flowing tears" of the slaves. Branagan's verse lacks the technical resources to approach a subject as morally complicated and economically prolix as the Atlantic slave trade, let alone America's shifting involvement in this phenomenon.

After Branagan, significant American poets appeared loath to take up the theme of the maritime slave trade. As abolition and slavery became increasingly important themes in American verse in the four decades leading up to the Civil War, the slave trade is indeed conspicuous by its absence. When the subject does make cursory appearances, it is in forms still completely constrained by the excesses, both stylistic and empathetic, of earlier British slavery verse. For example, Sarah Wentworth Morton's 1823 *The African Slave* is a torrid rehashing of various tried-and-tested British abolition tropes. The ordeal of the Middle Passage is both compressed and abstracted into the sentimentalized suffering of a single "princely slave," himself a devolved, distant, and distinctively shabby relation of Aphra Behn's Oroonoko. The poem is written in a paradoxically lurching yet racy variant of the classic ballad stanza. The a-b-a-b octosyllabic quatrains speed along with a gushing jollity, encasing the vast memory of a real suffering within a threadbare circumlocutory idiom:

> See how the black ship cleaves the main,
> High bounding o'er the dark blue wave,
> Remurmuring with the groans of pain,
> Deep freighted with the princely slave![10]

The verse is a strong example of how the theme of the Middle Passage had itself become debilitated in the imagination of American abolition versifiers, encrusted beyond functionality by the barnacles of decades of bellicose British abolition cliché.

When reading *O Navio Negreiro*, it is good to remember the extent to which extreme melodrama, theatrical excess, and demonstrative emotionalism appeared to be the only options when it came to treating the theme of slave death on the Atlantic. And these options were certainly in evidence in the verses two of America's most celebrated nineteenth-century poets composed in relation to the Middle Passage. Henry Wadsworth Longfellow with *The Witnesses* and John Greenleaf Whittier with *The Slave Ships* both weighed in with poems inspired by episodes on the Middle Passage. Whittier's poem, published in 1837, was inspired by a historical event of 1819 and reaches towards a tone of prophetic grandeur. The source narrative for *The Slave Ships* is indeed powerful and works well as a sort of gruesome parable of divine retribution. The French slave ship *Rodeur* endured a final Atlantic crossing that had entered medical history, and had been published as a curiosity in the *Bibliothèque Opthalmologique* for reasons that will become apparent. The facts were these: the slave cargo of the *Rodeur* were suddenly struck down with an eye disease in the middle of the Atlantic crossing and many of the slaves suddenly went blind. The captain of the vessel, still hoping to collect on the insurance of the slaves' lives, and in a gesture already familiar from British abolition's exploitation of the horrific fate of slaves aboard the *Zong*, had the blind ones thrown overboard alive. Subsequently not only the slaves but the entire ship's crew, with the exception of one man, went blind by the time the *Rodeur* finally reached Guadeloupe.

Whittier decided to configure his poetic version of the narrative in two dramatic halves, a sort of "before and after" construction of the tragedy. The first half of the poem is delivered by an omniscient narrator, who also poses ironically as the surviving eyewitness to the event. The captain is set out as a reassuringly piratical old sea dog, a callous devil, who refers to the murdered slaves as "worthless lubbers" and "dead dogs," and encourages his crew in strains preempting Robert Newton's hearty and exotic piratical performances as Long John Silver: "Overboard with them shipmates!" Yet the short journey of the blind slaves from below deck to the open, and their brief respite before being hurled to their deaths, is done with some pathos:

> Up from the loathsome prison
> The stricken blind ones came:
> Below all had been darkness,
> Above, was still the same.
> Yet the holy breath of heaven
> Was sweetly breathing there,
> And the heated brow of fever
> Cooled in the soft sea air.
>
> "Overboard with them shipmates!"
> Cutlass and dirk were plied;
> Fettered and blind, one after one,
> Plunged down the vessel's side.[11]

Whittier, a hands-on abolition activist and consciousness raiser, made no claims for his slavery verse as art, and openly constructed it as manipulative and emotionally charged propaganda that is narrowly occasional. In the preface to his slavery poems he bluntly stated that they were "written with no expectation that they would survive the occasions that called them forth: they were protests, alarm-signals, trumpet calls to action, words wrung from a writers heart, forged in a white-heat."[12] Here, however, he used the awkward and blunt tool of his 7-6-7-6 variant on the ballad stanza to fashion some effective shifts of perspective. It is the metrical unexpectedness that energizes the verse. The clever use of an irregular couplet constantly juxtaposing an opening seven-syllable line against an end stopped six-syllable second line, often dominated by harsh monosyllabic words, means that there is a constant foundering of any optimistic energy against a bleak cold rejoinder. The couplet "Below all had been darkness / Above was still the same" is a good example of how the stark diction and binary oppositions (below/above, slave/free, light/dark) convey the calculating coldness of the world of the slave power.

While Whittier and Longfellow were both popular among Brazilian abolitionists, translations of some of their antislavery verse appearing in Brazilian journals, their slave trade poems did not have an impact on Brazilian abolition propaganda, and were not known to Alves.[13] It is finally no exaggeration to say that *O Navio Negreiro* was, and remains, the only masterpiece in verse solely devoted to the subject of the Middle Passage.[14] After its initial success in performance, the work was only published posthumously in book form in 1880, twelve years after its composition, and well after the poet's death. In many ways the poem could be seen, to put it mildly, as belated. By 1880 the Brazilian slave trade had, at least officially, been abolished for three decades; no other Brazilian abolition writing, in any form in the 1880s, is much interested in the subject of the maritime slave trade. This is hardly surprising if one looks at the overall picture during that decade. By 1880 several of the slave states up in the North East were on the verge of abolishing plantation slavery. The coffee plantations of São Paulo and Rio were experiencing passive-aggressive slave sabotage, including spontaneous slave labor freezes and exodus from plantations.[15] Abolition and emancipation were seen to be, and existed in physical terms as, a mainland phenomenon. The maritime slave trade was ancient history: in the eyes of Brazilians it was a crime conducted by foreigners, and it was no longer part of the current official slavery agenda either when Alves wrote his work, or when it was published. A number of small fast ships were still running slaves from Senegal and even Mozambique, but this was a trickle compared to the trade's heyday. These late slave cargoes were illegal, unregistered, and unnoticed. They ghosted into small ports around Rio and were invisible to authorities because of their clandestine nature and the bribes paid to look the other way, and these slave imports consequently remain invisible to, or unregistered within, the slavery archive.[16]

O Navio Negreiro consequently poses a question—why did Alves turn back to the subject of the Middle Passage at this point? Writing in 1868, his central demand in the poem, namely that the slave trade be immediately abolished, appears anachronistic. Under intense British diplomatic pressure, the Brazilians had legally abolished the slave trade through legislation back in 1850 and 1852. This of course did not mean that inestimable numbers of slaves were not being illegally smuggled into Rio, Bahia, and Recife, not to mention other small ports up and down the Brazilian coast, from Fortaleza to São Paulo. But I don't believe the poem is referring, in a spirit of bleak irony or Heine-esque black humor, to the continuing illicit traffic. The details of the ship in Alves's poem clearly indicate a large boat taking a substantial cargo across the Middle Passage openly. An argument can be made that Alves had a current if ironic political message. Many Brazilians and most Brazilian politicians saw the slave trade as a completely European endeavor, and a crime from which Brazil stood absolved through non-participation. The fact that Brazilian slave traders bought the slaves when they arrived in Brazil was conveniently ignored. In insisting that his slave ship be Brazilian, even to the extent of flying a Brazilian flag, and in harping on the national shame of this fact, Alves was forcing Brazilians to confront their nation's mass involvement in the trade.[17]

Yet, viewed in terms not of immediate political pressure but of creativity and aesthetics, the decision to write about the Middle Passage after the official abolition of the trade needs no special justification and operates outside narrow historical perspectives. Alves's choice is an artistic one, standing naturally alongside another peculiar, willful, and brave gesture. I allude to J. M. W. Turner's painting *Slave Ship* (originally titled *Slavers Throwing Overboard the Dead and Dying, Typhoon Coming On*). This superb oil painting, first exhibited in 1840, is the only other work of high Romantic genius to dare to confront the Middle Passage, and the huge death toll it involved. Turner, like Alves, turned back to the unfashionable subject of mass murder, multiple trauma, and the suffering of slaves at sea. In the early 1840s, thirty-five years after the maritime slave trade had been abolished in Britain, Turner decided British atrocity and murderous greed as manifested in the mass murder of slaves (with the shadow of the Zong outrage hanging in the background) should be taken back on board British memory. With both men there was a decision to return to a dark place that had been hastily and messily disguised and overwritten with the cultural camouflages of abolition and supposed emancipation. Turner and Alves insisted on opening up this mass grave, thinly scabbed over, but floating deep down in the depths of the Atlantic Ocean. Both artist and poet also saw in the slave trade a corruption of maritime trade—of the normal mercantile procedures of exchange, profit, and loss—into something monstrous, which contaminated Nature herself, and which this powerful goddess would not endure without a colossal display of outrage. And with both men the decision had to do with a profound aesthetic inheritance embedded in the sea, and in a national inheritance revolving around voyages of empire and the establishment of maritime domination.

In taking on the subject of the slave trade at sea, Alves was in fact bypassing Anglo-American abolition of the second half of the nineteenth century. Turner aside, the propagandas generated in this period by English and American abolition had largely, as we have seen, turned away from the subject of the slave ship. When Britain had confronted maritime themes within the context of slavery, it was through the filter of a bellicose and self-serving nationalism, developed via a celebration of the British antislavery patrols. Visual art showed heroic English "Tars" liberating emaciated slave cargoes, or presented scenes of slave captivity and sale on the African coast, conducted by French and Spanish slavers.[18] Very few North American authors writing about slavery thought about the oceanic slave trade, and unless one considers Melville's *Moby Dick* a vast but metaphoric assault on the memory of slavery, only Longfellow produced any committed work of significance on the subject.[19] In choosing to take the transatlantic slave trade, and the slave ship in particular, as the theme of his masterpiece, Alves is in fact mainlining straight back into the origin of abolition in the last three decades of the eighteenth century and opening years of the nineteenth.

In Britain the slave trade abolition movement, beginning with Granville Sharpe's focus on the disgraceful insurance battle surrounding the slave ship Zong, and then developing into a popular and Parliamentary political crusade, was focused fairly exclusively upon the Atlantic trade and the horrors of the Middle Passage.[20] This campaign climaxed in the year 1807 when the act abolishing the British slave trade was finally passed. Visual propaganda of astonishing power had been produced as part of this political crusade. Images and texts appeared that brought home the inhumanity of the conditions of the Middle Passage with a confrontational directness that was never to be equaled. The *Plan of the Slave Ship Brookes*, which appeared in 1789, was of course the culmination of efforts in this direction. The image, widely reproduced in various forms in North America and Brazil, has maintained its status as still the most potent, long-lived, and most imitated and parodied piece of visual art ever to approach explicit representation of the trauma of Atlantic slavery in pictorial and ideographic form.[21] In its diagrammatic concision and the forensic coldness of its descriptive method, the work stands in stark, even absolute, opposition to the emotional hyperbole of Alves. Yet within literature, of any form, there had been almost nothing of any quality to come out of Britain or North America. By the time Alves wrote, the Atlantic slave diaspora, the slaving powers of Europe and the Americas, had had almost four hundred years to develop a work that could approach through verse what the Middle Passage meant, or had come to mean. This development quite simply had not happened. Alves alone stood up to the mark and composed a long work capable of the kind of creative amplitude and emotional extremity that in visual terms had been created by Turner.

The poem, as is the case with Alves generally, is not that well known outside Brazil. Within Brazil it is probably the best-known poem generated by Brazilian Romanticism. Alves wrote a lot of poetry devoted to exploring the issue of Brazil's slavery inheritance from a variety of perspectives and in several poetic forms and styles, yet *O Navio Negreiro* is the only piece of his slavery verse, indeed the only poetic work on the subject of slavery, to have remained truly popular and active within Brazilian cultural memory. It is still a poem taught to Brazilian school children, and it has also remained in popular adaptive cultural circulation and generated a series of works by visual artists and musicians, most famously the powerful interpretation of Caetano Veloso.[22] *O Navio Negreiro* is an elaborate, indeed fully blown, product of the most extreme imaginative exponent of Brazilian Romanticism. It is also a poem that in its extraordinary metaphoric ambition, and in the seemingly impossible moves it makes uniting extreme horror with sublime natural beauty, reaches out to mainstream European poetry. The work looks not only backward to Coleridge's *Rime of the Ancient Mariner* with its capacity to make nature and the cosmos embody traumatized human states of mind, but forward to Rimbaud's *Bateau Ivre* (Drunken Boat).[23] The qualities of surrealism, sublimity, metaphoric amplitude, and finally unashamed beauty make Rimbaud's terrific poem the creative soul mate of *Navio Negreiro*.

Alves and Ambiguity

O Navio Negreiro is an extremely dense and allusive poem that is founded upon paradoxes, and that understands that it may finally be impossible to develop a voice capable of capturing the suffering and effacement of Africans lost on the Middle Passage. It is a poem of great ambition in that it is as much about national identity, or the myths of national identity, and about the corruptions of trade, as it is about slavery. Longing, loss, an instinctive empathy with elegy, displacement, and the sorrow of migration and separation are peculiarly Brazilian qualities. The untranslatable concept of "saudade," a sort of impossible bittersweet longing for the place of origin, is a testimony to this, as is the even more powerful Afro-Brazilian concept of "banzo." "Banzo" describes an extreme condition of suicidal melancholia in the mind of the captive African slave when remembering African origins and evolves out of the Bantu word "banza," denoting acute homesickness caused by memories of one's ancestral village.[24] Alves manages to harness his culture's special languages of loss and nostalgia to the subject of slavery. *O Navio Negreiro* is consequently not only still relevant, but absolutely necessary, to the process of understanding slavery and memory within Brazil, and indeed the entire Atlantic slave diaspora.

O Navio Negreiro, like any other great poem, is finally untranslatable, but aspects of its strangeness can be explained. Minute treatment of the bizarre and often contradictory plays on words, double meanings, and etymological tensions uncover some of the unprecedented ways in which this poem combines extreme violence and extreme beauty. To understand the verse, it is essential to see it as grounded in ambiguities of an Empsonian muscular amplitude.[25] Consequently, the poem carries shifting symbolic and narrative meanings, and different parts of it can mean quite distinct things when read in isolation or in relation to other parts. In order to see this, it is necessary to have a keen sense of the poem as a whole complex narrative structure.

The poem is divided into six sections, and the following summary of the argument outlines the narrative structure. Sections one and two concern a celebration of the sea and of the characteristics of oceangoing nations. The first section presents an essentialized and idealized sailing vessel, which the poet seems to inhabit from the famous first words "Stamos em pleno mar" (We are in the open sea), as if reader, vessel, and poet are united on the ocean's surface, but a line that also has the effect of pulling out in a panoramic wide angle.[26] The first section is an extended plea by the poet to be allowed to enter the beautiful mysteries of the life of ships and of maritime exploration. The section ends with a plea to be allowed to become the spirit of the Albatross, the "Leviathan of space" whose wings the poet begs, as a sort of oceanic muse. Of course Alves knew Coleridge's masterpiece, and consequently the introduction of the albatross as symbol casts the shadow of potential natural spoliation, and of a European murderous guilt, across the verse. The allusion to the central act of pointless violence at the core of the *Ancient Mariner*, and Alves's dramatic desire to become the martyred bird, is an iconic shot across the bows, a warning to take heed that when it comes to Alves's imagery what you get, as the poem progresses, is a good deal more than what you are initially allowed to see. The second section shifts from the abstracted ideal of the boat on the sea as an embodiment of the spirit of inspiration to a series of brief meditations upon the national characteristics of the different seagoing peoples of Europe. The Spanish and Italians are remembered in imagery drawing on types of voluptuousness and indolence, and the English and French are similarly typified and caricatured according to national stereotypes. The English mariners emerge as "frio" (cold), and as obsessed with a bellicose nationalism, fastened to the worship of Nelson and his recent martial successes. At this point a hard and historically specific element enters the analysis for the first time. The section ends by opening up the perspective of the European maritime experience by alluding to the Greeks, with their ancient inheritance of the sea stretching back to Homer. The current Greek sailors are pictured singing out the verses that Homer created in agony ("que Homer gemeu"). Which verses exactly Alves is thinking of is left to the viewer to decide, but clearly we are led to think of Ulysses, and the travails of his maritime peregrinations, possibly the words he speaks when lashed to the mast and passing the Sirens' island. The most pointed aspect of this section lies not in what it says, but in what it refuses to say, for it shuts the Portuguese mariners out. The remarkable sailors who linked India, Africa, Europe, and Brazil at an almost impossibly early date, and who formed the inspiration and personnel for the *Lusíadas*, are consigned to a hugely significant silence. This silence will emerge in the incensed irony of the poem's conclusion as a quiet space of deep shame.

From the speculative and seemingly ecstatic celebration of the first two sections the poem plunges, in the six-line single stanza that comprises the third section, into a sudden evocation of a world of horror. The final words are written in a paired down language that is new, and alludes to an infamous and vile world, and in uncanny anticipation of the words of Kurtz ("The horror! The horror!") in Conrad's grim verdict on European colonial crimes in Africa in *Heart of Darkness*. Alves simply announces, "What horror!" (Que horror!). The reader is left on the brink and forced to anticipate what this unexpected vision of depravity might be.

The fourth section is another lesson in economy and compression, the entire horror of the Middle Passage telescoped into one dramatic vignette. Alves focuses on the spectacle of the slaves forced to "dance" on deck in order to maintain their health and strength. Alves may have got this scenario from the grim set-piece slave dance in Heine's *Slave Ship*, but if he did see this treatment he decides to come at the subject in a radically different manner. This one scene, in its grotesquery, perversity, buffoonery, and Dante-esque surrealism, sums up the monstrous inexplicability of the suffering engendered on the slave ships.[27]

The fifth section of the poem is a direct response to slavery's sins, triggered by the enormity of the previous section, and is constructed as a formal address to God, asking who these suffering people are, and answering the question with a compressed portrait of the suffering of the internal slave trade of Africa, and its connection to the Atlantic slave networks. The section also ideally constructs the Africans, whether desert or coastal dwellers, as a form of "noble savage," Rousseauean free spirits enjoying liberty by Natural Right. The section ends by pulling back out to its opening cosmic perspective, and again addressing God, who this time is dramatically called upon to cleanse both himself and the oceans by calling down apocalyptic natural destruction in the form of mighty tempest and typhoon. The invocation for a spectacular divine retribution is a well-established rhetorical trope of abolition. The device energizes a host of earlier British and American abolition poems, and indeed prose fictions. The interrogation of this narrative possibility, tempest as divine retribution, also lies at the heart of Turner's *Slave Ship*.[28]

The concluding sixth section moves into an almost entirely symbolic yet intensely ironic mode, taking up key positive images of Brazilian nationhood and burying them in a ferocious shame. Two central emblematic sights are chosen for assault: the first is the national flag, recent symbol of Brazil's liberty and newly established republic after the war with Paraguay, and the second is Columbus. The flag is now a filthy rag, disgraced, its green and gold drenched in slaves' blood. In the final six lines the myth of Columbus is shut down. The seminal moment of the "discovery" of the Americas moves from a "trail, opened like a beautiful rainbow [or eye] upon the uncharted seas" to something the poet wishes had never happened. The poem ends with a theatrical injunction for the clock to be turned back, and history to be reversed by the hand of the great navigator himself: "Columbus! Shut the gate of your seas!" (Colombo! Fecha a porta dos mares!). Alves demands that, given the horror of Atlantic slavery, it would be better had the so-called "New World" never been born in the mind of Europeans.

These then are the structural/narrative bones of the poem, and yet the trouble enters when one attempts to pin the verse down to a single interpretative base. The poem did become a popular vehicle for the abolition movement and, as mentioned, has enjoyed several reincarnations in the minds of black and white Brazilian musicians and artists down to the present day as a central statement of the suffering of the blacks, not only under slavery, but in the continued conditions of social disempowerment they endure in Brazil now. At this level the poem lives on as political art, but when one wrestles with the intricacies of Alves's densely allusive and contradictory style, its meanings emerge as unstable and even anarchic.

When considering its choreographed levels of meaning, it must always be remembered that this was a poem designed to be read out loud, performed. This element comes out powerfully in the transformation of words into layered musical and distinctively percussive modes in Caetano Veloso's adaptation of the opening of *Navio Negreiro*.[29] What would one give for a recording of Alves performing this work? The poem has the rhythms, the rise and fall, the rhetoric, and in particular the *repetitio* of great performance poetry and of call and response oral forms in particular. It is also at a profound level a poetry of natural mimesis, poetry about the rhythms of the sea, about the sea as conduit of life, and force of death. It is synesthetic poetry made for the ears as much as the mind, and a poetry of heightened emotions, emotions beyond sentimentality, designed to make us shed salt tears in the face of a purgative tragedy. It is designed to express, and to emote, extreme, impolite, explosive emotions through sound—sadness, longing, pity, joy, anger, and shame.

As narrative poetry *Navio Negreiro* has, as will become apparent, many qualities developed out of French Romanticism, but this verse is also close to less familiar models.[30] There is a quality of extreme compression that is much closer to certain forms of Catholic mysticism. The sacred allusive lyrics of St. John of the

Cross are often called to mind. Meaning is encoded in symbolic structures that are themselves so densely encrusted as to be beyond a single literal interpretation. One major problem with Alves is that he is capable of, indeed imaginatively set on fire by, the processes of setting up completely conflicting readings within his own verse. One stanza can quite literally contain two contrary sets of meanings: the ambiguity of the language; the convolutions, involutions, and evolutions of his wordplay; and his knowingly ironic deployment of contradictory etymologies shift language into an unstable space energized by oppositions. There is not room within the confines of this book to provide an adequate close reading of the entire poem, which would require a volume in its own right. Indeed, the poem will hopefully one day find its ideal reader and generate a Brazilian equivalent of Roland Barthes's mesmeric *S/Z*, creating for *O Navio Negreiro* an involved decipherment fully the counterpart of the hermeneutic code that Barthes evolved in order to uncover the mysteries of Balzac's *Sarrasine*. It is very hard to explain the workings of Alves's verse outside its Brazilian Portuguese language base. In the following attempt to translate or form an English language dialogue with the first three stanzas, I hope to explain some of the bewildering complexities generated by Alves's peculiar poetic language. His poetry communicates the trauma of the Middle Passage with a unique amplitude.

The opening of *O Navio Negreiro* is as good a place as any to attempt to explain the impossible economies and metaphoric compressions of this fizzing, fusive language. The first point to make about this opening is the unique approach Alves has to landscape as a resource. He has a peculiar ability to construct radically unstable natural landscapes, which are at one level naturalistic, but at another operate through conflicted iconic layers that become increasingly abstract. The justly celebrated opening quatrain is a fine example of such linguistic fission:

> Stamos em pleno mar . . . Doudo no espaço
> Brinca o luar—dourada borboleta;
> E as vagas apoz ella, correm . . . cançam
> Como turbas de infantes inquieta![31]

The first stanza exemplifies Alves's ability to produce poetry that, impossibly, does two things at once, giving dual simultaneous accounts, both of which are "true." This stanza can and must be read at one level as an expression of enjoyment of the sea, of the experience of being out at sea, and of being inspired by the nautical. But the stanza also entombs a quite distinct and unbearably sad memory as we witness a human imagination driven into visionary insanity by pain. We witness the workings of a mind that sees within the sea an unbearably violent and tragic sight, the bodies of drowning and drowned slave children. I will try to explain what is finally the impossible, and bring out how these contradictory readings are achieved.

Put simply as prose the stanza can read: "We are out on the high sea . . . the moonlight plays extravagantly in space like a golden butterfly; and the waves follow her [the butterfly], running . . . singing like multitudes of rowdy children." Yet the opening can also be translated very differently: "We are floating on open sea . . . the moonlight capers, a lunatic in space—a gilded stingray; and the waves behind it, running, chanting like crowds of terrified infants." What on earth does a rationalist empirical intelligence, let alone an English translator, do with such language? Both readings are true, both readings are interred in the poetry, although so different in sense as to appear, in bald English, completely different and apparently irreconcilable works. And yet they are not separate beings, they are linguistic Siamese-twins, sharing the same lifeblood within the body of this extraordinarily polyphonic verse. By setting up two readings—one innocent and happy that makes perfect sense as the reader first enters the poem, another that becomes true, or comes slowly into being, as the reader moves into the dark center of the poem—Alves demands retroactive reading. This poetry is almost analogous to living history, to a site of atrocity, to a mass grave; bodies are hidden, entombed, within the shifting language of the poetry, within the movement of the waves, but they will come out into the light.

Alves makes unusual demands upon those who take him up and inside their minds. The reader cannot escape the inclusivity of the verse. If both readings are true then both readings encompass "us" as readers in ways that cannot be avoided. In the plurality of that disturbing opening word "stamos," "we are" told that "we are," but who are "we"? The verb "estar" is the same as the verb "to be" in English, as in "to be, or not to be." So with this opening "we are" allowed by Alves to be a lot more certain about our existence than Hamlet; we are told that we exist, but who are "we"? Alves leaves the reader suspended: maybe "we" is all sailors, or all on the boat, including the slaves, or all human life. Is Alves opening with a big metaphor about all human life as an oceanic voyage? Maybe "we" is more complicit, a bond between the poet and the reader. He has taken us with him onto the boat, and now "we" stand together within his vision, looking out through the same eyes over the sea. In this sense "we" will only be able to see through the vision of the poet.

The next clause is equally hard to pin down. "Doudo" is an odd word, a variant of "doido," and "doido" is also a strange word and a very powerful one.

It covers a whole range of extreme emotions from violent destructive insanity, or a crazy, alienated state of mind, to prophetic enthusiasm. What is for sure is that someone described as "doido" or "doudo" is possessed by violent emotion poised to turn the corner into insanity. This word clearly gives a certain coloring to the accompanying "espaço" (a space, a gap, an absence). Here there is the equation of madness with vacuum, with emptiness, with absence or alienation. To be crazy is to be in an empty space, a non-place, to have no human status, like a slave. The otherwise unambiguous "brinca o luar" (the moonlight plays) again becomes tainted by the association with this madness. This play (and the word carries again a myriad of associated meanings, all to do with gamboling, dallying, cavorting, or even fondling, frolicking, and adornment) is not the innocent play of children, but the dysfunctional carryings on of the crazy adult.

Alves's games with sanity and stability continue with the "dourada borboleta," the "golden butterfly." Certainly at a primary level this is a delightful metaphor for the broken reflections of moonlight playing on the waves. When one takes up the associated meaning of "borboleta" to be the "butterfly fish," in other words any of the ray or skate family with their underwater "wings," the image can still be seen as celebratory. The light and joyous associations of the butterfly are extended to this fish, a bottom feeder that has somehow risen to the surface to play in the moonlight, or to become the moonlight. But this spirit fish also has by now a darker set of associations, if we return to Turner's great pictorial meditation on slavery and death by drowning. The bottom right-hand corner of *The Slave Ship* presents a feeding frenzy. The piscatorial assemblage that tears and mumbles at the human flesh contains a bevy of fanciful fish including adaptations of rays and dogfish, as well as sharks.

The ray is of course an ocean scavenger, part of the same family of fish as the shark and dogfish, and Turner places them centrally within the mythology of the slave ship and the grim feasts it bestowed. For Turner the shark is also the shark of financial rapaciousness that drives the trade on. This metaphoric construction of the shark as the voracious maw of mercantilism is also explored at length in Heine's *Das Sklavenschiff* and is a theme that, as we shall see, Alves develops in a series of puns in his second quatrain. But to return to the serious lexicographic games here, Alves ingeniously starts out his poem with an image hinting that the slave body will become food for fish. This lovely ray, a ray of golden light dancing in the moonlight, is also a scavenging opportunist, after the gold of profit. There is also in these words the continued link with mental instability: to call someone a "borboleta" is to intimate that they are flighty, daffy, completely unreliable or unstable. To call someone a "borboleta" could never quite be said to amount to a charge of insanity, but as the image chains link up in Alves's poem, this flightiness he has introduced is slowly fastened to madness. The link is grammatically quite specific, and naturalistically precise: it is the "borboleta" with its nervy flight, which is "doudo em espaço" (meaning erratic in movement but also mentally unstable, a madman, a crackpot encased in a mental vacuum). This will also not be the last time that the butterfly is used by a great Brazilian as a central metaphor for the collective memory of slavery, and for the instability of that memory.[32]

This imagery of mental vacuity, or being lost, and here lost on the open ocean, "lost at sea," takes yet another form in the words "E as vagas apoz elle, correm," which again looks simple enough: "And behind her [i.e., the golden butterfly] the waves run." Again the pun starts to surface: "as vagas" is not merely "the waves" or "the billows" but carries a whole slew of meanings to do with vacancy, vacuity, unfulfillment, and loss of identity. "Vaga" as an adjective is something a bit stronger than the English "vague"; it can mean wandering, vagrant, or gone, empty, vacant. Turned into a plural adjectival noun, "as vagas" would in this sense mean roaming ones, the empty ones, the vacant ones, the vague ones. These are of course the slaves, vacant in many senses, emptied of their life by enslavement, emptied out by trauma, emptied of their human status by being murdered, empty in the eyes of the Europeans who cannot see the slaves as people. "As vagas" suggests both lack of personality and madness, but it also contains the idea that these lost people (as vagas) may have entered into the waves (as vagas). This is Alves at his most tricky, the two meanings of "vaga" brought into coexistence to suggest that these vacant ones have become waves, and so the waves are the lost ones.

Here at the very outset, Alves establishes the beautiful metaphor at the heart of his lament, and indeed at the center of the metaphoric loss in Turner's *Slave Ship*. In both works the bodies of the slaves have been taken up into the form of the sea and now disport themselves, sadly, obscenely, and beautifully. The final line and a half of the stanza then fill in that aporia within "as vagas," by giving them a heartbreaking identity: "cançam / Como turbas de infantes inquieta" could be "they [the waves] sing like crowds of restless children," but it can mean many other things as well. "They ["as vagas," the "empty ones"] sing as [in other words because they are] hordes of distraught infants." "Inquieta" is not just "unquiet," or "restless," but carries meanings that suggest disturbed and dark states of mind, and these are taken up and developed in "turbas." In strict grammatical terms this word is simply the plural of the word for mobs, or hordes, yet it is also linked to the verb "turbar" (to disturb, to darken, to trouble, to dim). And of course, as these are the "vague" "wave-ghosts" of black children, they are bound

1. A feeding frenzy—detail from J. M. W. Turner's *Slave Ship* (*Slavers Throwing Overboard the Dead and Dying, Typhoon Coming On*), oil on canvas, 1840 (Museum of Fine Arts, Boston).

to be dark. The English "turbid," so often coupled with water, is useful here in terms of describing the association. Again, dark water, dark thoughts, dark states of mind, dark deeds, dark histories all sway alongside one another in Alves's associational mutabilities. The breaking of the Atlantic waves embodies the tragic elegiac voices of the thousands of children lost on the Middle Passage. This is what, by the end of the first four lines, we are forced to hear with the poet, all of us standing on the open sea ("em plano mar"). These children are a paradox. In one reading they are happy, carefree, playful, beautiful ocean spirits, chasing the golden butterfly of the moon's reflection. Yet in the same four lines they are sad, strange, terrified, lost, and absent victims of the slave-trade holocaust. They are full of sadness and joy, light and dark, life and death, emptiness and meaning, just like the memory of the Middle Passage itself. It is essential to Alves that both the celebratory and the tragic exist in impossible duality. A marriage of heaven and hell might be the only way to embody both the depravity of the Middle Passage and the idea that the suffering of the victims of that depravity still has an inestimable value, that these lost lives were beautiful. Alves sets out to reclaim that suffering, and to show that his art has a power not only to recover the trauma, but to transmogrify it. *O Navio Negreiro* has an awful opening, and under its transformative spell a breaking wave in the Atlantic will never sound or look the same again, will never be innocent nature at its cyclical work. Then comes the second quatrain:

> Stamos em pleno mar . . . Do firmamento
> Os astros saltam como espumas d'ouro . . .
> O mar em troca accende as ardentias,
> —Constellação do liquido thesouro . . .[33]

Again, in the second stanza Alves creates a parallel creative universe. On the surface the verse describes the amalgamation of sea and sky in a series of exotic light effects, stars become foam, and sea becomes fire, and the whole thing forms a single visual treasure. Read this way the lines translated literally are: "We are out on the high sea, from the firmament, the stars jump like golden foam, the changeable sea lights up with phosphorescence—constellations of liquid treasure." But there many puns drag in an undertow of dark meanings, building on the imagery of drowning and loss that appear in the first quatrain, but which also build in an element referring to trading and the loss of capital suffered by the slave owners when the slaves are drowned. Read this way the lines can be constructed: "We are in a vast ocean, from their foundation, the heavenly bodies jump about like a deranged golden scum, the sea in its infuriated trading is consumed with rage, constellations of precious people are liquefied [both in the economic sense of assets and the physical sense of turned into liquid]."

The central ambiguities here arise out of the multiple possible constructions of several words. While "espumas" can mean "sea foam," it carries meanings relating to the unclean products of cleansing and boiling processes, and in terms of emotional expression carries associations of rabid fury. "Espuma" can mean "scum" and "froth," and indeed the spoon used to take the scum off the top of the boiling sugar cauldrons was called an "espumadeira." The boiling sea transforms into cane juice within a vast sugar cauldron. The main product of the Brazilian slave plantations is metaphorically fused with the Middle Passage. The word can also mean "saliva," or bad stomach gas, and carries over to a number of related meanings in the verb "espumar," which can mean "to slaver, to slabber, to drivel, or to froth with rage or foam at the mouth." Indeed, there is another related verb, "espumajar," which means precisely this, "to foam with fury." Seen in this light, "we" are not being offered golden foam, but an infected, and maybe furious scum, the sea itself poisoned and deranged by the greed, the symbolic gold, of the slave trade. This toxic anger carries over into the firmament itself, via the simile introduced through the word "como"—"like" or "as." The line could even be taken to present the firmament as alive, or jumping with golden saliva, as if the stars are spitting down on the ocean in fury. And why are the stars spitting on the ocean? The answer comes in the next line. The sea, as the agent of the slave trade, has become an abominable trader in humanity. This reading grows out of the incorporation of multivalent meanings of the verb "trocar." While this can mean "to change, to turn, to alter," it also carries a raft of associated meanings embedded in trade negotiation: "to barter, to truck, to bank, to change, to exchange, and to interchange." So the sea here, in trade, or in the act of being a trader or banker, becomes "accende," an old spelling of the verb "acender," which here could mean either to become "incandescent, fiery, enthusiastic, lifted, ardent," or equally to become "provoked, infuriated, enraged."[34] The line can consequently hold both the meaning that the sea becomes enthusiastically inspired by its role as a trader, or that the sea, as a trader, becomes burned up with fury. The latter construction makes sense in the context of the final line. Here the ambiguity comes out of the extended meaning for "thesouro," the nineteenth-century spelling for "tesouro." This word primarily means "a treasure," but when extended to people means "a treasured or special human being." What is happening to each of these unique people is that they are being liquefied. "Liquido" is again a brilliant play on two senses of a word that, both as adjective "liquido" and verb "liquidar," carries meanings invoking the physical description of the sea as well as the economics of the slave trade. "Liquido" as adjective can mean both "liquid or fluid" and "net assets." But the verb "liquidar" (of which "liquido" would be the first-person present indicative, the past participle being 'liquidado") can mean "liquidated" in the sense of "sold up, wound up, or finished" for a business, and also, for a living thing or person, the sense of "destroyed, annihilated, murdered." And so this final compound "liquido thesouro" carries a network of pretty nasty meanings. The "liquid treasure" is the body of each special slave dissolved into the ocean, but it is also a liquefied treasure, in terms of the cash value of each slave, which has been ironically liquefied as an asset, in the sense that it has been destroyed by jumping into the sea. But there is yet another perspective operating and giving a new view onto the slaves' experience.

Slaves drowned themselves on the Middle Passage, not merely because of a suicidal misery, but because they believed that they would be returning to their homeland in Africa. From the point of view of the slaves who have died, they see themselves as journeying through death to the homeland. In this sense the slaves have spiritually cashed in their assets, in that they have taken back their humanity and their identity through the act of suicide and redeemed themselves as Africans. Here the suicidal melancholy of *banzo* as a state of mind generating an unbearable desire to return home to Africa is given a celebratory fulfillment: suicide provides an instant way home. If "liquido" is read as present indicative "I am liquidated treasure," the slave is proclaiming his or her own salvation through annihilation, and also the saving of their final human worth from the rapacious maw of the marketplace, concerned only with debit and credit. The slaves may finally be seen as constellations, resurrected into the eternal fire of the stars, by death.

Psychologized and personified landscape is of course an imaginative resource that was seen by John Ruskin as lying at the core of the Romantic imagination. In the light of Alves's transformations, it is pertinent to remember that Ruskin developed his seminal theory of the pathetic fallacy in relation to imagery in Charles Kingsley's "Alton Locke," a poem that reincarnates the ocean waves as cruel beings. According to Ruskin, the emotional force that generates such cruel transformative vision in this poem is grief at witnessing death by water, and specifically at seeing a drowned body in relation to waves:

> They rowed her in across the rolling foam—
> The cruel, crawling foam.

Ruskin, commenting on Kingsley's lines, writes: "The foam is not cruel, neither does it crawl. The state of mind which attributes to it these characters of a living creature is one in which the reason is unhinged by grief. All violent feelings have the same effect. They produce in us a falseness in all our impressions of external things, which I would generally characterize as the 'pathetic fallacy.'"[35] Alves also responds to drowned human bodies, and also experiences a grief so intense that it generates a vision that transforms inanimate nature into something living. Yet the vision here goes beyond the identifiable terms of the pathetic fallacy. Alves's seascape by this point has reached beyond the simple injection of human emotion into objective nature. Ruskin in his definition of the pathetic fallacy isolates Kingsley's striking line "The cruel, crawling foam" as a pure example of where imaginative fallaciousness is to be located. The untruth lies in the fact that the foam is in reality just cold salt water (as Ruskin points out, the sea always appears to Homer in this way) and consequently cannot be said to operate within the terms of either the adjective "cruel," which describes a human emotion, or the verb "crawl," which describes human or animal action. Yet what would Ruskin have done faced with Alves's foam, which is—simultaneously, impossibly, gloriously—cold seawater, human saliva, boiling scum, and froth? Again, how would his theory of the imposition of inappropriate emotion onto inanimate nature fare against Alves's sea, which is both constantly shifting and changing, as waves do, yet trading for gold, as waves do not? This writing is impossible to keep in intellectual or imaginative focus; it remains purely natural yet becomes metaphoric and symbolic at the same instant. Alves's writing, if there is a critical theory that can encompass it, in fact fulfills quite precisely the terms of Ruskin's fourth level of imaginative vision within his categorization of the pathetic fallacy. In attempting to describe the limitation of the pathetic fallacy as a creative way of seeing, Ruskin constructed an aesthetic escape clause, which he termed the prophetic mode. This mode occurs when great creative minds are "submitted to influences stronger than they, and see in a sense truly because what they see is inconceivably above them. This last is the usual condition of Prophetic inspiration." Ruskin then goes on to articulate how this visionary language operates in a manner that nicely encapsulates the nature or the rhetorical register of *O Navio Negreiro*: "however great a man may be there are some subjects which *ought* to throw him off his balance; some by which his poor human capacity of thought should be conquered, and brought into the inaccurate and vague state of perception, so that the language of the highest inspiration becomes broken, obscure, and wild in metaphor."[36] This way of seeing/writing astonishes through its capacity to maintain naturalistic truth in description while employing the most outrageous emotionalized descriptive distortions. Very few minds can operate within this reified creative atmosphere. Ruskin cites the poetry of the Old Testament prophets as one example. Alves, I would argue, constitutes another triumphant example. The terrible subject that pressures Alves's creative spirit into moving into this impossible space is of course the horror of the Atlantic slave trade.

The poem confronts the inapproachability of human depravity. It is in the fourth section that Alves meets the facts of the Middle Passage head on, and in what is one of the crucial passages of writing to come out of the slave diaspora gives a tremendous tragicomic account of slave dancing. As I have argued elsewhere, this so-called dancing scenario on the decks of slave ships is a cultural event packed with a particularly disgusting ironic charge, when the distance between Europe and Africa, in terms of dance culture, is brought to mind. For all the sub-Saharan dance cultures involved in the slave trade, and for all the victims who were traded into slave ships, dancing held a sacred place. From the cradle to the grave, whether we consider the cultures of Senegal, Sierra Leone, Angola, Ghana, Dahomey, Togo, or Nigeria, the crucial stages of life and love were marked by ritual dances of immense beauty and complexity.[37] When the slaves were hauled from the stinking holds of slave ships and commanded to caper and hop about, usually to the sounds of whatever motley musical assemblage the deck sailors could muster on fiddle, accordion, and makeshift percussion, what went through their minds? It is into this underresearched and pain-filled space of historical reenactment that Alves leads his art. The passage, as with the whole poem, is not strictly translatable.

I give below a version that attempts to render Alves into English, before indicating at some level, in prolonged commentary on each stanza, the manner in which Alves's art is constructed to resist such unilinear interpretation, let alone the painful reductions of translation. This fourth section of *O Navio Negreiro* has a claim to be the most far-reaching meditation ever written about the Middle Passage. These thirty-six lines take on the terrible theme of "useless violence," which Primo Levi uncovered as the bedrock of the Nazi method, or anarchically sadistic anti-method, in the death camps. Indeed, the forced performance, the existence of a surreal orchestra, and the conclusion that madness is the only sane survival mechanism within such a social Tophet-pit uncannily resonate with aspects of the ghastly performances that occurred within Auschwitz:

> Era um sonho dantesco! . . . o tomdadilho
> Que das luzemas avermelha o brilho,
> Em sangue a se banhar.
> Tinir de ferros . . . estalar de açoite . . .
> Legiõs de homens negros como a noite,
> Horrendos a dansar . . .[38]

> (It was a Dante-esque dream vision! . . . the quarterdeck
> Shining with brilliant vermillion lights,
> Bathed in blood.
> The clanking of irons . . . the whiplash
> Legions of black men black as night
> Perform their horrific dance . . .)

The first thing to emphasize is the violent stopping and starting rhythms of the original, which cannot be shifted into English. Formally and in terms of content, this section stands alone and creates effects of metrical fragmentation, and disjunctive rhyme, that describe the disorientation and mental dissolution of the slaves. The rest of the poem is written either in couplets (the majority in the singsong octosyllabic couplets of popular narrative verse) or in variations on the a-b-a-b ballad quatrain. The latter is a stanza form designed for the smooth logical progression of a teleological story line. The fourth section is composed in an unusual stanza. This has an external symmetry and runs for six verses of six lines rhyming a-a-c-b-b-c; yet the outward order enfolds an inward fracturing that can border on linguistic chaos. The two sets of ten-syllable couplets are interspersed with two powerful staccato end-stopped shorter third and sixth lines, which form an irregular, or delayed, rhyming couplet. The effect is to bring the smoother rhythms of the longer lines up against the brutal grammar and terse statements of the shorter lines. At some points these abbreviated lines seem to cut off at the knees any semblance of narrative ebb and flow, and at others disconcertingly they seem to support the softer cadences of the longer lines.

The opening stanza of the fourth section contains an intensely emotional description, but it is hard to say whether this emotion is outraged or ecstatic. The verb "brilhar" is a very positive one in Portuguese and is not really covered by the English "shine," for it is much showier and carries a strong feeling of ostentatious display, covering meanings including "to glitter, shine, sparkle, scintillate, spangle, flash, beacon." "Brilhar" also carries a subset of associated meanings relating to public performance, "to excel, to show off, to star in."[39] And this sense, disturbing and even disgusting, that the deck itself is brought alive by the blood of the slaves, and that it positively immerses itself in the experience, comes out with emphasis in the third line. I translated this line in an imposed passive form, in order to pick up on the conventional English idiom "bathed in blood," but in Alves the verb is active, suggesting a certain luxuriousness or indulgence, as the quarterdeck bizarrely cleanses itself in the leaking life force of the victims. Alves sets up this bath of blood as a performance in order to set it off against the public performance of the slaves in the second half of the stanza. Again, there are two levels running through the language, one descriptive and naturalistic, one empathetic. The phrase "Tinir de ferros . . ." on the surface could be translated as in my first rendition "the clanking of chains" or as "the chains jangle." But "tinir" is again a verb that carries a substratum of extended meanings with implications of human behavior: "to tremble" (with fright or cold), "to feel very hungry," and also to have auditory hallucinations, to hear "a buzzing in the ears." And all of these are relevant not to the sound and motion of the chains, but to the emotion of the slaves held by the shackles, and to their unstable mental state. Great poetry puts an associative quart into a pint pot, and Alves's compression is inimitable. It is the sudden shifts here, the utter strangeness of the language, that is hard to convey, as if we have been taken into another world where horror demands its own lexis. The fifth line, for example, carries the sense that the black men and the night are one. An English simile "negroes as black as night" does not convey this, and the final line suggests that dancing itself has become a horror, again an idea almost impossible to convey in English syntax. At this point the verse makes a dramatic gender shift from male to female:

> Negras mulheres, suspendendo ás têtas
> Magras crianças, cujas boccas pretas
> Rega o sangue das mães:
> Outras, moças, mas núas e espantadas,
> No turbilhão de espectros arrastadas,
> Em ancia e magoa vãs![40]

> (Black women, suspended from their breasts
> Famished children whose black mouths
> Are spattered by their mother's blood:
> Others, girls, still naked and astounded
> Within the maelstrom of drawling spectres
> Moving on in ancient desolation.)

The first half of this second stanza interrogates the imagery of breast-feeding within the context of Brazilian slavery. The second and third lines end with the words "pretas" and "mães," a powerful combination for the *mãe-preta* or slave wet nurse, which holds a mythic place within the Brazilian iconography of slavery. I have examined the complicated symbolism connected with this subject in Brazil in some depth elsewhere.[41] The majority of white males of Alves's generation, including himself, were brought up on the milk of their black slave nurses. At the turn of the nineteenth century José Verissimo, in his classic treatise on Brazilian education, looked back upon slavery with the following observation: "As the nurse the slave girl and woman suckled every Brazilian generation."[42] The image of the *mãe preta*'s infinite capacity to produce milk in order to sustain not only her children but those of the master is locked into a complicated space in the semiotics of Brazilian slavery, and indeed in the cultural afterlife of the institution.[43] The figure of the *mãe preta* signifies intimate exploitation but at the same time black female abundance and succulence and in a sense black productive, reproductive, and natural superiority. Yet she also symbolizes the intimate violence of slavery, the theft of the very stuff of life from the black female body by the white slave power, a theme powerfully interrogated within Afro-Brazilian folk art.[44] Alves, in taking the scenario of black female breast-feeding to its diasporic origin, in a hideous moment aboard the slave ship, makes an important intervention in this iconographic field. The first three lines violently upend the reassuring myth that, whatever the circumstances, black women will go on turning their blood into mother's milk for black and white alike. The first line could be read as "Black women, strung up or hung up (suspendendo) by the breasts," until it is linked with the second line, when the main subject emerges as "diseased" or "hungry" or even "dying" children, who are hanging from the breasts.

The commonplace sense of breast-feeding as unalterably healthy and life giving is overturned. The slave-mother's nipple enters this New World as a trauma point, or in Barthesian terms a visual *punctum*, manifesting a colossal insufficiency. The rhetorical shock tactics continue with the phrase "boccas pretas," because the infants' sucking mouths should not be black; African lips, together with the palms of the hands and feet, are a space in which black skin gives way to pink. If these mouths are black it is because they are diseased, or desiccated, or, as we are taken into the imagery of the third line, covered in the dried blood that has come out of the mother's desiccated breasts. There is even the shocking inference that in their rage of thirst the infants have bitten the mothers' nipples until they bleed. The use of the verb "regar" here is again peculiarly resonant in its ambiguities. It can mean "to water, to irrigate, to sprinkle, to make wet"—all meanings connected to the idea of the water of life, fertility, and the production of crops. Consequently, the word carries strong associations meaning "to feed" or "nurture," but it can also suggest violent "inundation," "flooding," and even the idea of a cleansing ablution, of washing and finally bathing. The meanings travel back full circle to the ironic blood and washing imagery of the first stanza.[45] It is not milk but blood that again forms the baptismal washing ritual for the enslaved mothers and their children. The image is an ingenious reappropriation of ancient Catholic mystical ritualistic imagery in which the idea of bathing the soul clean in a bath of Christ's blood was an intensely erotic commonplace.[46]

The second half of the stanza operates as a tragic coda to this unbearable opening, turning to females who exist suspended between infancy and womanhood. These beings, stripped naked, have a premature antiquity thrust upon them. Yet again it is not possible to translate the final line. Its condensation cannot really be rendered in English "They endure, or they go on [in the sense that the narrator in Samuel Becket's *The Unnameable* ends by saying "I can't go on, I'll go on"] in ancientness and misery." The lines carry the intimation that this female youthfulness has been horribly perverted, frozen within an immemorial sadness that is wholly inappropriate, yet inevitable, eternal, and completely inescapable. This conclusion prepares the way for the phantasmagorical vision that follows:

> E ri-se a orchestra ironica e estridente . . .
> E da ronda phantastica a serpente
> Faz doudas espiraes . . .
> Se o velho arqueja . . . se no chão resvala,
> Ouvem-se gritos, o chicote estala . . .
> E vôam mais e mais! . . .[47]

> (And the strident and ironic orchestra laughs at itself
> And from its fantastic circuit the serpent
> Makes crazy spirals . . .
> If an old fellow labors for breath . . . slips on the smooth deck
> Screams are ignited and the cracking of whips . . .
> And they go on, and on and on! . . .)

Who is this orchestra composed of? The slaves? The sailors who play for the slaves? A mixture of the two? The ambiguity is important here. In Heine's notorious treatment of the same theme in *Das Sklavenschiff*, the slaves also dance on deck. The German poet is factual and explicit that it is the white sailors, working across ranks, who form an impromptu quartet and turn their hands to the production of an extemporized racket. There is a certain German desire for organization about the whole thing:

> Die Fiedel streicht der Steuermann,
> Der Koch, der spielt die Flöte
> Ein Schiffsjung schlägt die Trommel dazu,
> Der Doktor blast die Trompete[48]

(The steersman/helmsman scrapes the fiddle
The cook plays the flute
A ship's boy bangs the drum
The doctor blasts on the trumpet)

Contemporary accounts suggest that in the extempore musical accompaniment to which the slaves danced, the performers were sometimes sailors with Western instruments, sometimes the slaves themselves playing whatever came to hand, and sometimes a mixture of the two.[49] Alves again creates a confused space. The first line could carry the meaning I have given it, or it could mean "The hysterical and desperate orchestra laughs at them." Both interpretations carry appalling intimations, depending on who we take the orchestra to be. If the orchestra is composed of sailors, then why do they laugh at themselves, at their own depravity? If it is composed of slaves, do they laugh both at the sailors' depravity and at their own complicity? It is also no easier to extract a clear meaning for the second and third lines. The ambiguities here emanate primarily from the word "ronda," which could carry any one of three powerful meanings that do not surface in my first translation. "Ronda" can mean a dance performed in the round, it can mean a roundup of cattle, or criminals or slaves, and it can mean a game of chance played in a circle. At this point the poetry has moved into a sort of associational fluidity that requires us to go with it and abandon literalness. The serpent is clearly many things. It is the form of the circular dance, as the slaves perform on deck, and as they become the body of the snake, making it move in the "crazy circles" of their own dance. But this is also a transhistorical and transcultural icon, the figure of the eternal circle, the ouroboros, the snake biting its own tail. It is an image obsessively returned to by major English Romantic poets, an emblem that can mean eternity, perfection, or perpetual torment depending on which culture you are coming from.[50] And of course the snake, both as the slaves dancing and as the system that has caused them to do this, is diabolical, a manifestation of Satan, who was turned into a serpent by God for causing the fall of man, and who appears laughing to himself in the final words of this lyric. Subject, object, cause, and effect are increasingly eroded in this stanza, suggesting a world of existential ruination where victims and oppressors, objects and people, sounds and feelings are conflated. It is in this context that the refusal to order the music or event along the lines of Heine's picturing of the obscene performance is significant. In the final line it is not possible to tell what "voam" refers to, who or what "goes on" more and more forcefully. Is it the sound of the cries and the whiplashes, or is it the suffering and falling of the old slaves, who cannot keep up with the dance? In this world of almost orgiastic suffering, it doesn't matter. This is the message of the increasingly abstract fourth stanza, which presents different forms of insanity, hilarity, and delirium as the only possible response to this world. The chain is taken up and transformed into a metaphor for the inclusivity and ubiquity of the suffering:

> Presa nos élos de uma só cadeia,
> A multitdão faminta cambaleia,
> E chora e dança alli!
> Uma raiva delira, outro enlouquece
> Outro, aue de martyrios embruce,
> Cantando, geme e ri![51]

> (Bound up in the links of a single chain
> The famished multitude totter
> And scream and dance there!
> One deliriously raving, another driven to madness
> Another animalized by the agony of martyrdom
> Singing, laments and laughs!)

Much of the power of these lines comes from the deployment of the impersonal "uma," "outro," "outro." These are humans with no names and no identity, either in the eyes of the sailors, or in their own mad eyes, which have been driven beyond human responses. I have written elsewhere, in the context of the great eighteenth-century slave sculptor of Salvador Bahia, Xavier Chagas, of the peculiar Luso-Brazilian aesthetic sensibility that operates around slavery and the animalizing effects of Christian martyrdom. Alves here daringly takes up that legacy, the slave finding refuge in a mad laughter born out of a pain that has driven him or her beyond humanity. The extraordinary density of the shorter third and sixth lines, with their utterly fragmented diction, and thumping end-stopped rhymes, take the verse into a region of linguistic ugliness, of brutal diction, which is quite unlike Alves. It is as if, in order to describe bestiality, the poet himself has been forced to write like an animal, grunting out increasingly primitive exclamatory mantras, "dança alli!", "geme e ri!". After this the return to the relatively conventional satiric attack on the relatively typical sea captain, hidden in the mists of tobacco smoke, and exuding a familiar monstrism, is almost reassuring:

No entanto o capitão manda e manobra,
E apos fitando e céu, que se desdobra
Tão puro sobre o mar,
Diz do fumo entre os densos nevoeiros:
"Vibrai rijo o chicote, marinheiros!
Fazei-os mais dansar! . . ."⁵²

(In the meantime the captain manipulates the manoeuvres
Beneath the frozen sky, which unfolds itself
With utter purity, upon the sea
Commands, from out of the dense fug of his cigar smoke,
"Strike harder with the whip, sailors!
Make them dance quicker! . . .")

What lifts this verse out of a conventional gothicization and demonization of the symbolic figurehead of the slave power, however, are the remarkable second and third lines. Alves intuitively lifts his caricature out of the world of melodrama and sets him down against a seascape that has a hallucinatory clarity reminiscent again of Coleridge's *Rime of the Ancient Mariner*. Indeed, the calm, intimate, and beautiful union of sea and sky, apparently oblivious of the horror unfolding in their midst, reaches out to the magical union with nature that happens at the climax of Coleridge's masterpiece, when the Mariner is capable of blessing the sea snakes. Yet the dialogue with the English Romantic is an ironic one, for in the context of Alves's poem the message is not the union of human consciousness with the natural world, but rather the complete separation of natural harmony from the depravity of human nature. The captain's insane attempts to whip the slaves into frantic activity is placed against the calm and innocent beauty of the natural world. And with this horribly painful glimpse of a calm, ordered, loving, and harmonious world outside the microcosmic inferno of the slave ship, Alves ends the lyric. The poem veers back into the seemingly unbreakable and eternal cycle of suffering, an ouroboros of trauma.

Alves is a poet who rarely repeats himself, but here in order to explain that there is no way out, to intimate that his tumultuous creativity has come up hard against an emotional dead end, he repeats the crucial three lines that opened the third stanza. Dante's damned souls suffer eternally, cyclically; Alves insists that, in the man-made hell of the slave ship, and in this manufactured circular revolving ritual torment that the slave power has evolved theoretically to preserve the health of the slaves, man has created the repetitive cycles of hell's agony here on earth:

> E ri-se a orchestra ironica, estridente! . . .
> E da ronda phantastica a serpente . . .
> Faz doudas espiraes . . .
> Qual n'um sonho dantesco, as sombras vôam! . . .
> Gritos, ais, maldições, preces resoam! . . .
> E ri-se Satanaz! . . .[53]

> (And the strident and ironic orchestra laughs at itself! . . .
> And from its fantastic circuit the serpent
> Makes crazy spirals . . .
> As in a Dantesque dream vision the spirits fly up! . . .
> Cries, curses, exclamations, prayers are offered up! . . .
> And Satan sniggers to himself! . . .)

The appearance of an amused Satan who observes the perfection of his kingdom achieved on earth by the abuses of slavery was a theme that had also been taken up in North American abolition verse. Lydia Maria Child's "The Devil's Walk in Washington" is in danger of merely literalizing the cliché of slavery as a "living hell."[54] Alves makes the idea of Satanic manifestation unsettling, for that last line can be taken to mean that Satan laughs (again "rir" is a verb with a multitude of possible meanings, and shades of meaning) at himself, or that he laughs to himself. It is essential that both meanings are taken to be true, or are kept in grammatical focus, for the final message is that the dance on the slave ship is the physical manifestation of hell on earth.

The long fifth lyric then sweeps out, above and back from the squalor of the slave ship to provide the slaves with a lurid backstory. The section is necessary to provide the space for the final coda, the devastating anti-imperial imperatives of the sixth section. Yet the fifth section sets out an Africa of behavioral binaries and geographic confusion, and is the weakest part of the poem. In response to the poet's rhetorical declamation to God, and his readers, "Quem são estes desgraçados" (Who are these disgraced ones?), Alves delivers a highly impressionistic and historically rather shaky account of the movement of the slaves from the African interior to the slave ships. Living in an oasis in grass huts among desert palm trees, members of the African village are kidnapped *en masse* by a passing camel caravan, and the slaves then are taken somehow straight to Sierra Leone. Alves's vision of an African homeland here is, to put it mildly, idealizing and rather more Saharan than sub-Saharan. His Africans inhabit some sandy land where the men and women are equally untenable exotic cutouts, all the children are beautiful ("crianças lindas"), all the women are noble ("moças gentis"), while the men live and fight naked, and wrestle big cats including rather unlikely spotted tigers:

> São os filhos do deserto
> Onde a terra esposa a luz,
> Onde viva em cambo aberto
> A tribu dos homens nús
> São os guerreiros ousados
> Que com os tigres mosqueados
> Combatam na solidão! . . .
> Hontem, simples, fortes, bravos . . .
> Hoje miseros escravos,
> Sem ar, sem luz, sem razão[55]

> (These are the sons of the desert
> Where the land espouses the light
> Where they live on the open plane
> A tribe of naked men
> They are the brave warriors
> Who with spotted tigers
> Wrestle in the wilderness
> Yesterday strong and brave
> Today miserable slaves
> Without air, without light, without reason)

It is only in the last line, snapping back into the desperate mental world of the slave ship, that the poem regains its earlier intensity. What makes the line so powerful is the ambiguity of that final "sem razão," where the lack of reason refers both to the inhuman extremity of the slave system and to the madness within the slaves' own minds. The section concludes by drawing, as briefly mentioned, upon the rather exhausted abolitionist trope whereby the poet demands that divine retribution destroy the slave ship by tempest. The slaves at this point appear to pay a rather high price as aesthetic collateral damage in the face of Alves's rhetorical strike.

Admitting the comparative weakness of the fifth section, the poem ends with one of the most stupendous assaults upon the cultural bedrocks of colonial nationalism ever penned. Alves takes on national symbolism at its most basic and emotional, namely the image of the national flag, and puts it through a series of highly ironic and inspired metaphorical transformations. The flag is first seen fluttering on the mast as a potentially obscene cover for the horror in the ship beneath. It is then transformed into some weird surreal cloak that floats on the back of a sensual but cold Bacchic Roman at an orgy, a "bacchante." This filthy vision inspires the poet to critique his own inspiration and to demand that his muse snatch this blood-soaked cloth and wash it clean with her tears. In the second stanza the flag is then resurrected and restored to the mast as a beautiful image of hope kissing the sun and breeze, only again to be buried in the final line as Brazil's winding sheet.

The final stanza launches into the celebrated attack upon the horror of a European colonialism based in the evil of slavery, climaxing in the justly celebrated order to Columbus to close down and shut out his own history: "Colombo! Fecha a porta dos teus mares!" (Columbus! Close the door to your seas!). Every schoolchild knows that "In fourteen hundred and ninety-two, Columbus sailed the ocean blue." Given what Columbus stood for at the epicenter of the Ur myths of Euro-American colonialism, given his mystical presence as the instigator and legitimator of Eurocentric colonization of the Americas, Alves's final command was and remains staggering in its violence and audacity. The slave trade, the Middle Passage, and the economic systems of greed and corruption lying behind that dirty business have, in Alves's unique art of moral confrontation, overturned and indeed replaced the self-serving narratives of European Renaissance exploration and their subsequent literary transmogrification.

O Navio Negreiro ends with Alves delivering a colossal rhetorical rewinding of history. Is there an aesthetic analogue for such a creative process? The justifiably sensational climax to Elem Klimov's 1985 film *Come and See* springs immediately to mind. The young boy-hero Florya (played with unforgettable intensity by Aleksei Kravchenko), despite witnessing the extremes of Nazi atrocity in Byelorussia, manages imaginatively to rewind history. In both these trauma masterpieces the ultimate horrors of history are finally taken back, taken away, closed down, shut out, by the triumph of a ruined but still morally focused humanity. Both poem and film take us through a lyrical configuration of absolute horror only to end up by saying, "Just demand that it never happened, go back and go deep in order to go beyond, you can if you try hard enough."

CHAPTER 2

Castro Alves, *Voices of Africa*, and the *Paulo Afonso Falls*: From Afro-Brazilian Monologic Propopeia to Brazilian Plantation Anti-Pastoral

From the moment it was first publicly performed by Castro Alves in September 1868, *O Navio Negreiro* had, and has maintained, a level of celebrity that has tended to eclipse his other poetic work on slavery. There are, however, two major poems, *Vozes de Africa* (Voices from Africa) and *A Cachoeira de Paulo Afonso* (The Paulo Afonso Waterfall, hereafter referred to as *A Cachoeira*), that negotiate slavery and Brazilian cultural memory in imaginative and technically ingenious ways quite as ambitious as his better-known masterpiece on the Middle Passage. These two works contrast with but also complement, and indeed in some ways bookend, *O Navio Negreiro*. As a formal unit the three works can be seen as a poetic triptych that embraces the entire Luso-Afro-Brazilian slave diaspora.

Vozes de Africa: A Callout for Adamastor

Vozes de Africa was first published in 1883 in *Os Escravos*, the anthology containing Alves's collected poetry focused on Brazilian slavery. It is uncertain if he performed the work before his death. The poem is in many ways a creative antidote to the relatively weak imaginative treatment of continental Africa in *O Navio Negreiro*, as briefly discussed in the last chapter. *Vozes de Africa*, an important, indeed vital, intervention into abolition propaganda, is a creative attempt to give Africa an articulate presence. The title of the poem and particularly the use of the plural "voices" is striking, given that Africa had a tightly controlled presence in the late 1860s within Eurocentric arts and literatures. When sub-Saharan Africa was spoken of, even in abolition verse, it was almost inevitably overwritten by a set of attitudes presenting it in disempowering forms. Some of these were blatantly degrading, others were superficially seductive and idealizing, and because sugarcoated may be an even worse form of disguised cultural poison.[1] In *Vozes de Africa* Alves gives the continent not one voice but several. His Africa seems initially to be a single entity, yet it emerges as a many-sided mythic construction. The continental subaltern that Europe had so narrowly imagined finally speaks in several ways through the mind of a Brazilian poet.

Alves's poem was consciously negotiating a European and American literary landscape already partially absorbed into Brazilian culture. This was an inheritance that contained and closed down the reality and imaginative possibilities of a complicated and as yet virtually unexplored cultural terrain. There is not space here to survey the multivalent prehistory of creative projections of Africa in the West. It is, however, important to note that by the time Alves was embodying Africa, Africa had already been constructed according to certain central tropes. Because this prehistory impacted Alves's approach to Africa, it is useful to summarize them, although such a summary must simplify. First, there were fantasies contained in travel literatures and focused on the exoticized peoples and wildlife of sub-Saharan Africa. Popular adaptations of Mungo Park, and subsequent derivative "Exploration" and "Discovery" narratives, most famously the publishing efflorescence that had evolved around Dr. David Livingstone, would typify this kind of imperial and expansionist propaganda. Second, there were fictions based in extreme negro-phobe fantasies fixated upon supposed African violence, libidinousness, and cannibalism. The kernel of this tradition is conveniently essentialized in Hegel's treatment of Africa and Africans in the notorious appendices to the *Philosophy of World History*. In the second half of the nineteenth century and the first decades of the twentieth, such work generated a cultural racist tsunami the ghastly results of which we still live with. Hollywood shows little sign of rejecting the ground rules of this cultural game whether it flourishes within *King Solomon's Mines*, *Tarzan*, *King Kong*, *Blood Diamond*, *Last King of Scotland*, *Casino Royale*, and so on. And third, there were Romantic fictions (often adapted by, or generated by, the abolition movement) intent to present the African female as noble, passive, and above all unthreatening, and African males as noble, aristocratic and, if rebellious, then inevitably doomed. Aphra Behn's male and female leads in *Oroonoko*, later stereotyped in Thomas Southerne's hugely popular stage adaptation of Behn's novella, are the *loci classici* for this subgenre. This final category could bleed into the forms of Romantic fiction involving the ruined love affairs of young idealistic slaves either on the slave-coast of Africa or newly transported to the diasporic plantations. The most celebrated, globally influential and long-lived example of this subgenre sentimentalizing the tragic love of the transplanted African slave couple is *Paul et Virginie* (*Paul and Virginia*). This appeared in 1788 and remained hugely popular across Europe and the Americas. *Vozes de Africa* can thus be seen as a strategic abolition intervention into Africanist literatures coming out of Europe. Alves is entering a complicated aesthetic and cultural terrain with its own established conventions, traditions, and expectations. Alves plunged in and created a confrontational work with unique perspectives on Luso-Afro-Brazilian themes and traditions.

Bearing in mind the larger European cultural perspectives devoted to processing African cultures, the most striking qualities of Alves's *Vozes de Africa* are its vast intercontinental perspectives, its polemic inclusivity, and the way it moves prosopopoeia into wholly unexpected places. The poem takes the form of an extended dramatic monologue, spoken in the disembodied voice of Africa and addressed, at the outset, to a god. As the poem continues, however, it moves out to embrace and indeed to question the other major continents involved in the Atlantic slave trade. In imaginatively embracing and simultaneously critiquing Asia and India, the poem extends a truly global perspective.

The question as to why, in formal terms, Alves decided to personify Africa in the first place and have it speak directly to the reader, comes out of the poet's relationship with the literary history of Portugal and its colonial inheritance. The great shadow hanging over any Luso-Brazilian artistic treatment of Africa and colonization is that of Luis Vaz de Camões's *Os Lusíadas*. This enormous epic poem takes the form of a fantastic narration of the voyage of Vasco da Gama down the west coast of Africa, around the Cape, back up the east coast, and out to India's spice coast. The story contains supernatural machinery involving the intervention of classical deities and the animated appearance of inanimate things. *Os Lusíadas* casts a specific and remarkably intense poetic shadow, to use Harold Bloom's great phrase an epic "anxiety of influence," which hangs above the literary construction of sub-Saharan Africa in the form of Camões's invention of the specter of Adamastor. Any subsequent poet writing in Portuguese about Africa and the sea had to take on this inheritance. Adamastor is a mighty male spirit who arises, at the narrative epicenter of the Lusíadas, quite literally out of the African soil, a chimerical hulk of earth and roots that veers up as da Gama's ship approaches the Cape. The Cape is not only geographically the southernmost point of Africa, but also the tipping point between sub-Saharan West Africa and East Africa. This divide was, and has remained, of huge significance for European perceptions of the African continent, for conceptions of

Atlantic slavery, and consequently for conceptions of Brazil, and of Portuguese maritime ambition.

Camões's introduction of a speaking Africa is itself intriguing, and by no means straightforward in terms of the perceptions of Africa it grants the Europeans, and the perception of Europeans and Africans it provides for the reader. In Canto V of the *Lusíadas*, having lost their bearings and desperate for landfall, Vasco da Gama and his mariners approach the Cape. After landing, the first African to appear to the narrator is a kidnap victim, a male whom the colonizers snatched as he foraged for honey: "I see a NATIVE come, black as the *Cole*: Whom *they* had took perforce, as in the *Wood*, Getting out *Honey* from the *Combe* he stood."[2] The African is shown gold, silver, and spices, but is not excited by these and only comes to life, as far as the narrator can see, when shown cheap trade goods, including beads and a liberty cap or *bonnet rouge*. These details appear to be adapted from the celebrated account of the first encounter with indigenous Brazilians by Pero Vaz de Caminha in 1500.[3] A group of Africans then appears, who the Europeans assume want more of this trade trash. Veloso (one of da Gama's men used at different points in brief exploratory incursions into the African coastland) pursues them with a band of soldiers into the forest in the hopes of finding gold. Yet the gullible and greedy Europeans are ambushed; fleeing an African attack, they barely escape back to the ship with their lives. Sailing directly on, they start to round the Cape, and it is at this point that Africa is again manifested, this time in the apparition of Adamastor. He is a terrifying gigantic specter, a personification of the *cabo tormentoso*, to use Bartholomeo Dias's striking early naming of the Cape as an agonistic space. Adamastor rises up before them, cutting the narrator off mid-sentence. This is how the "voice of Africa" appears in Sir Richard Fanshawe's translation, a work still unmatched for a rugged liveliness that is close in spirit to the original. Fanshawe gets over the combination of bulky, dirty, jerky physicality and the sheer immensity of Camões's vision:

> I had not ended, when a *humane* Feature
> Appear'd to us ith'*Ayre*, Robustious, ralli'd
> Of *Heterogeneal* parts, of *boundless* Stature,
> A *Clowd* in's *Face*, a *Beard* prolix and squallid:
> *Cave-Eyes*, a *gesture* that betray'd ill *nature*,
> And a worse mood, a clay *complexion* pallid:
> > His crispt *Hayre* fill'd with *earth*, and thick as *Wyre*,
> > A *mouth* cole-black, of *Teeth* two yellow Tyre.[4]

The visual impact of this vision of Africa establishes an unforgettable figure, barbaric, unkempt, as if he is not only from the wilderness but made out of the wilderness. He is a "most strange Colossus" (estranhíssimo Colosso); a "most rough/rude/rugged son of the Earth" (Filho aspérrimo da Terra); he is deformed, with a wild squalid beard, the color of earth, with crinkled hair, a black mouth and yellow teeth ("disforme estatura," "barba esquálid," "cor terrena," "cheios de terra e crespos os cabelos / a boca negra, os dentes, amarelos"). Adamastor then delivers a prophetic speech telling the colonizers that the Cape will be forever a cursed space for Europeans. He then outlines a series of violent disasters, including graphic visions of starving white children and abused white women. These ominous prophecies of Adamastor created a dark and ambiguous space around Europe's configurations of Africa, and in a way constitute an open challenge to subsequent poets attempting to evolve a creative dialogue with the continent. It is as if Camões had latched onto some deep and irrational terror embedded in the colonial imaginary when it came to conjuring up an essential metaphor embodying "the dark continent." Several generations of poets took up this challenge from European and African perspectives, and Adamastor has generated an entire dialogic subliterature consisting of poetic and artistic responses to and developments of this horrifying specter. Many of these are highly politicized and use Adamastor as a way into talking about the disaster of African colonization in the nineteenth century.[5] Alves's *Vozes de Africa* is, then, among other things a specifically Brazilian, and quite early, contribution to this ongoing literary dialogue with, or overwriting of, the Portuguese master, yet this aspect of the poem is not one that has been pursued in criticism. In many ways Alves's poem is not only framed by but also attempts to go beyond Camões's alienating and terrific specter, and the following analysis brings out this constant pressure.

Alves's very title *Vozes de Africa* is a charged one when set against Camões's personification, stuck down there right on the southernmost tip of the continent. Alves refuses the option of one mighty and foreboding African spirit. He proclaims that Africa has its own set of voices, and its own complex narratives relating to slavery, narratives that move up and down the continent and are not merely coastal but take in the ancient Arab inland slave trade routes. He gives Africanity a definite position that exists in relation to Europe, the Americas, and indeed India and the Indian Ocean slave trade. When reading the title, it is important to remember that Brazilian "voz," although it can carry something equivalent to the English word "voice," is a much more powerful word. It contains meanings alluding to the territory of vociferous remonstrance, or even lamentation, often conducted through the form of ritual song. It is a word denoting the basic right to speech, to utterance, to proclaiming existence through sound.[6]

As the poem progresses, it becomes evident that Alves allows Africa to exhibit an awareness of internal conflicts over slavery. The poem alludes to the fundamental division between sub- and supra-Saharan Africa, and the ancient Arab internal slave trading routes that preceded the arrival of the European colonial slave trade, and that have survived its demise and live on today. The poem opens with a series of dramatic moves playing with the reader's location of Africa and the iconography that might be appropriate to this vast continent. In this sense the poem is interrogating the reader and asking what Africa, the Dark Continent, the unknown continent, might mean to the Brazilian, but also pointedly to the European, imagination.

The first voice in which Africa is manifested in the opening stanza is that of Old Testament prophecy, of a despairing voice crying aloud to a silent god from the deep, or from the wilderness of its suffering. There is a deliberate echo here of the terrible opening of the first and greatest of what are known as the "Passion Psalms," and of course Christ's appropriation of this cry in Aramaic when he accuses God of having forsaken him, as he hangs and expires upon the cross. Indeed, the whole Psalm appears to have been appropriated by Christ in his agony, but it is the opening lines that Alves invokes where the Psalmist roars out his sense of betrayal like a lion:

> My God, my God, why hast thou forsaken me?
> Why art thou so far from helping me, and from the words
>   of my roaring?
> O my God, I cry in the daytime but thou hearest not,
> And in the night season and am not silent.[7]

The text of the Psalm, as one of the great experiments in the thought and language of the trauma victim, has particular advantages as a resource for the agonized personification of Africa. Although we are clearly hearing the voice of an individual in agony, the Psalm also articulates the suffering of a nation, in the Bible a personification of the Jewish people in exile, persecuted by the heathen, for Alves a personification of Africa, persecuted and ruined by the slave trade.[8] This combination of an abstract personification of nationality with a distinctly individual human voice of suffering has been seen as a wholly "novel element" in modern critical interpretations of the poem. Yet viewed from the perspective of its model in the Passion Psalms, Alves is to be seen drawing on a grand literary and indeed sacred tradition for articulating trauma on a cosmic scale.⁹

The second stanza then shatters the prophetico/Christological frame and introduces a wholly different form of victim and a different mythology. The biblical prophetic register shifts into neoclassical Romantic rhetoric, but with a twist. The second stanza begins with the simile "Qual Prometeu" (Like Prometheus), Africa choosing to personify itself in the form of one of the central icons of Romantic revolutionary masculinity:

> Qual Prometeu, tu me amarraste um dia
> Do deserto na rubra penedia,
> Infinito galé! . . .
> Por abutre—me deste o sol ardente!
> E a terra de Suez—foi a corrente
> Que me ligaste so pé.¹⁰

> (Like Prometheus, you fastened me down one day
> Took me out of the desert onto an ensanguined rock
> An eternal galley slave! . . .
> For a vulture—I was given the fiery sun!
> And the land of Suez—was the shackle
> Which bound my foot.)

Prometheus, who stole fire from the gods in order to benefit mankind, and who was eternally bound to a rock and tortured by Zeus for his efforts, a vulture perpetually consuming his liver, constituted a central touchstone for Romantic artists in Europe. Alves took up the subject several times in his verse and wrote a poem entitled *Prometeu*, which appeared posthumously in the volume *Os Escravos*.¹¹ Byron and Shelley, the two most influential of the English Romantics for Alves, and William Blake (who despite so many striking parallels with the thought of Alves was unknown to the young Brazilian), reinvented the figure in many ways in their work. Prometheus was also adopted in a variety of inferior abolition verse in the late eighteenth and early nineteenth centuries.¹² Yet Alves's treatment in this poem is quite distinctive, involving another lightning-fast shift of perspective. His Prometheus is both Titanic hero and historically located slave victim. The torture of this Promethean African body is compared to service in the slave galleys, the labor of rowing is presented as equivalent to the effects of sun and drought in the parched lands of the Sahara, the ankle shackle of the galley slave is presented as Suez, the isthmus that is the only land bridge, or link, physically between Africa and Asia. This is a complicated network of analogies. Enslavement in the galleys, originating with the ancient Greeks and Romans, had continued to survive as a practice within the navies of colonial Portugal and Spain. The famous treatment of galley slavery in Cervantes's *Don Quixote* is testament to the extent to which, even in the sixteenth century, this image lived as a resource within Hispanic literatures, and maintained its power as the embodiment of an ultimate form of human debasement.

The personification of Alves's Africa has then become, within the space of two stanzas, layered and difficult to disentangle. The self-dramatizing spirit of Africa stands outside itself, and looking down on the Sahara sees this as God's punishment, but punishment for what? The answer comes in the second half of the stanza with the reference to Suez. Suez was, of course, the point at which African and Arab/Asian trade routes met. The grammatical construction here suggests that not only the sun, but the land of Suez, the desert, is to be seen as a vulture ("Por abutre . . . a terra de Suez"). The Suez Canal had just been opened when Alves was writing, but he thinks of Suez in terms of its significance before the canal was constructed. Suez is a vulture, and Africa is chained to it, because the ancient Arab slave trading routes led up from the densely populated regions of central sub-Saharan Africa, through the Sahara and up to Suez, where the slaves were then dispersed across the Arab slave diaspora and also into Asia. Suez is logically a vulture because it feeds off the bodies of the enslaved blacks who are perpetually fed into its markets. The constantly renewed but tortured liver of Prometheus constitutes the perpetually refreshed supply of slave bodies coming up through Africa.

It is the thought of these Arab trade caravans, endlessly moving through the desert, no matter the cost in human suffering, that is logically taken up in the third stanza. These lines develop the imagery of the Saharan caravans more explicitly, and also develop an analogy between the suffering of the beast of burden, here the horse, and the slave, an equation that had been a staple of European abolition rhetoric, but which had never been so ingeniously developed in a context within central Africa:

> O cavallo estafado do Beduino
> Sob a vergasta tomba resupino,
> E morre no areal.
> Minha garupa sangra, a dôr poreja,

Quando o chicote do *simoun* dardeja
O teu braço eternal.¹³

(The Bedouin's exhausted horse
Collapses supine beneath the whip
And dies on the sand.
My haunches bleed, the pain oozed out
Cut by the whiplash of the *simoom*
Your eternally powerful arm.)

In this pitiless landscape, where the scope, the limitlessness of punishment is hard to determine, Alves's empathy also appears beyond bounds. Point of view is hard to work out. The first three lines show the horse perishing at the hands of the Bedouin trader, and the unstoppable forces of Nature. The choice of a single word "garupa" has the effect of suspending the suffering body of Africa between beast and human, and even suggests that the animal victim can talk. "Garupa" is a word that does not relate to human anatomy but describes the hind end, crupper, or haunches of a horse. The usage raises a series of intriguing possibilities: is the narrator Africa animalizing itself and its own suffering, or is it creating an empathetic model suggesting that the suffering of any tortured being, animal or human, is both equal and intolerable? The narrational voice becomes increasingly unstable, and in this fourth line it is hard to tell who speaks. Is this disembodied voice that of the horse, that of a slave, that of the personified continent of Africa, or are all of these incorporated into the voice of the narrator? The compressed, allusive, and inclusive style of Alves means, of course, that the speaker is each and all of these. Africa's haunches or rear end is both the desert and the horse's tortured body; it is a landscape soaked in blood, but the blood is also personified as pain—disconcertingly it is not blood that oozes here but pain itself. The torturer who whips this vast expiring animalized slave body shifts from Bedouin Arab to God, although it is not clear if this is the Christian god or some nonspecific universal being representing the eternal or literally the "arm of eternity." In this unredeemed and bleak vision, it is this eternal arm ("braço eternal"), in the form of blasts of the baking desert wind, the *simoom*, which unendingly inflicts pain. Indeed, the god who operates within this poem is decidedly unstable, as is Africa's attitude towards him/her. The irony sometimes seems to approach the comic. At the poem's conclusion, for example, Alves revisits this all-powerful arm, and apparently allows

Africa to have a go at God in exasperation, shouting out "Enough, Sir! Of your potent arm" (Basta, Senhor! De teu potente braço). Yet when the next grammatical element is introduced, an enjambment transforms the meaning. What was a powerful accusation from the voice of Africa to God becomes part of a plea for forgiveness and redemption, and Africa appears as conventional penitent: "Basta, Senhor! De teu potente braço, / Rolé atravez dos astros e do espaço / Perdão p'ra os crimes meus!" (Enough, Lord! Let forgiveness for my sins, roll down from your strong arm through the stars and through space). Because Alves is constantly setting up such charged rhetorical revisiting and revision of key images, nothing is quite as it seems.

Having initially located Africa in relation to the desert trade routes of Arabic North Africa, via the connection of the internal slave trade, Africa is then taken out of itself, and sees itself in relation to Occidental and Oriental perspectives. India is intensely eroticized as a female captive. Alves's geographical mapping here looks back to the heyday of Portuguese maritime supremacy and its intercontinental scope, to da Gama's quest for, and final triumphant passage to, the Indian subcontinent, and again unavoidably the shadow of Camões looms large. Well before Brazil was "discovered" and developed, Portugal had already reached out down the African coast, round the cape and up to Mozambique, before moving out to develop essential trade bases in India, and to set up a dazzling trading center in Goa. Camões published his poem just three years after returning from the Indies, and the poem is not concerned with, does not know about, Brazil. So when Alves refers to the Ganges at the opening of his fifth stanza, he does so in ironic dialogue with Camões, who has the river announce itself in the Lusíadas as the true cradle of life in the heavens and as a force of spiritual renewal that can cleanse the souls of mankind with its waters.[14] The earlier poet's noble mythologizing of the river is supplanted by a river that has become a force of amorous sexuality, intensely seductive, kissing its own beaches and suggestively inundating them in colored corals ("O Ganges amoroso beija a praia, Coberta de coraes"). The mainland of India is also characterized in sexual terms but, unlike the Ganges or Ganga, it is seen as erotically passive, as a female sex slave in the harem, contented and oblivious in her abandon: "Asia sleeps in the voluptuous shadows of the Sultan's harem" (Dorme a Asia nas sombras voluptuosas, Dos *harens* do Sultão). The construction of continents in terms of sexualized female forms is continued as Africa turns its attention to Europe. Europe is presented as incapable of change, Europe is always Europe, "Europa—é sempre Europa," and this constancy is revealed as rooted in a moral chaos and in a sexually voracious prostitution. Europe is a combination of power and lustfulness, "Rainha e cortezã," (queen and courtesan), and finally "grande meretriz" (vast whore). In the eyes of Africa Europe is confused and confusing, ironically glorious and desirable, but ideologically unstable and emotionally corrupted. The moral inconstancy of Europe, especially around notions of power and freedom, is summed up in the couplet: "Always taking on the laurels of each struggle, / Now a crown, now the *Phrygian-cap*" (Sempre a laurea lhe cabe no litigio . . . Ora uma c'rõa, or o *barrete-phrygio*).[15] Here the *bonnet rouge*, possibly recalling the red cap given to Camões's African, but certainly recalling the more recent emblem of French revolutionary idealism, is presented as interchangeable with the sign of absolute monarchy, the Crown. French vacillation between absolute monarchy and the extreme egalitarian ideals of Jacobinism is set out as two sides of the same coin. The Phrygian-cap was of course the symbol of universal social equality during the first stages of the French Revolution, but it was also an icon with origins in Roman slave manumission ceremonies.[16] The symbol is highly ironic in the context of the French engagement with the issue of slavery during the revolutionary period. Slavery was first idealistically abolished by the decree of the National Assembly, only to be brutally reinstated by Napoleon in a bid to regain San Domingo in the throes of the slave revolution. Napoleon himself dramatically moved from revolutionary idealist to absolute monarch. Alves, clearly playing with France's bitter historical inconstancy over its role in Atlantic slavery, gives Africa the voice to isolate this inconsistency.

Having set up this complicated foundation for the consideration of Africa's global relation to the slave diaspora, the poem then moves in its final stages into a violent interrogation of European justificatory myths for the operations of the Atlantic slave trade, and of their incorporation into Brazil by the slave power. The move is made initially through Africa's ironic internalization of the biblical myth of the curse of Ham, but the poem then takes up this myth and runs in some quite extraordinary directions with it. Alves, in taking on the curse of Ham, was not doing anything particularly new: he was attacking one of the foundational myths of pro-slavery discourse. The brief narrative in Genesis 9 had been used from the earliest phases of Portuguese and Spanish slavery. It then was maintained within the pro-slavery rhetoric of the Caribbean and North America.[17] Yet, within the poem, it is specifically in answer to the rhetorical question posed by Africa to God ("What terrible crime have I ever committed that I merited your two edged Vengeance?") that Africa supplies the shocking answer that this suffering began the day it, Africa, saw "A vagrant, negro, weak, enfeebled and panting, descend from Ararat" (Um viandante, / Negro, sombrio, pallido, arquejante / Descia do Ararat). The image clearly alludes to Ham's ejection from Noah's family in the wake of his sin of seeing the father naked. Ejected from the familial circle, Ham descends from Ararat into the wilderness. Africa then provides a quite bizarre narrative relating how the encounter develops. Africa confronts and addresses its own racist construction: "And I greeted the stranger with the words 'Ham! You are my most dearly beloved husband. I will be your Eloa'" (E eu disse ao peregrino fulminado: "Chan! . . . serás meu esposo bem amado . . . / Serei tua Eloá"). The mad extremity lying at the heart of this exchange has not been acknowledged. Alves interrogates Africa's relationship to the racist myths applied to it with unparalleled irony. These lines eccentrically fuse two very distinct and distinctive narratives, which logic would dictate cannot coexist. The first is the familiar biblical tale of Ham, condemned to be marked (with black skin according to the revisionist biblical interpretations of the slave power) and to wander cursed because he had looked upon his father Noah when drunk and naked. The second story is not so familiar now, although it would have been immediately recognized within the Brazilian Francophile intellectual circles in which Alves moved. The poem references the tale of Eloa, the central character in Alfred de Vigny's long, eponymous psychological narrative poem *Eloa*. Alves was deeply devoted to French Romantic verse, and Eloa, by the time he was writing, had become acknowledged not only in France but across the Francophone world as one of the great achievements of early French Romanticism. The long poem was a profound interrogation of the redemptive capacities of woman's love, and a very radical retake on the myth of the fall that gives Eve, in the guise of Eloa, a uniquely charged imaginative space. The poem also gives a grim account of the capacity of the male to seduce and abuse the beautiful potential of female love, Eloa's lovely spirit being corrupted and ruined by the ultimate evil angel, Lucifer. To give an inadequate précis of an infinitely subtle work, the bones of the narrative are that the angelic spirit Eloa attempts to redeem Lucifer through the sheer power of selfless love. She fails, is seduced by him, and finally falls into a terrible damnation, only establishing Lucifer's identity when it is too late.[18]

The gender implications of Alves's move in taking up and transferring Eloa into this peculiar Hamitic setting are radical, not to say weird. Let me summarize the narrational process here, because it is by no means straightforward. Africa, the narrator, answers its own rhetorical question to God, "What horrific crime have I ever committed that you oppress me with your terrible vengeance?", by presenting the sin in the following terms. Africa's answer on seeing the stricken figure of the cursed Ham presents itself/himself/herself as Ham's/Lucifer's Eloa. So Africa configures itself as a beautiful, morally good, damned sacrificial female, an innocent whose powers of love extend even to embracing pure evil. The evil that Africa/Eloa embraces in embracing Ham/Lucifer is the ultimate evil of Euro/Christian racism as founded in white supremacist perversions of the Bible. It is this embrace, the symbolic marriage of Ham and Eloa, of European corruption and the pure spirit of precolonial Africa, that constitutes Africa's sin. In this extravagant move Alves is implying that Africa is now aware that it has embraced Ham from the moment of his first appearance as the original European perversion of Africanism, and has claimed to be able to redeem this Ham/Lucifer fantasy. Africa has consequently, from the first contact, condemned both itself and all the "sons of Ham" to a fate anchored in a racist theory of African inferiority and justified persecution. The sin, the tragedy, the corruption of African racial and cultural innocence, lies in this internalization of European negrophobe mythology. In this bleak mythographic construction, Africa's demonic self-identification condemns all the sons of Ham. Simply because of their different color, they are subsequently doomed to exploitation and suffering at the hands first of the Arab, and then of the European, slave traders:

> Desde este dia o vento da desgraça
> Por meus cabellos, ululando, passa
> O anathema cruel.
> As *tribus* erram do areial nas vagas
> E o *nomado* faminto corta as plagas
> No rapido corsel . . .
> Depois vi minha prole desgraçada
> Pelas garras de Europa—arrebatada
> Amestrado falcão![19]

(From that day onwards the winds of disgrace
Because of my hair, weep, and pass
The cruel curse.
The tribes move across the open plains
And the famished nomad scours all regions
With his rapid mount . . .
And then I saw my disgraced children
Violently carried off by the talons of Europe
Well-trained falcon.)

Alves alludes back to the primitive identification of black skin as a sign of devilry, an association that had been made since the Middle Ages, and confirmed during the Crusades, and that fed into the attitudes particularly of the early Portuguese and African slavers.[20] In fact the first three lines of this quotation are open to two quite distinct possible readings, the one I have given in translation, but also the reading: "From that day onwards the winds of disgrace / Pass weeping through my hair / O cruel anathema." In this reading it is the sense of disgrace itself (disgrace at having entered into complicity with, or marriage to, the racist myth) of Ham that is weeping, and which inhabits the curly hair of the black people. There is in this verse the terrible inference that all black Africans and their descendants have become an embodiment of despair, a despair brought about by buying into the mindset of the blind persecutory and brutally racist vision of the people who enslave them. And so the Africans become a chain of unending victims, carried away through slavery in the talons of Europe's unending rapaciousness. And yet this rapacious bird of prey is not a chaotic or anarchic force of nature; as an "Amestrado falcão," a trained or skilled falcon, it, too, is obeying orders. So, who trained it so well: God or the slave power?

The poem finally turns to America, in the inclusive sense of the Americas, and plays tremendous variations on the image of the falcon, and on the bird imagery that has permeated the poem:

> Hoje em meu sangue a America se nutre:
> —Condor, que transformára-se em abutre,
>   Ave de escravidão
> Ella juntou-se ás mais . . . irmã traidora!
> Qual de José os vis irmãos, outr'óra
> Venderam seu irmão[21]

> (Today America nourishes itself with my blood:
> A condor which has transformed itself into a vulture,
> The bird of slavery.
> She approaches nearer, traitor sister!
> Which one of Joseph's vile brothers, or which other one,
> Will sell his own brother?)

The poem, condor-like, rises above the nationalist politics of the Atlantic diaspora, involving the whole of the Americas, South, Central, and North, in the blood-sucking crime of slavery. Both Brazil and North America have undergone aviary metamorphosis, the well-trained falcon, bird of princes, having devolved into buzzard and then vulture. These are birds that feed both on the dead and the dying, and of course, to return to the poem's mythic origins, upon the body of the perpetually dying, but living, Prometheus. The vulture was also in the second stanza seen as a symbol of the Arab slave trade, and so Alves is making a subtle analogy between the ancient Arab and more recent Atlantic slave industries. It is a particularly terrifying imaginative sleight of hand to transform the noble falcon and then the gorgeous form of the world's largest flying bird, the Andean condor, into a common or garden vulture. The condor is, of course, technically one of the vulture family of birds, yet its ethereal existence, riding the oceanic thermal currents thousands of feet above the earth, seems to have separated it from this dirty family relation, much in the manner that the albatross inhabits a very different imaginative space from the common seagull.

The final three lines of the stanza then move into a deeply troubling tangential take on perverse family relations by moving from the family of birds to the family of man, and most explicitly the biblical case of Joseph and his brothers. The Bible comes at slavery in many different ways in the Old Testament, but probably the most powerful narrative to take up the iniquitous subject, and to instill it with an intimate bitterness, is the story of Joseph, sold through greed and jealousy into slavery by his own brothers. The action is a complete betrayal of the sacred bond of family, yet in its utter corruption and immorality, and in Joseph's subsequent domestic sexual abuse by Potiphar's wife, has multiple very real applications to the practices of Atlantic slavery. The final question—who would sell their own family?—does not beg a single answer, but is open to many answers. Africans sold their own children and brethren into slavery to profit from the European and the Arab slave traders over the centuries. Within Brazil, especially during the final decades of slavery, when the internal trade from the North to the new coffee plantations of Rio and São Paulo became massive, not only slaves but also free blacks were commonly sold into slavery by masters. The great abolitionist firebrand the mulatto Luís Gama was such a figure, sold into slavery by his own father at the age of ten.[22] And then of course the question reaches out beyond the literal family relation to an idea of universal brotherhood. The idea that all of humanity constitutes one idyllic family, an infinitude of brothers and sisters, had been enshrined within the motto accompanying the renowned emblem of the antislavery society. This showed a kneeling male or, in another version, female slave asking respectively, "Am I not a man and a brother?" and "Am I not a woman and a sister?" The images enjoyed massive and immediate success in England, France, and North America in the late eighteenth century and continued an iconic life in the nineteenth century throughout Europe and the Americas, including of course Brazil.

Alves's final question in this poem answers the patronizing naivety of the earlier question with another, far more bitter one. When so many brothers have sold their own brothers into slavery, over such a long time, and in so many places, it is sadly pointless to ask the question "Am I not a man and a brother?" In the dog-eat-dog marketplace of Atlantic slavery, it doesn't matter a damn if you are my or someone else's brother. You will still be sold into slavery to make a fast buck. For all his apparent imaginative excess, there is a political hard edge to Alves's take on Atlantic slavery, and nowhere is this more apparent than in the conclusion to this poem.

The true power of Alves's verse comes from its combination of a furious sadness with a refusal to apportion blame in any simplistic manner. Embracing the full complexity of the trade nexus underlying the Atlantic slave systems, the poem does not provide easy answers, simply an overriding feeling of incredulous disgust and cosmic sadness. The work's continuing power stems from its refusal to allow religion any kind of reassuring function, and in this respect it is based in a bleak philosophical modernity. Alves draws on the heartrending pleas of the prophets of the Passion Psalms and of the book of Lamentations, but he is not prepared to offer any facile redemptive options. In the face of the horror of the slave trade, the voice of Africa articulates not merely a terrible sense of suffering, but a sense of abandonment, and the sense that the real suffering comes from the death of hope, that no matter what the victim says or does there is no reply from a higher power. The lamentation of the voice of Africa is met by a resounding silence. The thirsty land consumes the slaves' tears, which are locked away, hidden, forgotten forever in an earthly vault:

> ... Eu triste, abandonada,
> Em meio dos desertos desgarrada,
> Perdida marcho em vão!
> Se chóro bebe o pranto a areia ardente!
> Talvez ... p'ra que meu pranto, ó Deus clemente,
> Não descubras no chão! ... [23]

(... I am sad, abandoned
Disgraced in the middle of deserts

Lost, I march in vain,
If I weep . . . the hot desert drinks my tears/lamentation
Perhaps . . . all my weeping, O God of clemency,
Doesn't get discovered by you on the ground.)

The voice of Africa finally articulates the lost, silent, forgotten history of its trauma. In giving Africa such a terrific cry of lamentation, such a noisy way of commenting upon the processes of its silencing, Alves does at least try to create a space in which the subaltern can, if not speak, at least weep and wail.

The Waterfalls of Paulo Afonso

"E tudo se acabou!": Slavery and the Death of Love

In *O Navio Negreiro*, Alves made the Middle Passage reopen itself. In *Vozes de Africa* he created a new space for Africa to address Europe upon the theme of how slavery had ruined that continent. In *A Cachoeira de Paulo Afonso*, Alves created an epic love poem about the horrors of domestic slavery and the emotional and physical abuse of slaves. Sentimental narratives of doomed slave love on the plantation had of course been popular across Europe and the Americas for a century. The theme of tragic sexual relationships between slaves had been worked through in a variety of forms including poetry, drama, and of course the North American slave narratives. These in turn bled into the spectacular constructions of ruined slave families that lie at the heart of Stowe's *Uncle Tom's Cabin* and a plethora of subsequent plantation fiction. Aphra Behn's *Oroonoko* had established a violent and self-destructive narrative core for melodramatic novelistic treatments of the genre in the late seventeenth century. By the time Alves was writing, the most celebrated, globally influential, and long-lived novelistic example of this subgenre, sentimentalizing the tragic love of the transplanted African slave couple, was *Paul et Virginie* (*Paul and Virginia*), a work mentioned briefly in the contextualizing discussion of African representation at the opening of this chapter. The novel, by Jacques-Henri Bernardin de Saint-Pierre, first published in 1788, became a global best seller. The book remained in print throughout the nineteenth century. Its popularity in terms of scale and longevity was unprecedented and burst the boundaries of conventional publishing. The most beloved scenes were mass-produced, represented in the forms of decorations on ceramics and textiles, including wallpaper. Given the Brazilian Francophile elite's adoration of French Romantic literature, Alves must have

Chapter 2

2. Augusto Stahl, *Paulo Afonso Falls*, glass plate collodion print on paper, c. 1860.

been well aware of this text. Indeed, *A Cachoeira* could be read as an ironic interrogation of the fictional mechanisms that had made *Paul et Virginie* so attractive to a mainstream European readership as an approach to, and normalizing of, shattered slave romance. One of the most radical aspects of Alves's poem lies in its creation of a redemptive myth presenting slave suicide, not emancipation, as the ultimate act of liberation. It is an intimate, at times even an emotionally hysterical, poem. *A Cachoeira* is not afraid to confront female slave sexual abuse, or to celebrate suicide, indeed the suicide pact, as a political act of defiance. The work is formally disjointed and disjunctive, deliberately disrupted and disruptive. Formally, the work destabilizes the chronological and teleological conventions of linear narrative. It is composed of lyric fragments that narrate in new ways the emotional states of slave consciousness often on the threshold of traumatic dissolution.

Formal coherence in *A Cachoeira* is not to be found within conventional plot structures but emanates from extraordinary extended elemental metaphors. Castro Alves created his most intense and complicated slavery poetry around the metaphorics of death, slavery, liberation, and the movement of great waters. In the case of *Vozes de Africa*, it is the total absence of water in a desert landscape that frames the verse, the salt water of Africa's tears swallowed up in the parched land and silenced. Salt water and fresh water are of course elemental forces central to the symbolism of Brazilian syncretic religions. The two most powerful female deities within *Candomblé* are the goddess of streams and lakes, Oxum, and the goddess of the oceans, Iemanjá. The worship of these powerful female water spirits links Africa with its Afro-Brazilian slave heritage, and lies behind Alves's decision to base his two greatest slavery poems in the saline solution of the Atlantic Ocean (*O Navio Negreiro*) and the fresh water of rivers and waterfalls (*A Cachoeira*).

The waterfall of the title may, ironically, have been named after a notorious *bandeirante* of the eighteenth century who had penetrated the interior, hunting for Indians to enslave. The waterfalls were absorbed into liberationist Indian iconography and into imagery connected to black resistance over the next two centuries.[24] Waterfalls, slaves, and freedom are also umbilically connected in the imaginative culture of the Americas. Within the slave systems of North America, the Underground Railroad for a large number of escaped slaves terminated at Niagara Falls, and passage beyond the falls led into Canada and freedom. Consequently this great landmark was organically absorbed into the art and thought of slave liberation in the United States.[25] The nascent tourist industry merged with abolitionism in countless photographs showing newly arrived slaves, about to move into Canada, the real "land of the free," as the mighty falls smoked in the background.[26] In Brazil the Paulo Afonso falls became a focus for visual artists from an early date and enjoyed, in relative national aesthetic terms, an even higher profile than the Niagara Falls. The point at which the seven tributary rivers of the São Francisco unite to form one mighty cauldron of water became an iconic image when the French photographer Augusto Stahl, at the request of the Emperor Dom Pedro II, produced a stunning panoramic diptych of the scene as early as 1860.

The photograph communicates the sublimity of the scene in a truly Burkean manner (terror at the scale and energy of the natural forces combines with the sheer beauty of the rock formations and water currents). The image also, however, seems to cast a side glance at slavery and freedom. What really communicates both an idea of scale and of the triviality of human existence is the watching figure of a seated black man, in white shorts or loin-cloth, balanced upon a rocky precipice overlooking the steaming torrent, with the luminous spray rising behind him. This racially charged image was made in 1860, eighteen years before the abolition of slavery and five years before Alves began to assemble the lyrics for his narrative sequence *A Cachoeira*. Yet both this and the flood of subsequent photographs evoking the destructive potential of the falls were to become permanently inflected by Alves's work. Depictions of the falls were thenceforth saturated in an ecstatic yet tragic relation to slavery, and the falls became symbolically complicated, fraught, darker, more ambiguous, and finally more inspirational because of the manner in which Alves had imaginatively commandeered the natural phenomenon.

Alves's *A Cachoeira* is a highly wrought and hysterically ecstatic lyric sequence telling the tragic story of a young slave woman, Maria, and her lover, Lucas. The plot, simple and brutal, recounts a slave woman's rape and a male slave's inability to take physical revenge for the outrage, yet the poem comes at this familiar plot with a remarkable and disturbing set of ironic shifts. The bones of the plot are conventional and melodramatic and can be easily summarized. Coming back to Maria's slave hut in the evening, Lucas finds her gone. He searches for her and discovers her sailing down the river in a canoe, distraught. She confesses to him that she went bathing naked in a stream, and was suddenly set upon, pursued, and raped by her white owner. Lucas swears vengeance, but then remembers his deathbed promise to his mother. Lucas then recounts his mother's life story. She was persecuted and mortally wounded by her white mistress, because the mistress was jealous that Lucas's mother had a child (Lucas) with her slave master. Yet on her deathbed the mother made Lucas promise, because he was the son of a union between herself and her master, not to take vengeance on any of the family, or any white people. Facing the agony of his and Maria's current predicament, Lucas sees only one agonizing way out as the canoe drifts towards the edge of the Paulo Afonso falls. The poem ends with the two lovers facing death with a conflicted combination of terror and joy. In death they are taken up into the spirit of the mighty waters.

The theme is potentially highly compromised and relates closely to a set of canonical narratives that sentimentally indulge in the doomed and finally self-destructive love of young slave couples. Yet what saves *A Cachoeira* from sinking into the tradition of works that followed in the wake of *Oroonoko* and saturated the eighteenth- and nineteenth-century literature of sentiment with beautiful, doomed, and finally impotent slave lovers is the structure. This work, although close to the psychological monodrama of Tennyson's *Maud*, is not technically a monodrama, but a series of interspersed monologues, or lyric meditations, by the two central characters. The poet's narrative presence hovers about and above the interludes, making a series of interventions. Yet as a series of cleverly varied lyrics describing extreme emotional states, and focused on tragic love and insanity, the sequence in its entirety has much in common with the transformative landscapes of Tennyson's *Maud*. The power of Alves's long verse experiment stems from its fusing structure with geography and the natural world. The earlier analysis of *Vozes de Africa* revealed Alves's ability to create landscape descriptions that powerfully embody traumatic states of mind. Similarly, *A Cachoeira* describes emotional transformation and even spontaneous changes in thought through successive, wildly varied descriptions of nature. It is the literal course of nature that finally dictates the narrative very precisely as it follows the river through its origins in the arid *sertão* (backlands) out through the sugarcane land, to the mountains, and finally down into the waterfalls. This extended use of psychologized landscape to embody the journey of a people looks forward to the techniques of Euclides da Cunha. Because of this organizing principle, the poem is strangely poised between a teleological and cyclical structure.

Alves's most notable achievement in representing the slave body is that he does not present his lovers as tragic victims. They emerge as figures who choose death as the only logical and noble way to a life outside the geographical, physical, moral, and emotional imprisonment of slavery. Both are psychologically complex, indeed fragile and unstable characters, whose moods and motivations shift, as do the rhetorical registers in which these states are recorded. It is, consequently, a difficult and deeply disturbing poem to read. It describes processes of mental torture and pressures of suffering so intense that they threaten the psychological stability of conventional character. The poem's method anticipates the monuments of American and European experimental poetic modernism, and particularly the efforts to create a sort of lyric epic verse. Alves's construction of discreet but often dramatic lyric sections, whole in themselves but in deep communication with one another, often suggests that we are within the aesthetic ambience of Eliot's *Four Quartets* or of Pound's *Cantos*. Yet *A Cachoeira* has a confidence in the values and emotional commitments of nineteenth-century Romanticism, and an inspirational relationship with nature, that both Pound and Eliot in their different ways resisted and were frightened of. It is finally Pablo Neruda's *Canto General* that had the courage to compete with the legacy of Alves.

A Cachoeira is the most visionary, the most realistic, and the most idealistic of Alves's works. The weird, paradoxical antics of *A Cachoeira* come out in the terrific final lyric, evoking the last seconds of the lovers as they plunge over the falls to their deaths. These lines are as good a place as any to begin thinking about how the poem works and what it is saying. The lyric is representative of the astonishing emotional displacements that work through the poem as a whole. This climax shows how Alves's poetic vision can embrace contradictions and emotional chaos. Alves shares with Wordsworth an ability to conjure magical linguistic processes that make natural phenomena and human emotion part of the vast cycles of nature:

> Á BEIRA DO ABISMO
> E DO INFINITO
>
> A celeste Africana, a virgem—Noite
> Cobria as faces . . . Gotta a gotta os astros
> Colhiam-lhe das mãos no peito seu . . .
> Um beijo infindo suspirou nos ares
>
> . . . .
>
> A canôa rolava! Abriu-se a um tempo
> O precipio! . . . e o céu! . . .[27]

> (ON THE VERGE OF THE ABYSS
> AND THE INFINITE
>
> The celestial Africanness, the virgin—Night
> Covers their faces . . . Drop by drop the stars
> Fall from her hands to her breasts . . .
> An infinite kiss is breathed out into the air
>
> . . . .
>
> The canoe goes over! . . . Time opens itself
> The precipice! . . . and the sky!)

This double death becomes finally mythical, at one level a reference to the traditional belief of the slave that they return to the African homeland through death by water. This was, as we have seen, a theme Alves also explored in *O Navio*

Negreiro when explaining why so many slaves chose to drown themselves on the Middle Passage. In *A Cachoeira* Alves also again returns to the creation of Africa as a personification, but unlike *Vozes de Africa* the voice here is quintessentially female, even virginal. This female Africa is embodied as the night, a nurturing darkness, a proper dark, gently engulfing the faces of the doomed lovers. This conclusion enacts a semiotic revolution, upending the time-honored and superstitious European associations that see night in terms of negativity, obscurity, blackness, and fear of the unknown. The darkness, the blackness, engulfing these trusting children of Africa is maternal, loving, embracing, protective, womanly, and beautiful. The metaphoric amplitude of the verse is equally ambitious, the water of the Middle Passage, the water of the São Francisco river, the water of Maria's tears, of Africa's tears, and the milk from Africa's breasts are all taken up in this open language. The infinite kiss is both the final ecstatic kiss of the lovers, united in a Brazilian *liebestod* and the motherly kiss of Africa as she takes back her children.

The conclusion is violent death for the lovers, but it is also simultaneously a rebirth, or perhaps even something more mysterious. What are we supposed to take from those magical last words: "A canôa rolava! . . . Abriu-se a um tempo / O precipio! . . . e o céu! . . ."? They describe the movement into a state both inside and outside what is understood as human existence; we are in the space of death and a space beyond death. "Rolar" is a nuanced verb of motion, embodying a variety of meanings that taken together seem to describe the final process of the boat's and the lovers' fate. It can mean "to go forward steadily, to sway, to cause to revolve, to spin in circles, to tumble and fall precipitously" and consequently embodies the destruction of the boat and by extension the violently shifting states of mind of the lovers, on the verge of simultaneous annihilation and apotheosis.[28] Similarly "abrir," even without the passive inflection, is a verb that carries a network of relevant intimations. It commonly means "to open," but also means "to cut, to tear open, to pierce, to unlock, to unfasten," all meanings suggesting both an end of one state and the beginning of a new one, and a verb that also clearly carries a sexual charge in its present context. These various meanings of the verb convey a revolutionary movement into a new social mode: "to found, to establish, to initiate, to begin."[29] We are in a moment out of time, or an achievement of a state of consciousness in which all existence, pain and joy, terror and peace, love and hate, fall into a strange harmony, an ecstasy, an orgasm. Time opens up to absorb all space, the space below and the space above. The conclusion is Alves's own very special version of the marriage of heaven and hell as *liebestod*, a brilliant retake on "ertrinken, versinken, –unbewusst, –höchste

Lust!" (drown, be engulfed, unconscious, supreme joy/pleasure!), the climactic words of Richard Wagner's *liebestod* in *Tristan und Isolde*.

Alves, throughout the poem, fuses an ecstatic and redemptive vision for the lovers (the climax of which I have just set out) with a hard-nosed and even cynical dimension. Several lyrics articulate the sordid and hopeless conditions of slave life that had to be surmounted in order to enable this final moment of Romantic and uncluttered ecstasy. The uncomfortable daring of such a forced set of disjunctive aesthetic unions makes *A Cachoeira* a deeply disconcerting creation. It is as if the Shelley who wrote the final lyric sequence that concludes the fourth act of *Prometheus Unbound* has been fused with Maupassant, at his most dismally unrelenting.

Alves has the ability to take the language of Romantic banality, or cliché, and elevate it into something beyond itself, both by ironic juxtaposition with another register that is transformative, or simply by a sheer force of belief in his own capacity to raise the old terms from their death-bed of overfamiliarity. For example, the opening three sections of the poem that introduce the character of the idealized slave girl Maria begin conventionally enough, celebrating her loveliness by describing her harmony with nature. Yet the third section suddenly shatters such formal familiarity and takes the celebration into a space of Alvesian excess that throws form and emotion to the winds and possesses a Blakean capacity of universalist animation. The joy the girl generates enlivens nature, reaching down to the smallest insect:

> E em lindos cardumes
> Subtis vagalumes
> Accendem os lumes
> P'ra o baile na flor . . .
>
> Os grillos em festa
> Começam na orchestra
> Febris á tocar
>
> E as breves
> Phalenas
> Vão leves
> Serenas
> Em bando
> Girando

Walsando,
Voando,
No ar! . . .[30]

(And in beautiful unison
The subtle fireflies
Ignite flames
For the flowering festival

The crickets
Celebrate
And begin to play
Their feverish
Orchestrations

And the transient
Moths
Delicately
Serenely
In unison
Spin
Waltz
Fly
In air! . . .)

Has anyone written about human joy by describing the life of insects in this way before? This is poetry that sees into nature with the prophetic animationist spirit of Christopher Smart's *Jubilato Agno*, or maybe it is a Brazilian variant upon William Blake's visionary hymn in celebration of the transformative power of freedom, and the necessity of revolutionary violence, the dance around the wine presses of Luvah, in Book IX of *Vala* or *The Four Zoas*:

> The Sportive root, the Earthworm, the small beetle, the wise Emmet
> Dance round the Winepresses of Luvah. The Centipede is there,
> The ground Spider with many Eyes, the Mole clothed in Velvet,
> The Earwig arm'd, the tender Maggot, emblem of Immortality,
> The Slow Slug, the grasshopper that sings & laughs & drinks:

> The winter comes, he folds his slender bones without a murmur—...
> ... Naked in all their beauty, dancing round the Wine Presses.[31]

Similarly, Alves orchestrates and choreographs his cosmic insect artists who perform, make music, dance and light, providing a synesthetic moment of natural harmony. The section works as a tragically uplifting coda before the catastrophic onset of the sexual violence that is the narrative mechanism around which all the lyrics rotate, in a sort of perverse aesthetic Copernicanism. Fire, an ancient symbol of destructive lust, but a much more open metaphor for Alves, first appears in the poem in this gentle prelude, and takes the form of the phosphorescence of the fireflies, who delicately illuminate this ephemeral spectacle. As the poem progresses, this scene stands for the fragile perfection of the relationship the lovers Lucas and Maria have constructed for themselves amid the brutal traps slavery sets for human emotional bonds. Against all the odds, this precious spectacle exists, and seems to offer the hope of a natural world that reflects, and indeed embodies, the most uplifting of human emotions. The idea of the lovers as part of this prelapsarian harmonic unity, oblivious, innocent natural forms, playing their gentle and loving games against the backdrop of an inevitable immolation, is taken up in the next lyric. The concept condensed in the line "Alegres sob o abismo ... os passarinhos! ..." (Ecstatic above the abyss ... the songbirds!) both embodies the sense that the lovers can enjoy a genuine moment of bliss lifted above the abysm of slavery and simultaneously intimates that nature's creatures exist and celebrate existence oblivious to the suffering of others, or the outrages of human cruelty. Turner taught us that sunsets will continue to be beautiful no matter what abominations are perpetrated against the slave bodies that are so gorgeously illuminated. Alves knew that the songbirds go on singing no matter what abominations are happening around them.

It is with this complicated prelude that the poem moves suddenly into the section entitled "A Queimada," the "The Forest Fire," a title that can also be translated as "The Raging Fury." Alves's description of the fire resonates with Piero di Cosimo's astonishing depiction of the same subject painted over three hundred years earlier.[32] Both works meditate on the seemingly useless violence and destruction of innocence that these natural holocausts involve. Both works are deeply sensitive to the pain and terror of the sufferers but realize it is the very destructive grandeur of the fire that enables this pitiable spectacle. And of course this is not just a forest fire, this is a fire of the mind:

Nas rubras roscas estorteja as mattas
Que espanadam o sangue das cascatas
Do roto coração! . . .[33]

(The jungles writhe, ensanguined severed worms
Which expel blood in cascades
From the ruined heart . . .)

Suddenly the gentle fireflies of the forest have been replaced by these monstrous incendiary worms, themselves mutilated and tortured. The fire becomes the essential symbol for the way slavery feeds on itself, cycles full of sound and fury generating sadness: "O estampido estupendo das queimadas / Se enrola de quebradas em quebradas" (The stupendous stampede of fire / Coils itself up, in ravine after ravine). The casual but engulfing violence of the fire is also given a subtle human dimension because the final phrase carries an echo of the colloquial Brazilian Portuguese expression "quebra quebra," which means "to cuff about, to rain blows down, to have a street fight." Yet again, however, my translation gives less than half the story, for the second line is not to be pinned down to one English version. It could equally be translated in a manner that brought out erotic ecstasy rather than destructive violence, not that these two are of course mutually exclusive in human emotional life. The verb "enrolar" could be translated as any of the following: "curls itself up, rolls itself up, wraps itself up, twists itself up, swells itself up, engulfs itself, or fondles itself," while the final phrase could mean "in curve after curve." These are curious creatures, worms of fire, which also suggest the salamanders of Spanish and Portuguese medieval erotic lyrics, which like the lover's tortured heart live inside the hot flames: "Qual vive salamandra in fiamma ardente." The reptiles that live within the fires of love, embodying a fraught fusion of opposites, are both victims and destroyers, agonized and agonizing. Like slavery itself, they are locked into a cycle of self-consuming violence, a spectacular, arbitrarily beautiful, but finally pointless immolation. There is a terrible sense that in the emotional inferno generated by slavery, and generated explicitly in the mind of Lucas and Maria, destructive pain is the only emotion that survives, that means anything, that is in fact real.

The entire lyric sequence is at one level an examination, indeed exhumation, of the fantasies that have been generated around the slave body, an insistent questioning of what is "real" when it comes to the fictionalization of the slave body. Both Maria and Lucas are initially idealized, or in fact hyper-idealized, according to the stereotypes of sentimental abolition literature coming out of the Anglo-American tradition. Maria is overabundantly beautiful, virtuous, delicate, and loyal, the "casta flor do sertão" (the pure flower of the wilderness), and appears initially in a conceit that might have been adapted out of Wordsworth's early pastoral poetry, almost as an extension of her dwelling place. Her charming, clean, welcoming slave cabin, "tão pequena e bella" (so petite and beautiful), is an embodiment of herself. Lucas is initially equally overbrimming with predictable qualities of handsomeness, virility, and creative vision. He is, ironically, an illustration of the completely happy, healthy, and seemingly contented slave:

> Um bello escravo do terra
> Cheio de vico e valor
> Era o filho das florestas
> Era o escravo lenhador . . .[34]

> (A beautiful slave from the earth
> Over-brimming with strength and gracefulness
> He was the son of the forest
> He was the slave woodsman)

Yet Alves rapidly develops the portrait in ways that start to raise questions. How much is too much? When does praise become parody? Alves's idealization deliberately sets out to take Lucas beyond the merely human, to thrust upon him an almost absurd mythogrification, whereby he is not only godlike, but emerges quite literally and ludicrously as the bronze statue of a god or ancient hero:

> Aquelle vulto soberbo
> Vivamente alumiado
> Atravessa o descampado
> Como uma estatua de bronze
> Do incendio ao fulo clarão[35]

> (What a superb figure
> Illuminated with the life force

> He passes through the wilderness
> Like a bronze statue
> Forged from a fire of fulvous lightning)

These lines explicitly look forward to the unashamedly celebratory later lyric "Sangue Africano" (African Blood) when, having heard Maria's pitiful narrative of her rape, Lucas rises up "como o tigre bravo" (like a wild tiger), becomes "a estátua terrível da vigança" (a terrible statue of vengeance), and is explicitly idealized as the statue of a Greek hero in the act of quintessential revenge:

> Com o gesto bravo, sacudido, fero,
> A dextra ameaçando a immensidade . . .
> Era um bronze de Achilles furioso[36]

> (With a ferocious gesture, elegant, violent,
> His right hand confronting the surrounding immensity
> He was a bronze statue of the infuriated Achilles)

Alves's use of hyperbole is quite deliberate, part of an aesthetic calculation designed to produce a celebratory absolute against which Lucas's mental dissolution and emotional ruination a few lines later on, and indeed in the remainder of the lyric sequence, can be measured. Yet Alves seeks not merely dramatic effect but the constant buffeting of the easy idealizations so beloved of abolitionist poets and novelists. What makes the verse so powerful is that at one level Alves is committed to the very traditions of slave valorization he interrogates. He will not throw the aesthetic baby out with the bathwater, but he demands that his verse think about exactly what the appropriate terms for the celebration of slave violence might be. The final effect is also intimately related to the manner in which Alves forces the reader to empathize with this initial poetic vision of the slave. The couplet representing the statue forged from bronze in a lightning strike looks forward to the imagery that combines Achilles and the tiger in a single monument. The lines are not merely description, but the poet's entry into a myth of origins. Alves in beholding his own creation, the slave Lucas, imagines what it must have taken to create him in this form, and what forces led to such an extraordinary consummation.

There are many ruses Alves uses to entice the reader into his opening vision of slavery. These ideals are set up with an eye to their bitter ironic dismantling in the latter stages of the sequence. Alves draws the reader in with frequent dramatic exclamations commenting upon the nature not only of Lucas's appearance but on the nature of his art. Lucas is presented singing improvised ("improvisara") slave songs as he walks toward Maria's hut. This African-evolved music has the power that so much Romantic verse craved, to carry the poet back to his childhood mind:

> Eu gosto dessas cantigas
> Que me vem lembrar a infancia;
> São meas velhas amigas
> Por ellas morro de amor[37]

> (I like these songs
> That carry me back to the memory of infancy
> They are my old friends
> I would die for the love of them)

This irony is bitter. What is worth dying for? Would the poet die for the art of the slave? Alves seems caught in his own trap, taken up in the excess of the moment to which he links himself through the slave's song with the idea of dying for true love, of the Romantic death pact, which is to be the lover's final lot. As the poem progresses, these lines appear increasingly problematic; we are not sure whether the poet's excess is foolish, insensitive, or indeed aligned in a tragic harmony with the desperate act of suicide.

The constant pressure of these moments of idealization provides an elaborate setting for the climactic scene of emotional despair, in the lyric "Desespero" (Beyond Hope) where Lucas, confronted with the reality of Maria's rape, and its implications for both of them, violently deconstructs the myth of the noble slave. Lucas provides a psychologically brutal account of what it means, at a day-to-day level, to be enslaved. The lyric opens by calling up more animal analogies in order to justify immediate violent revenge. Lucas compares his predicament to that of sublime beasts, which repay any injury with immediate and fatal violence, asking rhetorically, "Is it a crime if the jaguar takes in his teeth a perfidious rodent stolen from an Indian?" Yet he immediately condemns these analogies as pointless if set in relation to the slave's status. The lines that follow summarize slave existence as a form of what Orlando Patterson in his breakthrough 1990 monograph *Slavery and Social Death: A Comparative Study* would famously insist to be a form of degraded and invisible life outside a white defined social contract of any visible or meaningful human existence:

> Sim! Nós somos reptis... Qu'importa a especie?
> A lesma é vil,—a cascavel é bravo
> E vens fallar de crimes ao captivo?
> Então não sabes o que é ser escravo!...[38]
>
> Ser escravo—é nascer no alcouce escuro
> Dos seios infamados da vendida...
> Filho de perdição no berço impuro
> Sem leite para a bocca resequida...
> A terra—sem amor!... sem Deus—o espaço!
>
> Ser escravo—é, do homens repellido,
> Ser tambem repellido pela fera;
> Sendo dos dous irmãos pasto querido
> Que o tigre come e o homem dilacera...
>
> —É do lodo no lodo sacudido
> Ver que acqui ou além nada o espera
> Que em cada leito novo ha mancha nova...
> No berço... após no tóro... após na cova[39]

> (Yes! We are vermin... What species exactly, who cares?
> The slug is vile, the rattlesnake is fierce
> And you come to talk about crime to the slave?
> Such a one doesn't know what it means to be a slave!...
>
> To be a slave—is to be born into a dark brothel
> From wombs made polluted by sale
> A son of perdition human filth from the cradle
> Without any milk for the frantic mouth...
> An earth—without love!... A godless firmament!

> To be a slave—is to be rejected by all men,
> To be continually rejected like a beast;
> A tasty morsel fought over by two brothers
> Delicious to tiger and man alike . . .
>
> And wiggled from one shit heap to another
> Knowing it's pointless whether it happens here or there, it's
>   all hopeless
> In each new resting place there's a new shame
> From cradle . . . to maelstrom . . . to grave! . . .)

These are horrible lines, and this is the hole lying in the heart of the poem, a set of unanswerable truths about how slaves are perceived and how they are forced to live. Lucas's analysis articulates an appalled and appalling verity that the rest of the poem will struggle to question and to overturn. Alves has touched bottom here with no way back from this particular vision of social damnation.

Yet Alves has other, less bleak but perhaps more audacious, strategies for bringing home the impossibility of really communicating the slaves' existence. The poem maintains a constant ability to turn the platitudes of abolition literatures on their head. Alves dares to be outrageous with cliché and employs an almost Whitmanesque extravagance and, like Whitman, is prepared to court tastelessness as an aesthetic option. Instead of the nihilism of Lucas's astonishing vision of the slave's existential position, take for example the climax to the Gothic lyric *Diálogo do Echos* (Dialogue of the Echoes). The main body of the lyric presents the desperate Lucas moving through the deserted slave cabin of Maria. As he sees signs of her distressed departure, he declaims his fury and lust for vengeance with each new discovery. Yet each oratorical outburst is met with a single obscure word from the echo that inhabits the room. This echo does not merely repeat what has been last said but, by taking the final syllable of much longer words, transforms meaning and context and meets overblown rhetoric with impenetrable, sphinxlike monosyllables. To the massive question directed at Maria "Que fazes tu sobre a terra" (What are you doing on this earth), "E o echo responde:—Erra!" (The echo replies:—Wrong!). Lucas, as passionate avenger, is drowned in an ambiguity of fathomless economy, for that final word could mean a whole host of things. "Errar" is a verb with myriad meanings and inferences in Brazilian Portuguese, some of which could apply to Lucas's perception and some to Maria's fate. Here in disembodied imperative form it could mean all or none of the following: "Mistaken!" "It's a mistake!" "You made a mistake!"

"You are mistaken!" "You have taken one thing for another!" "Ramble!" "Gone astray!" "Gone roaming!" "Sin!" "Failure!" "Offence!" "You have offended!" The meeting of Lucas's melodramatic extravagance and the laconic terseness of the echo becomes increasingly saturated with black humor. This climaxes in the final exchange:

> Onde ha sangue, sangue escorre! . . .
> Villão! Deste ferro e braço,
> Nem a terra, nem o espaço,
> Nem mesmo Deus te soccorre!! . . ."
>
> O echo responde:—Corre!⁴⁰

> (Where there is blood, blood will run out
> Villain! From this arm and machete
> Neither the earth, nor space,
> Nor God himself will protect you!!
> The echo replies:—Run!)

Again the verb "Corre," extracted from the longer word "soccore," is multidimensional. I have translated it in its most immediate meaning, as the simple but open-ended imperative "Run!", but it could mean a whole slew of other things. All these meanings are intensely ironic when set against the word that has generated them, "soccore," meaning to protect or to offer succor. One set of meanings relates explicitly to tracking something down: "Pursue!" "Chase!" "Hunt!" Yet the same verb also carries the inverse meaning and could command precisely the opposite: "Flee!" "Fly!" "Take to your heels!" And, most significantly for a slave, "Run-away!" The verb is used repeatedly in different forms by Maria in the lyric "Nos Campos" (On the fields) during the description of the young woman's desperate flight from her rapist, before he finally gets her. "Avante! Corramos! / Corramos ainde!" (Go! Let's run! Run faster!) urges the poet narrator as he simultaneously comments upon and recounts her flight. And then finally come the terrible one-word series of lines describing the rape: "Na douda / Corrida / Vencida / Perdida" (Into insanity / running / taken / lost). Given the astonishing and dark work Alves calls upon this verb to perform during the account of the rape scene, it is therefore not clear what the echo advises Lucas to do. If it is advising rapid pursuit, then is this pursuit of the roving Maria, or of the slave master who raped her, or of both? If the echo is advising Lucas to run away, is he advising him to run away from slavery to Maria, or to run away from the agonizing dilemma of her rape, in other words to forget about it and to abandon her? In this sense the echo is articulating that long-held truism so dear to the heart of the runaway slave that there is no problem in life so big that you cannot run away from it. It is at this point that Alves makes the truly outrageous move of backing off from the dialogue of Lucas and the echo to introduce the observational narrative voice of the poet who declaims:

> Como o cão elle em torno o ar aspira
> Depois se orientou;
> Fareja as hervas . . . descobriu a pista
> E rapida marchou.[41]

> (He turned like a dog and sniffed the air
> After having oriented himself;
> Nosed the grass . . . discovered the track
> And rapidly sprang off.)

How on earth does this function within the semiotics of slave literature? The paragon of black slave masculinity, the outraged lover desperate to find his abused lover and avenge her abuse, is suddenly converted into a slave-hunting hound. The naturalistic details of dog behavior (the specific use of the verb "farejar"), and of the hunt, are brought in to operate what on the face of it seems an obscene animalization. What Alves is doing here, however, is confronting the reader's own prejudices and expectations. Bizarrely, in turning the noble Lucas into a slave-dog, Alves articulates the completeness of the transformation that the outrage of Maria has occasioned. At another level the movement is one of empowerment, for the slave hound operated within one tradition of abolitionist representation as a sign for the slave power.[42] Read this way, Lucas is assuming the guise of his tormentors at their most empowered and inhuman. Yet one cannot finally retreat from the most basic level of meaning. As a slave Lucas has been considered on a par with domestic animals all his life, and so at a moment of crisis he reverts to type.[43] It takes a tremendous amount of daring to make such an imaginative equation, and it is at this point of comic monstrosity that Alves approaches a sardonic-comic impasse reminiscent of Whitman's farcical mimicry of the role of slave auctioneer in his section from *Leaves of Grass*, "I sing the body electric": "A slave at auction! I help the auctioneer . . . the sloven doesn't know half his business."[44] For both Alves and Whitman, the creative command is not merely "know your enemy" but "enter your enemy." When it comes to poetry, as with any other art form, slavery makes excruciating demands on its muse.

CHAPTER 3

Obscure Agency: Machado de Assis Framing Black Servitudes

Rigid behavioural alternatives have never existed in the history of slavery, and the stress on them stultifies any enquiry.

—M. I. Finley, *Ancient Slavery and Modern Ideology*

Assis and the Presumed Responsibilities of "Mixed Race" Authorship

From the time Machado de Assis first gained a literary reputation until now, there has been much debate, often vitriolic, among readers, writers, and scholars concerning the extent to which he did and did not engage explicitly, morally, or sympathetically with slavery in his work. Much of this writing has descended into debates over the extent to which Assis's racial hybridity functioned or failed to function within the work. My analysis is not interested in questions of whether or not Assis's racial identity inflected his writing. Given the man's protean ingenuity and innate capacity for disguises, the configuration of his racial identity must remain a critical dead end. In the following set of close readings, it will become apparent that Assis is an ingenious artist and not a social propagandist, or indeed any kind of ideologue. It will also become apparent, however, that slavery and its inheritance within Brazilian urban society remained a profound concern, even though Assis chose to come at slavery with cunning invention and indirection. My detailed readings of the short stories and of the late and formally boldly experimental novels *Jacob and Esau, Counselor Ayres' Memorial* and, most importantly, *Posthumous Memoirs of Brás Cubas* establish that Assis uncovered the dark pressures and intimacies generated by urban slavery in Rio with creative amplitude and a uniquely complicated social vision. Assis was above all an ethical and creative investigator of urban slavery and its legacies. His deferred and camouflaged approaches to slavery continue to generate lively speculation, particularly within Brazilian criticism, over the extent to which he can be seen to have confronted or indeed critiqued not just the issue of Brazilian slavery but any of the important sociopolitical concerns of his day.[1]

Very shortly after his death, bitter accusations started to fly. Hemetério dos Santos, who considered himself a fellow mixed-race Carioca, upbraided the mulatto Assis for having betrayed Brazil's black population and black heritage. This is typical of a certain approach to Assis that demanded, and in some quarters still demands, that his art follow obvious abolitionist and Afro-Brazilian agendas.[2] The manner in which the recent rediscovery of mixed-race authors who did devote their life and work to the recovery, recording, and explication of Afro-Brazilianism in very direct ways has also informed the debates around Assis's race agendas. Past distrust and indeed current hatred of Assis can still bleed into the popular media's construction of Brazil's late nineteenth-century literary landscape. The great Afro-Brazilian mystic and father of Brazilian symbolist poetry Cruz e Souza is a fascinating case in point. A victim of racism at many levels, and certainly a neglected genius in his own harsh life, Cruz e Souza has emerged as the most brilliant and experimental Brazilian poet of the late nineteenth century. He was also an author who not only violently criticized the inheritance of slavery but who celebrated blackness and particularly female Afro-Brazilian beauty and sexuality with an unmatched lyrical intensity. The recent exciting and highly erotic treatment of Sousa in the film *Cruz e Souza o Poeta do Desterro* (Cruz e Souza the Banished Poet) deals very harshly with Assis. It is a fact that Cruz e Souza was vetoed from entering the Brazilian Academy of Letters while Assis was its president. In one scene of the film, friends and supporters of Sousa shower a bust of Assis with rice flour while they chant the following street ballad:

> Machado de Assis, assás,
> Machado de assás, Assis;
> Oh! Zebra escrita com giz
> Pega na pena faz "zás,"
> Sae-lhe o "Borba" por um triz
> Plagiário do "Gil-Blás"
> Que de Le Sage por trás,
> Banalidades nos diz,
> Pavio quem arde sem gaz,
> Carranca de chafariz,
> Machado de Assis, assás,
> Machado de assás, Assis

This translates roughly as "Machado de Assis, too much, / Machado enough already, Assis / Oh zebra written with chalk (i.e. an impermanent medium), / When you try to write (entrap) with a quill, zoom (it, the zebra, disappears) / You almost did not produce (generate) Borba / You plagiarized *Gil Blas* / You talk banalities to us imitating Le Sage, / You're a wick without gas, / You figurehead fountain. / Machado de Assis, enough already, / Machado, too much."[3] Apparently this was a popular street song of the day. It attacks Assis for being trivial, a product of miscegenation (the zebra reference) and, above all, in literary terms no better than a plagiarist of unremarkable bourgeois French literature. These charges are, as we shall see, not just unfair but inaccurate assessments of the work. But this exuberantly bitter little *pasquinade* does get across the vital point that Assis was, and is, viewed with a lot of suspicion around his race agenda, his moral positioning, and his qualities as a truly "Brazilian" author. Yet Assis was not, and is never going to be, aligned with fin de siècle cultural archaeologists of creolization; he had and has nothing to do with Manuel Querino's mighty project. In aesthetic terms he is producing a completely different form of art from that of the visionary Cruz e Souza.[4] Saying this is not to devalue the achievement of any of these authors. As we shall see, Assis does introduce the black body as a physical entity into his novels. This was inevitable given the manner in which every aspect of the social world he describes is serviced by the slave.[5] Yet because his black characters often appear, on a superficial reading, to be peripheral, anonymous, or even silenced, many of his contemporaries and near contemporaries, and a bevy of subsequent critics, saw him as refusing or side-stepping responsible engagement with slavery and post-slavery debate. This presumed absence in the work continued to be seen by many as particularly reprehensible because of the mixed-race status of Assis. The first extended criticism of his work, included in the magisterial five-volume history of Brazilian literature by the now almost completely forgotten Sílvero Romero, not only attacked Assis but also listed a host of negative early appraisals that highlighted Assis's apparent lack of commitment and refusal to talk about social and racial issues. These included negative polemics by the mystical lyric poet Cruz e Souza, and a host of minor figures including Múcio Texeira and Agripino Grieco.[6] Romero, if he is remembered at all, has become something of a figure of fun. His celebration of Tobias Barreto as infinitely superior to Assis has inevitably damned him in the eyes of later literary critics. Yet Romero remains interesting as an extreme example of the kind of critical ambience in which Assis wrote; recently described tactfully as a writer "steeped in an ethnological and sociological determinism," Romero might less tactfully be designated as a primitive white supremacist.[7]

Assis was writing, and then was received, during periods when intellectual and philosophical speculation on race and Brazil's future was something of an obsession in intellectual and literary circles.[8] By the mid-twentieth century no less a figure than the titan of Brazilian cultural history and passionate celebrant of Jorge Amado, Gilberto Freyre, basically accused Assis not only of selling out over his engagement with slavery, but also, because of his cursory engagement with the minutiae of Afro-Brazilian folk cultures, of not really representing Brazilian culture at all.[9] In Freyre's reading he emerges as a sort of European *literateur* in disguise. Freyre also dismissed Afro-Brazilian appreciation of Assis as based in a superficial counterracism, a sort of blind *negritude* construction that celebrated Assis as a black in ways he would not have appreciated. Freyre concluded: "Particularly among Negroes ... [Assis] is appreciated now perhaps not so much for his social analysis of the bourgeois society of the Brazilian Empire as for his status as an Afro-American. Though this sort of appreciation does not after all affect an author's literary merits, it is hardly the sort of tribute Machado or any of his contemporaries would have seen or even wanted."[10]

Other critics see Assis's deliberate embrace of certain formal European models (Cervantes, Sterne) as providing a way out of the narrow determinist or regionalist approaches of the critics and authors who surrounded him.[11] These debates and their history are well rehearsed in Assis studies and do not need reiterating here. The extent to which Assis was or was not a didactic social critic with a recognizable agenda on race is not a line of Assis studies that has much bearing on the following analysis. Such debates do not concern themselves with the close reading of Assis's texts and tend to relate the work to his biography and its relation to daily politics in ways that close down Assis's profoundly ambiguous art.[12] With the possible exception of the short story *Pai contra Mãe*, a test case that literary criticism has latched onto as quite clearly confronting the horror of urban slavery in Brazil head on, it is fair to conclude that Assis, in the later works, did not write in any straightforward or partisan manner about the social operations of slavery.[13] His insights and creative responses to this dark institution need to be teased out with the utmost delicacy; if the reader pulls on Assis's connection to slavery too hard, it snaps and disappears. That Assis's consistent engagement with slavery in the short stories and the four great late novels continues to remain invisible to many of his critics is borne out by the fact that slavery barely features within the pages or index of David Jackson's otherwise comprehensive and thoroughly researched 2015 *Machado de Assis: A Literary Life*. What the following analysis emphasizes is the manner in which the creative exploration of slavery and intimacy was taken into new, darkly delicate, and still little-understood aesthetic territory by Machado de Assis. It is argued that slavery's shadow falls across the later works, and that the subject infiltrates the last novels that he wrote on both sides of the great divide of 1888. Slavery also inhabits those peculiar stories composed at the end of his life, as slavery officially dragged towards, and then beyond, its demise. In the mature work again and again, the body of the domestic slave hovers around the bourgeois and erotic concerns of his white, socially paralyzed and morally vapid Carioca cast of characters. His fictions suggest that slave bodies can be outwardly ignored, but that they cannot be hidden from the inner consciousness. Slaves weirdly inflect the moods, thoughts, and actions of the nominally free whites. Assis existed in a slave-saturated city, and he explored the domestic impacts of slavery in ways that stand apart from the often melodramatic and extreme hierarchies of the Anglo-American traditions of slave fiction.

His approach to slaves and slavery was also very different from those taken by, for example, Lima Barreto, who dealt with race in a crudely direct and satiric manner.[14] Assis's most extreme reaction to this specific tradition was to crystallize around his response to the Brazilian celebration of its own emancipation moment in 1888.[15] Throughout his late work Assis's concerns might be seen, indeed have been seen by recent critics, to reach outside the paradigms of Brazilian provincialism towards Europe's modernist and protomodernist experiments with the novel.[16] Some critics see a sinister Europeanizing that has converted Assis into a Latin American resurrection of Laurence Sterne or even into something "Proustian before Proust," and these literary makeovers have also been seen to involve his literal "whitening," for a Western audience.[17]

Assis's late work has also been read in relation to structuralist and poststructuralist debates on authorial "authority" and intentionality under the rather tired shadow of post Barthesian/Foucaultian debates concerning the "death of the author," and what has been termed Assis's "discovery of his own removability."[18] The accretion of critical superstructures onto Assis serves no useful purpose.

Assis's habitual irony in the late novels, his narrative distancing and fragmentation, his parodic questioning of the limits of conventional novelistic plot structures, and his interrogation of the moral collapse of his bourgeois Rio milieu, are all in sympathy with major experimental European fiction of the period. His central white characters are recognizable, indeed unsettlingly familiar, to a European middle-class bourgeois readership at the end of the nineteenth century. His cast of intellectually exhausted, socially embalmed urban sophisticates could naturally rub shoulders with the inhabitants of the early Henry James and Virginia Woolf, or Ford Madox Ford, and preeminently, of course, Flaubert.

His characters would have been able to hold a spiritual conversation with the inhabitants of Chekhov's mature short stories or the performers in Joyce's "The Dead." And yet the society in which these jaded, emotionally corrupt and corrupting beings slide and idle about approaches humanity and power through an economics of ownership that Europe and North America did not share at this stage. Assis's society is a slave society, and Brazilian slavery was unique. As the oldest, largest, most long-lived and most endemic Atlantic-diasporic slave society to have been generated, Brazilian slavery threw up unique social structures organized around absolute power and its related social caprices, and Assis's fiction constantly circles around, probes, and searches this reality.

Brazilian slavery, and urban domestic slavery in particular, is also a reality that throws Assis's literary and formal placement into contradictory and confusing spaces. The revolutionary work to bring out precisely how ideologically complex Assis's engagement with the social and power implications of different slave systems might be was of course that of Roberto Schwarz, who remains, and will remain, an intellectual giant within Assis studies. The appearance of Schwarz's *Ao Vencedor as Batatas: Forma literária e processo social nos inícios do romance Brasileiro* and the outstanding *Um Mestre na Periferia do Capitalismo: Machado de Assis* transformed the theoretical landscape around Assis, and continues to do so.[19] The brilliant 2001 translation of the latter book, with an equally superb introduction by John Gledson, *A Master on the Periphery of Capitalism: Machado de Assis*, took Schwarz into a theoretical space that included Europe and North America.[20] Schwarz's supra-Marxist two-part analysis revolutionized understanding of Assis's sophisticated critique of the economic operations of slavery within the nascent capitalism of late nineteenth-century Brazil, and brought out the construction of social classes within the mature fiction. He also focused on Assis's engagement with power and the behavioral camouflages that systems of absolute power enforce. Schwarz had had to confront the workings of absolute power, and the compromises it enforces on its victims, because he lived through the Brazilian dictatorship. Much of his formative thinking about slavery, power relations, and behavioral mimicry in Assis's earlier fiction happened while he lived in forced exile in Paris. Above all Schwarz almost obsessively demonstrated how the combination of "caprice and volubility" within the mentality of the master class operates to contaminate every level of society.[21] The translation also established *Posthumous Memoirs of Brás Cubas* as a masterpiece with a global reach.

Schwarz's work is enormously creative in seeing how Assis's particular form of modernist social critique worked. He brought out how essential parody was, as a political tool, in Assis. When confronted in an interview with the contention that parody endangered political engagement, or encouraged "an excessively contemplative position," he flatly replied: "I don't see why it should. Parody is one of the most combative of literary forms."[22] This is an important insight in relation to Assis because his laconic, ironic, and loquacious disguises had hitherto prevented critics from seeing how ferociously Assis is engaged in all manner of violent satiric combat. Schwarz's hard-hitting analysis of the first page of *Posthumous Memoirs of Brás Cubas* describes writing that is "a firework display of impudence, in which one provocation follows hard on the heels of another."[23] He stressed for the first time the strange Brazilian intimacy, the ability to reach out to the universal through social minutiae, peculiar to Assis.[24] Schwarz was also the first to observe that legal/technical slavery abolition in 1888 did not remove the unique structures of power and vulnerability between masters, white dependents, and ex-slaves.

It should be evident by now that Schwarz is no hard-line Stalinist-Marxist critic. He is, however, a dialectical theorist working out of the shadows of the monuments of the Frankfurt School. His work is permeated by the certainty that "the basis of Marxist theory lies in the dialectic between the literary form and the social process."[25] My work is not predicated on the same certainty. I have no complete faith that the literary form and the social process are fused by an adamantine dialectical bond. As a humanist manqué, or maybe a theoretical humanitarian, I put ethics and morality at the center of my readings in ways Schwarz would consider perhaps woefully "fetishistic," not to say sometimes overemotional. Schwarz's *A Master*, superb though it is, does not finally consider in detail Assis's multivalent constructions of the inheritance of slavery, particularly in the areas of evil and moral chaos. And so it remains the case that to date there is no extended analysis of Assis's powerful moral position over slavery, or of his unique focus on the excesses of emotional, ethical, sexual, and moral depravity within the mentality of the urban bourgeois slaveholder. Although not easily acknowledged by orthodox revolutionary Marxism, Atlantic slavery is a unique problem within world labor systems and their resultant social structures. The writings of Che Guevara are perhaps the purest demonstration of the fact. It is relevant that very little of Schwarz's text discusses slavery explicitly, as attested by the index to Gledson's translation of *A Master*.[26]

Maybe such neglect of Assis on slavery reflects the common perception that Assis says far less about direct engagement than many of his literalist readers over the last two or three decades would have liked. Criticism revolves around whether this indirection is a deliberate tactic or a political carelessness bordering upon moral amnesia. Mercurial, wry, and sly in his approach to human motive and human cruelty in whatever contexts they are manifested, Assis avoids simple political categorization over any issue, and often seems to come at politics back to front.[27] I argue that there is, finally, no moral or ethical confusion over his stance on slavery. False trails are laid, and moral traps are set, in order to entice a potentially complacent and white readership (which assumes that it knows how to pronounce upon slavery and race) to enter into places they/we have never been, and if given the choice would rather not go. Assis gets under the skin of slavery, but more importantly he gets under the skin of the reader. With a cruel and incessant familiarity, he corrupts us, he takes our decency down, he depraves us. The act of reading Assis is a more complicit process than most reading of fiction, and we emerge from the experience having become participants in something dirty and ethically usurious. Assis can force a reader to be disgusted by him or herself.

Assis, like all the best creative thinkers who have approached the abject memory of slavery, does not manifest himself as an antislavery crusader, let alone as proto-Marxist dialectical ideologue. He does not wear his political heart on his sleeve, which is not to say he is a stranger to confronting evil and showing how it happens in the midst of human blindness, both willed, but more terribly and more frequently unwilled. Evil can quite simply be the result of boredom, of inactivity, of exhausted mimicry. Consequently, those who come to Assis with agendas, be they postcolonial, or Marxist, or post-structuralist, or even a simple, and quite frankly ridiculous, desire to hear the subaltern speak directly, will be disappointed. Assis is very rarely dogmatic, and when he is his art is at its weakest. He provides no easy formulas for separating out good from bad, black from white, victim from perpetrator, the guilty from the innocent. But this is not to say he rejects moral responsibility over Brazil, or over slavery and its inheritance. Morally locating oneself around the late fiction of Assis is tiring work for a reader. Slaves are apparently evanescent, barely mentioned presences moving in and out of rooms, town houses, people's lives. Yet these figures, some of the most terrific specters in literature, simultaneously move in and out of the reified realm of the Brazilian awareness of skin color, and of the different levels and forms of servitude that embrace black and white. Assis hovers around a complicated metaphorics of suffering that in its turn evolved around slavery, an unstable territory he approaches at times with an almost insane subtlety. Assis shares with Faulkner, or at least the Faulkner of *Absalom, Absalom!*, a fascination with forcing us to think through the possible limits of what it would have meant for black and white to actually live with each other, day in and day out, under the crazy rules and constant pressures of enslavement. It is, however, only recently that his radical approach to slavery has been seen as prefiguring American fictional responses to slavery by half a century and more.[28] Indeed, Assis has a capacity to abstract the black body, to see it and present it as an object. The processes of willed self-blinding and human objectification, which recur in his fictions, manage to mimic the manner in which the slave power lived a lie and could use the slave body, feed off it, and depend upon it, while all the time refusing to see it. In order to uncover the full subtlety of Assis's techniques for describing slavery and cruelty, it is useful to begin this analysis by thinking about whether he possesses a concomitant capacity for directness.

The Psychopathologies of Denial, or How Assis Gets His Readers Inside the Mind of the Slaveholder

If the violence and emotional extremity of slavery are rarely directly treated in Assis's writings, "The Case of the Stick" is a good lesson as to why. Here Assis in fact developed a specific creative agenda around slavery. "The Case of the Stick" shows Assis operating in the same lurid fictional domains as the slavery fictions of so much North American abolition, and the work of Stowe in particular. Stowe's *Uncle Tom's Cabin*, as hugely popular among the literate classes in Brazil as it was across Europe, provides an ample demonstration of how easy it is to enter a world of sentimental projection when treating slave abuse. Within Stowe's manipulative imaginative domain, slaves are innocent victims, and those who brutalize them are demons. It is the abolitionist's duty to raise the consciousness of all moral readers around these moral polarities, to make the reader weep over the martyred slave and hate the slave torturer. As James Baldwin pointed out long ago, this world of abolition moral binaries is a Gothic Evangelical model peopled by reassuring fantasies of good and evil.[29] Assis's important writing on slavery confronted something far more difficult, the emotional liminalities engendered under slavery. His project is finally directed at uncovering the corrupted consciousness of the slaveholders, and those disempowered whites bound in their nexus, rather than at the exhibition and examination of the traumatized consciousnesses of the slave victims. This is, in moral terms, a hugely responsible move, but it is also deeply troubling for the powers that be. It is easy and often pleasurable to weep over a suffering externalized slave victim; it is very different to be constantly forced into, or projected into, the conflicted, deceived, and deceiving mind of the slave owner. If that slave owner exists as a character who is well mannered, urbane, reasonable, sensitive, and apparently in almost all respects "just like us," then the reader may have to face some unpalatable home truths. That is also why so many of the stories approach the condition of slavery, and the mindset of the slave owners, in such abstruse, tangential ways. Assis does not want to allow his readers the luxuries of melodramatic alienation. It is easy to hate an out-and-out monster, a moral Other. Yet if you are gently seduced into inhabiting the psychological world of the white Cariocas, only to find that it is they who run the show, it is they who profit from it, then you must learn to react to a much more terrifying, intimate, proximate form of slave-monstrism.

The Horrors of Slavery on Public Display in *Pai contra Mãe* (Father against Mother) and *O Caso da Vara* (The Case of the Stick)

The short story that deals most flatly with the physical violence of slavery and free-white privileged denial of this reality is *O Caso da Vara* (1886; The Case of the Stick/Wand). In its somewhat crude emotional machinery, the story stands apart from Assis's other work on slavery and is finally an artistic and moral failure. Yet the terms in which it fails are useful in the way they highlight how the majority of Assis's fiction avoids the obvious narrative and symbolic traps sentimental abolition had established for the creative containment of slavery. This story concerns the manner in which the situation of a young white man leads him to contribute, albeit tangentially and against his moral judgement, to the abuse of a slave. The plot is spare, instructional, indeed almost fablelike. A young seminary student, Damião, who can't stand the idea of becoming a priest, runs away and hides out at the house of his uncle's mistress hoping that she will buy him out of his predicament. The woman, Sinhá Rita, operates a lace-making business at home run on slave labor. While she supports the boy's case, and dotes on him, she simultaneously acts with vicious cruelty towards her girl slaves. One slave in particular gets behind in her work, in part because she has been listening to the stories with which Damião has been entertaining Sinhá Rita and her friends.

This girl is sick, weak, inefficient, pathetic, and utterly passive. The prose describes her with a cold objectivity, the narrator apparently speaking for or through the eyes of Damião. The girl is called Lucrécia, the name of arguably the most renowned suicide/rape victim in classical mythology. This Lucrécia is, however, in the eyes of her owners an utterly worthless victim, and only identifiable via the visible scars left on her body by her mistress's abuse. She is described as "uma negrinha magricela, frangalho de nada, com uma cicatriz na testa e uma queimadura na mão esquerda" (a scrawny little black female, a worthless rag, with a scar on her head and a burn on her left hand).[30] The phrase "frangalho de nada"—"a tatter of nothing" or "a worthless rag"—brutally suggests that this human is a nonbeing, not even a thing, not even a dirty, debased thing.

The story climaxes in a moment of agonized decision-making for the young white man. Sinhá Rita demands that Damião hand her a cane with which she will whip this girl:

> Give me the cane Signior Damião.
> Damião got as far as going towards the settee. Then the girl begged him for the sake of everything he held most sacred, his father, his mother, Our Lord himself . . .
> "Help me young master!"
> Sinhá Rita, her face on fire, and her eyes starting out of her head, demanded the cane, without letting go of the girl, who was now paralysed with a fit of coughing. Damião felt a pang of guilt; but he needed to get out of the seminary so badly! He went over to the settee, picked up the cane, and handed it over to Sinhá Rita.[31]

This climax works dramatically and is clever because it suddenly activates a secondary meaning in the word "vara." "Vara" in Brazilian Portuguese, as well as meaning "stick," could mean "court"—hence the phrase "vara criminal" (criminal court), and indeed this ending creates a parodic mini–court scene.[32] Suddenly the object of punishment forms the focus for a judgmental decision by Signior Damião. He should demand justice and try to prevent the abuse of the young slave woman, but instead he goes along with the corrupted verdict of the mistress. Yet despite the clever word play, the conclusion is in danger of slipping over into melodrama. This story is a good warning against approaching slavery with a simplistic moral map. This is Assis at his most flagrantly didactic and brazenly manipulative. He sets up a moral dilemma the reader is then invited to enter and solve. This is as close as he gets to writing empathetic antislavery propaganda. The story lacks the rhetorical maneuvers of *Pai contra Mãe*, and exploits characterizational clichés to familiar ends, activating a wholly predictable pathos. The older woman transforms into a familiar monster of abolition fiction, a cruel, volatile, sadistic slave mistress who takes out her frustrations upon her black female victims. The slave girl is equally the creature of stereotype, a pathetic, passive, pure victim, who is only allowed to speak when she begs for a white male to save her, and who is then shut out of further speech in a paralytic convulsion of coughing. Her only function is to enable Assis to establish the dilemma of the morally compromised young white male; she is a plot element, a catalyst, not a character. No complex subterranean narrative connections are set up between slave and free, black and white, as they are for example in the story *Pai contra Mãe*. In *O Caso da Vara*, black and white, slave owners and slaves, victim and torturer, are treated in terms of the binary oppositions that Assis so meticulously avoided in most of his later fiction. The ending is predictable, and strangely overwritten: it is not necessary for the narrator to explain the dull, conflicted motives of Signior Damião with such leaden insistence. To tell the reader that Damião "felt a pang of guilt; but he needed to get out of the seminary so badly" is superfluous.

The short story *Pai contra Mãe* is one of the few pieces of writing that appear, or have appeared to a host of literary critics, to directly address the practical operations of slave torture. This piece has been widely understood to constitute the one place where Assis uncompromisingly presents the harsh realities of the slave system without shirking. Yet as I will argue, even here, maybe especially here, things are not what they seem. Assis gets up to some of his most ingenious chicanery just when his narrator seems to be looking us straight in the eye and telling it how it is.

The plot is as follows: the central character, a thirty-year-old poor white called, with perhaps a little too much Dickensian symbolism, Candido Neves (White Snow) is a feckless failure, jumping from one failed trade to another and never able to hold down a job. He falls in love with and marries Clara ("purity," "white," "bright," or "cleanness"). They find happiness and are determined to have a child, against the advice of Clara's aunt Monica, who lives with them, and who argues that they will never be able to support a child. Clara duly gets pregnant and has the child. Candido has been making money as a slave catcher, but the market becomes competitive, and all but dries up. Clara is a seamstress, but they have no safety net around their existence and are not far from living in the streets and from starving. Aunt Clara advises them that the only thing to do is to give the child, a boy, away to a convent who will then pass it onto a foundling hospital. The couple love the child passionately but after they are thrown out of their house and are reduced to living on almost no food in one filthy room, Candido finally agrees to carry the child to the convent. On the way there he spots a female runaway mulatto slave, a young woman he has been fruitlessly trying to find for some time because there is a large reward on her head. He takes his chance, dumps his baby in a shop, and returns to capture the hapless woman. Despite her protestations, he violently drags the slave woman back to her master, and just when he has been paid off, she collapses in the street and aborts a baby. Candido rushes off, collects his child, takes him back home, and delightedly explains to Clara and Monica that he now has the money they need, and that he consequently has not given their infant away.

It is uncommon to see Assis bringing the nuts and bolts of slave abuse, the real languages and objects used to police and torture slave bodies, into the foreground of his fiction, although the careful work of Eduardo de Assis Duarte has brought to light several early stories and some early poetry that are prepared to consider slave trading, and the sexual abuse of slave women, directly, if melodramatically.[33] Yet even when Assis seems to be at his most historically literal, he frequently maintains a queer capacity for abstract suffering. I will conduct a detailed reading of the remarkable opening to this story because it shows how Assis can mimic, and satirically infiltrate, the utilitarian and economic languages evolved around slave ownership, slave breeding, and slave flight. Far from being a straightforward description of "the horrors of slavery," the opening is a merciless dissection of the mechanisms of circumlocution, of sanitized doublespeak, which the slave power evolved in order to sidestep the reality of sadism.

The opening of *Pai contra Mãe* contains a discussion of slavery that is unusually direct but simultaneously peculiarly distantiated. The story opens with Assis providing a master class on the semiotic potential of objects of slave torture—the tools of the torturers, those iconic and shocking iron shackles, elaborate hand-beaten collars for runaways, and formally beautiful hand-forged punishment masks, now on display in slavery galleries, and hanging as paradoxically beautiful sculptural objects on the walls of museums, across the Atlantic diaspora. I quote the passage at length because it opens up a crucial space with regard to Assis's imaginative engagement with slavery:

> Slavery arrayed itself in trades and tools as must surely have happened with other social institutions. I will mention some tools only because they are connected to certain functions. One of them is the neck iron and another is the leg iron; there is also the tin mask. The tin mask stopped the evil of a slave's drinking [alcohol] by stopping up the slave's mouth. It had only three holes, two to see and one to breathe, and it was locked behind the head. Together with the vice of drinking they also lost the temptation to steal because it was usually with the master's pocket money that they got what they needed in order to quench their thirst. Thus two sins were extinguished and honesty and sobriety were ensured. Such a mask was grotesque

but human and social order cannot always be arrived at without grotesqueness and some cruelty. The tin-smiths hung the masks up in the doorway of their shops to sell. But we must not imagine things about masks.

The neck ring was applied to fugitive slaves. Imagine a big collar with a big handle on the right or on the left, coming up as high as the head and locked behind with a key. Naturally it was heavy, but it wasn't so much a punishment as a sign. A slave who ran away in that state, wherever he went, showed that he was a reoffender, and so he was very quickly retaken.[34]

This description, and indeed the story as a whole, have been constructed by critics as a place where Assis breaks his own rules around slavery. We are told that here he "addresses the problems of race and slavery in fiction frontally," he is "blunt," he is "uncharacteristically stark and direct," but even here he is not being direct, he is playing games with an apparently forensic factuality, he is layering up irony upon irony.[35] Here the objects of terror, the objects of torture used by the slave power to break the slaves' resistance, are set out initially in a descriptive language that is precise and apparently unemotional. Yet crucially they are also unexceptional, they are not peculiar, they exist in a normalized and generalized discursive environment concerned to think about what typifies certain "social institutions." Assis elegantly takes up that oddest of descriptive epithets, for in North America slavery was exceptionalized as "the peculiar institution." Assis suggests that this institution is not "peculiar" at all, but typical of the way humans organize themselves.

The opening sentence is anything but objective, indeed rather baroque. Slavery appears as a personification, a vain personification interested in personal adornment, but the way it decks itself out, the heavy-duty jewelry with which slavery "arrays itself," are elaborate instruments of torture. These objects are, in their turn, described initially in terms of their physical appearance in a prose of great precision and apparent objectivity. They are then, however, described a second time in terms of their function, and the manner in which they are perfectly suited to the behaviors they punish. The narrator patiently explains exactly how nicely the punishment, or the tool of punishment, fits the crime. The narrator adopts the precise yet interested tone of a connoisseur. This tone is the logical and distanced voice of the slave owner himself meditating upon a necessary evil, a cruelty required to maintain slave morality. Yet as the discussion of torture implements develops, Assis finally has his narrator push the prose out just a little too far, into a space where we have to ask the question: what sort of a mind can happily justify the existence of such objects through what is basically a businessman's logic, a pure theory of profit and loss? The normalization of torture is effected through philosophical platitude, necessary evils are catalogued, the ends are shown to justify the means. The cruel and grotesque become unexceptional parts of a social equation in the wholly reasonable assertion that "human and social order cannot always be arrived at without grotesqueness and some cruelty." This is an assertion we hear down the centuries as a justification for all systems of absolute power no matter how debased they are. We are invited to agree with this wise and rather dull commonplace about what appears to be the necessity of the threat of violence within a social contract. The irony of course is that within slavery and the slave codes, there is no social contract for the slave. The slave is merely property, not a social being.

The shift in the narrator's style, as he drifts into a casual realism, communicates a mind recollecting having seen these torture devices hung out for sale at many hardware shops. So the narrator reframes torture within a reassuring social pattern of going shopping, or window-shopping. We are back with the suggestions of display and conspicuous consumption encoded in the opening words, slavery arraying itself. Here the shopping is for madly cruel, utterly depraved objects. Their being casually displayed, belonging to a mundane visual world of trade goods, makes these baroque emblems of horror unexceptional, available, functional, and useful. You buy a runaway collar or a dirt-eating mask in the same trading space and in the same spirit that you buy a rattrap, or a spade, or a horse shoe, or a machete, or a frock, or a hat. Having indicated this vista of banal and ubiquitous horror, Assis then calmly shuts it down again, with the extraordinary and economic pronouncement: "But we must not imagine things about masks" (Mas não cuidemos de mascáras). What is he (the narrator? Assis?) up to here? Is he being disingenuous or bitterly satiric? If we must not imagine things about masks, then why is the narrator doing this, and then self-censoring himself before the reader's very eyes? Clearly the prose has moved on from a straightforward technique of factual description offering a simple catalogue of trade goods.

There are many kinds of masks in the world and Assis is at one level a consummate manufacturer of fictional ones. The mask is of course not a simple disguise. Assis as an author is always wearing masks, he is addicted to them, he cannot write without them; they enable his irony, the instability of his characters, his layered social critiques. The statement that "We must not imagine things about masks" leads the reader into what is undoubtedly Assis's most confrontational and obviously horrifying, even melodramatic, story about the trauma of slavery. Yet the story is not directly concerned with any of the torture objects he describes so carefully at the outset. And so this opening is a rhetorical sleight of hand that underlines that we will have to read what follows symbolically, tangentially, that we will have to forge the connections ourselves as readers. Assis's indirection finds a way to get inside the shadow of these terrible engines of pain, and he will invite his readers to inhabit them.

The strength of this introductory passage also grows out of its ambiguity, and Assis's writing is so endlessly open-ended that his double and triple entendres are frequently impossible to fully translate. Take, for example, the phrase I just focused on about imagining masks. This translation turns on "cuidar," a verb not easily pinned down in Brazilian Portuguese, and if, like a mask, Assis can never be taken at face value, this truism comes out with a particular literalness when he is talking of masks. "Cuidar" can mean many things: "to consider, to judge, to cogitate about, to pay attention to, to take care of, to think about, to take charge of, to bother oneself about"—all are possible contenders here.[36] I chose "imagine things about" because I feel it reflects the narrator's mercilessly precise mind. It seems he does not want to move either himself or his audience into speculation or recollection, but just to give the facts. The narrator is correcting himself for having wandered off the straight and narrow. Of course the voice is also ultimately the satiric voice of Assis, forever behind the mask of his narrational persona, implying something extra, something different. Here the final critical inference is a faintly detectable disgust at the idea that the voice of the narrator is imagining ways of justifying the use of the mask. The horror then is not simply that the mask is used, but that it can be logically justified by the users, and that it is so familiar that it doesn't need noticing; it is a tool of the trade, a part of the furniture of slave torture.

Melodrama and schlock horror are constant dangers when attempting to write about slave trauma. The traditions of Anglo-American abolition fictions are heavy with examples of superficially theatricalized and satirical violence. Assis strives for a rather different effect, even I would argue a horror beyond Sade. Assis's narrator casually takes us into an imaginative world of pain that tests the limits of the Sadean imaginary. For all its confrontational shock tactics, Sade's world of pain and trauma is reassuringly monstrous, and gains its impact by straining for abnormal status. Sade wants to shock, and he also wants to hurt his readers in the process of describing the torture of his victims. Sadists enjoy the pain they inflict, but if they are to gain fulfillment they must see how pain works on the victim. The victim's expression of suffering and the spectator's enjoyment of that dramatized exchange is the *sine qua non* of the Sadean equation. The Sadean tormentor strives for ever-increasing levels of performative exploitation of the victim. The Sadean approach finds analogies in much abolition writing that presents the prolonged torture of the slave body. Simon Legree's conversion of the death of Uncle Tom into a ritualized flagellation scene that he watches and reacts to with increasing fury and pleasure is quintessentially Sadean in structure and emotion. From this perspective, Assis's method is new; to recast an older book title, he has created an aesthetic beyond, or outside, Sade. Sade's descriptions of trauma are highly theatrical, clamorous, and excessively theorized when compared to the thought and language of Assis's narrator. This consciousness seems to exist in a world of cruelty where Sadean spectacle and performance are *de trop*, even irrelevant. In the mindset of the colonial slave power, there is no Sadean excess or superfluity. Pain is purely functional. Cruelty, the infliction of pain, and restraint operate in crudely educational terms. They teach lessons in a proto-Pavlovian manner: they are intended to train, as you would train a dog. Assis's narrator enables enormity by being so matter of fact, or one could say sensible (in its devolved modern meaning), about it. Pain becomes normal and cruelty ubiquitous because these elements occur in a society that has so fully ingested, digested, and incorporated them. Black bodies are acknowledged only in terms that are purely mechanistic and utilitarian. It is this smooth and calm acceptance, where horror exists outside melodrama and does not cause a ripple, that defines a particular form of evil.

There is a similar calm and expansive irony at work in the description of the slave collar, which involves a highly sophisticated semiotics. What has seemed to recent critical readers a safely detached hyperrealist style rapidly becomes unstable. The reader is instructed that, horrible though this object is, its real value lies not in the physical pain it inflicts but in its signification, in its power as a pure sign: "but it [the collar] wasn't so much a punishment as a sign" (mas era menos castigo que sinal). What does this strange announcement mean? Why "a sign," and what sort of signification is called up? What this serious sign tells the white observer in later nineteenth-century Rio is that this slave has run away, attempted to liberate itself from its bond as property. Consequently, this slave body has defied the social and more crucially economic mechanisms of the world of the slave power. Assis's irony projects slave suffering as a totally irrelevant concern when set in the context of the power exerted by the symbolic function of the collar. Suddenly the "social institution" of slavery appears through the eyes of the slaveholder. Objects, maybe most especially objects of torture, do not represent the theatrics of Sadean terror and pain, but symbolize law and order, the status quo, the necessary evil required to keep everything running smoothly. Slave bodies, if they behave in certain aberrant ways, bring these symbolic objects into play. Assis does something very difficult, and something abolition writing very rarely does without falling into the stylistic traps of melodrama and monstrism. He articulates the vision of the slave power, makes us see the world operated by the slave torturer. What emerges is a vision founded in a capacity to render the slave invisible as human presence and indeed to obliterate the possibility of slave agency, slave emotion, slave culture. Slaves are only brought to life, or registered as living, by the objects used to torture them. It is in this context that the object becomes its sign. The collar is pure signification; it identifies the slave within a certain category as a runaway, and has a further practical function in making it impossible for him to run away again without being seen and found. Assis in this opening compels us to understand that when we interpret the visible world, all things are relative. This relativity is what makes slavery's radical destabilization of morality possible. A slave collar means one thing to a slave, another to an abolitionist, another to a slave owner, another to a tinsmith, blacksmith, or hardware store owner. The true horror lies not in its interpretation but in the fact that it was invented and then used at all. And yet the narrator cannot see this; Assis leaves it for the reader to discover, if the reader can penetrate deeply enough. There is, however, a lot more significance in this sign.

In Brazilian Portuguese, the full meaning of the strange phrase "mas era menos castigo que sinal" emerges if "sinal" is read according to the full weight of possible meaning it carries, and not translated merely as "sign."[37] The word has many other relevant significations: it can mean "a portent, an omen, a token of something, a manifestation." It can also mean an intimate identifying mark such as a birthmark or a mole, both of which are referred to as "sinal." This meaning has particular resonance in the context of a later discussion within *Pai contra Mãe* of runaway slave advertisements, and the publication of the slaves' distinguishing marks including "o defeito físico," namely physical defects. "Sinal" can also mean a stigma, in other words a holy sign of Christ's suffering, and consequently within the significant development of martyrological symbolism, a sign to be given to Christ's most exceptional and deserving followers. This meaning would have vast ironic repercussions here, especially when one remembers the penchant of certain white Brazilian abolitionists for spectacular performances equating Christ's physical suffering with that of the slave.[38] What seems initially like a precise and objective description of a physical object consequently emerges as anything but this. While the collar is a collar, it is also a sign, and a very promiscuous sign because the cloud of meanings that hang around the word "sinal" make it virtually impossible to tie down.

Assis's bipartite prefatory apparatus to his story then moves, with a ruthless semiotic logic, from the signs of the captured runaway, punishment mask, and collar to the commercial sign systems describing the active and absent fugitive, the runaway slave advertisement. There is a precise description of how slave advertisements work, what they contained, and the visual sign that was attached to them:

> When someone's slave escaped they offered a sum of money to whoever returned them. They put advertisements in the newspapers with distinguishing marks of the escapee, name, clothes, physical defects if there were any, the neighbourhood where he might be, and the amount of the reward . . . Often the advertisement carried above it or at the side a little vignette of a black man, barefoot, with a stick over his shoulder and bundle at the end. Anyone who gave the slave shelter was threatened with the full rigour of the law. Well then, catching runaway slaves was a trade of the time.[39]

This passage is stylistically different from anything else in the story. It is not speculative as in the earlier paragraphs, and it is not fiction, not even realistic social fiction of the sort that fills up the remainder of the story. What Assis has written is in fact very good social history, explaining, apparently with no edge at all, and through short factual sentences, the conditions within a slave society that created and enabled the job of the slave catcher, and how a slave advertisement was constructed and functioned. Assis wishes to create a flat historical space, to point up the day-to-day problem of the runaway in an urban slave society, and into this setting he then casts the horrors that follow.

Pai contra Mãe was written in the early twentieth century and was published in 1906, eighteen years after slavery had been legally, officially abolished in Brazil. The story unflinchingly shows civilized white people behaving with an abstracted cruelty to slaves while simultaneously behaving with tenderness and love to their immediate families. Following the introductory paragraphs, the tale moves into a discussion of how slavery created an underworld, a twilight world in Rio populated by runaway slaves, and by slave catchers. The narrator to an extent sets himself up as an apologist and explains that slave catchers do the work because they are desperate, poor, and powerless themselves. Assis is of course taking up, or taking on, the fictional representation of a profession that had been hyperbolically traduced in North American abolition fictions over and over again. One of the most notorious and globally marketed visions of a slave catcher is the character of Shelby, as set out in the opening chapters of

Stowe's *Uncle Tom's Cabin*, a figure who constitutes a high-water mark in this process of fictional demonization. Assis, who knew Stowe's novel well, sets out a counterfiction.[40] He creates a slave hunter who is not monstrous but pathetic. Assis's narrator explains that this dangerous, degraded activity is nobody's career choice, but a desperate option for the desperate. After vividly setting up the social background in the passages just analyzed, the rest of the story is written in a familiar narrative mode. It describes the day-to-day travails of a poor couple, part of the white social underclass of a big nineteenth-century city that happens to be Rio. The plot has the simplicity of a parable, yet the story is written in a style of joyless and ironic dirty realism strongly reminiscent of Maupassant at his most relentless and unforgiving.

As the synopsis above indicates, in immediate terms most of the story is not directly about slaves or slavery at all, but about the hard life of poor whites in Rio. As we have seen, slavery is addressed in great and explicit detail in the introduction, but this part of the story seems radically disconnected in formal and narrative terms from what follows. It is only at the very end of the tale that slavery directly appears again in the only detailed account of Candido at his trade, actually taking a runaway. Assis's narrative method up to the story's end has been to present the job Candido does as the last resort of the desperate. The slaves are only relevant in relation to the money they have the potential to generate for Candido. Their vulnerability and suffering, and their construction not as humans but as property, are no concern of Candido. Yet Candido exists in a peculiarly intimate relationship to the slaves. If he is to hunt them down successfully then he must be streetwise and familiar with black low-life himself. Candido is shown to understand the haunts and habits of the runaways in the same way that "it takes a thief to catch a thief"; he must enter the mindset of the runaway to succeed at catching runaways. Assis carefully controls the narrative, so that all we have heard about his "trade" before the explosive final paragraphs of the story are terse lines concerning the efficiency of Candido's method. He tries to impress Aunt Monica by boasting of his authority and bravado within his chosen profession: "the runaway slaves know I am not to be trifled with; hardly any of them put up any fight, many of them give themselves up there and then." And one paragraph later the narrator, in that strange voice that is half third-person and half Candido's confessional monologue, tells us: "He didn't always get away without losing some blood, for the victim's teeth and nails did their work, but usually he tamed them without the least scratch." Candido's job, it emerges, ironically involves him in an intimate identification with the thought and behavior of the slave and also reduces him to fighting with them in the streets, like an animal. He may "tame" his wild prey, but what becomes of his humanity in the process, as he battles, red in tooth and claw, with fugitive slave bodies?

The scene where Candido captures the pregnant woman shatters the fictional world of the preceding pages and plays with the expectations Assis has set up in the reader's mind in unexpected ways. Candido approaches her in an alley, and at this point she is given a name in a process conducted via horrific irony. Candido himself names her, or rather calls her by her name, and in the act of giving her a name, an identity, he simultaneously entraps her: "It was her it was the runaway mulatta. 'Arminda' he shouted, using the name in the advertisement. Arminda turned round without suspecting ill intent."[41]

Assis shows the intimacy necessary if Candido is to succeed in his chosen work. The anonymous runaway only gains a name and a personality, indeed a minibiography, in the runaway slave advertisement. It is this intimacy, the detailed personal description contained in the advertisement, and his understanding of the woman's nature, that enables Candido to trick "Arminda" into declaring her identity, and into initially coming quietly. That's his trade, he wants to get the job done as quietly and quickly as possible. The perpetrator of horror does not want to cause a scene: it is well-rehearsed behavior, and he wants everything to go off smoothly without unnecessary emotional mess. The motive of the SS Guards who told female arrivals at Auschwitz that they were going off for a shower in order to avoid a scene is perhaps not that dissimilar.

The moral force of the story comes not from the actual horror of the capture, or the woman's heartfelt pleas, or her collapse, or even her abortion, but from the corrupted reactions of Candido to these processes. The scene climaxes as follows:

> Arminda fell in the corridor. At the same moment the master of the slave opened his wallet and took out the hundred *milreis* of the reward. Candido Neves put away the two fifty *milreis* notes, while the master again told the slave to get inside. On the floor where she was lying, transported by fear and pain, and after a short struggle, the slave aborted.
>
> The fruit of a short time's growth entered into this world with no life amid the lamentations of the mother, and the gestures of despair of the owner. Candido Neves saw the whole spectacle. He didn't know what time it was. He knew what he had to do, to run urgently to the Rua Ajuda, and that's exactly what he did without wanting to know the consequences of the disaster.[42]

In a story about runaways, it is finally Candido who runs away from the consequences of his actions and from the horror he has instigated. The prose at the opening is coldly observational. Only in the last words of the first paragraph does Assis move away from objective description of the facts to enter the emotional world of the slave. Instead of telling us "Arminda aborted on the floor where she lay," we are told two pieces of additional information. First, that she is transported with grief and terror, and second that she, or her body, struggles to keep the child. This is one of those rare moments where Assis, as omniscient narrator, cracks, and cannot hold back his indignation, albeit it is introduced through sardonic circumlocution. And the tone is developed at the opening of the next paragraph where the child is elaborately described as "the fruit of a short time's growth." Then the mask snaps shut again, and we go back into cold hard fact. Events are seen again through the mind's eye of Candido; his motives are set out, not the reactions of a disembodied narrator. He has no interest in what he sees, now that the money is folded away. Arminda is not seen again, because Candido has no further interest in her, but the reader is nonetheless left to ponder this opacity.

The scene raises terrible unanswered questions. What does the master's reaction mean? Is he despairing for the plight of the woman or because she may be damaged physically, which will affect her value or indeed wipe it out if she too dies? Does he care that she has lost her child, or that he has lost something that would mature into another valuable piece of property? And again, the task of the translator is not straightforward in terms of uncovering how all of these meanings could be harbored within Assis's text. The word "desespero," which I translated as "despair," can equally mean "fury" or "anger." Is the owner in despair or feeling furious, or both? Is the woman about to suffer a terrible retribution for her dual crimes of removing herself and involuntarily destroying the master's property—her own fetus? In the world Assis lays before us, Candido could not care less. He is blinded by the tunnel vision of his own love for his family. This love has been presented in intimate and apparently unironic ways. We have seen a relationship grow at close quarters earlier in the story; we have seen human love expressed between the parents and transferred onto the child. The final aphorism "Not all children come to fruition—the heart beat out to him" (nem todos as crianças vingam, bateau-lhe o coração) leaves the reader in an impossible position. Whose heart is beating out the message here, his own or that of the dying fetus? Who is speaking to whom? This combination of pat fatalism (the line delivered by a supposedly sympathetic friend to the mother who miscarries) and the objective affirmation of the life force in the form of Candido's beating heart, an organ that goes on beating as the little heart of the fetus fails, is stark. Candido's heartlessness is, with a bitter irony typical of Assis's insights into the terrible moral confusions generated by slavery, expressed in a heartfelt and heart-wringing prose that in its turn is encased within an utterly calculating aesthetic frigidity.

Finally the critical consensus has got it right in that *Pai contra Mãe* is eccentric within Assis's oeuvre in dealing in so head-on a fashion with the physical realities of slavery. What has not been recognized, however, is the formal radicalism of the tale. The compartmentalized nature of the opening, the didactic purpose of the description of the torture implements followed by the slave advertisement, is brought back into brutal focus only in the final paragraphs. For the remainder of the tale the reader is invited to sink into the emotionally empathetic space of a dirty realist narrative focused on a struggling white family. The result is an impossible fiction to read at any level of consistency. Willing, or indeed positively willed, suspension of disbelief is barely achievable against the proto-Brechtian violence of such ghastly bookending.

Servants, Slaves, Companions: Assis and the Interrogation of Domestic Labor

The short story "The Companion" ("O Enfermero," 1884) is a strong place to begin thinking about Assis's techniques as an indirect aesthetician of the traumatic.[43] This story emerges as an interrogation of the plight of the house slave under a cruel master. Yet the process is managed through disguise and deferral, the house slave victim in fact being apparently and disconcertingly white and nominally free. In fact, this technique of obliquely introducing issues around slave treatment through the presentation of white characters was one that Assis used, with ingenious variations, elsewhere. There is, for example, a remarkably abstruse experiment along these lines in the story "O Espelho, Esboço de uma teoria da Alma Humana" ("The Mirror, Outline of a New Theory of the Human Soul," 1883).[44]

"The Companion" has not to date been read as the allegorical discussion of master–slave relations that the following analysis argues for. As with most of the late stories, the plot of "The Companion" is minimal, the story line as such merely a reminiscence of a single incident, an excuse to go somewhere else. The dramatic framing of the story is as follows. Relating an "accident" in his past, the narrator addresses an unidentified reader, who may be a friend, or who may be Machado de Assis, or who may be us, the readers. The narrator tells how as a young man at a loose end in Rio, he was offered the job of being the companion of an old colonel who lived in a village in the backlands of the interior. The narrator takes the position, finds the old man violent and malevolent, and on being attacked by the old invalid strangles him in a moment of passion. The murder goes undetected, the young man finds he has been left the old man's entire estate, and after some moral qualms he settles into enjoying the inheritance.

This is basically a story about two ignoble and immoral white men neither of whom does one admirable thing, and both of whom are morally deeply flawed. Yet the story deals with the psychological damage induced by being tied to an insanely cruel master in ways that set up a direct commentary upon the plight of the domestic slave. The didactic brilliance lies in telling this tale as the story of a dependent white male, rather than as the story of a slave. Assis ruthlessly exploits the ironic potential of the narrative situation. In this sense the story is also locked into dialogue with the uniquely staggered power relations in Brazilian slavery society involving *clientilism* or dependent whites who existed in a limbo between slaves and masters.[45]

From the first the old Colonel is reported as a figure who uses up his servants/companions/slaves as a casual resource. For this man, dependent people become things that may be abused in any manner. The narrator, and consequently we as readers, are warned: "He used up more companions than medicines, two of them had had their faces bashed in." The relationship itself between master and "companion" is carefully constructed via a series of incidents that constitute a direct commentary upon what it means to have total control over another human being in a domestic setting. The Colonel first appears as an embodiment of the indolent planter, stretched out, obsessing over the corrupt character of his minions, and almost erotically enthused about the possibility of having found another servile victim to persecute, intimately, in private, for as long as he likes. The initial exchange sets up with great ingenuity the unending possibilities for abuse that are locked into the relationship:

> I found him stretched out in a chair on the veranda, breathing heavily. He didn't receive me badly. At first he said nothing. Then as he turned his watchful cat's eyes on me a sort of malevolent smile lit up his severe features. Finally he said all his former companions had been insolent good-for-nothings, always sleeping on the job or sniffing after the maids. Two were even thieves.
> "Are you a thief?"
> "No sir."

> Then he asked me my name. I told him and he looked startled. "Colombo?" "No, sir, Procópio José Gomes Valongo." He found Valongo a strange name and proposed calling me simply Procópio. I replied that whatever name suited him was fine with me. I mention this incident not only because it gives a good idea of his character, but because my answer made an excellent impression on him . . . The fact is we had a regular honeymoon that lasted a week.
>
> On the eighth day I began the life of my predecessors—a dog's life. I no longer slept. I wasn't supposed to think about anything but his needs. I had to swallow insults and laugh at them from time to time with an air of resignation and submission, for I learned that this was a way of pleasing him.[46]

Although a slave is not being ostensibly described here, the reader is being ingeniously shifted in and out of the intimate social structures operated by domestic slavery. Assis moves us from the bourgeois world we thought we were dealing with—that of a young white Carioca serving as the male "companion" of a provincial retired colonel—into another world, repressed, forgotten, and now brutally thrust before us: that of the domestic slave at the mercy of a sadistic master. The process is let loose by that one brilliant metaphor, "cat's eyes." This master has the eyes not of a man but of a domestic animal that, peculiarly among other domesticated land mammals, loves to torment its prey before it kills it, and then play with the body afterwards, as if it were still alive, as if life and death cannot interfere with the humor. This is a world where the strong prey perpetually and cruelly upon the weak, where they play with them before and after killing them, because powerlessness exists to be toyed with.

The next move is intimidation via categorization: if the victim is not a toy, and exists in a volitional space beyond placidity, then it must exist in another fictional extreme, as a threat. In this world the assumption is that all who serve are, by nature of their position, consequently dishonest, lazy, and lascivious. These are, of course, the charges traditionally leveled at slaves by the slave power, familiar in literature since at least the dramatic comedies of ancient Greece and Rome. The pressure of these inevitable assumptions within the mind of the master naturally generates the initial words addressed to the servant, a question that is an accusation: "Are you a thief?" The next move takes us to the heart of slavery and power by introducing that seminal event in so many North American slave narratives, the renaming of the slave body by the master, as the linguistic stamp of ownership.[47] The grandly named Procópio José Gomes

Valongo is first misnamed Colombo, then renamed simply as the familiar and condescending Procópio. That Assis intends us to see Procópio in relation to slavery comes out in the encoded full name, for Valongo was notorious to all Cariocas as the location of the notorious slave market of Rio, which kept going long after the slave trade was officially abolished.[48] What pleases the master and leads to the initial "honeymoon," with its lingering sexual undertow (note the heavy breathing), is Procópio's acceptance not merely of this name but of the slave owner's principle that the slave will be delighted to accept whatever name the master decides to bestow on him or her. Assis, customarily so economic in his words, and so shy of unnecessary expansion, takes the pains to digress on the precise significance of this act of renaming and its acceptance: "I mention this incident not only because it gives a good idea of his character, but because my answer made an excellent impression on him." Of course, the character being described here is that of the slave owner. To take it a step further, given Assis's cunning deployment of nomenclature, the strange name is obviously not a triviality. Slaves throughout the diaspora were often named after classical authority figures, most typically Roman emperors, unending Caesars, Augustuses, Pompeys, and Neros. Procopius (Procópio) is not an imperial household name, and no wonder. He burned brightly but briefly, a figure who having gained favor with the Emperor Julius then went out and betrayed him, and briefly claimed the title of Emperor of the East. After an eight-month military spree, and a successful usurpation, Procopius was then beheaded by Julius's successor. The name Procópio is both an ironic allusion to the processes of slave renaming, and a gesture towards a space of political corruption and ambition. Ancient Rome as it runs out of steam is horribly redolent, it seems, of the world in which Assis's central character obliviously lives through the collapse of the last great slave power.

By this point Assis is hovering on the edge, waiting to immerse us, softly, within the genuine hell of a domestic slave's existence. With the phrase "On the eighth day . . ." he signals that what he is giving us is nothing less than a parodic inversion, or extension, of the biblical act of genesis in which the creation of paradise is replaced with the creation of the hell of slave existence. God created the heavens and the earth in six days and rested on the seventh. We don't know what God got up to on the eighth day, so Assis fills in the gap and tells us that the devil, manifested as the slave power, created the life of the slave, which is one of misery, torture, and endless waiting. Assis indeed literalizes the identification of slave owner and devil by the story's end, for we are told that the locals state: "He's dead and gone now. But he was the very devil!"[49] Does Assis intend us to take this literally? He had played at length with the phrase in relation to slave abuse in *The Posthumous Memoirs of Brás Cubas*, where the narrator earns the nickname of "Devil Child" through his abuse and torture of domestic slaves.[50] Certainly the hell this "very devil" creates is one of total control where sleep deprivation, verbal abuse, and finally physical abuse are endemic. Assis then makes an even more unsettling move, taking us from the mechanics of this world of abuse into the psychological mechanisms it generates within the mind of the slave, a complicity, a comically ironic tolerance, "an air of recognition and submission" generated with the sole desire "of pleasing him [the master]." By making a young free white man suddenly appear as the psychological manifestation of the enslaved consciousness, Assis has slipped slavery into a tender white psychological space normally denied it. When is a companion a slave, when is a slave a companion, when is a servant a slave, when is a slave a servant, when is a slave a slave? Assis's great achievement here is to bring slavery home, to make it close to us, to blur the boundaries we like to set up between slavery and freedom, slavery and free labor, black and white. In the world of power abuse and moral suspension engendered by slavery, these are not easy boundaries to maintain, or maybe even possible questions to answer.

As the story progresses, the assumed power of the master over the slave is shown to be grounded in a seemingly limitless desire to maintain control. This thirst for an eternal power over the slave body comes out with an extremity that is almost surreal. After a caning, Procópio has threatened to resign and the old man comes back with the following:

> Here I am with one foot in the grave. You've got to go to my funeral, Procópio, under no circumstances will I release you. You've got to go and pray over my grave. If you don't, he added laughing, I'll come back to haunt you.[51]

The idea of giving up power over the slave body, even in death, is unthinkable for the slave master. The fantasy of extending power over the slave body beyond death is worked out in various ways in the psychology of the masters if one surveys the archive of the Atlantic diaspora. On more than one occasion white slave captains fed the organs of executed rebel slaves to the surviving slaves in an attempt to have their power reach out beyond the space of death. Closer to the example of Assis is that of the slave-owning patriarch Bryan Edwards, who desired to be buried in his own slave's burial ground. Edwards even wrote an inscription to be placed over this grave which made it quite plain that his role as master and overseer of his slaves would extend quite literally into, and then hopefully beyond, the grave.[52]

Of course, when the slave owner's death does come, the Colonel has no control over it at all. His corpse is now physically in the hands of the enslaved. The only appearance of the actual slaves who run the Colonel's household, as opposed to the metaphoric slave Procópio, comes just after the Colonel's murder. The narrator tells us how he used the slaves to help him cover up the crime: "Then I called a slave, told him the Colonel had died in his sleep and had him notify the vicar and the doctor . . . I laid out the corpse myself with the help of a nearsighted old negro."[53] Why are these slave figures introduced at this point, and this point alone? Partly to show that in real terms Procópio and the slaves share an equality in their victimhood, that they are, for the didactic purposes of this story, one and the same. Yet there is a deeper meaning in making the slaves put in this crucial appearance. They float into the story as the silent powerless bodies upon which the Colonel practiced a lifelong sadism. When Procópio returns to the Colonel's village to collect his ill-gotten inheritance, he attempts to invent an ironic myth emphasizing the old man's generosity and warmth. The villagers will have none of this and develop a different narrative, one based in depravity and violent cruelty: "And they described perverse cases of cruelty and brutality some of them quite extraordinary . . . Then other stories followed and the old man's entire life was reviewed. The old people remembered his cruelties as a child . . ."[54] In opening up these vistas of abuse the prose also opens up vistas of silent suffering. If the Colonel was a genuinely evil sadist, then what of the suffering of his victims? It is left to the reader to make that terrifying connection between these buried crimes and the silent anonymous slave bodies who put in their brief appearance around the fresh corpse of their tormentor. There is a dissembling moral tact in the way Assis takes us into slave suffering by taking us into the hurt and bitterness of the white "companion" Procópio, who functions as surrogate slave consciousness. The final master stroke is to leave the slaves themselves as opaque and ephemeral icons, standing silently outside the voice of testimony. To conjure up the mute forms of the slaves at the conclusion is not to reassert their powerlessness but to enforce awareness that the inheritance of their suffering will not go away.

The Slave Body as *Punctum*

"The Companion" provides one technique for making the invisible house slave visible, a discourse that operates through parallelism, silent black characters whose predicament is lived out in the mindful words of a white. Yet there are many other stories where the reader is not offered so much assistance, where the slave body is introduced as a sort of semiotic *punctum* which it is the reader's task to locate, enter, and search.

The story "Dona Paula" (1884; "D. Paula") is a fine example.[55] The eponymous Dona Paula arrives unexpectedly at her niece Verancinha's house in Rio and creeps up on the weeping young woman. The story is from the start one of voyeurism and vicarious exploitation. Finding out that her niece is in danger of losing her husband who has seen her flirting with another man, the aunt goes immediately to the husband's office. She arranges with the husband to take her niece out to her house in the country and sort her out, in order for a reconciliation to take place. It turns out, however, that the young man in question is none other than the son of a man with whom Dona Paula conducted a passionate affair over several years of married life, an infidelity that was never discovered. After the affair was over, Dona Paula became a model of respectability; both her husband and her ex-lover died, and she had been left ever since with a combination of piousness and repressed sexual memory. The young niece's innocent infatuation with the son of Dona Paula's lover has the effect of unleashing a memorial floodgate, charged, disturbing, erotic, yet creepily titillating for the older woman. In order to reanimate the dead memory of her passion, Dona Paula then adopts the role of confessor to the young woman, forcing her to divulge every detail, every sexually charged instant, of her interaction with the young man. Like some perverted female priest in the confessional, Dona Paula ruthlessly manipulates the young woman to her own pornographic ends, achieving a parasitic satisfaction that is finally almost complete. Dona Paula, while voraciously feeding off her niece's frustrated desire, never herself confesses a single detail of her own former excesses with the young man's father. After the niece is forced into a confessional climax, precipitated by the aunt's inquisitorial thoroughness, the older woman approaches some form of retroactive fulfillment. At the story's end the older woman stands desolate, staring out into the night. She realizes that her ability to relive her passion is entirely the product of her vampiric relationship with the niece, and that this relationship is now at an end.

So where does slavery fit into this unpleasant little soap opera? Maybe the metaphor isn't quite right. Maybe it's not a question of where slavery fits in, so much as how Assis makes a black frame out of slavery in order to provide some very threatening boundaries for this particularly depraved vignette. In this story every instant of extreme white female emotion is conditioned and policed by the silent presence of the slaves. When Dona Paula first arrives and desires to spy on her emotionally stricken niece, she must first deal with the slaves. We are told: "A slave who saw her wanted to announce her arrival, but Dona Paula told her not to—to avoid rustling her skirts, she tiptoed ever so slowly to the parlour door...."[56] As is the norm in Assis, the slave does not speak, but is there as a presence who witnesses everything, and who must be negotiated and silenced. When the aunt's initial interview with the niece is over, and she sets out for the husband's office, she has only one parting instruction: "I'm on my way, and don't let the slaves see you looking like this."[57] White emotion, white passion, white vulnerability are not things slaves should see, but, as the prose insists, they do and can see all the time. Dona Paula's instructions, her almost instinctive ability to detect the slave presence and to shut it out when it might be dangerous, is born out of her own former affair, and the manner in which she successfully hid her infidelity for years. At the climax of the story, when the aunt has worked herself into a climactic state by using the niece's emotions, we are again made aware of the presence of a silent slave who witnesses everything:

> Verancinha finished. Her Aunt, in a state of rapture, said nothing. Then she came to, took her niece by the hand, and drew her closer. She didn't talk right away. First she stared intently at her niece's deep set eyes, fresh mouth, and restless, palpitating youthfulness.... Tea was served, but it wasn't really an appropriate time for tea. Verancinha retired immediately—as it was still quite light, she left the room with eyes lowered so that the servant wouldn't see her in such a state of emotion. Dona Paula remained seated at the table, in the presence of the servant. She spent about twenty minutes drinking tea and munching on a biscuit. As soon as she was alone, she went to lean against the window....[58]

How do the slaves impact on this scene, where both white women are so emotionally aroused by each other and yet where they must pretend, because of the slaves' presence, that they feel no emotion at all? Can there be any emotional veracity when one set of people have to spend all their time living in houses where they pretend they do not see another set of people who spend all their time silently watching them? White emotion, white intimacy, white love, seems compromised, distorted, constantly damaged by this visible but silent pressure of a perpetual black surveillance. Assis brings home another great silence within slavery studies, the constant pressure placed upon the slave masters, or here mistresses, by the countersurveillance of the silent populations of black domestic slaves who inhabit every wealthy household in Rio.

As the story ends, the frustrated older woman gazes out into darkness in a state of melancholy desolation, yet Assis rounds off the story showing us yet again that even now the aunt is not alone. Her sad meditation may seem private to her but is achieved at a cost to the slaves who must sit up, watching and waiting, and telling their own stories, stories Assis tells us exist, but that he will not let us overhear: "But she gazed out anyway and in the kitchen the slave women fought off their drowsiness by telling stories. Now and then they commented impatiently, 'seems like the old missus ain't never going to bed tonight!'"[59] The ironies mount again outside the slaves' commentary, for of course it is the slaves also who will never get to bed if the old lady decides to stay up. It is the slaves who get the last word, and the slaves who see things as they are. A tired old lady is keeping them up, the thought that her grief might exact a price, that it is selfish, could never even cross the mind of the "old missus." The slaves are shut out from her world, she is shut out from theirs, and yet day in and day out, they live together. This is another way of thinking about the horrors of slavery and intimacy. Slaves and owners exist according to a rigorous set of domestic rules and social rituals, but they communicate through exhausted half-truths, in an atmosphere of unending domestic tension where everyone watches and is watched, where everyone waits. The paralysis, the claustrophobia, and the sheer misery that Assis communicates in this short story quietly embodies the living hell urban domestic slavery can generate for all concerned.

Another example of this use of the black body as a form of punctuation that linguistically and symbolically overpowers the text occurs in *Eternal* ("Eterno," 1887).[60] In this strange story a black wet nurse appears silently and suddenly, and then disappears in much the same manner, and yet her imaginative legacy is almost infinite. A first-person narrator relates the tale of his friend Norberto's obsession with a young married woman called initially the Baroness de Magalhães. Norberto comes to his friend distraught that the baroness is leaving with her husband for Bahia. The narrator, who is forced to leave for Bahia at the same time, agrees to keep in contact with the baroness and plead Norberto's case to her. Inevitably, over time the narrator falls in love with the beautiful baroness, while Norberto loses interest. After the baron's death, Norberto marries the widow and returns to Rio. He visits Norberto only to find him married with two children. Norberto ends the reunion by declaring his eternal love for his wife. The narrator leaves, and in a ruminative state of mind returns to his wife, the baroness. He asks her what is eternal, and she replies her love for the narrator.

On the face of it this seems a straightforward, preachy little piece about human frailty and the inconstancy of male ardor, all wrapped up in a pretty ending. Yet at the charged moment when the narrator returns to meet Norberto and finds him married with young children, again Assis is asking some central questions about the nature of, indeed the limits of, black and white love within a slave society:

> I learned that Norberto lived in the vicinity of the Rio Comprido. He was married which was so much the better. I rushed off to his house. In the garden I saw a black wet nurse suckling a baby. Another child of about one was squatting on the ground gathering pebbles.[61]

Looking for his friend, the first thing the narrator "sees" is "a black wet nurse suckling." She is immediately dropped as a subject in favor of the children, and once Norberto arrives his affection for the children seems to drown out awareness of all else. Yet Assis refuses to shut down the black subject; both the father and the narrator, almost unaware, circle back to her a few lines later:

> Giving a nod of assent Norberto attended to his son, who was pulling at his face and asking him for more kisses. Then he went over to the wet nurse who was suckling the baby girl. He looked at his daughter with admiration as he called her endearing names and told me to come and see her. Enraptured he saw something of himself reflected in the child, but if I returned in fifteen years he said I would see a beautiful young lady. What lovely arms and chubby fingers! Unable to contain his delight he bent over to kiss her. ["Não podendo ter-se, inclinou-se e beijou-a."]
> "Come in and meet my wife, you'll dine with us."[62]

What the narrator sees, what Norberto sees, and what we are allowed to see through the double puncture created by the two appearances of the slave wet nurse are very different versions of reality. The prose is explicit: although Norberto goes over to the black woman who is in the process of feeding his daughter, he has eyes only for his daughter, and he apparently does not visually register the woman or the black breast and nipple on which the child sucks. The prose is full of commands from the father to see, and to look, and even to imagine seeing and looking at the objects of his adoration. What he cannot see at all is that the life of this little girl, as with her brother before her, has literally been made out of slave milk. As the father expresses his love and deep admiration for the baby, he invites the narrator to see not his baby, but to imagine her a beautiful young woman. He then bends over and kisses her, while she sucks on the black slave's breast. Things could hardly get more intimate and confused, in terms of what, at a physical level, is happening. Why does he imagine his daughter as a young woman when she is feeding from a young black woman he apparently cannot acknowledge? When he is unable to restrain himself (Não podendo ter-se), the syntax begs a question. Why would there be need of restraint if the baby did not have the nipple of a black woman in its mouth? Other questions follow, for example where does he kiss the baby? If he kisses her on the head his lips will be an inch or two from the black nipple from which she sucks, if he kisses her on the lips, then his lips will also be in touch with the black nipple. With a typical slyness masquerading as decency, Assis leaves us to visualize or enact the scene. The casual propriety of the last sentence of dialogue serves merely to underline the extravagant impropriety with which the lactating young black woman has been treated. The story ends with the narrator's ironically amused questioning of his wife as to what constitutes the "eternal" in human life. The reply is as follows:

> I arrived at the Hotel dos Estrangeiros late in the afternoon. My wife was expecting me for dinner. When I entered the room I took her by the hands and asked her "Iiaiá Lindinha—what's eternal?"
> "How ungrateful you are, my love for you of course!"
> I dined without remorse, quite the contrary: I was cheerful and comforted. But that's Father Time for you! Give him a handful of mud and he'll reimburse you with gems . . ."[63]

Proverbs are dangerous things, imprecise, allusive, what does it mean this: "Cousas do Tempo! Dá-se-lhe um puhnado do lôdo, êle o restitui em diamantes . . ." Who does it refer to, and what? Certainly there is the obvious meaning that the young man, thinking he was merely doing some dirty business for his friend, ended up loving a beautiful and seemingly virtuous widow, and being loved. Yet "lodo" is a particularly nasty word to apply to the woman of your dreams. In Brazilian "lodo" can mean "mud, shit, filth, mire, clay, slime," and by association figuratively carries the meanings "ignominy, disgrace, dishonor, degradation." Then again who is this woman named first Baroness de Margalhães and then incongruously Iiaiá Lindinha? This is an odd title for a grand lady, a sort of racially charged double diminutive. Assis comments on the peculiarity that once she returned to Bahia, and to the very black area of Bahia, Bom Fim, where she and the baron lived, and presumably met, everyone addresses her with this familiar term: "The Baroness—or Iiaiá Lindinha which was the name everyone still used when they addressed her."⁶⁴ We are also told that she was twenty-four when they married, that he was fifty-four, and that he bought his title in order to please her. Today in Brazil the epithet "Iiaiá" is as good as banned because it carries degrading race associations; it was the term generally applied to young slave women and especially to mistresses, and even prostitutes.⁶⁵ When Assis was writing it could still be applied respectably, in very intimate circles, to girls, and young women, within a family context, as a term of endearment. It was certainly, however, not a term by which a white aristocratic woman would be known generally. Clearly there are enough straws in the wind for us to be left to wonder who this fascinating young widow of the baron is, with her Bahian background, her residence in Bom Fim, her desire for status, and her very unaristocratic insistence before she remarry that the young man finish his degree, for as she says "I'll only marry a doctor," as it would seem she would only marry a baron, whether he bought the title or not. If Iiaiá Lindinha is, like the great majority of beautiful Bahianas, not entirely white, then it would make perfect sense that she would constitute the *lodo*, or piece of dirt, that changed into a diamond. She may even be a piece of dirt capable of turning her white partners into diamonds. Then again why talk about what dark things turn into or how to manufacture diamonds? Is Assis going so far as to intimate that those little white children who suckle from their black mother are making themselves into diamonds by growing on milk made from a black slave woman's blood? For those with eyes to see, slavery has saturated every aspect of life, but Assis is determined to make us suck the bitter truth out for ourselves, drop by drop. The final message seems to be that the only thing that remains eternal in this world is how slavery deforms the lives of those who live within it. The final bitter pill is the message that slave society has been formed precisely to ensure that its deformation of life remains invisible to those who live within it.

Assis's Satiric Interventions into Antislavery Legislation

The style of darkly amused and bitterly ironic detachment that Assis cultivated so meticulously when it came to unraveling the workings of the slave power led him naturally to consider slavery, the law, and the processes of slave emancipation. His inquisitive mind, which delighted in pursuing moral paradoxes with a proto-Borgesian sophistry, generated a series of parodic engagements with the state's judicial machinations and tomfoolery. Three major pieces of emancipation legislation passed in Brazil while Assis lived and wrote in Rio. The first of these was the so-called Law of the Free Womb, which was supposed to give all newly born children of slave mothers freedom. The second was the "Law of the Sixty Year Olds," a particularly cynical move that gave all slaves over sixty their freedom. Finally, there was the passage of the "Golden Law" of 1888 supposedly abolishing slavery. Assis's novels comment on all three pieces of legislation in subtle ways, and relentlessly reveal these pieces of judicial trickery for the empty promises they are. Yet he is also fascinated by how they are cynically constructed by the urban bourgeois slaveholders who watch them pass. As ever, it is the processes of white corruption around slavery and power that fascinate him. He exposes how these legal lies are digested, consumed, and excreted.

Assis wrote with a furious and confrontational irony about the "Law of 28 September", also known as the "Law of the Free Womb." Although met with general euphoria, this was in reality a confused, indeed deliberately compromised, piece of legislation. It was claimed that the law granted all newly born children of slave mothers their freedom, yet it was hedged about with compromise and indemnity clauses that in actuality rendered it totally ineffective.[66] Assis, in his role as journalist, meditated bitterly on the meaninglessness of such gestures, if the attitudes of the whites remained the same:

> The law of September 28 is now five years old. God giveth health and life. It was a great step in our life. If it had come thirty years before we would find ourselves in different conditions. But thirty years ago the law did not come, slaves came, instead, smuggled, and they were sold openly at Valongo. Beside the sale there was a public prison. A man I know sighs, thinking of the whip. "The slaves nowadays have become proud" he says often. "If you give a beating to one there is always someone else who intervenes and calls the police. Ah, the good old days! I still remember the time when the people saw a *preto* all bloody walk by and they would say: 'Keep going devil, you deserve it!' Nowadays . . ." And the man sighs deeply from his heart . . . it is touching. *Le pauvre homme*[67]

What is the point of legislating freedom within a society where it can never exist, especially in the minds of the whites? As Assis said elsewhere: "Now the slave is emancipated the master has to be emancipated too."[68] Yet like Joaquim Nabuco before him, and Gilberto Freyre after him, Assis understood that the behavioral codes of slavery penetrated so deeply that the white mentality might never be liberated from these profoundly internalized structures, and that whites might never liberate themselves from mental slavery. Even here the commentary is not transparent, and it is not in direct confrontation or demonstrative outrage that

Assis comments on the hypocrisy and ineffectiveness of this legislation. He sets up a satiric dialogue between himself as narrator and an imagined conservative he claims to hear mouthing off about how different things were in "the good old days" of slavery. Assis's final comment casts the whole paragraph ironically and consists of an aside, a pointed satiric literary allusion, which links back ironically to the phrase "God giveth peace and life." Why the French quotation, and who is this *"pauvre homme"* who suffers so because slaves do not suffer? He is of course the inheritor of the new mouthpiece for Molière's Tartuffe, in that celebrated passage where the phrase (which has since become a French sarcastic idiom) ironically mounts into a cyclic roll call revealing Tartuffe's selfish hedonism and obscene devotional hypocrisy.[69] And Assis's work contains other, even more bitter asides on this legislation. The most effective occurs in the story "A Celebrity," where Assis dealt the Law of 28 September a final satiric death blow, in a manner of such fine raillery that it almost slips by unnoticed.[70]

"Um homem célebre" (published in the year of abolition, 1888; "A Celebrity") is a potent little meditation on serviceable creativity, or inventive banality, and its pitiable distance from genius.[71] In this sense it is akin, as a work of art made out of deep engagement with the horror of technical perfection imprisoned within artistic mediocrity, to Robert Browning's *Andrea del Sarto*. The story deals with Pestana, a young musician who is the illegitimate offspring of a liaison between his mother and a priest. He is notorious in Rio for writing fashionable polkas but yearns to write great music that could stand alongside the masterworks of Beethoven and Mozart, which he worships. He exists alone apart from an old black slave whom he barely acknowledges. He marries in the hope that his wife will inspire him. She dies tragically of tuberculosis, yet even this experience of real sorrow and loss cannot raise him to write a requiem in her honor. Yet whether he likes it or not, his knack for writing vastly popular little dance tunes will not leave him. He finally dies, visited on his deathbed by his publisher, who has throughout appeared treating Pestana's creations with a pragmatic contempt, and emphasizing the importance of the title over the substance. When it comes to giving the works titles, his publisher will only ever give Pestana two options, to name them salaciously or to name them after a topical event. So it happens that his first published polka ever is to be named either *Sweethearts Aren't for Fondling* or *The Law of September 28th*.[72] What is the effect of this enforced yet arbitrary collision between popular entertainment and the botched Law of the Free Womb (as the Law of 28 September was more popularly known)? If the sweetheart you fondle is also the slave woman you rape legally as her master, then there will be more fruit created for the Law of the Free

Womb to deal with. It is hard to say if Assis is asking serious questions about the social function of music, or if he is just laughing darkly when he considers what the polkas might mean to the betrayed infant slaves. We are left to make out meaning as best we can. In this context it is worth pointing out that illustrated sheet music of polkas in Rio contained racist assaults on black figures, and also created hybrid forms involving the polka and Afro-Brazilian dances including the highly erotic lundu. The following broadside shows a black street vendor, almost certainly a slave, advertising "Polka-Lundus."[73] The slave holds his goods on a board above his head. They consist of miniature figures of male clergymen, priests, and bishops, in their ecclesiastical robes. They all have wings and the text asks "Who are they? Who are they?" The text also calls for the Polka-Lundu to be excommunicated. The work is a hard comment on the hypocrisy of the Catholic Church, which celebrated the passage of this bill, remaining oblivious to the reality of its ineffectiveness.

There is a similarly creative approach to the satirizing of the so-called Law of the Sixty Year Olds in the story "Among Saints." The law was a brutal and crass piece of legislation passed in 1885 that granted freedom to all slaves over sixty. In reality this meant that slaveholders were now able to liberate all their old infirm and unproductive slaves, and consequently had no commitment to looking after them in their old age.[74] There was a mass of popular print propaganda that reacted to the law and played around with ideas of the slaves being liberated when they were as good as dead or even after they were dead. The image by the great Brazilian visual satirist Angelo Agostini showing the corpses of the so-called Free Sixty Year Olds being dragged by their chains into a mass grave by a plantation owner is a bleak satire. It appeared on the front cover of the greatest graphic satiric journal of nineteenth-century Brazil, *Revista Illustrada*. The design is pertinent in that it shows the metaphoric world of visual satire in which Assis was writing. The usurious hypocrisy underlying this cynical piece of emancipatory legislation led Assis into one of his more extreme experiments with corrupted logic. In "Among Saints" Assis inserts an anecdote concerning a slave owner who emancipates the freshly dead corpse of an old slave, because then he would no longer feel under obligation to pay for a funeral of any sort. In many ways "Among Saints" operates in creative dialogue with Agostini's pungent irony. Both artists think about what the Law of the Sixty Year Olds, also known as the "Saraiva Bill," really did in granting freedom to ancient slaves provided they agreed to work for another five years with no pay as compensation to their benevolent masters.

The brilliance in Assis's story lies in the manner in which he has isolated and

Obscure Agency: Machado de Assis Framing Black Servitudes

3. A. J. W. Azevedo, *Polka-Lundu*, sheet music, c. 1880.

then uncovered the brutal driving motive behind the actual law of 1885, namely a monumental meanness that would seek to avoid financial responsibility for old slaves. Assis merely extends the grotesque logic of this parsimonious cruelty one stage further, and has it reach out in bitter satire beyond the old and infirm to the deceased. Assis is a satiric soulmate of Agostini imagining the emancipated ancient slaves as already dead and thrown into open graves.[75]

Assis and the "Golden Law": Satiric Ruses in the Longer Fiction

Assis was at his most potent as a social critic of slavery in his refusal to be sucked into the easy and universal optimism within the public response to abolition when it was finally manifested in a nationwide carnival greeting the passage of the so-called Golden Law of emancipation in May 1888. This chapter ends with a detailed consideration of how Assis approaches what I have elsewhere designated "The Horrible Gift of Freedom" as manifested in the Emancipation Moment. Assis began fully to explore his ironic stance with regard to Brazil's emancipation mythology not in the short stories but in the late novels. A brief analysis of Assis's ironic approach to the passage of the Golden Law in *Esau and Jacob* (*Esaú e Jacób*, 1904) leads into a more extended reading of the same theme in *Counselor Ayres' Memorial* (*Memorial de Ayres*, 1908).

In the late chapter of *Esau and Jacob* entitled "Disaccord in Accord," politician and populist orator Paulo Ayres greets the emancipation decree of 1888 with a public speech in which he announces, "Abolition is the dawn of liberty, we await the sun: the black emancipated it remains to emancipate the white."[76] When his mother reads this in the papers she is appalled, thinking it a revolutionary statement, "a threat against the Emperor and the Empire." But Assis has his narrator then explain that it is merely a commonplace, a piece of worn out linguistic currency with no clear origin, no clear political meaning, and which vacuously circulates because it sounds good, a sort of emancipationist "Chinese whisper":

> Someone said it one day in a speech or a conversation, in an article, or during a journey over land or sea. Another repeated it, until many people made it their own. It was fresh, it was forceful, it was expressive, finally it became public property. There are felicitous phrases like that... Each man lays hold of them, improves them as he can, and carries them to market where all take them as their own.[77]

4. Angelo Agostini, *Law of the Sixty Year Olds*, lithograph in *Revista Illustrada*, 1885.

This is Assis distancing himself from any idealizing approach to the sudden demise of slavery, stepping out of the glare of the emancipation moment. As a social critic he wrote elsewhere that external influence, things as they are, exert a terrible weight of inertia on society, on ideals, and on language: "It is external influence which determines the way things go: for the moment, in our context, the power of inventing new doctrines does not exist."[78] It is not that nothing changes, but that people cannot change things suddenly by an act of will or the invention of a new theory. By incorporating slavery and emancipation into the hazy outlines of his "theory of misplaced ideas," a conceptual territory that has generated a mass of heated discussion by Brazilian Marxists, Assis throws a pall over the idea of a new birth of freedom.[79]

Assis, Heine, and the Mendacities of Emancipation in a Global Marketplace

Die schwarze Ware ist besser. (The black trade goods are better)

—Heinrich Heine, *Das Sklavenschiff*

Assis had not finished with 1888, however, and reserved his most profound meditation on its form and function for his final published novel, *Counselor Ayres' Memorial*.[80] This determinedly nostalgic work lets its poison drain out softly. It is set back twenty years in the past, and consequently deals centrally with the effects of the 1888 Golden Law of abolition, and more disturbingly with the consequences of emancipation. The book takes the form of a confessional journal written by Ayres, a widowed and retired Brazilian diplomat who spent much of his career in Europe and who has now returned and is living out his twilight years in Rio (is Joaquim Nabuco floating in the background here?). He is a complicated personality who is witty, sentimental, laconic, yet who is also ironic, urbanely cynical, incapable of love, and suspicious of outward displays of emotion. Assis makes this emotional vacuity spectacularly clear as he has Ayres obsessively repeat a line of Shelley's, "I can give not what men call love," whenever he is with Fidelia, a young widow he is obsessed with.[81] Ayres makes a statement concerning his feeling about tears: "I do not like them myself, nor do I know that I ever shed any, except at my nurse's teat as a baby; but those are long since gone."[82] In this one confessional fragment we learn a lot, for the teat to which Ayres refers would of course have been that of a black slave wet nurse, maybe the only person he ever loved. Although critics have tended to see

Ayres as a rather attractive and fulfilled old charmer, or as voluble and vacuous, and this novel as softer than the three great late satiric novels with which it is joined, this fragment highlights what Assis is really up to.[83] Where the critique of slavery and emancipation is concerned, *Counselor Ayres' Memorial* is a wolf in sheep's clothing. Ayres is in fact probably the most delicate, refined, and horrifying portrait Assis created of the slave owner morally and emotionally crippled by the world that created him. Ayres's "memorial" constitutes Assis's bleak prophecy concerning what the inheritance of emancipation will, in reality, bring—both for the slaves and the slave owners. The unredemptive and brutal reality of what the Golden Law of emancipation meant, or more importantly didn't mean, is set out with extraordinary sophistication. Assis's most disconcerting move is to present an individual act of emancipation by a slave owner that anticipates the Golden Law and that sets out with ruthless precision how emancipation will, in practical terms, change very little.

In formal terms the novel contains a fictive journal written by Ayres, the entries for which cover 1888 and 1889 and at the level of surface narrative concern the old man's sentimental and erotic fascination with the young widow Fidelia. The entries also contain his disguised but fixated reactions to her bourgeoning love affair with the young Tristão, who has returned to Rio from Portugal. Fidelia is presented on the conventional narrative surface as an ideal heroine, charming, sensible, practical, beautiful, and to a degree artistically gifted, yet she is also pretty poison. Fidelia finally operates as Assis's seductive weapon for anatomizing the operations of slavery and the Golden Law of 1888. The young woman is entirely the creation of old-fashioned plantation slavery, having grown up on her father, Baron Santa Pia's, slave estate in Parahyba do Sol, and having married against her father's wishes and been cursed by him. The journal opens with the baron coming to Rio to sign legislation emancipating his slaves, and still set against his daughter, although her husband is now dead.

The first time we see Ayres and Fidelia conjoined over the issue of slavery is in the context of the Baron Santa Pia's visit to negotiate the ins and outs of emancipating his slaves. Having found out that the government is inevitably going to pass a law of universal abolition, the baron has decided to go in for a bizarre preemptive strike. He will express his absolute and continued power by formally and legally freeing his slaves before the government issues its own legislation of liberation.

Ayres writes a series of long journal entries on the baron's thought and behavior over this issue, in which Ayres emerges as a cynical casuist who is amused by the motives that lie behind such a seemingly contradictory act by a confirmed slave-ocrat. Ayres is fascinated to find that the baron's motives are the expression of a monomaniac desire to continue the exercise of his power over the slaves, or as the baron puts it in ornate legalese: "I want to furnish definite proof that I consider the government's act a spoliation because it interferes in the exercise of a right that belongs solely to the proprietor and I now exercise this right to my own loss because I can and will do so."[84] Ayres reacts to these words with the sophistry: "I am not sure whether they [the baron's motives for drawing up his own law of freedom] are subtle or profound, or both, or neither." The baron has his brother, a judge who deeply disapproves of the gesture of legally freeing the slaves, draw up the emancipation decree. Pocketing the document, the baron observes with a fierce fatalism and raw realism: "I am certain that few of them [the slaves] will leave the plantation; the greater number will remain working with me for the wages I will set for them, some ... even without wages—for the pleasure of dying where they were born."[85] The baron and Ayres it seems share a conviction that although you can legally take the slave out of slavery, you will never take slavery out of the slave, or more precisely erase its effect from the mind of those who were once enslaved. When Fidelia hears of her father's action, she is profoundly delighted, seeing him in her limited and easily assumed idealism as an emancipator. She has no insight at all into the old tyrant's true motives. When Ayres meets Fidelia subsequently, he simply goes along with her fantasy, although he knows that the baron is nothing short of evil:

> Yesterday with the father, today with the daughter. With her I felt a desire to speak evil of him, so much good did she say of him apropos of his emancipation of his slaves. Desire without action, pure velleity; instead I found myself obliged to praise him, which gave her a chance to prolong her panegyric. She told me he is a good master, they are good slaves; she related anecdotes of the time when she was a girl and a young lady, with such openheartedness and fervour that I was seized with a desire to catch hold of her hand and kiss it in token of applause. Desire without action.[86]

The slaves exist only as an emotional catalyst for this triangle of slave owners. In Fidelia's mind they enjoyed an idyllic existence under slavery and are now part of the young widow's impregnable anecdotage. Their emancipation merely proves the moral worth of the slave owner; they do not exist at all as a social reality—a fiction that all emancipationists in the slave diaspora are prone to fall for. The next journal entry completes the process of abstraction by setting the Golden Law beside not only the baron's individual act of emancipation but alongside American emancipation, as if all these processes are interchangeable:

> There goes the Baron with his slave's emancipation in his portmanteau. Perhaps he had heard something of the government's intention, that as soon as the parliament opens a bill will be proposed. Come, it is time! I still remember what I read about us when I was abroad on the occasion of the famous proclamation by Lincoln: "I, Abraham Lincoln, President of the United States of America . . ." More than one newspaper alluded to Brazil by name . . .[87]

Assis is using Ayres to articulate the sort of cultural slippage and historical conflations that allow slavery to suddenly mean nothing more than the nationalistic and rhetorical processes fictionalizing its abolition by signing a piece of paper.

No matter what critics and cultural theorists think about what happened to slavery before and after emancipation, there was, and I would say remains, a general consensus among Brazilians that the hours directly following the signing of the law by Princess Isabel were some of the most ecstatic and genuinely optimistic that Rio has ever witnessed. Photographs of the massed celebrations testify to an atmosphere that was, even by the exceptional and excessive standards of the Brazilian capacity to enjoy a street party, truly carnivalesque.[88] Rio, and Brazilian urban centers generally, seemed to have followed the English and then American models for celebrating the emancipation moment through a carefully choreographed propagandistic delirium, but in Brazil the hedonism dial was turned up to maximum. The evil of slavery and its entire memory is erased, and immediately replaced by a celebratory rhetoric that is determinedly non self-reflexive in its triumphalism. The myth that an emancipation decree could wipe out the dark memory of slavery and provide a slave-trading and slave-owning nation with an historical tabula rasa had obvious attractions for any former slave society. It is in this context that Assis's return to this moment in his final fiction is so powerful. Assis, an eyewitness to the events he was to fictionalize, left a short, uncharacteristically confessional account of how he felt and behaved during the emancipation celebrations:

> There was sunshine, great sunshine, that Sunday of 1888 when the senate voted the law, which the Regency approved and we all went out in the streets. Yes, I myself went out in the street, the most closed of all the big snails, I entered the parade in an open coach, the guest of an absent fat

friend, we all breathed happiness, it was all a delirium. In truth it was the only day of public delirium I ever remember having seen.[89]

Machado de Assis, the secretive, epileptic, mulatto author and journalist, is confusedly swept along in the public rejoicing. The transformation is expressed with wonderful imagistic sleight of hand, and verges upon the surreal. The shy Assis, existing as a giant tropical land snail, is turned out of his private shell, and into another more public one, the coach, in which he will, however reluctantly, form part of the official celebrations for the passage of the Golden Law. And yet he seems isolated and unreal. He shares the coach with a ghostly figure, the absent presence of the "fat friend" who had invited him along but then not appeared. Although the emotion of Assis and the crowds is intense, it is still presented as a diseased fantasy. The word "delirium" is carefully reiterated, Assis's private delirium part of a public delirium as emancipation erupts briefly as the fevered fantasy of a great writer and of a whole nation. This personal, deeply skeptical version of the experience of emancipation was to be revisited, and reshaped into something infinitely darker, when Assis came to confront the event again in the journal entries of Ayres.

In this final settling of the cultural accounts of abolition, Assis in the guise of Ayres begins by reiterating the established order of events. The Golden Law finally materializes:

> Eventually the law. I've never been, nor did my duty allow me to be, a protagonist of abolition but I confess I felt a great pleasure when I heard of the final vote of the senate and of the sanction of the Regency. I was at the time in the Rua do Ouvidor where there was a great turmoil.[90]

The liberation of the slaves is purely a legislative move, the voting through of an overdue law. The narrator admits that he has never been involved in active antislavery, but that nevertheless he is caught up in the public pleasure initially generated by the voting through of the law in the Chamber of Deputies and then climaxing when the law was finally sanctioned by the signature from Isabel's jewel-encrusted pen.[91] As the account continues, however, Assis casts a dark shadow over this mass jubilation: he refuses the easy option he had given us before, the infectious vision of an untroubled societal rebirth. When it comes to this particular piece of legislation, he sees the skull of slavery beneath the skin of emancipation:

An acquaintance of mine, a journalist who found me there, offered me a seat in his coach which was in the Rua Nuova and would line up in the organised parade to drive around the royal palace and make an ovation at the Regency. I almost accepted, such was my astonishment, but my quiet habits, my custom as a diplomat, my very nature, and my age, kept me back better than the reigns of a coachmen kept the horses back, and I refused. I refused with displeasure. I left there both my acquaintance and the others who joined and left from the Rua Primeiro de Março. They told me later that the demonstrators stood up on their coaches, which were open, made great acclamations in front of the royal palace where the ministers were. If I had been there I probably would have done the same and even now I would not have understood myself . . . no, I would have done nothing, I would have put my head between my knees.[92]

This writing is saturated with Assis's terrible honesty, and by having the narrator create a series of multiple fictions of the imagined effects of the emancipation moment, the writing makes typically unsettling demands on the reader's moral position. As the text forces us to live through the narrator's/author's confusion and guilt, again and again, implicit questions pop up: "what would we have done, what is the right thing to do?" Initially the narrator tells us that his social position, his age, his basic personality, force him to withdraw from this quintessential moment of Brazilian political carnival. But the moment is not so easily avoided, nor are the narrator's motives, as he is forced to relive the emancipation moment in increasingly painful ways. The narrator imaginatively reinserts himself back into the moment not once but twice. He first sees himself as a joyful participant, but then refuses this option, as he had in "reality" refused it a few sentences before. The final version, and insofar as it is relevant, the "true" version, is then given. The narrator envisions himself as a paralyzed figure, given over to despair and darkness, his head abjectly placed between his knees, turning away as if in sickness from the grand parade and its living lies.

Assis then changes perspective again, pulling even further away. His narrator adopts a seemingly dispassionate tone, sitting back bearing no kind of creed but contemplating all, including that *rara avis* German antislavery satire:

It is a good thing we got rid of it [slavery] it was high time. Even though we have burned all the laws, the decrees, and the announcements, we will

> never be able to erase the private acts, the contracts, and the inventories, nor to erase the institution from history or even from poetry. Poetry will speak of it, particularly in those verses by Heine in which our name will remain forever. In them the captain of a slave boat tells of having released 300 *negros* in Rio de Janeiro where "the Gonçalves Pereira House" had him pay 200 ducats per head. It doesn't matter that the poet alters the name of the buyer and calls him Gonzales Perreiro; it is the rhyme or the bad pronunciation that brings it about. Besides this we don't have ducats, but in this case it is the seller who changed into his language the buyer's money.[93]

Critics have rightly seen the clever introduction of Heine's great poem as evidence of Assis's ability to cast Brazilian slavery within a global trade nexus, and to abstract the slave body within a language that can equate coins, slave bodies, and the slippages that result from creative linguistic translation.[94] Yet the passage has also been singled out as an example of Assis's tendency to digress and lose his way when it comes to confronting big political realities. He is seen to bury the memory of slavery in indirection as he "digresses endlessly towards poetry and irony, still avoiding any forms of more involved consideration."[95]

Of course the big mistake here is to take the words of Ayres for the thoughts of Assis. It is Ayres who, true to his character, finds it delightful to "digress," and to cloud the moral atmosphere. Ayres's digressions parody the slave power, its prevarications, elusions, delusions, while simultaneously commenting upon its potential for self-deception and bad history.

Assis's writing here is anything but an example of an author hiding from moral commitment within the thickets of his own stylistic prolixity. There is a tremendous moral rigor, and didactic focus, and not least a satiric thrust, behind these seeming digressions. This passage constitutes one of the great meditations on the relation of the slavery archive to the emancipation moment. It begins with the assertion that slavery has gone, or rather that "we have got rid of it" as one might remove a nasty rash or local infection. The rest of the passage is an increasingly furious assertion that slavery, its inheritance, its social structures, and its cruelties are something you can never "get rid of," no matter how elaborate the cultural fictions erected around its abolition. Assis is quite accurate when he has Ayres refer to a vast act of archival arson perpetrated on the history of Brazilian slavery. The official policy on the passage of the Golden Law demanded that all public records relating to slavery be burned, as a symbolic gesture confirming the fact that a new beginning was not only possible but achievable. Of course, this demand also constituted a vast destruction of evidence, an auto-da-fé conveniently obliterating the details of how every institution had been connected to slavery, its economic minutiae, its vast profits, and its cruelty. Yet Assis has Ayres comment on the futility of the gesture. The second sentence in this passage sets the official attempt to quite literally burn up the official records of slavery against the cold observation that the myriad "private acts" that passed between slaves and masters, the dark memorial "inventories" of slavery carried inside the imaginations of so many, slaves and masters, cannot be so easily burned away. In truth it will never be possible "to erase the institution from history" or Brazilian cultural memory. The sentence ends by pointing out that the memory of slavery also saturates the highest artistic forms evolved by the slave power. Far from being a digression, the ensuing discussion of Heine follows on logically from this position. Assis is dealing here with a vast communal outburst, a street theatre that is in fact facile emancipation propaganda, with all its distortions and erasures. As with the abolition laws of England and then North America, the Golden Law was met in Brazil, and across Europe, with the now standard propagandistic pyrotechnics: poems, songs, plays, orations, hymns, eulogies, prints, paintings, sculptures, and photographs. Above all stood the climactic jubilation of crowds responding to the public signing of a document by a Princess with a diamond-encrusted quill. With one scratch of her little pen she unleashed one delirious blast that shut out pain, suffering, guilt, culpability, torture, memory—in short, the truth. But Assis has Ayres insist that the infamy of Brazilian slavery has already gone out into the world and been recorded in European art and letters in ways that not only confront its infamy in general terms but, in the case of the Heine poem, name and shame Brazilian individuals.

Assis's canny injection of Heine's great poem at this crucial juncture into the imagination of the erudite and Europhile Ayres, is a superb satiric ruse. Far from being a digression, or maybe precisely because it appears an aesthetic tangent, Assis focuses attention on the extent to which art can or cannot engage with the true enormity of the Atlantic slave trade and labor systems. There was in fact very little German art or literature produced around Atlantic slavery and abolition compared to that of France, England, and Spain, a fact reflecting Germany's relatively small hands-on engagement with either the slave trade or plantation slavery. Heine's poem, as has been argued above, is exceptional in its committed satiric stance, its bleak black humor, and its superbly German fixation upon the economic practicalities of the trade. Of course, as Assis and more crucially his creation Ayres very well know, the most influential and well-known poem by a Brazilian on the subject of the slave ship and its passage from Africa to Brazil is Castro Alves's *O Navio Negreiro*. It is also relevant to remember that Alves had indeed sought out Assis in 1868 and read the whole of *O Navio Negreiro* to the master in a private tête-à-tête before launching into a hugely successful set of public performances of his slavery poetry in Rio in September 1868. Yet Alves's persona, language, thought, and aesthetics could hardly be further from Heine's bitter humor, and precise engagement with the facts of slavery on the Middle Passage.[96] So why does Assis have Ayres choose Heine over Alves at this crucial point? It is the cold German practicality that drew in Assis as well as the sustained ironic humor, a quality Assis shares with Heine but Alves did not. There may also be a sideswipe at the Brazilian elite's reluctance to equate their own Romantic literature with that of the literary big guns of Germany, France, and England. And that humor continues into what Assis has Ayres make of the poem. It is with typical slyness that he has Ayres airily pronounce not upon the celebrated strengths of Heine's poem but upon the inaccuracies within an obscure section, the few lines dealing with the slave's destination.

Ayres in many ways may as well not have bothered to read the poem at all for all he seems to take from it. He is revealed to us as a lazy, partisan, and morally blind reader. The poem's most remarkable aspects, the ghastly mercantilist vision of the captain and the ship's doctor, interest him not at all. The extended metaphoric discussion of the sharks that pursue the slave ship and are encoded into the captain's economic negotiations are also passed over, as indeed are the bodies of the slaves themselves. What interests the whimsical Ayres is, initially, Brazil's international reputation down the ages. He also, however, articulates a dread that the immortality of great art has a capacity to make the memory of iniquity live on, despite the attempts of bureaucrats and abolitionist propagandists to wipe it from the face of the earth. Ayres in his persnickety way focuses in on Heine's assumed mistakes, highlighting his claimed factual inaccuracies when introducing Brazilian slave dealers into the global equation. Heine gets his facts spectacularly wrong in the verses Ayres alludes to:

>Ich hab zum Tausche Branntewein,
>Glasperlen und Stahlzeug gegeben;
>Gewinne daran achthundert Prozent,
>Bleibt mir die Hälfte am Leben.
>
>Bleiben mir Neger dreihundert nur
>Im Hafen von Rio-Janeiro,
>Zahlt dort mir hundert Dukaten per Stück
>Das Haus Gonzales Perreiro.[97]

(I swapped for them [the slaves] brandy, trinkets and beads,
It's such a bargain I'm driving;
I'll come out ahead eight hundred percent,
With only the half surviving.

If only three hundred negroes remain
By the time we reach Rio de Janeiro,
I'll be getting a hundred ducats per head
From the house of Gonzales Perreiro.)

Ayres's analysis of these lines is revealing. He claims Heine's account to be error strewn, but his own account of Heine's account introduces another level of falsity: "the captain of a slave boat tells of having released 300 *negros* in Rio de Janeiro where 'the Gonçalves Pereira House' had him pay 200 ducats per head. It doesn't matter that the poet alters the name of the buyer and calls him Gonzales Perreiro; it is the rhyme or the bad pronunciation that brings it about. Besides this we don't have ducats, but in this case it is the seller who changed into his language the buyer's money." Heine doesn't know Brazilian Portuguese, and transforms the name of his emancipatory hero into something with Spanish elements. Heine doesn't know what Brazilian currency is, so imagines it to be the romantic ducat, so beloved of Shylock and various Caribbean pirates. Yet when Ayres tells us with rhetorical flippancy that these errors of fact do not matter, he does so in the light of his own mistakes. Heine's verses state not that the slaves have been or ever will be delivered to Rio, but that the captain fantasizes that if even three hundred survive he can sell them to Perreiro at 800 percent profit. Whether he did so cannot be foretold. Heine also states that the slaves will sell for one hundred ducats while Ayres's account weirdly doubles the value. Ayres's protestations that Brazil's infamy will live on under mistaken identities of nomenclature and international currency are of course absurd. What Assis is sending up here is Ayres's contradictory take on things. What concerns Ayres is not the horror of the slave trade per se, or its morality, or the fate of slaves, but the fact that it is Brazil's part in it, and a particular Brazilian slave trader's house, that will live on through the poem's celebrity. Worse still, the memory of the slave dealer and the money he paid will live on with false identities. What Assis's satire demands is that we see Ayres, for all his mercurial superiority, to be a man without a moral compass. This is a brilliant satire on the erudite delusions that could allow the educated Brazilian elite to bypass slavery's real history. What Assis finally demands here is that the details do matter, they matter terribly, and that accurate memory, accurate fact finding, is the basis of historical record. Art, be it the satire of Heine, or the satire of Assis, must make sure that it does not live in lies designed to destroy true memory. The final sentence in the above quotation is hard to pin down, but I take it to mean that Heine, the cultural salesman, is complicit with the buyer, the Brazilian reading public, who want to buy into a certain shared lie. Assis is uncovering an international cultural marketplace devoted to the erasure of the memory of slavery. Slavery turned people into commodities, and that was bad enough; now emancipation turns the reinvention of the memory of slavery into a conveniently priced set of shared lies. Assis's horribly refined satiric humor was never harsher, more honest, or more aesthetically focused.

As the novel progresses, it emerges that Assis uses the passage of the 1888 law as a fulcrum upon which to balance his analysis of slavery through the thought and action of Fidelia and Ayres's reaction to it. Right after the Golden Law is passed, the baron dies of a stroke and Fidelia inherits the plantation with its population of emancipated slaves. Ayres is allowed to read a letter Fidelia writes to her friend Dona Carmo in which she relates her return to the plantation. Ayres sets down his recollection of the letter and reaction to it in strangely layered prose:

> The letter speaks at length of him [the baron] and of the haunting memories she found there, memories awakened by the wall of the bedrooms and of the great rooms downstairs, by the columns of the veranda, the stones in the well, the old-fashioned windows, the rustic chapel. *Mucamas* and *moleques* she had left as children, she now found grown and free, and with the same affection for her they had had as slaves; these received several lines of remembrance in passing.[98]

This writing articulates the conflation of all forms of property, including slaves, in the mind of the young woman. The fabric of the house seems able to speak, although what dark memories it evokes remain ambiguous. What does the reference to the memories evoked by the wall of the bedroom allude to, the baron's miscegenetic sexual unions with chosen slave mistresses perhaps? The thoughts of the now ex-slave mistress cannot differentiate between slaves and objects. The wet nurses and slave children are as much part of the fabric of the place as are the well, the chapel, and the walls. The slaves may have grown physically, but their emotions have remained completely frozen. Their passive adoration of the mistress is presented as eternal. The law of 1888 is just a piece of paper; it does not affect domestic relations within the big house or inside the head of this young white woman, one jot. The only value of the letter for the deluded Ayres is that it proves the moral and aesthetic worth of Fidelia, that she can both generate and then articulate such devotion, and such emotion proves her worth. She emerges as a sort of egotistical sublime for Ayres's adoring contemplation. Fidelia then decides to sell the plantation, and this leads Ayres into a further fantasy that sets out the bewildering labyrinths he is capable of erecting around enslavement as a trope:

> It seems the freed slaves are going to be unhappy. When they learned she was going to sell the plantation they begged her not to, not to sell it, or to take them all with her. There you are, that's what it is to be beautiful and to have the power of enslaving! In this kind of enslavement there are no emancipation laws or papers to free you; the bonds are eternal and divine.[99]

Here the experiences and plight of real slaves, unable to confront the social reality of their new overpowering state of enforced freedom, is conflated with Ayres's own maudlin fantasies of romantic obsession. The slaves' terror at being left without their erstwhile owner, and their unwavering devotion to this woman, is reconstructed as on a par with the erotic enslavement Ayres sees himself to be a victim of. The conflation of the trope of romantic love as enslavement, with the state of plantation slavery, had already been played out in some of the most corrupt and decadent literature to be generated by the pro-slavery authors of the eighteenth century. What Ayres says here is ideologically identical to the revolting conclusion to James Boswell's *No Abolition of Slavery, or the Universal Empire of Love*, where he winds up his love poem to a young lady with the words:

> The rhapsody must now be ended
> My proposition, I've defended;
> For slavery there must ever be,
> While we have mistresses like thee.[100]

The cynical but enamored mind of Ayres chimes with that of Boswell in seeing emancipation as impossible while sentimental white males are still capable of enslaving their hearts to lovely young women. Ayres in fact simply does not care about any aspect of the life, memory, experience, or future of slaves, emancipated or not, beyond the ways in which their plight might be capable of embellishing his fantasies of Fidelia. And as his memorial moves towards its conclusion, Assis forces this bitter pill down the reader's throat again and again. When Fidelia learns of the slaves' feelings, she and her betrothed Tristão decide that the best course of action is to give the plantation over to the slaves to run themselves. When Ayres first hears the plantation may not be sold, he confesses: "I do not remember if I made some observation in regard to liberty and slavery, but it is possible since it is of no interest to me whether Santa-Pia is sold or not. What *is* of interest to me is the plantation mistress—this plantation mistress." The vast irresponsibility of this solipsism appears to know no bounds; slavery and liberty mean nothing outside the context of Ayres's frozen erotic fantasy of his plantation mistress. His final gesture towards these ex-slaves and the realities of emancipation takes the form of one of the shortest journal entries of all, a fragment he cannot even be bothered to finish: "April 28 There goes Santa Pia to the freedmen who will probably receive it with dances and with tears; but it may be that this new or first responsibility . . ."[101] And so Ayres's engagement with slavery slips off the page with three of the most terrifying dots in publishing history. When it comes to imagining what freedom might actually mean for these people who must live through the shadow of their slavery, Ayres just does not want to know. The brilliantly reticent Assis gives us one of his most appalling speaking silences. Ayres will not go there: he ducks out of the picture, he shuts up his imaginative shop, he quite simply can't be bothered. Assis leaves both the reader and Ayres in a terrible darkness, a "darkness-visible" with which Brazilian society is still coming to terms.

CHAPTER 4

"The child is father to the man": Bad Big Daddy and the Dilemmas of Planter Patriarchy in *Memórias Póstumas de Brás Cubas*

Brás Cubas, a Devilish New Anti-Patriarch

Brás Cubas, the curious and curiously deceased narrator of Machado de Assis's *Posthumous Memoirs of Brás Cubas* (*Memórias Póstumas de Brás Cubas*, 1881) might be seen as a parodic response to a certain extreme stereotype. The grotesquely sadistic plantation owner had been established by abolitionist fictions in both eighteenth- and nineteenth-century Europe and America. The moral suasion arguments against slavery embraced the idea that one of the best ways to show the failure of slave systems lay in uncovering the manner in which they corrupted their members, and the patriarchal head of the household was a primary target. This creation of slavery's monsters had long been an option for abolition polemicists. The novelty of what Assis created in the character of Brás Cubas questions the fictional limits and uses of monstrism.

By the time Assis created his Brás Cubas, the planter as a caricatured amalgam of inhuman beastliness had appeared again and again in extreme form in popular abolition literatures to the point where the figure was a cliché. A standard element within single-sheet print satires, whether English etchings by James Gillray, Isaac and George Cruikshank, or Richard Newton, he continues to appear within American print satire up to the end of the American Civil War.[1] He is prevalent in white abolitionist-sanctioned North American slave narratives, including Solomon Northrup's *Twelve Years a Slave*. The figure still haunts the popular mythography of American slavery. The Oscar-winning film adaptation of Northrup's narrative took the sadistic planter back into Hollywood's heart. A more impressive variant of the type appeared in more garish and caricatured extremity in the character of Monsieur Calvin J. Candy, played with an excessive parodic brio by Leonardo DiCaprio in Quentin Tarantino's 2012 film *Django Unchained*.

In mid-nineteenth-century abolitionist fiction, the monstrous planter's most spectacular manifestation had been in the guise of Simon Legree, the evil plantation owner in Harriet Beecher Stowe's *Uncle Tom's Cabin*. This late Gothic sadist finally has Uncle Tom whipped to death. The book, hugely popular in Brazil as it was globally, was translated and published in two Brazilian Portuguese editions shortly after the year of its appearance in 1852 and was constantly reprinted. Assis knew it well.[2] Legree, the ruined planter, living in a decaying and broken world of Gothic excess, sadistic insanity, and sexual violence, is held up as the ultimate warning of what happens to the human spirit empowered and depraved by slavery. But compared with Assis's Brás Cubas, Legree is, in imaginative terms, a reassuring fantasy, a safe and easy option for the judgmental reader. Legree is two-dimensional, the devolved end of a melodramatic tradition. It is logical that he ended up being literally a cardboard cut-out villain in the board game version of *Uncle Tom's Cabin* that was one of the profitable nineteenth-century merchandising spinoffs from the book.[3] Simon Legree, when set against Brás Cubas, is most reassuring, a comfortably alienated being, stumbling, blustering, and beating his way around in a stunted brutish imaginative terrain, and a morally dumbed-down world. Legree has been generated by, he is the child of, the primitive Evangelical didacticism and easy self-righteousness of the Anglo-American abolition tradition. Stowe's easy horror was ruthlessly isolated by James Baldwin in the middle of the twentieth century.[4] Brás Cubas may be many things, but he could never become a cardboard cutout of evil within a self-righteous toy theatre. He is infinitely more troubling than that.

Brás Cubas does, however, have something of a fictional precursor within *Uncle Tom's Cabin*. Legree exists in binary opposition to another parodic planter stereotype named with uber-Dickensian irony Augustine St. Clare. The wealthy owner of a substantial slave plantation, St. Clare lives off the proceeds of slavery in a fine urban villa in New Orleans. At a superficial level he could be seen as an American proto-Brás Cubas, sharing many characteristics with Assis's patriarch. He is a hyperrefined, educated, laconic, and morally confused plantation owner, delighting in philosophical speculations and social experiments focused on slavery and the compromises it enforces on slave owners. He is also interested in considering the emotional outfall of slavery and racism. For example, he purchases Topsy, a very black and "heathenish" small African slave girl, and then gives her as a challenge to his Northern abolitionist cousin Miss Ophelia to educate, convert, and civilize. In setting up a social experiment deliberately pitting Southern intimacy with slaves against Northern racist disgust at the physical reality and proximity of the black body, Stowe uses St. Clare to test the limits of Northern racist hypocrisy. Yet Stowe emerges as personally confused over what she had created in St. Clare. In the bizarre compilation of source material for her novel, *A Key to Uncle Tom's Cabin*, Stowe's ninth chapter "St. Clare" presents him in ideal terms as a paradox, an "aristocratic democrat." She concludes that she "has been astonished to see how under all the disadvantages which attend the early possession of arbitrary power, all the temptations which the reflective mind will see arise from possession of this power in various forms, there are often developed such fine and interesting traits of character."[5] Yet the St. Clare in her novel is a far darker, more tainted, more cynically speculative character than her celebratory analysis in the *Key* would suggest.

In the final analysis, however, St. Clare is not a prefiguration of Brás Cubas. Despite the possible shadows and echoes of St. Clare as a source for the laconic, morally chaotic slave owner, Assis finally created a wholly new kind of white male slave-owning patriarch. Brás Cubas is not a planter, or a variant on the Southern chivalric aristocrat, but a bourgeois urban gentleman who happens to have inherited slaves. Stowe's creation is a relatively straightforward didactic tool, and of course finally an orthodox and sentimentally trite Evangelical Christian. He is a very different creature from Assis's slothful, highly sensitive sophisticate. Brás Cubas is a profoundly lazy being who lives in and around slavery and is intimately corrupted by it in ways his ethically suspended worldview prevents him from understanding, but not from enjoying. St. Clare may do some ambivalent things, but Stowe is incapable of taking us into his consciousness. Assis's achievement lies in the way he makes us intimate with the fascinating and urbane inner mind of Brás Cubas. In his laconic ennui he remains a very modern consciousness, not only urbane, but distinctly urban and infinitely cynical. Brás Cubas's solipsism, his unending capacity to dress up and disguise his failings, and those of his immediate family, and to be delighted by the very processes of his own self-deception, make him familiar, a confider with the reader. This is a new kind of slave-owning animal. Almost testosterone-free, he talks to us from beyond the grave in a voice of sinister camaraderie and confessional intimacy that has in it very little of assertive male patriarchy. In taking us into his confidence, Brás Cubas slowly drip feeds the reader his complicated moral poisons, an ethical honey trap way more dangerous to the reader's moral health than anything Stowe could come up with.[6]

"Decifra-me ou devoro-te" (Decipher Me or I'll Devour You)

This gentle but terrible instruction from Brás Cubas to his readers—"Decipher me or I'll devour you"— which ends the first paragraph of the second section of *Posthumous Memoirs*, places a sinister responsibility, not to say necessity, upon the individual to find the truth beneath the fictive puzzles and traps that Assis has Brás Cubas so cunningly create and set.[7] The statement is a terrific provocation, both a threat and a challenge, warning that if you don't read deeply or ironically enough then you will be swallowed up by Brás Cubas's corruption. Assis was well aware that he had moved out of conventional novelistic structures in this work, and as many critics have pointed out he explicitly refers us to Laurence Sterne. In the prologue to the third edition of the *Posthumous Memoirs*, he has Brás Cubas announce, "It is a question of a scattered work, where I, Brás Cubas, have adopted the free form of a Sterne," and immediately continues "but I may have put a few touches of fretful pessimism into it." Assis, who only ever repeats himself when there is an aesthetic necessity for the gesture, returns to this theme of worried darkness at the book's center, when in the next paragraph he repeats: "What makes my Brás Cubas a singular author is what he terms 'a few touches of fretful pessimism.' There is in the soul of this book, for all its merry appearance, a harsh and bitter feeling, that is a far cry from its models."[8] Assis sets himself up in dialogue with Sterne at a formal level, and draws on Sterne's whimsical engagement with, if not perversion of, the theory of moral sentiment. Yet Assis has created a very different emotional world, one saturated with "um sentimento amargo e áspero."[9] Where does this bitterness and bleakness, where do these "touches of fretful bitterness," come from? The book is a sort of historical puzzle: he will not tell us, but the revelation slowly bleeds out, that it is the ever-present overhanging shadow of slavery. The world that surrounded him as he grew up, and the world he must live in and share with his domestic slaves, gives the book, or rather its narrator, this feeling of corruption, hopelessness, and moral impotence. Assis gives a strong hint right here at the start. The adjective "amargo" is powerful and relates to feelings of bitterness, distaste, profound sorrow, or sadness. These emotions come out of a set of more literal sensory stimuli to do with taste, and in Brazilian Portuguese the word refers not only to a lack of sweetness, a lack of sugar, but explicitly to beverages without sugar. The word leads us straight into the productive world of slavery, Brazilian slavery, founded on sugar and coffee.

This is a book that comes at the exhausted corruption of a slaveholding elite with forensic detachment, or perhaps, to return to that disturbing opening aphorism, the cold devouring desperation of a parasite. The ability of the book to get under the skin of a slaveholding society, and to take us as readers with it, to the extent that it makes us feed on the corrupted body of the slave power, comes out of a paradoxical fusion, or perhaps collision, of subject and style, of exhaustion and energy. The bored depravity of slavery, and the effects of this corruption on every aspect of the life and thought of a civilization at all social levels, are uncovered by the voice of a dead man who is bored to death with himself and the memory of his life. It is very important that he is not dead, that his voice lives on, and that we, in the act of imaginative necrophilia that constitutes reading, constantly bring back the memory of slavery in the act of consuming its memory. It is in this sense that by actively decoding Brás Cubas as a slave owner we can devour him, rather than have him devour us in endless detour. But the terrible ironic pact Assis sets out between literary producer and literary consumer is that the reader's act of consumption, if it is successful, keeps revivifying slavery. Slavery, its inherited workings, its memory and its horror, are not so easily killed off.

In this work Assis builds upon Laurence Sterne's experiments with empathetic complicity not only in *Tristram Shandy*, but perhaps more crucially in *A Sentimental Journey*. Our relation to the posthumous narrator, and to the author who lies outside and inside this voice, is however very unlike that orchestrated by Sterne's more jovial but melancholy narrational prototypes, in that the relation is never allowed to be a comfortable one. We are deeply, irredeemably implicated and simultaneously insulted throughout. The processes of complicity start with the dedication: "Ao Verme Que Primeiro Roeu as Frias Carnes Do Meu Cadáver Dedico Com Saudosa Lembrança Estas *Memórias Póstumas*."[10] Unlike the dedications of Sterne's *Tristram Shandy*, which in accordance with Sterne's obsessional disjunctiveness refuse to take their place at the beginning, Assis seems to be straightforward and places his dedication right at the front. But the more one ponders it the more slippery this dedication becomes. It is a cunning warning that in my beginning is my end. The dedication translates superficially as "To the worm which first gnawed the cold meat of my cadaver I dedicate, as a nostalgic memorial, these Posthumous Memoirs." But who is this worm, and what exactly is the meat it gnaws on? Assis's dedication is clearly aimed at everyone who reads the book. The dead body is the book, and the worm that feeds upon it is the reader. Readers are a form of bookworm, as we continue to consume, to gnaw, at the body of the text, and so in the act of reading we make ourselves into parasites. "Verme" and "carne" are words with many meanings, figurative and literal. "Verme" is an open designation: it does not simply mean earthworm (minhoca) or ring worm (lombriga), but it can mean any grub, larva, or form of vermin. As a general epithet for anything that feeds on corruption, it is consequently a very precise term for the imagination that consumes this most corrupt of texts. "Verme" also has a figurative meaning of great power, connoting inward torment, the idea of being consumed or undermined alive from within. There is then the sense from the outset that the processes of corruption are embodied in this text. This memorial from the slave past passes memories on to the reader. In the act of reading the book Assis locks us into a disgusting compact that necessitates our consumption of the corpse of this rotten text. Assis seems to have anticipated, and gone beyond, the limited and celebratory conclusion of Barthes's rather optimistic little formula that "The death of the author is the birth of the reader." You can't kill an author off that easily, especially when he invents a narrator who embodies the living dead. And in this context it is worth noting that the word "carne" does not just mean meat, but the meat and muscles of the human body, and that it also carries a series of fascinating figurative meanings. "Carne" in colloquial Brazilian means "a rich loafer, a stupid common rich person, a good for nothing." "Carne" then embodies a set of ideas precisely applicable to Brás Cubas himself, a wealthy, lazy man who achieves nothing, and then tells us all about his extended failures. Beyond this, "carne" also carries the figurative meanings of sensuality or lust (hence "carnal," "of the flesh"), and the idea of blood kinship or consanguinity. To consume the memoirs is to be locked in a lustful union with the corruption of Brás Cubas and the slaveholding world in which he is embedded. To read this tainted text is to feed off, to become familiar with, the corpse of the slave master. To read is to enter an imaginative necrophilia that brings the rotten meat back to life. It is a central contention of my deciphering of Assis's book that it is the variously manifested intimacies with which Brazilian culture uncovers the operations of slavery that so often separates the Brazilian memory of slavery, and Assis in particular, from other diasporic cultures. With the *Posthumous Memoirs* Assis takes this intimacy to a terrible point, a point that engulfs not just the memory of the past, but the imagination of the future and the contamination of the reader's imagination.

The book suggests that we may never break out of the inheritance that slavery cast upon us. The curious use of the past tense in that verb "roeu" comes back to haunt each new reader, or each new reading, which starts once again to gnaw at the vitals of this text. The stakes are high when you read the *Posthumous Memoirs*; you are being taken inside the body of the slave power, and if you don't read the signs you will be consumed by it. It's not as if we are not warned at the beginning, firstly with that dark dedication, secondly with the terrific command: "decifra-me ou devoro-te" (Decipher me or I'll devour you).

When does slavery enter this book? It is no exaggeration to say that slavery is everywhere; it is an atmosphere that everyone and everything has no choice but to breathe. Slavery emerges from the very start as a plague breath saturating everything no matter how assiduously the consciousness of the white slaveholder tries to shut it out, or to normalize it. The first ostensible entrance of slavery into the book is the muted and disturbing climax of the "orquestra de morte" (orchestra of death) that passes through the mind of Brás Cubas at what should be his moment of extinction:

> Now I want to die peacefully, methodically, listening to the ladies whimpering, the men talking softly, the rain drumming on the caladium's leaves of my country home, and the grating sound of a knife which a knife grinder is sharpening outside by a harness maker's doorway. I take my oath that this orchestra of death was not as sad as it might appear.[11]

In this peculiar passage Assis moves from the intimate deathbed scene, populated by bourgeois whites and focused on the dying man—the women sobbing, the men murmuring, the soft rain on the leaves (rain that has already been parodically constructed in an overblown metaphor as Nature weeping for the death of a great man)—to the external and discordant sound of the knife being sharpened. This violent noise penetrating from outside is described with peculiar detail. Rather than just refer to "the sound of a knife being sharpened outside," we are given the knife, the knife grinder, and the act of sharpening, through distinct parts of speech: "o som estrídulo de uma navalha que um amolador está afiando lá fora."[12] The prose, in its intense and reiterative particularity, its concentration of hard *í* and *á* sounds, creates the effect of something troubling, or annoying. The effect is emphasized by the fact that the adjective "amolador" means not merely "sharpener," or "grinder," but by extension "annoyer, pesterer, plaguer," and the verb "amolar" carries a variety of meanings from the irritation of "to bother, to annoy" to the violence of "to harangue, to molest." Indeed, the verb is used colloquially in a number of ways such as "vá amolar outro!" (buzz off and bother someone else).[13] What is being stressed here is that the emotional life of the affluent whites, and the mind of the dying slaveholder himself, at this most intense and intimate threshold moment, cannot be insulated from the poor black life of the streets. The slave owner's last sensory experience is to hear the noise created by an itinerant knife grinder, almost certainly the labor of a slave working for hire. That the knife grinder is working outside makes it certain he is "amalodor ambulante," a wandering knife sharpener, a stock figure of Rio street life, depicted in superb detail by Jean Baptiste Debret, but also illustrated in countless tourist souvenir booklets depicting typical urban slave occupations.[14] Assis shares with James Joyce the ability to conjure enormous symbolic transformations out of a hypersensitive observational accuracy. What he does in this passage is to create a most troubling variant on the figure of the clichéd grim reaper. Death enters this quiet suburban space, not in stereotypical symbolic guise as a black shrouded deaths-head bearing a giant scythe, but as an offstage sound effect, the insistent presence of a black slave laborer, whetting a knife. And the reader is left to ponder Brás Cubas's enigmatic announcement, that this orchestra of death is not as sad as it might seem. Is this because the slave is very much alive, although oblivious to the theatre of death he contributes to, but is shut out from?

The two sentences purporting to give the final thoughts of a slaveholder who is also a very unremarkable urbanite provide an intense introduction into the layered ironies with which Assis approaches, and then gently prises apart, the enfolded and enfolding grip that slavery possesses over his characters. The prose is mercurial, and part of the method is seduction. It is hard to resist the consciousness of Brás Cubas, it is hard not to sink into his world, to think the way he and his circle so often are shown to think, and to inculcate both his, and their, methods for shutting slavery out of their lives, despite its palpable, its undeniable physical presence.

As slavery is introduced shrouding Brás Cubas at the moment of death, so this effect is delicately balanced at the moment of his birth. The birth, so unlike that of Tristram Shandy, is physically straightforward but described in terms that bring in elements of which Sterne would have approved. Assis again cleverly entangles the elevated worlds of the slaveholders with that of the slave laborer, while the process of Brás Cubas's birth is shown to have a certain value in the marketplace:

> On that day the tree of the Cubases blossomed with a gracious flower. I was born; the arms of Pascoela received me, the distinguished midwife from Minho, who bragged of having opened the door to the world for an entire generation of nobles. It is not impossible that my father was familiar with the declaration, I believe finally however, that paternal sentiment was what induced him to show her his gratification with two half-doubloons. Washed and swathed I immediately became the hero of our house.[15]

The scene of the birth of Brás Cubas is a clever transformation of one of the most notorious satiric birth scenes in world literature, the agonized emergence of Tristram Shandy. It is not, as expected, the extended arms of the family that greet this infant, and new flower on the family tree, but the possibly black arms of the midwife.[16] Pascoela is a superb replacement for Sterne's brutal and blundering Dr. Slop, who causes such trauma to Mrs. Shandy, and who crushes Tristram's nose with his birthing forceps. Pascoela effortlessly receives the infant body from its mother, as she has received so many tiny, bloody slaveholders' babies from between the bloody legs of innumerable slave mistresses. She cleanses and wraps up the infant, who only at this point becomes the slightly ridiculous "heroi de nossa casa."

As news of the infant's birth circulates, the effect is described in ways that again insist on the presence of slave labor, while denying the slave body social agency or visibility: "I know that the neighbourhood sent greetings or came to see the newborn and in the first weeks there were many visitors to our house. There wasn't a single sedan chair that wasn't hard at work, many frock coats and many pairs of breeches were floating about."[17] In Brás Cubas's social circle, all public visitors would have to arrive in sedan chairs carried by slaves, and the social position of the occupants was further emphasized by the manner in which the slaves were decked out in elaborate livery, often wearing morning coats and velvet breeches, despite the searing heat.[18] The very grammar here is satiric: the sedan chairs are described as laboring or being at work ("trabalhasse"), not the slaves who do the real work of lugging their white owners about. The slaves remain implicit, and their bodies become even more conspicuous by their absence when the coats and breeches are described as floating about the place, as if they had a life of their own. The technical brilliance of the critique here again relates to Assis's ability silently to slip into the vision of the white bourgeoisie, while effortlessly taking his reader into that same compromised space. The slave owners see what they want to see, they are aware of the objects defining their social status, but not the black bodies that inhabit and enable those objects. Again, Brás Cubas's birth, and the social acknowledgment of that birth, comes at a price for the slaves. This is a price that Assis does not allow his characters to register, but he leaves the reader with the moral imperative of reading and registering it. Here, and throughout the book, we as readers are invited to open our eyes, to find out if we have the capacity to see slavery for what it really is.

Assis repeatedly shows how the Brazilian elite can easily understand and talk about slavery in theory, while remaining blind to it in practice. Yet within such an apparently morally suspended narrative, and such repeated scenes of willed ignorance, Assis soon bears his teeth and exposes the horrors of domestic slavery, and domestic slave abuse. He does so by entering a taboo area, and exposing the moral corruption inculcated within the children of the slave power. The short section that immediately follows the account of Brás Cubas's birth is entitled "O menino é pai do homem" (The child is father of the man), a direct translation of a line from a celebrated and celebratory short Wordsworth lyric. The reference is not superficial; the engagement with Wordsworth is profound and extended. As the chapter, and indeed book, progress, Assis's ruthless exploitation of the Wordsworthian theory of the childish imagination points up the depravity of domestic slavery in starkly unsettling and harshly satiric ways.

The section begins by referencing Wordsworth, stating: "a poet says that the child is father of the man. If this is true let us see some of the lineaments of the child." This is no Wordsworthian child, endowed with visionary innocence and trailing clouds of glory from its divine creator. This child, born within slavery, is infernal, cruel, vicious, and corrupted. Just in case we are in danger of missing the point that the slave child is evil, Assis has Brás Cubas confess that from the age of five the infant Brás Cubas had earned the nickname "Devil Child" (Menino Diabo), and in order to illustrate how the name was acquired there is a confessional paragraph. This is worth quoting at length because it forms a launching pad for a sustained anatomization of the debilitating effects slavery exercises on the slaves and the slave owners. It is this analysis that reaches out over the subsequent chapters:

> One day I broke the head of a slave because she refused to give me a spoon of the coconut sweet she was making, and not content with that evil, I threw a handful of ashes into the bowl, and not satisfied with that prank I went and told my mother that it was the slave who had ruined the sweetmeat ["estragara o doce"] out of ill-will, and I was only six years old. Prudêncio, a little black house slave ["moleque de casa"[19]] became my horse every single day. He put his hands on the ground, took a rope into his chops, as a sort of bridle, and I'd mount his back with a whip in my hand. I would beat him, make him do a thousand turns in every direction, and he obeyed—at times moaning—but he obeyed, without saying one word, or when he couldn't bear it, just "Ah, little master!" to which I retorted, "Shut your mouth, beast!" Hiding the hats of visitors, fixing paper tails on distinguished visitors, yanking ponytails on heads of hair, giving pinches to the arms of matrons, and many other acts of this sort, were evidence of a perturbed temperament, but I must also believe that they were also expressions

of a robust spirit, because my father held me in great admiration; and if at times he would tell me off in front of people, it was simply for appearance's sake: in private he would give me kisses.[20]

The truly terrifying aspect of this passage lies not in the sheer violence that the infant Brás Cubas is capable of inflicting, habitually, and day after day, on his slave victims, but in the moral confusion still permeating his recollection of the acts, and which we finally see is engendered by the moral chaos in which his father operates. The paragraph is divided into two halves. The first describes in apparently objective detail the involved cruelty of the infant towards the house slaves. The examples are carefully chosen to highlight the manner in which the vulnerability of the domestic slave is abused with infinite finesse by the infant's sadistic ingenuity. The first victim is an adult woman whom he physically assaults but then "sets up" as a victim before the adult powers running the house. Having split her head open, he then ruins the dessert she will have labored over for hours and which he craved, in order, it seems, simply to cause the slave untold suffering. He informs the parents that the slave's supposed act of destruction was carried out "por pirraça," out of spite, or evil intention. Within the world of slavery, this is a terrible charge; he is informing on his victim and presenting her as a rebel, a domestic saboteur, ruining the food of the masters. The word used to describe the slave's imagined act of spite is "estragara." "Estragar" is a very powerful verb meaning not simply "to waste," but "to destroy, ruin, damage, vitiate, deprave, rot, corrupt."

Because we are seeing the event not in terms of an account of the words actually spoken by the infant to the mother, but in terms of how the narrator remembers his actions, we cannot be sure exactly what he accused the slave of doing. Contaminating food was of course one deadly area of slave resistance. Slaves could poison their masters and mistresses in many ways, either by adding poison to the food, or just by serving food that had gone slightly off. Cooking was an intimate area of slave behavior around which slave owners were intensely neurotic and anxious. Some owners would even insist that the cook or servants taste the food first, to prove it was uncontaminated. The suspicion of poisoning in any form brought down the most severe of punishments. Of course, the slave victim remains anonymous, invisible, and Assis leaves it for the reader to pursue the terrible repercussions of this literally poisonous action to its imagined conclusion.

The next scene, the scene where the small boy is forced to become a horse for the perverted pleasures of the infant Brás Cubas, is equally dark and ominous.

Slaves were often called upon to perform as improvised pets or beasts of burden for the children of slave owners. There are even photographs recording the practice.

One ghastly studio photograph clearly does not show a child at play with an adult, but rather a young white infant who is the child of slave owners "riding" a female slave as if she is a horse or ox. Neither performer looks exactly happy: there is boredom and a certain anxiety in the child's face, trepidation and an unspeakable submissive terror in the black woman's face. Why this photograph was made will never be known, but the image enters precisely the domain of terror that Assis was intent to extrapolate in the notorious slave-riding scene in *Brás Cubas*.[21]

Assis's narration again includes fastidiously observed detail. We are told, for example, that the slave boy is forced to take a rope in his mouth as a bridle. But new elements are added to this vignette, which shifts this time into a more testimonial style. The slave is given a name, and there is direct speech on the part of both the slave and master. The horror of the sequence lies in the fact that the slave, in being forced to act and to suffer like a dumb beast, must behave like a dumb beast. When he breaks into the infant Brás Cubas's fantasy by speaking the single word of agonized rebuke "Ah, little master!" (ai, nho-nhô) the hysterical response is to shut down language and communication, and to insist that the slave is quite simply an animal, and that as an animal it should not speak as a human: "Shut your mouth, beast" (Cala a boca, besta!).

These dramatic and extended examples are immediately offset by the second half of the paragraph, in which extreme cruelty is absorbed into a series of dilatory contexts that are supposed to normalize it. The violence inflicted on the slaves is immediately set out as mere detail in a catalogue of subsequent childish pranks practiced on visitors: hiding guests' hats, pinching ladies' arms, tugging girls' plats, pinning paper tails on pompous gentlemen's coats. This is all normal childish behavior, still recognizable today, still tolerated if not approved of, and possibly explained away by indulgent parents as healthy high spirits, or mischievousness. And that is the point of Assis's satire. Slavery creates a domestic world where the normal rules do not apply, or where they apply sporadically, weirdly, yet where they are nevertheless applied. The treatment of the guests is, in terms of civilized urban society outside slavery, within the bounds of healthy childish behavior. The torture of the slaves most definitely is not. Yet for Brás Cubas, as he thinks back, there are no moral limits to his understanding: all this counts as "mischief" to his indulgent father, and consequently to him, both as a child and as an adult. The most debased and most hopeless aspect of Brás Cubas's

Dilemmas of Planter Patriarchy in Memórias Póstumas de Brás Cubas

5. J. H. Paff, "Slave Performing as Carrier for Child," albumen print, c. 1860 (George Ermakoff, Casa Editorial).

retroactive construction lies in the manner in which he can still see these acts, including the torture of slaves, as the expression of a healthy childish inventiveness, of a robust nature, "um espirito robusto." And he puts this spin on his memory within the golden glow of parental love and approval. His father, although he might reprimand him in public for the torture of the slaves, would kiss him and congratulate him in private for his energy and inventiveness.

The passage does not return to explicit detail concerning the abuse of the slave body, and it doesn't need to. Assis, with customary moral economy, has made the point. As we shall see, the "Devil Child" has planted a seed that will be cultivated later on in the book in the most horrific ways that will give a wholly terrifying spin to Wordsworth's idea that "the child is father to the man." What he does go on to expand in this key passage is the general corruption of the domestic milieu that surrounds and forms the infant Brás Cubas. Brás Cubas as narrator increasingly draws back to reflect on the rotten nature of his educators. He sums up his parents' contribution with the words: "Through the collaboration of these two creatures my education was born, which, though it contained certain good things, was in general vicious, incomplete, and in most parts, negative."[22] He then goes on to describe the education he receives at the hands of his uncles, one of whom spends his time seducing the slave women who do the washing and talking filth to them, and the other of whom, a canon, operates a sterile and corrupt form of Catholicism. He concludes that he grows up in a domestic world reflecting "vulgarity, love of appearances, noise, decayed will power, the domination of caprice, and more." And concludes by feeding off and inventing a long-established Romantic cliché: "from this earth, this dung ["estrume"], this flower was born."[23]

Which takes us back to Wordsworth. What exactly is Assis doing in calling up a line from the great English Romantic, and poet of childhood? The lyric from which Assis quotes is one of the most intense distillations of Wordsworth's celebratory and revolutionary theory of child consciousness. The line needs to be quoted in the context of the famous lyric in which it appears if the full extent of Assis's furious satire is to be understood. The lines run:

> My heart leaps up, when I behold,
> A rainbow in the sky:
> So was it when my life began;
> So is it when I am a man;
> So be it when I shall grow old,
> Or let me die!

> The Child is father of the Man;
> And I could wish my days to be
> Bound each to each by natural piety.[24]

Wordsworth here compresses into a few words an intensely optimistic version of his philosophical construction of the childish imagination as a privileged and beautiful state of mind. Able to respond to nature's beauty (the rainbow) from the moment of birth, the poet maintains, and will maintain, this inspired response into adulthood and old age, if he can continue to go back to, to draw from the well of, his uncorrupted childhood perception. This is what the line "The Child is father of the Man" means: the adult, if he thinks healthily and beautifully, can be constantly instructed by returning to or recapturing the tremendous imagination of his infant self. Assis produces a bleak and envenomed rereading of this message within the context of urban slavery. From the moment of birth, the child is surrounded by corrupt and vitiated sights and behaviors. He is saturated in visions of the ultimate abuse of one set of humans by another, and he is corrupted by these sights from the outset. And so, logically adapting Wordsworth's theory of the influence of the infant imagination on the life of the adult, this fallen and inhuman child's mind will constitute the mentality that forms and informs and reinforms the consciousness of the mature Brás Cubas. Assis has turned Wordsworth's redemptive theory of the infant imagination into something damned and damning, indeed infernal, hence the sobriquet "Little Devil" that Brás Cubas acquires.

And yet this is only half of the message, because the horror of this theory of moral influence is pushed out into a far darker space. It is not merely one child's imagination Assis shows as ruined, but two. What of the infant Prûdencio and his experience at the hands of his "little master," what sort of man will this childish imagination father? In one of the darkest corners of the fiction of Atlantic slavery, Assis pursues this question to its bitter and inevitable conclusion. Chapter 68, "The Whipping," provides a sudden vignette where the full effects of the young Brás Cubas's corrupted imagination and moral being are seen to bear the kind of fruit that would have disgusted Wordsworth but delighted the heart of the Marquis de Sade.

By this stage, now a gentleman of leisure in Rio, having inherited his father's estate, the physically alluring but feckless and self-serving Brás Cubas has taken a long-term mistress, Virgilia, the wife of a close friend of his. Terrified that he will not be able to maintain a regular secretive contact with her, he thinks up the ruse of setting up a love nest for the two of them, with a slave servant, whose service and soul he buys, to look after them and the little house. Walking along the street, he pleasures himself with the fantasy of how this secret space, a sort of perverse recreation of the Garden of Eden, will allow him to control his adulterous love. He can now retire to one rotten space of perfect sexual fantasy: "one single world, one single couple, one single life, one single will, one single unity—the moral unity of all things through the exclusion of those that were contrary to me."[25] It is at this precise moment that his imaginative control over this fantasy is shattered as the real world, and the real effects of the decadent sadism in which he has always floated and performed, fall in on him. The passage, central to Assis's unsparing vision of how slavery corrupts the inner core of the slave power, is a crucial articulation of the imaginative contamination slavery generates:

> Such were the reflections I made, as I went along the Valongo, after I had seen and made arrangements about the house. They were interrupted by a crowd: there was a black who was beating up another in the square. The other one didn't try to flee, he only moaned out these unique words: — "No, pardon me master, master pardon me." But the other didn't answer, and with each supplication responded with a new beating.
>
> "Take that you devil!" — he said — : "here's 'pardon' for you, you drunk!"
>
> "My master!" sobbed out the other.
>
> "Shut your mouth, beast!" — the whipper replied.
>
> I stopped to look . . . Good Heavens! And who was this whipper? None other than my black rascal Prudêncio—who my father had liberated several years before. He recognized me; stopped what he was doing, came over and asked for my blessing; I asked him if this black was his slave.
>
> "He is, yes, little master"
>
> "What thing has he done?"
>
> "He's a loafer and a terrible piss-artist. Just today I left him in the shop, while I went downtown, and he sloped off to get a drink."
>
> "It's fine, pardon him," I said.
>
> "No problem, little master, your wish is my command. Get into the house you drunkard!"
>
> I left the crowd, who looked at me questioningly and who were whispering conjectures. I went on my way, taking up a multitude of reflections which I am sure I have subsequently lost; moreover they would have proved material for a good chapter, maybe joyful. I like joyful chapters, they are my weakness. Viewed from the outside the Valongo episode was appalling, but

only from the outside. Once I forced the knife of rationality deeper into it I found it to have a mischievous entertaining and yet profound core. It was a method Prudêncio had developed to free himself from the beatings he had received—he transmitted them to another. I as a child, mounted him, put a cord in his mouth, and beat him without compassion; he lamented and suffered. Now that he was free however, he had the free use of his arms, and legs, he could work, rest, sleep, unfettered from his old condition, now he could really break the bank: he bought a slave, and paid him back with the highest interest, precisely that quantity which he had received from me. Just look at the subtlety of the scoundrel![26]

This is indeed a study in the operations of a completely immoral capital, and one of the most terrific indictments of the seemingly limitless immoral outreach of the slave–master relationship. The choreography and theatrical setting are superbly managed. It is no coincidence that Brás Cubas witnesses this scene and then analyzes it standing in the Valongo. Valongo meant one thing to Cariocas; it was Rio's massive Valongo slave market that dominated the area, the space where the majority of Rio's slave trading went on. Assis gives us the final scene of "the child becoming father to the man," and an unflinching revelation of how the effects of slavery can destroy an individual's capacity to enjoy, or even to comprehend, freedom. When Prudêncio is physically manumitted (not by Brás Cubas, be it noted, but by his father), the only form his corporeal freedom can manifest itself in is to continue the cycle of absolute abuse in which he was imprisoned by Brás Cubas as a child.

The basis for slavery is revealed not merely as morally toxic, but as mad. The system is enabled by a dynamic of monetary exchange, where people are reduced to investments, and where physical force and terror are the bottom line. Applying his vaunted "rationalism" in order to disguise the trauma of the events he has just witnessed, Brás Cubas merely extends this economic system into the realm of suffering. In this emotional model, the violence Brás Cubas "invests" in torturing Prudêncio as a child builds up a compound interest over the years. When Prudêncio is in a position of freedom himself, he can cash in this investment in misery by purchasing his own human subject and then reinvesting on that helpless creature the violence he had suffered as a child. And so Prudêncio emerges as a type of antimorality, becoming the totally ironic fulfillment of his name. This young man is indeed Prudence itself—judiciousness, common sense, foresight, all the elements that his conceptual name incorporates in Brazilian Portuguese are embodied in what he has evolved into. Prudence we are told in

Portuguese dictionaries is "the virtue which is carried by the man who knows and understands what is appropriate for him," and in the bleak world created by Assis, Prudêncio fulfills this vision of virtue to a fault.[27]

In this obscene moral closed circuit, the child is indeed father to the man. Brás Cubas can shield himself from the emotional and physical horror of what he has witnessed by uncovering the systematic and rational basis for this pattern of behavior. The ironies pile up as Brás Cubas congratulates himself in the role of child torturer, for having produced a victim whose consciousness is so poisoned that it will continue to spread, and indeed to increase, the depravity in which it was nurtured. Assis gives us a narrator who when it comes to performing evil has gone deep down into basics, and who reveals what the final social relations of slavery boil down to. The fact that he does this, if not unwittingly, then certainly only half consciously, serves to make the disclosure more horrid. The frivolous sophistication of Brás Cubas's moralizing exists in a world of nihilistic and fascistic sadism, where the useless objective is no more than the gratification of a pervert's theoretical whimsy. We are seeing, in the context of nineteenth-century urban slavery in Brazil, a variant on that same mental type that de Sade revealed far more crudely and directly, in the latter stages of *One Hundred and Twenty Days of Sodom*. The difference is that Assis's monster is furtive, and has only started to understand how to enjoy the fruits of his perversion. Assis is uniquely disturbing in his depiction of what slavery does to human thought, because he only allows the reader a glimpse of the depths that exist beyond the garish Sadean human-beast. Brás Cubas is not a Sadean monster most of the time, but he can think like one when he chooses to turn philosopher.

Brás Cubas is all the more unsettling because he approaches the enjoyment of his depravity through an amused and almost befuddled obscurity. In Toni Morrison's *Beloved* there is a bleak moment when ex-slave and convict Paul D stares at a piece of black scalp, with hair attached, and a red ribbon, which floats down a river. This is all that remains of a violated little back girl. The character asks incredulously, "what sort of things are they [the whites]?" The question is one that Morrison's art cannot, or does not want, to answer. Her white characters remain opaque enactors of blank forensic cruelty and horror. Her scientifically detached character of "schoolteacher" with his notebook and experiments is a plantation Mengele who views his slave victims as specimens. It takes the cool ironies of Machado de Assis to take us into the self-blinding processes that operated in the minds of the slave masters. These people did not appear to be monsters, either to themselves or their contemporaries, or frequently to the generations that followed them. Occasionally, a finely tuned creative mind emerges capable of finding an artistic language to describe the evil at work when human beings are reduced to exchangeable commodities within a cash nexus. Jane Austen manages to develop a language that simultaneously incorporates aesthetic and economic terminology in order to explain how the English slave power could justify the dehumanization of Atlantic slavery to itself.[28] With Assis, Brazil found its own artist capable of doing something similar but in a completely Brazilian mode. Brás Cubas is, on the face of it, no more melodramatically monstrous than Jane Austen's slave-owning patriarch Sir Thomas Bertram. They are both sophisticates who can approach the ownership, the sale, and the exploitation of humans for gain by applying a vision that deals with emotional and monetary concerns in the same terms. They are both, incidentally, equally immoral and cruel in their treatment of slaves and free white women. It is finally the systemic coldness, and the misplaced ingenuity, of these figures that constitutes their depravity. Yet what separates Brás Cubas from Sir Thomas is his laconic involvement with the processes of his own corruption. Slavery is finally about the capacity of investment to usurp ethics, and in this context the love of money does emerge as the route of this man's particular evil.

Assis brings out the unusual finesse of Brás Cubas's corruption by embedding it in a setting of cultural clichés. The elaborate disguises he erects around the harsh operations of slavery and money, around slavery as an economic system, exist in relation to the brutal but far more practical approach to the subject of his brother-in-law Cotrim, who appears at crucial points in the book. Initially he hovers around the moment of parental death, the key threshold moment in a slave society when human emotion and human property are brought into ghastly union. When slave owners die, their property becomes vulnerable, and Cotrim, Brás Cubas, and Prudêncio are brought into fortuitous union at the death of both of Brás's parents. The first extended moment in which we become aware of Cotrim is when Brás's mother has just died:

> On the seventh day; when the funeral mass was over, I gathered together a shotgun, some books, clothing, cigars, a houseboy—the Prudêncio of Chapter XI—and established myself in an old house we owned. My father made an effort to make me change my mind but I couldn't and didn't want to obey him . . . My brother in law was on the point of carrying me off forcibly. He was a good lad that Cotrim. He'd gone from profligacy to circumspection. Now he was a food merchant toiling with perseverance from morning 'til night. In the evening sitting by the window and twirling his sideburns that was all he had on his mind. He loved his wife and the

son they had at that time, who died a few days later. People said he was tight-fisted.[29]

This portrait, bringing Cotrim, Brás Cubas, and Prudêncio together by chance, and stressing Cotrim's obsession with business transactions, and his doomed dynastic ambitions, acts as a prologue for the next extended treatment of his character. When Brás's father dies, Cotrim and Prudêncio are brought into a more tightly focused proximity. Brás, his sister Sabina, and Cotrim argue gently, then more violently, about the inheritance:

> Reader look at us now, eight days after my father's death—my sister sitting on a sofa—Cotrim a little in front of her, on his feet, leaning against a sideboard, his arms folded and nibbling on his moustache—I pacing back and forth with my eyes on the floor. Deep mourning. Profound silence.
> "But in the end," Cotrim was saying, "this house can't be worth much more than thirty *contos*. At the most thirty five . . ."
> "It's worth fifty," I thought . . .
> " . . . Come on brother let's stop this," Sabina said, getting up from the sofa. "We can work everything out in a friendly fashion, and in good faith. For example Cotrim won't take the slaves, only father's coachman and Paulo . . ."
> "Not the coachman," I replied. "I'm getting the carriage and I'm not going to buy another driver."
> "Well I'll stick with Paulo and Prudêncio."
> "Prudêncio is free."
> "Free?"
> "For two years."
> "Free? How could your father have arranged things like this in the house without letting anyone know? That's great! What about the silver? . . . I suppose he didn't liberate the silver?"[30]

The silence may be profound, but it does not seem to relate to the sadness of mourning. This is a classic bourgeois tiff over the terms of an inheritance, the needy son-in-law with the practical business mind trying to inveigle what he can out of the situation. The slaves emerge as an incidental part of the property. Prudêncio, who will use his liberty so cruelly, is as we shall see saved a terrible fate, by the mere whim of Brás's father. Why he has been set free, we are never told. Did the father feel guilty about the way his son had tortured the slave as a child? The only meaning of freedom here is that it takes Prudêncio out of the economic equation, or to put it another way, as a free black he is, quite literally, no longer worth anything to the whites. There follows an intense argument over who should get the silver, which Brás Cubas will not give up. Cotrim ends with the outburst:

> "You want the carriage, you want the coachman, you want the silver, you want everything." . . .
>
> He was so irritated that I actually thought of suggesting a means of conciliation, dividing up the silver. He laughed and asked me who would get the teapot and who would get the sugar bowl . . . In the meantime Sabina had gone to the window that looked out onto the grounds—and after a moment she turned and proposed giving up Paulo and the other black on the condition that she get the silver. I was going to say that this wasn't convenient for me, but Cotrim anticipated me and said the same thing.
>
> "That, never! I don't make charitable donations," he said.[31]

We are witnesses to a world where slavery appears to operate its own rules of logic. While it appears mad to Cotrim to want to divide up a silver tea set, it seems a matter of no concern whether the slaves are divided up or not. The silver it seems possesses some kind of unity, or integrity, as a set, while the slaves enjoy no such distinction. We never find out who gets the silver and who gets the slaves, all we know is that this argument over property drives the relatives apart. The slaves appear to have a precise value, but only in relation to the family silver. After several years, Brás Cubas is reconciled with his sister and Cotrim and increasingly takes the brother-in-law's advice on intimate matters concerning his mistress or his choice of a suitable wife. The final discussion of Cotrim sets him up as a model citizen:

> I recognised he was a model. They accused him of avarice, and I believe they might have had reasons, but avarice is only the exaggeration of a virtue and virtues should never serve as calculations. Surplus is better than deficit. Since he was very dry in his manners, he had enemies who even accused him of being a barbarian. The only fact alleged in that particular was the frequency with which he sent slaves down to the dungeon, from where they would emerge streaming with blood; but as the ones he sent were vicious or runaways, it so happens that having long been involved in the smuggling

of slaves, he'd become accustomed to a certain way of acting that was a bit harder than is usually needed in the business, and one can't honestly attribute to the original nature of a man what is simply the effect of his social relations. The proof that Cotrim had pious feelings can be found in his love of his children and the grief that he felt when Sara died a few months after that. Irrefutable proof I think and not a unique one.[32]

The whole slave society suddenly opens up here. Within this society, conventional morality still seems to operate. The seven deadly sins are still part of the picture, and Cotrim is accused of avarice, because he is, as we have seen, a mean man obsessed with money. In the opinion of Brás, however, Cotrim's avariciousness could be constructed as excessive parsimoniousness, an old-fashioned virtue. As Brás Cubas attempts to defend his brother-in-law, horrific vistas suddenly unravel. Yet again it is the narrator Brás's obliviousness to the dark place he has taken us, to his own moral blindness, his own cold vision of the world the slaves inhabit, that emerges as truly ghastly. Cotrim tortures his slaves, or rather more horribly, orders them to be tortured, yet Brás Cubas cannot let the fact stand, wants to excuse this behavior, to find an explanation. Cotrim does this because he has intimate experience of illegal slave trading, which has made him oblivious to the emotional life and the physical agonies of his property. Brás Cubas argues that Cotrim's activity has corrupted and brutalized him, that he is not essentially a bad man. Brás Cubas argues that his brother-in-law is actually a victim within a world where the normal rules of human rights do not apply. This is the first we have heard of Cotrim's career as a slave smuggler, but not the first time the subject has appeared in the book. Suddenly we are taken back to Brás's account of a dinner party at his house when he is a boy. To commemorate the fall of Napoleon in 1814, the Cubas family has a grand banquet. Brás Cubas relates the behavior of the guests:

> In the midst of the great and common interest the small and private ones were also moving about. The girls spoke about the *modinhas* they were going to sing to the accompaniment of the harpsichord, the minuets, the English airs. Nor was there any lack of a matron who promised to perform an eight beat dance just to show how she had enjoyed herself in the good old days of childhood. One fellow next to me was passing on to another a recent report on the new slaves who were on their way according to letters he'd received from Luanda, one letter in which his nephew told him that he had already made a deal for about forty head . . . and another in which

... he had them right here in his pocket, but he couldn't read them on this occasion. What he guaranteed is that from this one shipment we can count on some one hundred and twenty slaves at least.

"Hush . . . hush . . . hush," Vilaça was saying, clapping his hands. The noise quickly stopped . . .[33]

We can never be quite sure if this dinner guest provides us with our first introduction to Cotrim. It doesn't really matter. What Assis wants to reveal, as in the explanation of Cotrim's apparent barbarousness, is the seamless integration of the most appalling realities of slavery with the everyday social life of the Rio bourgeoisie. In this world gossip about slave smuggling is just gossip. The "Hush" of the main speaker, clearing a space for his oration, is directed equally at all the "noise," including this terrible confession that took the form of a boast. Slave smuggling has precisely the same social currency as a fashionable song, or an old dance.

Assis is deeply involved in the interrogation of how the social reality of slavery encloses, erodes, and decomposes conceptions of freedom. The ultimate end of his critique of slavery aims to articulate how it closes down the imagination of the enslaved and the enslaver. As the example of Prudêncio illustrates, Assis is capable of carrying out this critique in a realistic setting with great thoroughness. Yet he was also capable of taking his interrogation into more abstract territory, indeed of producing what might be described as philosophical fabulist satire. Technically the most complicated and the deepest example of his meditation on how the environment of the enslaved operates on the limits of abstract thought comes in the chapter "The Black Butterfly" in *Brás Cubas*. This astonishing development of the animal fable is best approached via other treatments of the same theme using the same form. The adapted beast fable occupies a special place within Assis's critique of slavery.

The Yellow Canary Precursor to the Black Butterfly: Assis, Sterne, Slavery, and Animal Fables

The late short story "Ideas of a Canary" ("Idéias do Canário," 1895) and the chapter "Incident of the Donkey" in *Esau and Jacob* are developed out of the tradition of animal fables.[34] The imaginative and mythic depiction of animals is as old as human art; the wall paintings at Lascaux might be the first animal fictions. A literary tradition evolved in Europe, the moral beast fable being worked up into satiric form by Jean de la Fontaine and John Gay among many others.[35] The use of animals in short narratives that teach a moral, or give a warning, reach back into preliterate societies. Sub-Saharan Africa possessed and possesses some of the richest oral traditions of educational animal fables, the Anansi spider tales becoming the most well traveled and adapted. These tales became absorbed within and then celebrated in the context of slavery and found their way into the work of Joel Chandler Harris and Charles Chesnutt in the context of slavery. The Brer Rabbit tales of Joel Chandler Harris in his *Tales of the Old Plantation* introduced a carefully policed version of the stories to a global readership. The conjure tales of Charles Chesnutt elevated the African fable into the realms of high art in postbellum North America. With this history behind him, Assis takes the beast fable into new territory in the context of the form of the short story. His canary, donkey, and butterfly are good demonstrations of how Assis shares with Rudyard Kipling, Franz Kafka, and Clarice Lispector an ability to expand the beast fable, or the animal parable, into wholly new didactic and surreal territories within the frame of the short story. Assis is also involved in all three of these slavery/animal fables in a detailed creative dialogue with Laurence Sterne and his use of animals to raise political issues focused on Atlantic slavery.

"Ideas of a Canary" is a striking example of how far Assis could push the form of the animal fable. In this story an ornithologist called Macedo wanders into a junk shop, where among the rubbish he sees an ancient cage with a canary in it. He buys the bird and keeps it on his veranda in a big new cage. While he is ill through overwork, the bird escapes due to the neglect of a servant. Macedo is distraught, but visiting a friend's estate he comes across the bird one more time perched in a tree. The interest of the story then is clearly not in the action per se, but emerges from the fact that Macedo finds he can talk to the bird and it can talk to him. Their developing magic realist conversations constitute one of Assis's most profound meditations on slavery, cruelty, empathy, spiritual development, and the perception of freedom.

The narrator is revealed to be both a bird lover and a slaveholder. When he enters the curio shop, he sees the frozen remnants of middle-class life in Rio. These are presented with intense stylistic economy in the form of an inventory of objects described later as a "cemetery": "pots without lids, lids without pots, buttons, shoes, a black skirt, straw hats, fur hats, picture frames, binoculars, dress coats, a fencing foil, a stuffed dog" and so on.[36] These personal relics form a setting that brings to life the cage with the canary in it. The contrast of the vivaciousness, color, and sound of the bird, when set against the moribund stasis of the personal human and inhuman relics, climaxing in that stuffed dog, excites Macedo's imagination as he ruminates aloud on the bird's plight: "What detestable owner had the nerve to rid himself of this bird for a few cents? Or what indifferent soul, not wishing to keep his late master's pet, gave it away to a child, who sold it so he could make a bet on a game of football?" This series of fantasies on the bird's probable biography and on the moral responsibility that goes with the ownership of another's life provide commentary on the vulnerability of the slave as property. The slave lives a captive, a caged, life and can be bought or sold at will, because of any arbitrary desire on the owner's part, or any trick of fortune. At this point the reader of Laurence Sterne can see that this story is a development of that great sentimental ironist's most involved discussion of slavery and freedom. At one level "Ideas of a Canary" is a dialogue with Sterne's famous caged starling in *A Sentimental Journey*, but Assis extends the terms of Sterne's analysis of the psychology of liberty in those chapters.[37]

The influence of Sterne is, as briefly observed above, something of a commonplace in Assis scholarship. Assis himself set the ball rolling with his famous tribute to the Anglo-Irishman in the preface to *Brás Cubas*.[38] While Assis's relation to Sterne's mammoth masterpiece of divertive chicanery *Tristram Shandy* has been the focus of much commentary, formally, technically, and morally the most central model is Sterne's final work, *A Sentimental Journey*. This short episodic fiction was written just before Sterne died in 1768 in the form of a series of mock travel anecdotes, narrated by the emotionally unstable and maudlin Yorick, who is a fascinating prototype for the voice of Brás Cubas himself. Structurally the piece is divided up into short chapters each with a staccato title in a sort of newspaper headlinese. Assis adopted this structure quite precisely and deliberately in his *Brás Cubas*. Indeed, one can make a case that Assis is referring to *A Sentimental Journey* in the celebrated preface to *Brás Cubas*. When he refers ambiguously to adopting "a forma livre de um Sterne" (the form of a book by Sterne), critics have immediately jumped to the conclusion that it must be *Tristram Shandy* when the "livre" might just as easily be *A Sentimental Journey*. Assis is typically open ended on the issue.

Assis continued to use the episodic structure, anecdotal self-contained chapters, and the headlinese of *A Sentimental Journey* in the late novel *Esau and Jacob* (1904). Assis's novel contains several set pieces, which are in precise dialogue with sections of Sterne's travel-novella. For example, chapter 41, "Incident of the Donkey," is a typically bleak development of Sterne's section entitled "The Dead Ass," and in method is close to "Ideas of a Canary."[39]

The part of *A Sentimental Journey* that clearly inspired Assis to write "Ideas of a Canary" is the rightly celebrated section on the caged starling. Sterne provides a typically laconic analysis of the self-serving basis of empathetic theory. Assis takes the theme up where Sterne leaves off, and Macedo's fantasy history of the bird's sad life being "sold down the river" from one owner to another, until it ends up with the schoolboy, is a direct tribute to Sterne's account of his caged bird. In the chapter entitled "The Starling," Sterne gives the bird's entire history, including his own morally suspect part in it. Yet Sterne's account stops short of entering the satiric space of the bird's consciousness, and this is the fantastic space Assis decides to develop, ironically. Sterne's starling hovers around anthropomorphism but finally ends up on this side of realism. Yorick hears: "a voice which I took to be of a child complaining 'it could not get out.'"[40] Investigating, he finds the bird in a cage repeating this one stock phrase over and over, "I can't get out—I can't get out." So Yorick believes first that the bird has a human voice, then hears it speak, only to find it merely mimics the sound of four words, which we eventually find it was taught by an English boy, who both saved its life as a fledgling, and who became its first owner. Yet these words arouse Yorick's pity, and in a passion of sentiment he attempts to break open the cage. With comic irony he fails, and trails upstairs to his hotel room, there to use the bird as a symbolic focus for his meditations upon human slavery. Macedo's Sternean ruminations consequently exist in a precise relation to this sentimental literary prehistory, and Assis is in a sense taking his revenge on Yorick's hypocrisy by subjecting it to further brutally ironic assaults. Macedo's impassioned fantasy of how the bird's enslaved existence constitutes an outrage elicits a sharp response from the canary itself, who is a very different creature from Sterne's avian passive victim.

The canary is a real character; the little songbird is self-confident, if not pompous, and has a complete assurance in its world vision. It consequently opens up by telling Macedo he must be insane. Macedo then asks the bird to tell its story, ending with the question, as he indicates the shop owner: "Has your master always been that man sitting over there?" Macedo's view of the situation is again immediately turned on its head as the bird replies: "What master, the man over there is my servant. He gives me my food and water every day, so regularly that were I to pay him for his services it would be no small sum. But canaries do not pay their servants. In fact the world belongs to canaries . . ."[41] At this point Sternean sensibility is left behind, and the reader enters a more difficult moral space as Assis effortlessly enters the mind of the captive, but the happy captive, the privileged captive. Rather than have it express bitterness or pain, Sterne has his canary appear as pampered house slave, articulating or parroting (if canaries can parrot?) the classic pro-slavery theory of benevolent trusteeship.[42] The slave may be owned by the master, but the slave also exists as a trust. If a master looks after the slave well, then the slave enjoys complete contentment, and moreover it is the master who in fact serves the slave because of his or her moral duty to the creature that is owned. Because the bird has known nothing but contented captivity, that is what constitutes its experiential and moral universe. Macedo, fascinated at the notion that this creature has no theory of freedom because it has no experience of freedom, asks the bird if it "is not lonely for the infinite blue space?" When the bird replies that it doesn't know what he is talking about Macedo asks "What is the world to you?" and in return gets a description of the bird's immediate surroundings. The canary ends the description with a perfect control fantasy, which would fit the mindset of any domestic slave who had committed to the fiction of their own relative privilege: "The canary is master of the cage that it lives in and the shop that surrounds it. Beyond that everything is illusion and deception."[43] This is, if you want to read it that way, an explanation as to why so many slaves were content to live their lives within captivity. Assis may also, however, be referring to the closed mind of the slaveholder, since it is not only prisoners who see only the bars of their cage, but the jailer as well.[44]

The story goes on to take the form of a classic quest narrative arranged in the pattern of a riddle repeated three times before it is solved. The next stage involves Macedo purchasing the bird, and once it becomes his property he builds it a huge new cage and places it on his veranda, with a view of "the garden, the fountain and a bit of blue sky." The bird then becomes Macedo's project, his obsession, and he studies its life, language, and habits, precisely as a scientific racist would study an African slave enclosed in a plantation mansion: "When the philological and psychological study was done, I entered specifically into the study of canaries, their origin, their early history, the geography and flora of the Canary Islands, the bird's knowledge of navigation and so forth." On asking the canary to repeat, for the second time, its definition of the world, Macedo finds that the canary now defines the world as its new environment, concluding however with the old words "Everything else is illusion and deception." The canary then escapes, due to the deliberate neglect of the slave who Macedo has set to look after it. When shortly afterwards the distraught Macedo sees his canary on a tree branch in a friend's beautiful estate, he asks it a third time for its definition of the world, to be told this time that "The world is an infinite blue space with the sun up above." When the infuriated Macedo declares that according to this relativism "the world can be anything . . . it can even be a second hand shop," the bird finishes the story with the question "But is there such a thing as a second hand shop?"

The story is, as with most fables, open to many interpretations. Is the bird a representation of the perceptual and philosophical limitations that slavery imposes on the mind of the slave, and therefore an ultimate victim? Is the bird an articulation of the satiric intelligence of the slave, which tells the master what he wants to hear while always being one step ahead of him? Is the story really about Macedo's obliviousness to the real human slaves he keeps in his house and requires to sweep out the bird shit? While Macedo can feel extreme emotions of wonder and sorrow in the context of his canary, and get into profound philosophical debate with it, when the bird escapes he confesses, "my first impulse was to strangle the servant."[45] This superb aside is the point at which the narrator reveals how slavery has utterly corrupted his own moral compass.

A Theory of Immoral Sentiment: Sterne, Slavery, and the Black Butterfly

Et les carolles de papier, racornies, se balançant le long de la plaque comme des papillons noirs, enfin s'envolèrent par la cheminée.

—Flaubert, *Madame Bovary*[46]

Assis's irony, this time a tragicomic irony, as he meditated on slavery's capacity to destroy human imagination, climaxed in his fable, or allegory, or myth, of "The Black Butterfly." The reader has been elaborately prepared for the thirty-first chapter entitled "The Black Butterfly" by the event that concludes the previous chapter. In a garden Brás Cubas comes across Eugênia (a young lame girl he flirts with, and vaguely but briefly pursues, early in the book) and her mother Dona Eusébia. The mother is trying to get Brás Cubas interested in her daughter, and as the mother "sings her praises" he watches the girl's eyes and describes the effect through an elaborate simile. Her eyes appear "as if inside her head a little butterfly with golden wings and diamond eyes were flying around . . ." Brás Cubas then immediately moves from fancy to reality, observing: "I say inside because outside a black butterfly was flying around." As soon as Eusébia sees it she bursts into frantic curses crying out: "Keep away! . . . Go away Devil . . . Holy Virgin Mary," while the daughter "goes pale with fear," which she tries to conceal. Brás Cubas notes what he describes as the "superstition of the two women," and then laughs inwardly with what he describes as a "philosophical, disinterested, superior" laugh.[47] But where does this terror come from, and what superstition has Brás Cubas detected? In this initial encounter with the black butterfly, it appears that the two women are interpreting the animal through popular black cultural beliefs related to witchcraft and devil worship. Among the poor and the slaves, the butterfly carried folkloric associations as the devil's familiar, as a daemon. Witches could turn themselves into butterflies, and butterflies could embody Satan himself.[48] It is difficult to translate into English what the exclamations of Eusébia fully connote. My initial translation is valid but does not tell the whole story. When the mother screams "T'esconjuro! . . . sai, diabo! . . . Virgem Nossa Senhora! . . ." she is in fact carrying out a spontaneous exorcism.[49] The verb "esconjurar," as well as carrying a series of meanings related to entreating, is a powerful verb related to conjuring, and explicitly to exorcism through the pronunciation and adjuration of a holy name. So what she is actually saying in a heightened emotional form is "I conjure you to come forth . . . leave this body Satan . . . I command it by the Holy Virgin's name."

The next chapter, "A Borboleta Preta," extends the infernal and horrifying imagery of the black butterfly into a series of much more tense and intimate contexts, producing a disturbingly beautiful metaphoric exploration of the neuroses and power fantasies generated by Atlantic slavery. The key passage opens as follows:

> On the following day, as I was preparing to go down, a butterfly entered my bedroom, a butterfly as black as the other and much bigger than it was . . . the butterfly after fluttering about me settled on my head. I shook it off. It went on to land on the counterpane and because I chased it off again, it left and settled on an old portrait of my father. It was as black as night. The soft movements with which it began to move its wings after alighting had a certain mocking / jeering / derisive ["escarninho"] way about it that disgusted me a great deal. I turned my back, left the room, but when I returned a few minutes later and found it in the same spot, I was taken with a nervous shock. I seized a towel, struck it, and it fell.[50]

The account begins factually, yet as soon as the insect makes intimate contact with the painted face of Brás's father, anthropomorphic emotion suddenly floods in. The insect's wing movements are irrationally interpreted as powerfully, almost obscenely, disrespectful. Is this because complete blackness is hovering over, obliterating, the white slave owner's features? His father has a black devil sitting on his face. Brás Cubas then goes through a cycle of extreme emotions, leaves in disgust, returns, and seeing the butterfly still smothering his father's face, is given a nervous jolt, which generates an instinctive reaction to kill, but what is he killing? It is clear by this point that we are not dealing with a butterfly, or simply with a folkloric association of the butterfly with the devil, but with an allegorical sign, a dark memorial nexus, a creature which, if one takes the definition that "in the simplest terms, allegory says one thing and means another," means many allegorical things.⁵¹ The account then takes narrative wing and moves into a provocative discussion of what it means to have power of life and death over a black creature:

> It didn't drop down dead. It was twisting its body and moving its antennae. I regretted what I'd done, took it in the palm of my hand, and went over and put it on the window sill. It was too late. The poor thing expired after a few seconds. I was a little upset, bothered.
> "Why the devil wasn't it blue?" I said to myself.⁵²

Assis again pits himself against Sterne at this point. Sterne explored the relationship between macroaesthetics and human emotion in dramatic scenarios involving human interaction with animals. He embarked on a quest to discover the workings of human sentiment, and sentimental theory was after all eighteenth-century Britain's principle contribution to empathetic theory. A man, or woman, of *sentiment* expressed the refinement and quality of their empathetic resources, indeed expressed their basic humanity and goodness, through the intensity and profundity with which they could respond to the suffering of another. This *other* could be manifested in any form of life, human or animal, but of course the more remote the sentimental target the greater the imaginative challenge. Consequently, animals and black slaves were both important elements within sentimental and particularly abolition discourse.⁵³ If an individual could imaginatively enter the mind of a tortured slave on a slave ship, then they should also be able to enter the mind of a tortured cow at Smithfield market.⁵⁴

Empathetic theory raised all sorts of philosophical and ethical questions concerning the relative suffering and importance of man and animals, and their place in creation. As the example of the starling above suggests, Sterne was capable of using a quizzically satiric approach in order to search these questions to the quick. Yet he could also discard his gentle skepticism and fully commit to a sort of incontinent soppiness. Sterne's animal vignettes often evoke feelings and scenarios that give rise to the devolved notion of the sentimental as something emotionally false, self-indulgent, spongy, and saccharine, qualities that now define the word in common usage. Both *Tristram Shandy* and *A Sentimental Journey* abound in the type of weepy, morally uncentered exhibitionism that lives off the transference of emotion from an elevated human subject to a household pet, or even an insect in peril. Probably the most celebrated and unadulterated single scene devoted to this kind of demonstrative, indeed theatricalized, hypersensitivity is the notorious moment when Uncle Toby releases a household fly in *Tristram Shandy*. The celebrated description, which Assis felt compelled to return to and parodically assault several times in his work, runs as follows:

> He was of a peaceful placid nature; my uncle Toby had scarce a heart to hurt a fly. —Go—says he, one day at dinner, to an overgrown one which had buzzed about his nose, and tormented him cruelly all dinner time,— and which after infinite attempts, he had caught at last, as it flew by him;— I'll not hurt thee, says my uncle Toby, rising from his chair; and going across the room, with the fly in his hand,—I'll not hurt a hair of thy head:— Go, says he, lifting up the sash, and opening his hand as he spoke, to let it escape;—go, poor devil, get thee gone, why should I hurt thee?—this world surely is wide enough to hold both thee and me.[55]

At a direct level Brás Cubas acts brutally as the antithesis of Uncle Toby. Unnerved by the insect he faces, Brás Cubas feels horror, not benevolence, and casually destroys it. Then he picks it up and carries it to the window it will now never be able to fly through, drops it, watches it die and, we later learn, eventually flicks its corpse outside into the garden, for the pragmatic reason he doesn't want it to attract ants into the house (a constant problem in Rio, where the ants are big and dangerous).

Assis was clearly deeply interested in the potential of Sterne's scenario for analyzing the emotional life of Brás, as well as his approach to power and its abuses. Assis in fact circles around Sterne's fly scenario several times in *Brás Cubas*, and he places Brás Cubas into close conjunction with insects at various points in the book. Apart from the black butterfly, there is another episode later on in chapter 103 entitled "Distraction," in which Brás Cubas performs an elaborate variation on Uncle Toby and the fly. Brás Cubas, arguing with his mistress Virgilia because he is late meeting her, becomes transfixed with the spectacle of a fly crawling across the floor dragging along an ant that is biting its leg. The image is clearly a symbol for Brás's fretful, mutually abusive, and claustrophobic relationship with Virgilia, but it is also a picture of nature red in tooth and claw at its brutal work. At this point, however, Assis breaks away from the heavy symbolism to move into a fully blown parody. Brás, unlike his earlier manifestation, behaves towards the fly as a classic Sternean man of sentiment:

> Then I with the inborn delicacy of a man of our century took the two mortified creatures in the palm of my hand. I calculated the distance between my hand and the planet Saturn and asked myself what interest there could be in such a wretched episode. If you conclude from this that I am a barbarian then you are wrong because I asked Virgilia for a hairpin in order to separate the two insects. But the fly guessed my intentions, opened its wings and flew off. Poor fly! Poor ant! And God saw that it was good as scripture says.[56]

Brás physically attempts to mimic Uncle Toby, yet he cannot commit to the process and thinks, in his own skeptical and cynical terms, of a brute natural creation forever violent and doomed. His actions come to nothing anyway, and are comically thwarted by the insect, which flies off, as far as he can see, to maintain its tormented relationship with the ant, whether Brás Cubas wants it to or not. It seems that the delicacy of Brás, his sentiment, is worthless and futile. This is a world of the powerful and the powerless, of masters and slaves, and the only reason for indulging sentimental fantasy is to uphold the hypocrisies of the power structure. Brás Cubas might mimic and cynically parody elevated modes of thought and behavior, yet he arrives at a dead end.

Conversely, when Brás Cubas rejects sentimentalism for random, useless violence, when he kills the black butterfly and literally creates a dead end, the act has fertile results and leads him into an unfettered flight of fancy that he finds immensely heartwarming. Having responded to the butterfly's murder with the racist, or pigmentationalist, outburst "Why the devil wasn't it blue?" he continues:

> And that reflection—one of the most profound that has been made since butterflies were invented—consoled me for the evil deed and reconciled me with myself. I let myself contemplate the corpse with a certain amount of sympathy. I must confess I imagined that it had come out of the woods after having breakfast and that it was happy. The morning was beautiful. It came out of there, modest and black, having fun butterflying, under the broad cupola of a blue sky, which is always blue for all wings. It came through my window and found me. I suppose it had never seen a man before. It didn't know, therefore, what a man was. It executed infinite turns about my body and saw that I moved, that I had eyes, arms, legs, a divine look, a colossal stature. Then it said to itself, "This is probably the inventor of butterflies." The idea terrified it, subjugated it, but fear, which is also suggestive, hinted

to it that the best way to please its master was to kiss him on the forehead and it kissed me on the forehead. When I drove it away, it went to land on the counterpane. There it saw my father's picture and it's quite possible that it discovered a half-truth there. To wit that this was the father of the inventor of butterflies and it went over to beg his mercy.

Then the blow of the towel put an end to the affair. The blue immensity was of no use to it, nor the joy of the flowers, nor the splendor of the green leaves, against a face towel, a foot of raw linen. See how fine it is to be superior to butterflies. Because it's proper to say so, had it been blue or orange its life would not have been any more secure. It's quite possible that I would have run it through with a pin for the pleasure of my eyes. It was that last idea which gave me back my consolation. I put my middle finger against my thumb, gave a flick, and the corpse fell into the garden. It was time. The provident ants were already arriving. No, I go back to my first idea, it would have been better had it been born blue.[57]

This is a complicated development of Sterne that again takes us back to the idea that "the child is father to the man." In order to understand what Assis is doing here, it is necessary to return to *Tristram Shandy*. Sterne followed his anecdote about Uncle Toby and the fly by having the narrator immediately observe that he was ten when he witnessed this event and that it changed his sensibility forever, it made him good:

> I was but ten years old when this happened: but whether it was that the action itself was more in unison to my nerves at that age of pity, which instantly set my whole frame into one vibration of most pleasurable sensation I know not;—but this I know, that the lesson of universal goodwill then taught and imprinted on it by my uncle Toby, has never since been worn out of my mind.[58]

Indeed, the anecdote became adopted into popular children's fiction as an ideal of infantile moral rectitude. By 1789 the best-selling children's publisher John Newberry had brought out *The Life and Adventures of a Fly*. In this an eight-year-old Master Laurence Sterne helps the central character Tommy decide what to do with a fly he has caught: "Go to the window which you see is open, put him out, and say, 'Go thy ways, poor fluttering thing; it were very hard indeed, if in this wide world there were not room enough for *me* and *you* to live'; and then shut down the window and let him fly a-way." When Sterne was writing, an entire moral literature was generated around the notion of the crucial importance of avoiding pointless cruelty to lesser beings: "Unchecked, vicious impulses in children may lead to a lifetime of wickedness. Some of the most execrable tyrants that ever disgraced human nature began their career of cruelty with killing flies, and progressively went on to kill their fellow men," warned the *Young Gentleman's and Lady's Magazine.* Commenting on this passage, Lynn Festa makes an observation with precise relevance to what Assis will do with this tradition: "The child is father to the man in this domino theory of moral corruption."[59] Festa goes on to observe that the entire didactic tradition of literature aimed at children and warning of cruelty to animals dealt with power and responsibility in terms intimately related to slaveholding: "The morality of benevolent responsibility and paternalistic master-ship described in these texts draws younger readers into the roles of loving master and mistress, and creates powerful emotional bonds that lock person and things together in relations that super-cede the claims of mere property."[60] Assis is a slaveholder and has no interest in ever superceding the "claims of mere property."

The parody is precise and vicious. Where Sterne imagines Tristram formed by the influence of his sensitive and loving Uncle Toby, Assis has already given us Brás Cubas, vitiated by his debauched, cruel, and obscene Uncle João. And in that chapter "The Child is Father to the Man" we are told: "from the age of eleven on, I was admitted to his anecdotes, true or otherwise, all contaminated with obscenity or filth."[61] And the result is that as a morally ruined slaveholder, Brás Cubas gives his imagination over to a brutal assault on the tradition of benevolent sentimentality, which he develops in his fiction of the butterfly's life and thought. His reason for pretending to enter the creature's head, the justification for creating this self-serving version of "the life and adventures of a fly," is to overpaint his earlier feelings of terror and disgust with a narrative of reassurance. Brás Cubas does not approach his own violence, or the terror he felt at the black creature's chance erasure of his father's features (the fact that lay behind the violence). Instead, he shows the creature as a willing, even a necessary victim. The slave/butterfly emerges as the humble servant, who not only instinctively loves and worships the master as a god, but who desires to make itself the master's slave. In Sterne's world, humans, adults, and children alike are duty bound to enter into the imaginative world of the weak, or the victim, in order to protect and love them, be they slaves or flies. Brás Cubas does not do this, but rather takes his revenge on Sterne and the ethics of the Age of Sentiment, by creating an empathetic fantasy with a sting in the tail. He gives us a vision of the spontaneous self-enslavement of a free spirit, where the only love expressed is the devotion of the slave for the master. The butterfly/slave feels awe and fear before the colossal masters, father and son, and kisses both of them as a gesture of abjection. This solipsistic take on the mind of the slave is then made even more horrible by Brás's subsequent conclusion that he may well have killed the butterfly no matter what color it was. Why do people occasionally kill insects, irrationally? Because they can. Why do masters sometimes kill slaves, irrationally? Because they can. Yet Assis in bringing up the butterfly on the pin has extended the discussion and is not talking about mere physical death but a spiritual and social death.

If Brás Cubas had considered the creature beautiful, he would have killed it to keep its corpse near him, for his pleasure; if ugly, he would kill it anyway. This is the fate of the slaves. The pure Africans sail in from the blue of the Atlantic Ocean and, completely black and unassimilated, they go out to the plantations to be worked to death. But the exotic slaves, the beautiful, interesting mulatto or quadroon, will be kept, pinned down and golden skinned, inside the precious and privileged case of the *casa grande*, or Brás's town house, as prized specimens of domestic slavery, transfixed for the master's aesthetic perusal and use. What Assis is giving us is the depraved sophistry of the urban slaveholder's mind. It uses its intellect and creativity to invent stories that justify absolute power, ultimate cruelty, and what Primo Levi has termed "useless violence."

Assis has Brás Cubas present himself again as a form of post-Sadean super-ego, a creature who is completely free to enact any enormity he likes on the objects that are enslaved or, in his mad vision, have enslaved themselves to him. Brás Cubas presents himself in fact not according to the fiction of Sterne, but according to one of the most bleakly economic fictions in Shakespeare. The ur-text lying behind Brás's action and his subsequent fantasy, the ultimate fly-torture-fantasy as moral parable, is a line and a half from *King Lear*. Assis's whole butterfly chapter can be read as a spectacular extended parody of the blinded Duke of Gloucester's famous and bleak aphorism. When Gloucester has reached an ultimate point of physical abuse and mental despair, he declares: "As flies to wanton boys are we to the gods; / They kill us for their sport."[62] In Assis's parody Brás Cubas has taken this idea, namely that the gods treat humans as cruel boys treat flies when they torture and destroy them for fun, and given it a bizarre twist. Assis has imagined Brás Cubas imagining his victim, the fly, imagining Brás Cubas, the torturer, as a god, who behaves as a wanton boy, and kills the fly—that is a terrific set of inversions. The final and almost unbearable irony is that the "sport" lies in the imaginative games that Brás Cubas plays with the fly's memory once he has killed it. The fantasy of the butterfly's life and thought is a contaminating act of reinscription that gives a full insight into how effortlessly and frivolously the slave power can rewrite evil.

The narrative returns full circle to the abandoned and sadistic fictions with which Brás Cubas responded to the spectacle of Prudêncio's moral ruin. We are back with Brás Cubas the boy, who has been demoralized and poisoned to the spiritual and imaginative core, by witnessing how the adults around him live within slavery. Tragically, "the child is father to the man," and Brás Cubas destroyed this beautiful butterfly/slave, not because he has godlike powers and a godlike presence in the view of his victim, but because he was, and will always remain, the slave power's perfect creation—a wanton boy. That is Assis's final message in this terrible and beautiful book. Brás Cubas preaches an amoral message, namely that it would most certainly not have been better to have been born blue. In real terms it would have made no difference, assuming you were born a slave. Brás Cubas is out of moral and, more crucially, aesthetic control. That is what slavery does to you: you end up physically depraved and intellectually wanton. Slavery is a blind force that pulls everyone involved in it apart.

CHAPTER 5

Magnifying Signifying Silence: Afro-Brazilians and Slavery in Euclides da Cunha, *Os Sertões*

The martyrdom of man is here reflective of a greater torture, more widespread, one embracing the general economy of life. It arises from the age-old martyrdom of earth.

—Os Sertões

Os Sertões: Slavery and Brazilian Cultural Memory?

Antônio Vicente Mendes Maciel was popularly known, and has been passed down to posterity, as Antônio Conselheiro—"Anthony the Counsellor," "the Advocate," "the Adviser." Conselheiro was the mystical leader of the Canudos community, a vast social experiment that established itself, or perhaps more accurately spontaneously evolved, towards the end of the nineteenth century in the arid North Eastern scrublands of Brazil. There is unreliable and scant biographical information on him, and his writings survive in meagre and fragmentary form. Conselheiro is as much a glorious myth as a man, and even his name is not stable for he was also known to his devoted and often religiously fanatical supporters under several other appellations, including *Santo Antônio dos Mares, Santo Antônio Aparecido,* and *Bom Jesus Conselheiro.*[1] This man was central to the founding of a substantial community, which established a distinct set of religious beliefs, was relatively well organized as a social unit, and which, at its height in 1895, was estimated to have a population as large as thirty thousand.[2] There is argument over the social makeup of Canudos. With a rapidity that the authorities found disconcerting, Canudos had grown almost randomly. It drew in a remarkably diverse population of backlanders, cattle traders, beggars, bandits, mestizos, mulattos, *malandros, curibocas, cangaçeiros,* Indian *indigenos,* and newly freed slaves. Conselheiro was the inspirational force behind the production of a social phenomenon designated by some as "the last *quilombo*."³ He named the disused farm at the center of the settlement *Belo Monte*, or "Beautiful Mountain," but the popular name of the place, *Arraial de Canudos*, meant that it came to be known then, and down through posterity, as Canudos. It was in the years immediately following the passing of the Golden Law of May 1888, officially abolishing slavery in Brazil, that this strange experiment, part commune, part mystical monarchy, part religious order, developed in the backlands of Bahia. The foundation and evolution of Canudos and its widely documented and spectacular decimation in the autumn of 1897 at the hands of a military expeditionary force, which combined national and Bahian state troops and *jagunço* mercenaries, generated significant interest in the press and several extended neo-fictional accounts. Among the many narratives of Canudos, one epic treatment stood out, *Os Sertões* by Euclides da Cunha.

Da Cunha completed the manuscript in 1900, and from its first appearance in 1902 this vast text was hailed as one of the foundational works of Brazilian literature and cultural identity.⁴ Indeed from being an almost unknown author, da Cunha was within a year of publication taken into Brazil's most prestigious cultural institutions, being elected to Brazil's Academy of Letters, and also made a member of the Brazilian Geographical and Historical Institute. Yet despite its growing celebrity and its place at the heart of debates on Brazilian racial intermixture and national identity, slavery and Afro-Brazilianism have remained peripheral issues in the cultural reception of *Os Sertões*. How Canudos and slavery interface in da Cunha's work is not a question that has generated much interest or direct discussion inside or outside Brazil. It is fair to say that the question of whether *Os Sertões* engages with slavery as a part of Brazilian cultural memory has not been answered. It is also true to say that there has been pitifully little historical work devoted to considering the extent to which Conselheiro's followers before 1888 consisted of runaway slaves and from then up to the Canudos massacre were composed mainly of freed slaves.

Canudos, Conselheiro, and Martyrological Popular Fictions Before da Cunha

The substantial Canudos settlement grew up under the organization of the itinerant mystic Conselheiro, who had by the mid-1890s been wandering the arid backlands lying within the northern seaboard for over a quarter of a century. Having been subjected to concerted pressure over the decades from the authorities and the church, including physical abuse, a brief deportation, and continued harassment, he continued as a sort of Brazilian ancient mariner of the scrublands. Dressed in a simple robe of deep indigo blue, with long hair and beard, he was a powerful charismatic with a woeful and apocalyptically uplifting story to tell, and a magnetic pull on his socially disparate following. His ideas exist in no stable, extended, printed archive and cannot ever lead to an authoritative edited oeuvre. Indeed his ideas, whether in relation to his enthusiastic and messianic religious thought, or his political and social theory, were never coherently set out in any extended document and have to be pieced together from reported fragments of his extempore sermons, and from the ballads and statements of his followers, enemies, and persecutors.[5] These ideas appear to have been based upon a combination of influences: religion, explicitly millenarian fanaticism; a reverence for the monarchy and nostalgia for princess Isabelle; and a sympathy for Sebastianist revivalism.[6] He was set against the new Republic of Brazil and adhered to a primitive agrarian protocommunism, while undoubtedly setting himself up as a prophetic leader. His speeches and his movement could also encompass a savage colloquial satire, directed at the new republic, but not the Brazilian Catholic Church.[7] Moving through vast areas, and setting up camp in many towns—Algoinhas, Inhambupe, Bom Conselho, Geremoabo, Cumbe, Macumbo, Massacara, Pombal, and Tucano— Conselheiro, with his shifting but ever expanding band of followers, delivered sermons, agitated, restored derelict churches, and supposedly worked miracles. He appears to have focused his attentions frequently on rural slave populations and preached to large crowds of slaves in the slave quarters.[8] By the mid-1890s he had established the impromptu Canudos commune along the foothills of the Favela mountain. Conselheiro's following was subaltern, consisting almost entirely of the destitute, the suffering, the dispossessed, the criminal, the discontented, and above all the mystically inclined.[9] Brazil's new republic saw this social experiment as deeply troubling. Above all, Conselheiro's monarchical nostalgia was potentially dangerous, in a nation that had found the recent loss of its imperial identity, not to mention its slave property, traumatic. Because of his tolerance for the Catholic Church, initially priests had been sent in to attempt to infiltrate Conselheiro's followers and implement a state-backed policing form of Catholicism. When their efforts failed, it was only a matter of time before a "military solution" to Conselheiro and his fanatical adherents was seen as the best, or at least the only, option. Three rather badly organized and undermanned military expeditions were sent to snuff out the Canudos settlement, a sort of vast proto-*favela* in the wilderness. When these successively failed, finally state and government troops combined in a mass military campaign. In the subsequent bloodbath, Canudos was unceremoniously and

Chapter 5

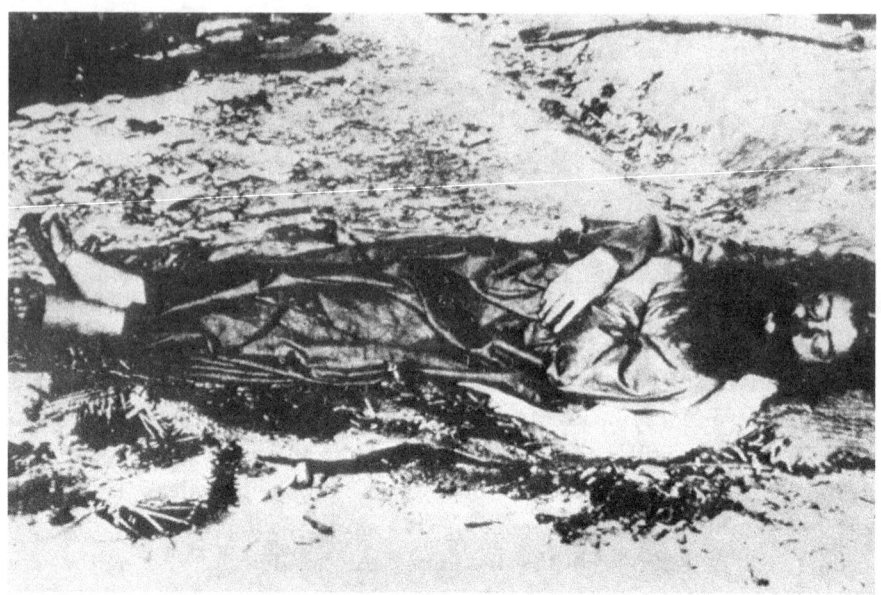

6. Anon., *Corpse of Antonio Conselheiro*, glass plate collodion print, 1879.

brutally obliterated. An estimated twenty-five thousand were massacred. The last four defenders of Canudos died in combat on October 5, 1897.

The last stand of the inhabitants of Canudos, and the images of the dead leader and of the captured women and children, were not without a certain martyrological and heroic element that rapidly gave Conselheiro and his inner circle mythical and martyrological status. Propaganda, printed in Salvador Bahia before the final assault, produced exaggerated accounts and apocryphal stories relating the extremity, strangeness, and brutality of the Canudos inhabitants.[10] Yet the processes of their destruction, so uncompromising and brutal, generated unusual fascination and strong sympathy among some Brazilian intellectuals, including Brazil's greatest living author, Machado de Assis. Assis indeed wrote a short newspaper article stressing the extent to which Canudos had entered the popular imagination via popular mass media including illustrated broadsides, fliers, and the *literatura de cordel*. The latter (cheap mass-produced pamphlets bound with a single stitched cord) often took the form of popular ballads designed to be performed.[11] *Cordel* readily accommodated the rising mythology of Conselheiro and Canudos and embedded them within extant popular forms of Brazilian folk tale, sensational crime narratives, Romance, and miracle

7. Anon., *Surviving Prisoners at Canudos*, glass plate collodion print, 1879.

literature.¹² Indeed there was a whole tradition of *Cordel* literature devoted to the hardships and horrors of life in the backlands, often with striking titles such as "The Devouring Drought and the Tears of the Sertanejo," which Canudos naturally fed into.¹³

The photographs that documented the end of the commune had perhaps the strongest impact on the popular national and international imagination. On October 6, 1897, literally the day after Canudos fell, the corpse of Conselheiro was exhumed and photographed as proof that he was indeed mortal and very dead (fig. 6). The legendary photograph of his corpse expanded the myths surrounding him and his martyrdom, much in the way that the photographs of the murdered Che Guevara in Vallegrande, Bolivia, on October 10, 1967, laid out Christ-like on a grim autopsy slab, contributed to his popular sanctification.¹⁴ The photographs of the women and children who survived are powerful.

The middle ground of one image (fig. 7) is filled with a chaotic bundled nest of suffering humanity, which is increasingly anonymous the further it gets from the wide-angled lens. What emerges is a teeming morass of victims, vulnerable and threatened because marked off and sealed in by an outer border of armed men. Standing off in the distance in their hats and scruffy uniforms, these are the hired *jagunços* responsible for the mass murder of these women's husbands and for the razing of their homes to the ground. These men, distant and anonymous, carry the threat of infinite violence. Another noticeable feature of this crowd is how black it is, the majority of the faces African or having African elements.

Da Cunha's Reappropriations of the Canudos Myth

What this mass of popular material emphasizes is that da Cunha, in deciding to take on the Canudos narrative and to mythologize it in his own way, was also taking on an already powerful set of popular symbols and images of refined artistry, made using the latest technology, which foregrounded the suffering and dignity of the commune.[15] Da Cunha triumphantly succeeded in putting his own stamp on what had already assumed the lineaments of a national myth of heroic suffering. His mercurial and unstable approach to Conselheiro, the Canudos commune, and the makeup of its inhabitants exhibits a love–hate relationship with the sentimental and melodramatic history he had inherited. It is da Cunha's confusion and ambiguity that finally give his work the aesthetic charge that raises it above and separates it out from all other treatments.

In terms of national mythologies, and the ramifications of race theory, not to mention the cultural history of Brazil's North East, *Os Sertões* was far and away the most popular and influential text to be generated by the Canudos affair. The reputation of *Os Sertões* within Brazilian literary history has only grown with time.[16] The book has now generated a substantial academic literature in Portuguese and led to the production of exhaustive scholarly editions, as well as colonizing popular visual media. *Os Sertões* formed the inspiration and basis for a variety of Brazilian feature films and a television miniseries. The work was translated into English by Samuel Putnam in 1944, and a new English translation by Elizabeth Lowe appeared under the dignified imprimatur of the Penguin Classics in 2010. *Os Sertões* is finally developing some sort of international fan base.

Coming out in 1902, some five years after the obliteration of Canudos, this vast and uncategorizable text was the *magnum opus* of da Cunha, an engineer and journalist/war correspondent who had firsthand experience of the final campaign, and who was indeed sent out to report on the events. What Canudos inspired this uniquely talented author to compose was certainly not mere journalism, although *Os Sertões* contained journalistic elements of reportage and certain linguistic elements, most notably headlinese, normally restricted to newspapers, print captions, and broadsides. *Os Sertões*, generally held out to be the first, indeed arguably the only, national epic of Brazil, is also categorized by some as a novel, although it does not really fit this label. No matter what its form might be, the colossal status of this text within Brazilian letters, historiography, race history, and intellectual life remains unshakable. Indeed, the book is one of those texts that immediately generated, and still generates, effects far beyond its covers. It has a mythic power and in many ways remains a sacred text within Brazil, and in other parts of Latin America. Some idea of its continuing hold on the South American creative consciousness outside Brazil comes out in the way it formed the core for Mario Vargas Llosa's plagiaristic best seller *The War at the End of the World*.[17]

What is undeniable is that da Cunha's book uncovers the Brazilian national consciousness in uniquely varied ways. Because of his scientific and technical training, da Cunha was able to draw upon a variety of disciplines that inflect not only his thought but his narrative options. These registers include geography, geology, botany, natural history, climatology, nineteenth-century race science, classical military history, and anthropology. The book is fearlessly digressive in terms of content, and diverse in terms of form. Da Cunha thinks nothing of presenting vast geological and botanical tangents in his opening hundred pages. The book has several styles that operate formally as a kind of literary stratification, and da Cunha develops enormous chains of extended metaphor. The book might be seen as formally in some profound spiritual sympathy with the cumbersome metaphoric genius of Melville's *Moby Dick*. Like Melville's literary leviathan, it slowly builds, like a vast natural destructive phenomenon—an avalanche or an earthquake—towards its sublime and violent conclusion. In appropriating the *sertão* as the geographical setting for his masterpiece, da Cunha was the last in a long line of artists and authors fascinated by recording the bare, arid, angular beauty of the *sertão* and the *caatingas* of the North East, a land that, because of its forbidding and impenetrable aspects, had long generated some of the most beautiful natural history and landscape studies of colonial Brazil.[18]

The opening sections of *Os Sertões* appear to consist of minute descriptions of landscape, rock formations, and weather. Yet what these powerful and extended descriptive set pieces really constitute are weirdly metaphoric anatomizations of a certain kind of Brazilian socio-geographic consciousness. The *sertões* or backlands of Brazil's North East are not just an area, or a place; they constitute something of a state of mind, or a shifting spiritual state of being.[19] These arid drought-stricken regions with their *sertanejos*, tough little men and women, with tough little horses, all clad in rough leather armor to protect against the heat and the vicious thorns of the *caatinga*, have their own mythology, and have been the basis for a series of remarkably powerful fictions of which da Cunha's is only one.[20] The cinematic masterpieces of Glauber Rocha, so influential on Martin Scorsese's early style, *Deus e o Diabo na Terra do Sol* (1964), *Terra em Transe* (1967), and *Antônio das Mortes* (1969), established the *sertão* as a charged sociopolitical arena that is essentially permeable and unstable, a sort of highly stylized focus for thinking about Brazil as a racial and social cauldron. From the 1950s through to the end of the twentieth century, the *sertão* emerged as what Ismail Xavier has nicely termed Brazil's "identity reservoir," a creative and cultural space locked into a series of regionalist and nationalist agendas. These saw Brazil's identity as sunk in the preservation of regional popular culture, and the adoration of the outsider and the bandit, typified by Lampião and Maria Bonita.[21] But it is essential when assessing da Cunha's approach and values to remember that he wrote at the turn of the nineteenth century and, as will become apparent, he had a very different set of cultural agendas relating to race and social displacement from those of Brazilian authors and cineastes of the later twentieth century.

The book's enduring and symbiotic appeal to Brazilians is difficult to grasp and justify. Not only is the text to be located around the post-history just sketched out, but it existed in a prehistory to which it also appeared immune. As stated, it was more than four years after the violent end of Canudos that da Cunha published his account. The event was itself celebrated in terms of the popular history it generated, as is evidenced by the fact that it had, via the wonders of wireless telegraphy, gained international attention in 1897–1898.[22] Canudos, and the final massacre in particular, had dominated the Brazilian popular newspapers. A sensational exhibition, projecting twenty-five "life sized" photographs of the final stages of the war and its aftermath, was advertised in February 1898, and two of the most effective are analyzed above.[23] As far as the domestic publishing market was concerned, *Os Sertões* appeared, given the illiteracy of nearly ninety percent of the Brazilian population and the small number of books published, in what had become a somewhat crowded publishing arena. A plethora of works providing narratives of Conselheiro's mystical mass movement, and of the military campaigns sent to destroy it, had come out before the publication of *Os Sertões*.[24] Yet none of these works generated mass appeal, let alone anything approaching the vast and enduring popular devotion that hung about da Cunha's epic from the moment it appeared. In focusing upon a minor religious maniac, the low-life disciples who followed him, and the successive coves of politicians who sent waves of adventuring soldiers to destroy these deliberately marginalized beings, da Cunha has been seen by one strand of historiography as laying bare the tectonic plates whose furious collisions enabled post-slavery Brazil to evolve.[25]

The book, as with any sui generis literary achievement, is in many ways beyond criticism both within and outside Brazil.[26] The book's first English translator, the American Luso-Hispanophile left-wing publisher and translator Samuel Putnam, made vast claims for the text. He stated as long ago as the 1940s that never, "in the history of world literature," had there been "such unanimity on the part of critics of all shades of opinion in acclaiming a book as the greatest and most distinctive which a people has produced [and] the most deeply expressive of that people's spirit." Putnam continued with the claim that the book was "the Bible of Brazilian nationality," and expanding upon this theme he concluded emphatically that *Os Sertões* was "the definitive early-century statement of the national-racial question in Brazil, a problem that is a vital one today."[27] Putnam was writing over half a century ago, but of course the question of racial, or as we should now say, ethnic identities, remains vital, and da Cunha's intervention might still be seen above all as a work about the evolution of racial consciousness in Brazil. Yet exactly what da Cunha's "statement," or take, on race in Brazil might or might not be is not as easy a question to answer now as it appeared to a confident North American in the 1940s. The more deeply one looks into da Cunha's race agendas, the more his book remains peculiarly suspended in, and simultaneously at odds with, the prejudices of the day. The work is particularly ambiguous over one crucial area of Brazil's attitudes towards race, namely Atlantic slavery and the generation of an Afro-Brazilian population.

Given the vast claims of his critics, given his subject and the time he is writing, and given historical claims for the number of newly freed slaves to be found among the numbers of his followers, it would appear essential, if not inevitable, that da Cunha's book must confront race and the inheritance of Atlantic slavery.[28] But does it, and if it does why has slavery been so silent or silenced in the theoretical and critical reactions to *Os Sertões*?

Critics have significantly swerved away from any concerted attempt to think through the silences and ambiguities of da Cunha's take on Brazil's saturation in slavery and its evolution of powerful Afro-Brazilian cultures and syncretic religions. His book has been read increasingly as invested in speaking for a certain set of communities to have lived and developed in the rural backlands of the North East, a population not easily connected in any direct way with Afro-Brazilianism, or the predominantly black slave-evolved populations of Brazil's great coastal cities of the North East. Yet da Cunha does deal with both slavery and Afro-Brazilian cultures throughout *Os Sertões*, and in fact displays an agonistic relation to these subjects. Slaves, ex-slaves, and their cultures in fact threaten da Cunha's specific mythographies of the *sertanejo*, and his extreme constructions of blacks and of African inheritance are violently tailored accordingly.

Da Cunha was twenty-two years old when slavery was officially abolished in 1888. Within a year, and partly as a result of the idealism and social destabilization unleashed by abolition, and the political debates it had generated in the decades leading up to abolition, Pedro II was forced to abdicate and the empire gave way to a shaky republic. As important as the sociopolitical dimensions of slavery was the manner in which the slavery and race debates had transformed Brazilian literature from top to bottom. Da Cunha had grown up and developed intellectually during a period when the greatest political and artistic texts had been generated around slavery and written by people who were black and white.[29] No creative consciousness of the mid-1890s could easily remain insulated from the literary monuments generated by thinking about Atlantic slavery within Brazil. Yet because da Cunha wrote after the abolition of slavery and appeared centrally, indeed almost exclusively, concerned with *mestizo* culture and the religious mysticism of the backlands, and not with Afro-Brazilians, or their syncretic religious cultures per se, *Os Sertões* has not been seen as a central text when considering the literary manifestation of slavery and its aftermath in Brazil. What has so far bamboozled the critics is that slavery does not function in *Os Sertões directly* as a central significant political or cultural phenomenon. But that is not to say that the book does not come at the memory of slavery, and the presence of different Afro-Brazilian elements, in extraordinary ways.

While there have been innumerable academic studies focused on the social groups within Canudos—the *jagunço*, the *sertanejo*, *cangaceiro*, and even indigenous "Indian" elements within the movement—Afro-Brazilianism and slavery continue to be largely absent and silent.[30] When slavery and Afro-Brazilianism has been raised in the context of da Cunha, it has frequently been done in terms of an exclusionist Manichaeism borrowed, or indeed implanted, from da Cunha's own ideological race agenda. Such readings present the *sertão* as a social and imaginative space that exists in precise contradistinction to the world of the *casa grande* and the lush coastal sugar plantation. The "backlands" of the interior and the "big house" of the slave coast are completely discreet entities and never the twain shall meet.[31] An extension of such polarized takes on da Cunha and race see him operating a crude approach to the *mestizo* that reads coastal *mestizaje* coming out of slavery as negative and the racial admixtures of the backlands *mestizaje* as positive.[32] There has also been subtle and important recent work attempting to bring the lessons of that branch of postcolonial literary theory known as "Subaltern Studies" to bear on Canudos and da Cunha and its cultural location of race. Campos Johnson's vital decision to reread da Cunha's imagined Canudos through the filters of contemporary novels that predate *Os Sertões* (Afonso Arinos, *Os jagunços*; Manoel Benício, *O rei dos jagunços*) is hugely significant.[33]

Os Sertões and the Paradoxes of Slavery and Abolition

The key question, as with every slave revolt or indeed social revolution, is not necessarily how did it happen, or even what happened, but how do those in power, within the society that generated such violence, explain it away, both then and now? *Os Sertões*, one of the strangest books ever written, and the continuing conflicting readings it generates, would indicate that is has many agendas, hidden and revealed, creative and political, but one constant pressure within it relates to containment, and cultural dismantling. The text, like so many early histories of slave revolts and violent subaltern acts of resistance across the Atlantic diaspora, has some investment in reassuring the powers that be that their prejudices are intact. At one level the book is devoted to explaining away Canudos in ways that make it seem safe: it is written off as a diseased and happily deceased aberration. Part of this agenda also involves containing and explaining, which may also involve finally ignoring, mainline connections between Canudos and the inheritance of Brazilian slavery.

For da Cunha the key forces enabling or energizing the Canudos rebellion are regression and atavism. In this sense *Os Sertões* is testament to the fact that Brazilian intellectual terror of the primitive, the compulsion to be living in an ever-present modernism, in line with those imagined to have evolved in Europe and North America, is clearly not a new one. In terms of defining what emerges as the outmoded, not to say fatally belated, nature of the thought and philosophy that generated Canudos, da Cunha takes some extreme narrative options. He sees the disciples of the visionary leader Conselheiro as ostensibly a walking dead, an army of zombies, or as a bunch of galvanized corpses: "What we had to look for here was the unlooked-for resurrection under arms, of an old society, a dead society, galvanised into life by a madman."[34] This is metaphorically Conselheiro configured as a primitive Dr. Frankenstein, and his followers/disciples emerge not as living social rebels, but as a risen dead, as the fanatical Portuguese charismatics of the Middle Ages, curiously shocked back into life and resuscitated as Conselheiro's "galvanised" monsters. Canudos is presented not as a new form of social experiment, let alone a cutting edge proto-Marxist commune, but as something paradoxically both wholly other and wholly familiar. Canudos is other in terms of time; it relives in perfectly preserved form the religious fanaticism of other, earlier systems.

As the search for origins and analogues continues, da Cunha's Canudos emerges not as a new social life-form, but a horribly resurrected body. At one point it appears as a return of, and simultaneously a return to, the primitive slave systems of Russian serfdom, at another as a version of the extremes of sadomasochistic medieval visionary experience. His methods involve the construction of peculiar transhistorical and cultural analogies, and some bizarre special pleading. The following extended attempt to explain what Canudos really *was* attempts to head slavery and its inheritances off at the cultural pass:

> We were not acquainted with this society [Canudos], it was not possible for us to have been acquainted with it. The adventurers of the seventeenth century, it is true, would encounter in it conditions with which they were familiar, just as the visionaries of the middle ages would be at home among the *demonopaths* or Varzenis or the Stundists of Russia; for these epidemic psychoses make their appearance in all ages and in all places, as obvious anachronisms, inevitable contrasts in the uneven evolution of the peoples—contrasts which become especially evident at a time when a broad movement is vigorously impelling the backward peoples towards a higher civilized way of life. We then behold the exaggerated Perfectionists breaking through the triumphant industrialism of North America.[35]

What makes da Cunha's analysis so important as a way into traumatic memory is his multivalence. In so relentlessly looking forward and then immediately in gazing back with such awestruck horror, da Cunha finds a way to articulate Brazil's denial of its slavery inheritance, while simultaneously opening this traumatic wound for all time. A constant firmness and vigilance hover over this text as da Cunha at one level tries to shut out the recent reality of the slave industries, and the huge social dislocations their legislative abolition generated. The account just quoted is both an act of containment and a diversion, which works through that tried and tested favorite of racist discourse, disease metaphor. Canudos is presented both as a colossal psychic infection, as a recurrent "epidemic psychosis," and as something entirely strange and alien, as a flashback to Brazil and Portugal's medieval and mystical past, as a case of "obvious anachronism." Yet this is an extreme and exclusive model to foist on such a complex social experiment as Canudos, especially when it is remembered that there are possible social contexts that make Canudos very recognizable.

Canudos could be, and indeed has been, constructed in terms of a continuation of historical and social models generated by slavery. Reading da Cunha one would never surmise that Canudos has been considered as a legitimate *quilombo*, essentially a final flowering of a series of social pressures and behavioral modes that had developed within the context of Brazil's long history of active and organized slave rebellion.[36] In this reading it is a glorious final flowering of a particular form of organized extra-colonial community that finds its celebrated *locus classicus* in the legendary seventeenth-century free slave state of *Palmares*.[37] Yet da Cunha ruthlessly shuts down the memory of *Palmares* and carefully polices the social theory underlying his fiction. His version of events, his reading of this revolt, wants nothing to do with historical narrative options that valorize organized and violent slave resistance.[38] Such models had emphasized, since *Palmares*, the sophisticated revolutionary ideas behind slave resistance, and a capacity for advanced social organization using African models introduced by slaves within the *quilombo*. Rather, he wants to take the whole phenomenon of Canudos as far back from, and as far away from, slavery, and the history of the *quilombos*, as possible. He wants to isolate Canudos, to take it out of Brazilian slave history and into the comparative world of religious fanaticism whether in ancient Portuguese colonialism, or in recent Russian or North American experience.

Canudos it seems at this stage is only to be understood via comparisons foreign either in time or in place. It is highly significant that when contemporary comparisons for the religious fanaticism of Canudos are set up, they are drawn in from outside Brazil. In the above passage, extreme recent Christian sects of the Christian Ukraine, the Stundists, are referenced. North America makes its presence felt through reference not to slave rebellions, or even the Civil War, but to the Oneida community and the obliquely referenced "Perfectionist" cult of Humphrey Noyse. Again, the move is profoundly defensive, and for a population that had just freed a vast slave population, very reassuring. The enthusiasts of Canudos, like the polygamous Oneida Perfectionists or the Tartar Stundists, are figured as a primitive aberration, a liberationist freak show lumbering in the spiritual scrublands as the new tide comes in establishing a New Brazil that joyously and furiously embraces the republic, and that will forge ahead embracing industrialization, urbanization, education, democracy and, above all, modernism. In this vision of history, Noyes, like Conselheiro, emerges as a dated fanatic who looks only backwards to the dark ages. This is of course a rather partial take on the Perfectionists and significantly fails to mention the central concern with slavery abolition within the philosophy of the community, or of the serious elements in Noyes's utopian socialism. Conselheiro, like Noyes, is shown as an ideological fossil, not just a conservative but as an example of an epidemic psychosis, in the form of anachronistic religious collective mania. Da Cunha has a leveling approach to religious enthusiasm that appears as a transhistorical and transtemporal virus. Maniacal outbursts or primitive religious millenarianism seem doomed to blindly repeat themselves "in all ages and in all places, as obvious anachronisms." That da Cunha, well before he composed his epic, had already been exposed to printed materials that presented the rebels of Canudos as weird outsiders, and that he developed this propaganda in extreme ways verging upon the surreal in his journalism, before he embarked upon the text of his great work, has been noted.[39] Da Cunha's strategies for discrediting the Canudos rebels were extreme and ingenious and not restricted to religious analogues. He also had other false political trails to set, and strange traps to lay. He had, for example, early on developed a counter thesis to his religious arguments in which he compared Canudos with Victor Hugo's melodramatic fictionalization of the violent Vendée peasant revolt against the French Republic. Here a fanatical Royal Catholic Army launched a pro-Catholic, pro-Monarchist counterrevolutionary war in 1793 and massacred tens of thousands before themselves being brutally repressed.[40]

Within the covers of *Os Sertões*, Conselheiro is then consistently configured as an ultimate outsider, and as the new republic's worst nightmare in terms of a force that would throw Brazil backwards into the mire of religious enthusiasm and monarchist superstition. Of course, the ultimate pressure behind the thought and writing relate to making Conselheiro appear as finally an impotent and futile bogeyman. This form of demonization is a tried-and-tested rhetorical method for defusing the threat of extreme revolutionary leadership. Conselheiro emerges, as Nat Turner emerged in the hysterical journalism with which the South met news of the Virginia slave revolt in the United States, as a deluded and violent false prophet. He was seen as a being lost in mystical fantasy and beyond the pale of conventional social analysis and sane thought process.[41] When it comes to analyzing Conselheiro's sermons, he is presented as an intellectual brute, an amusing fanatic whose irrational insights have no sociopolitical rhyme or reason. His sermons are presented in the most generalizing terms as extreme enthusiastic rhetoric divorced from political reality: "Every line of them [Conselheiro's sermons] was vibrant with the same vague and incongruous religiosity, but there was very little of political significance to be found in any one of them."[42] There is a strange impasse between the theory and the practice here, between religious ideology and political ideology. What on earth was Canudos all about if it was not a social experiment, if it was not "politically significant" of its essence? On the face of it there are strange, indeed epic, contradictions here. Da Cunha devoted years of his life to producing a vast and complex text about a minor social rebellion in the backlands of Brazil, led by a man for whom his text exhibits, in terms of open rhetorical protestation, nothing but contempt and often a horror bordering on loathing. In the process da Cunha produced a text widely acknowledged to be the greatest sociopolitical anatomization of Brazil as it emerged into the twentieth century. So what was his artistic purpose in producing so obsessive, so conflicted and politically confused a work? Was he deliberately transforming a lump of coal into a diamond, or did he see into and under the spectacular ironies that inform his peculiar endeavor, and the internecine social contradictions that both enabled and saturated Canudos?

Black Bodies in da Cunha's Rhetoric: Slave Presence, Absence, and Protestation

And so, after a prolix but unavoidable contextualizing discussion, the question emerges: what of the black bodies, the ex-slave bodies, the Afro-Brazilian bodies in Canudos?

Taking da Cunha's book as a whole it is fair to say that although it tries so hard, so constantly, so extravagantly to ignore, to erase, to negativize black bodies, it exhibits a horror of blacks, and finds it traumatic to incorporate them directly within its narrative or metaphorics. Which is not to say that the book, like any great work of art, is not finally, and triumphantly, capable of breaking its own rules, even its race rules, but this is to get ahead of my argument. When it comes to Afro-Brazilians and Canudos, da Cunha creates a peculiar presence and prescience for them just because he protests rather too long and loud about their irrelevance. *Os Sertões* contains repeated, sometimes crude, sometimes ingeniously constructed arguments denying that Brazilian blacks, mulattoes, *cafusos*, or indeed that African blood of any type, played any significant role in Canudos.[43] And yet his sources are quoted in ways that keep slipping in references to freed slaves and blacks as central actors in the unfolding drama. The traces of these sources take strangely altered forms within his writing. Slavery's memory is then to be located within the instances when black characters do break through da Cunha's cultural defenses to disturb or blemish the smooth grain and texture of his account. These moments of cultural suture are highly significant, and it is the task of the following writing to pick at these rhetorical racial scabs and, *puncta*, to make them bleed. What lies beneath may be nothing less than the mortified form of the memory of slavery.

In taking on this task of close reading, I am not interested in entering debates about the degree to which da Cunha, in our twenty-first century, was in academic, moral, humanistic, or any terms, a racist. At a level of basic translation, his text is indeed replete with dismissive analyses of blacks (and particularly *cafusos*) that are all too obviously evolved out of contemporary race theory.[44] This brute racist element needs acknowledging, but it is no more an impediment to unpacking da Cunha's deep insights into the continued legacies of Brazilian slavery in the context of its immediate abolition than Stevenson's or Conrad's "racism" prevents their investigations of the myths and power structures enabling some of the most horrific manifestations of European colonialism.

The second section of *Os Sertões* entitled "Man" consists of an extended attempt to define the character and racial stock of the *sertanejo*, or backlander in particular. It is in the context of this specially located racial narrative that the first set-piece discussion of Africans and Atlantic slavery systems occurs. Da Cunha begins with a statement couched as relative historiography, but is typically vague when it comes to naming names or book titles:

> Some historians, distracted by the coming of the African on a large scale, an event which, beginning at the end of the sixteenth century, continued uninterruptedly down to our time, have felt that the latter was the best ally of the Portuguese in the colonial epoch and, accordingly, attribute to him generally an exaggerated influence upon the formation of the inhabitant of the northern backlands. However, as far as any invasion by these conquered and unhappy beings is concerned, taking into account their extraordinary fecundity and their qualities of adaptation as tested by the burning suns of Africa, it is still debatable as to whether they exercised any profound influence on the back-country regions."[45]

The vocabulary gives several clues to the caste mentality underlying da Cunha's take on Afro-Brazilian culture. The opening is a masterpiece of circumlocution in which the mass participation of Brazil in the African slave trade is referred to as "the coming of the African on a large scale," although of course how the Africans in their millions "came" to Brazil was via the trauma of the Middle Passage. Equally revealing is the admission that despite various waves of legislation going back decades, the Brazilian slave trade was never really abolished, or as da Cunha puts it, this mass trade "continued uninterruptedly down to our own time." The subtext here is that the illegal slave trade continued to smuggle in hundreds of thousands of Africans not only up until 1888, but even afterwards. This is the final intimation, a shocking truth itself smuggled in so casually, that the process continues, even after abolition, "down to our own time" (that is the late 1890s). The passage also opens with a brilliant and again sly dismissal: African slave importation is written off as a "distraction," an alien figure sneaked into accounts of the formation of backlands culture by deluded historians. For da Cunha it is the enslaved status of the Africans that rules them out of his narrative, and they must be ruled out because they are a threat to his master narrative. The giveaway phrase is "any invasion by these conquered and unhappy beings." Da Cunha is writing an epic that celebrates his race fantasy of a certain kind of half-Indian, half-Portuguese *mestizo* population. Tested in an environment of unparalleled harshness, these Brazilians exhibit a capacity for stubborn fortitude and religious fanaticism. Their qualities, and above all their fierce unvanquishable spirit, which has thrived since the heroic days of the *Bandeirantes*, exists in precise binary opposition to black thralldom and passivity. To understand the full weight of that descriptive compound, "these conquered and unhappy beings," da Cunha's first fully fledged adjectival phrase devoted to the description of the slave diaspora in Brazil, it should be placed against the climactic lines describing the fall of Canudos. One of the distinctive stylistic traits of *Os Sertões* is the use of headlines throughout the massive text, in order both to direct and to shock the reader. Much in the mode to be adopted in Assis's late novels and in the "Aeolus" section of James Joyce's *Ulysses*, some thirty years later, each key idea is set out under a banner headline. The justly celebrated final chapter opens with the staccato headlinese THE END, followed by:

CANUDOS DID NOT SURRENDER

Let us bring this book to a close.

Canudos did not surrender. The only case of its kind in history, it held out to the last man. Conquered inch by inch, in the literal meaning of the words, it fell on October 5, toward dusk—when its last defenders fell, dying, every man of them. There were only four of them left: an old man, two other full-grown men, and a child, facing a furiously raging army of five thousand soldiers.[46]

This is Canudos taking on, or forced to wear, the glamour of tragic myth. Brazilian heroes don't, any more than the intractable and opaque backlanders in Borges's mythical protoexistential Argentina, live on after they have been conquered. They are conquered inch by inch and die in the struggle. Liberty is preferable to death or, faced with conquest, liberty is found through the choice of death. If viewed through the perspective of that earlier account of blacks, this stoic heroism in Canudos operates a precise overturning of the enfeebled defeatism of the conquered black. For da Cunha, the very fact that the African can live in and through slavery, indeed adapt happily to slavery and breed in captivity (this is the weight behind the reminder to "take into account their [the African's] extraordinary fecundity"), banishes them from his official version of the Canudos myth. Da Cunha is waging a constant rhetorical war on the cultural memory of Africans and Africanity in Brazil. It hovers over his master narrative like a terrible black shadow, or as he will later configure it, a great border, hemming in his fragile triumphalist fiction of the *sertanejo*.

Initially da Cunha, with his strange capacity to attempt to systematize his own fictions, tries to explain why blacks will not function in Canudos. He tells us that the first substantial interbreeding of whites and blacks happened a long way away, not in Brazil at all but in Lisbon. Blacks and whites are mixed up in an urban setting, da Cunha declaring via an undisclosed source that "in 1530 there were more than fifteen thousand negroes on the streets of Lisbon."[47] When slavery and Africans do come to Brazil, they exist in da Cunha's imagination exclusively on the seaboard. They exist as "beasts of burden" on the coast, within the sugar plantations, or within jungles set just barely inland. In the following passage da Cunha's thought is saturated with an inherited set of tried and trusted race tropes. The social function and geographical dispersal of slave populations are described as follows:

> A powerful organism, given to an extreme humility, without the Indian's rebelliousness, the Negro at once had the whole burden of colonial life placed on his shoulders. He was a beast of burden, condemned to labour unceasingly. Old ordinances setting forth "how one may rid himself of slaves or beasts upon finding them sick or maimed," show the brutality of the age. Moreover, and the point is incontrovertible, the numerous slaves imported were concentrated onto the seaboard. The great black border hemmed the coast from Bahía to Maranhão but did not extend far into the interior. Even in open revolt the humble Negro, became a dread *quilombola* foregathering in *mocambos*, and appeared to avoid the heart of the country.

Palmares with its thirty thousand *mocambeiros*, was after all only a few miles distant from the coast.[48]

There could be no clearer enunciation of da Cunha's colonial pecking order within the mythology of Canudos, or of his almost pathological desire to separate Canudos and the backlanders from any geographical, historical, or ideological proximity to the *quilombos* and the memory of Palmares in particular. Blacks are powerfully marginalized via the metaphorics of textile production and cartography. The black slaves are, intriguingly, hardly a part of the country at all. They exist as a "great black border," a border that, in terms of a racial map, marks the end of civilization, of land, and the beginning of the unknown, the ocean. Yet this geographical border is also literalized and also "appears" to function as some sort of black margin, or self-imposed exclusion zone, connected to the grand robes of Brazilian colonial adventure undertaken inland, in the backlands. Black slaves "hem the coast," always on the edge of things, on the edge of being, marking their relation through separation to this meaningful interior colonial enterprise.

Surprisingly, given that this passage clearly reveals his understanding of the phenomenon of the *quilombo*, da Cunha only mentions the legendary *quilombo* of Palmares once in his entire narrative. The omission is odd because in terms of extant national mythology, not to mention size and social organization, Palmares—if not an obvious precursor of Canudos—does suggest narrative and symbolic parallels. The great, late, historically mysterious and unstable sixteenth-century slave settlement called Palmares, with its cult religious and military leader, Ganga Zumbi, prefigures several aspects of the Canudos settlement. Zumbi's followers, just like those of Conselheiro, come to number, according to da Cunha's estimate, thirty thousand. They constructed a brilliantly fortified independent settlement, or in fact group of settlements. They engaged successive military campaigns in guerrilla warfare before being finally overrun by enormous forces who considered their existence a threat to the established colonial order. They also, like the inhabitants of Canudos, fought to the end, and by the time da Cunha wrote they had featured centrally in several histories of Brazil.

Given what he might have done with it, it is worth thinking about what da Cunha chooses to do with Palmares. For him Palmares does not feature as a probable analogue for the military tactics, or liberation mythologies, of the Brazilian freedom fighter. Despite his casual certainty on the matter, the geographical location of Palmares has never been precisely known and is much disputed. The historical location is still up for grabs, and several contemporary tourist sites, given current cultural celebrity of Zumbi and Palmares, claim the distinction of being the original. The weight of evidence suggests, however, that a settlement of this size would not have been stuck out on the coast, but situated well inland in inaccessible terrain in Alagoas. For da Cunha Palmares exists simply as a final demonstration of the black incapacity to leave the "great black border" of the seaboard, and enter the real Brazil, the heartland that is also the backland. For da Cunha black Africans, even when as roaming *quilombolas* they have the choice to go anywhere, "appeared to avoid the heart of the country." This phrase suggests that the black slave chooses not to be part of the beating vital organ embodying both love and life within the Brazilian nation. Given what Palmares has now come to mean for Brazilian national identity and the place of Afro-Brazilian culture at its present symbolic heart, da Cunha's fiction does appear an intensely comic upending of today's cultural orthodoxies. Palmares is now at the center of Afro-Brazilian myths of identity. Indeed, since its exotic construction in the 1984 Carlos Diegues film *Quilombo*, Zumbi has gained truly mythographic status. *Os Sertões* as a whole ruthlessly excludes the history of black resistance in the Quilombos of the seventeenth, eighteenth, and nineteenth centuries. It might be stressed here that nineteenth- and early twentieth-century histories of Brazil tend similarly to play down Palmares, or even excise it and Zumbi altogether. It was left to foreign historians, initially in fact to the English poet and historian Robert Southey, to foreground within Romantic narrative history an event that was to become so central to the definition of late twentieth-century Brazilian black consciousness. Yet although da Cunha's references to the *quilombos* are meagre, they are, as we see, intensely revealing.[49] The only other reference to this aspect of Brazilian colonial history comes as an aside, when da Cunha is celebrating the unorthodox methods of the troops invading Canudos. He talks of their efficacy as guerrilla fighters coming out of two centuries of experience with "rebellions put down" and "the *Quilombos* broken up by these diminutive armies."[50]

Having established this central and wildly inaccurate premise, namely that blacks operated in the geographical margins of Brazil and never left the Northern Seaboard for the backlands in any significant numbers, da Cunha officially sticks with it throughout, even in the face of multiple counterfactual accounts in his sources. Again and again he reiterates the fictional truism that the backlanders, who were to make up Conselheiro's followers in Canudos, are *curibocas*, the result of Portuguese and Indian unions, while the blacks remained broken and docile along the Northern coast:

A thoroughgoing distinction arose between the intermarriages in the backlands and those on the seaboard. As a consequence, with the white element the common denominator in both cases the mulatto appeared as the principal result in the latter and the curiboca in the former, instance.[51]

Da Cunha embraces miscegenetic union within Brazilian cultural formation, yet he delimits it in accordance with a set of miscegenetic master paradigms. In his world of fictional interracial sexuality, whites may only sexually mingle with one nonwhite population at a time, while Indians and Blacks are not permitted, within this sectarian fantasy, to mingle at all. We are a very long way from the miscegenetic democracies of the Mexican *Castas* paintings, or come to that from the interracial sexual cornucopia of Jorge Amado. Da Cunha's imaginative apartheid is all the more strange given the fact that black/Indian racial admixture had long been commented upon and celebrated within Brazilian culture and art. The Brazilian Portuguese term *cafuso* explicitly described the offspring of the union of African and indigenous Indian. Celebrated travel books, including those of Debret and Rugendas, dealt openly with the distinctiveness of *cafusos*. Gilberto Freyre later wrote at length of the necessity of these fusions of African and Indian blood for the health of the emergent Brazilian population, and of the complex and intimate fusions of African and indigenous Brazilian cultures resulting from this branch of *mestiçagem*.[52] There are, as some examples below indicate, places where da Cunha does use the word "cafuso" to describe individuals, in ways that exhibit a full knowledge of what it denoted racially. He also finds ingenious ways of eradicating these characters from the fictional landscape. He will refer to a "full-blooded Cafuso," indicating the unadulterated fusion of African and *indigeno*, but despite these lacunae da Cunha's take on Afro-Brazilians is unwavering. Africans are always dull, biddable, passive, and coastal, while Indians are rebellious, noble, active, and inland. It is the Indian populations, as racially admirable, who interbreed with the Portuguese settlers, the neo-mythical Bendeirantes and their powerfully independent descendants, to form the stoical, unswerving martyrs of the Canudos narrative. What underlies this fierce determination to establish the barriers of miscegenation within such suspect geographical barriers and fragile imaginative fictions?

Old-Fashioned Race Stereotypes and Racial League Tables

One answer lies in the way da Cunha enacts, and to an extent resurrects, a quite orthodox hierarchy that had saturated the construction of race in Latin America and the Caribbean for centuries. A hierarchy of the colonized had been established in European thought and culture from a very early stage. This hierarchy idealized the indigenous populations of the Caribbean and Latin America as noble savages, prelapsarian innocents, and simultaneously demonized Africans as subservient, inferior, and morally rotten. This two-tier attitude to the populations of the slave diaspora begins with its inception, and is enshrined within the political economy of Bartolomé de Las Casas. Las Casas of course was the first to advocate the introduction of black slaves to the Indies on the ground that this would save the innocent indigenous populations from the insane sadism of the Conquistadores. This was a story that Jorge Luis Borges then mischievously reconstructed in his early fiction.[53] The metaphorics of the Spanish *Leyenda Negra* or Black Legend in French, English, and Dutch literatures developed the theme, demonizing and indeed sadistically elaborating Spanish barbarities against the Indians. The eighteenth and nineteenth centuries continued the literary and cultural refinement of the tradition. It remained strong within the fantasies of European and American Romantic poets, and within the grim social policies of government servants. The mindset is typified by the notorious Governor Eyre of Jamaica. Eyre's total belief in the superiority of indigenous populations (particularly ones wiped out by the British), and the concomitant inferiority of all African-evolved slave populations, underlay his brutal response to the social complaints of ex-slave populations.[54] An Eyre style intracolonial apartheid remained imaginatively enforced, and may be seen as an analytical backdrop for da Cunha's thought. In the following example he confidently reinforces this age-old European orthodoxy as he declares of the backlands:

> The African element, in any event, remained in the vast canebrakes of the coast, fettered to the earth and giving rise to a racial admixture quite different from the one taking place in the recesses of the captaincies [areas of the backlands being colonized by colonial Portuguese, and the neo mythical *Bandeirantes*]. In the latter place the free Indian roamed, unadapted to toil, and always rebellious . . .[55]

The division between an "African element . . . fettered to the earth" and a "free Indian" roaming "unadapted to toil and always rebellious" is a direct continuation of the polarities within which the tradition and elongated fantasies of the Spanish *Leyenda Negra* operated in da Cunhas's racial map. He is somewhat eccentric in relation to the mainstream in insisting upon the insurrectionary initiative of the "always rebellious" Indian. Texts stemming from Las Casas's comparative race paradigms insist on the mildness and complete passivity of the indigenous populations they describe. But apart from this anomaly, da Cunha is perfectly orthodox in his racial stratifications and typifications. In fact, da Cunha nicely segues into European literary constructions of the indigenous "Indian" after the discovery of the "New World." A genicido-literary set of correlations seems to exist that might be summarized as follows: the more extinct an indigenous population X becomes at the hands of colonizer Y, and the more time separates the nasty realities of what Y did to exterminate X, the more celebratory and idealizing the mythologies of Y become in relation to X. In his "Preliminary Note" to *Os Sertões*, da Cunha ingeniously accretes himself to this equation and develops his own variation on a theme in his treatment of the backlanders of Canudos. By keeping the backlanders up to the 1890s as separate and fragile "sub-races," the product of Indian and Portuguese interbreeding, uncontaminated by blacks, da Cunha effects a variant of the established patterns for the degradation of blacks. For him the peoples of the backlands represent so many endangered species of noble savage. Black and mulatto immigration from the coasts will wipe out these unique race formations, and "The fearless *jagunço* the ingenuous *tabareo*, and the stolid *caipira* are types that will soon be relegated to the realm of evanescent or extinct traditions."[56]

Viewed from this perspective, *Os Sertões* is nothing more than a vast elegy to a series of wholly fantastic miscegenetic racial subsets that totter on the verge of extinction. Their identity, and paradoxical "purity" within hybridity, is defined by the inclusion of whiteness and exclusion of blackness.

Of course his sources did not always mirror the hard and fast lines of racial demarcation that form one of the structural frames for da Cunha's huge edifice. One can learn a lot about da Cunha's imagination by considering the determinism with which he attempts to shut blacks and mulattos out of the text. In many places he is extreme, and in rhetorical terms markedly in tune with the most elementary building blocks of nineteenth-century antiblack discourse. Take the following example, a description of a charge on the artillery during the first big military expedition sent out against Canudos. Descriptions of this early skirmish throw up a glimpse of a black guerrilla leader who, because he is so visible in all the source accounts of the episode, da Cunha cannot ignore:

> There could be seen moving about among them [the Canudos guerrillas] a burly but active Negro, a short rifle in his hands. This was their leader João Grande. He, it was, who designed their manoeuvres, making use of all the wiles of a bandit long skilled in hinterland warfare; and it was his

movements, his running leaps and primitive stratagems, that the backland rebels imitated . . . Finally the crude rebel chieftain proceeded to draw his men up for what he believed would be the decisive hand-to-hand combat. With his gorilla like features, he could be seen striding boldly at the head of his suddenly congregated band. With a fine display of heroism, they now advanced upon the artillery but were stopped by the explosion of a case of shot, which blew the nearest of their leaders to bits . . ."[57]

Here an inventor of guerrilla warfare is reduced to the status of gorilla. João has a certain animal fearlessness, and is troped entirely according to nineteenth-century race codes. He is a common or garden criminal, not a farmer or maroon, but a "bandit." He begins as a leader, but is soon a "chieftain," who is "burly," "wily," and "primitive." The implication that he is in fact not a man but a large primate is made explicit with the reference to his "gorilla like features." Suddenly a great black ape appears in "the hinterland," is briefly mimicked by the backlanders, and is then blown to bits, never to break the surface of the narrative again. If da Cunha's hackles start to rise when he is forced to introduce, however briefly, blacks into his narrative, his descriptive armory really starts to fire on the very rare occasions when he has to deal with his own special taboo, and when a *mulatto*, or worse a *cafuso*, crops up in the narrative. Discussing the pursuit of government troops by the Canudos fighters, the following passage begins as a celebration of bravery but develops into something very different:

> Upon perceiving what was afoot [the retreat] the *Jagunços* promptly gave pursuit. They were commanded now by an unusually fierce mestizo whose bravery was unexcelled, Pajehú by name. A full-blooded *cafuso*, he was endowed with an impulsive temperament which combined the tendencies of the lower races from which he sprang. He was the full-blown type of primitive fighter, fierce, fearless, and naïve, at once simple-minded and evil, brutal and infantile, valiant by fine example of recessive atavism, with the retrograde form of a grim troglodyte, stalking upright here with the same intrepidity with which, ages ago, he had brandished a stone hatchet at the entrance to his cave.
>
> It was this wily barbarian who now distributed his companions through the *caatingas* . . ."[58]

The descent into a particularly extreme racist hyperbole appears to be sparked off by the word "cafuso." A "pure" *cafuso* is the product of the union of a full-blood

Indian with a full-blood Negro, a miscegenetic zone of prohibition throughout the rest of the text. This is an area of Brazilian interbreeding to which da Cunha has a pathological aversion. The idea that nonwhite sections of Brazilian society might be breeding in the backlands unleashes the most fantastic imaginative distortions because it is a refutation of one of the centralist race fictions he adheres to. The rebels of Canudos cannot be thought of as an incubator of African blood, and most especially not African/Indian sanguinary admixtures. Racist rhetoric tends across time and place to operate through a limited and repeated set of major tropes. One of them is animalization, which we have already seen da Cunha operate; another is infantilization, and da Cunha uses it in the present example, but introduces a further twist. It is not enough to put Pajehú outside adult humanity by virtue of his "infantile" ferocity. He is placed outside history as well, bizarrely metamorphosed into a prehistoric cave dweller complete with stone hatchet. Tone is always hard to detect in da Cunha. At what point does genuine outrage shade into a kind of pantomimic blather? The bitter humor that pervades da Cunha's vision of human endeavor and that can make his approach to human violence and suffering look cynical is often difficult to read in Os Sertões. Has this passage gone beyond social analysis and into a full-blown parody, where the mechanisms of racist thought operate in a realm of irrational giganticism? Does da Cunha step into the role of conscious ironist, creating a narrator who is finally and deliberately alienated from the reader in the absurdity of his racist extremity? If the fantasy is generated out of a theory, then it is a singularly eccentric one. Da Cunha's serious point, if he has one, seems to be that if you conjoin Indian and African blood, a spontaneous process of "recessive atavism" operates. Here two human racial negatives make, not a racial positive, but a colossal negative, and the issue of this union of two "lower races" leapfrogs back through human development to end up with an explicitly prehistoric mythical "troglodyte."

In etymological terms "troglodyte" (Greek "trog," meaning hole, and "dyein," to dive into) was supposed to be a primitive cave dweller. The term then got taken up, via shaky Linnaean taxonomy in 1758, to mean "homo troglodytes," a primitive cave-dwelling being not entirely human and sometimes equated to the orangutan or, via another linguistic sidestep, "pan troglodytes," a neologism for the chimpanzee. The descriptions of a black being who is "simple-minded and evil, brutal and infantile, valiant by fine example of recessive atavism" does not appear to describe any flesh and blood character who ever fought at Canudos, but the nature of the narrator's own confused but enthused regressive terror fantasies. Instead a new monstrous hybrid is created, the "troglodytic *cafuso.*"

The myth of the troglodyte as a subspecies beneath the indigenous American Indian in fact remains very much alive within the myths of Hollywood, as is evidenced in the undiluted, darkly comic racism of S. Craig Zahler's 2015 film *Bone Tomahawk*.

Think Like an African: Fetishizing Fetish Religions in Canudos

Da Cunha's approach to the description of physical crossbreeding, especially in relation to the products of black miscegenation with Indians, seems simultaneously to be stylistically unhinged and theoretically cut and dried. In this context it is intriguing to see what happens to the language when da Cunha approaches cultural cross-fertilization in the context of Afro-Brazilian culture, and to religious syncretism in particular.

When the expedition of Colonel Moreira Cesar is routed and put to flight, having briefly entered the Canudos settlement, the event is interpreted as a form of divine intervention. Da Cunha presents the population of Canudos as becoming superstitious. The superstition is described as resulting in "a revival of their barbarous instincts to the deterioration of their character." In order to back up this generalization, da Cunha inserts an illustrational vignette, which is again richly revealing in its race agenda:

> There was a strange occurrence which bore witness to this, a kind of sinister diversion reminiscent of the tragically perverted religious sense of the Ashantis, which came as a sequel to the events narrated . . . the jangunços then collected all the corpses that were lying here and there, decapitated them, and burned the bodies, after which they lined the heads up along both sides of the highway, at regular intervals, with the faces turned toward the road. Above these, from the tallest shrubbery, they suspended the remains of the uniforms and equipment, the trousers and the multicoloured dolmans, the saddles, belts, red-tipped kepis, the capes, blankets, canteens, and knapsacks.
>
> The barren, withered *caatinga* now blossomed forth with an extravagant-colored flora . . ."[59]

This is wonderful writing, which deftly expresses the unspeakable terror at the heart of this theatre of cruelty. The desecrated corpses are reanimated as fetishes, the physical bodies burned and the heads united to the brilliantly colored uniforms. Does the gesture mean that to the rebels the soldiers are inhuman, uniforms without bodies? Rather than try to explain how this gesture works in terms of an Afro-Brazilian semiotics, da Cunha deftly transforms the outlandish dolls into flowers. The desert is finally made to bloom in a gesture of darkly surreal humor that would not be out of place in *Les Chants de Maldoror*. But why is this ritualized exhibition of the remains of the defeated government troops described as a "sinister diversion" to be placed alongside "the tragically perverted religious sense of the Ashantis"? Where does African religion come into this, and what religion is being referred to? To answer this, the reader needs to be alert to da Cunha's continuing dialogue with the Ashanti. This passage relates directly back to an earlier set piece where violent and elaborate sacrificial ritual is again aligned with the Ashanti.

When discussing the cultural conditions that enabled the rise of Conselheiro, there is an extended discussion of the religions and superstitions of the backlands. As has already become apparent, qualities of naïve credulity, primitivism, and superstition are seen as underpinning all mestizo religious thought. The text emphasizes that the origin of these elements lies, not merely in the comparative cultural phenomena already noted and connected with white colonial religious fanaticism, but explicitly in African fetishism. Of the backlander or *sertanejo*, we are told that "his religion is a monotheism which he does not understand marred by an extravagant mysticism, with an incongruous admixture of the fetishism of the Indian and the African." Da Cunha describes the religious fusion of the backlanders in precisely the terms that lead to such extravagant fulminations when he is describing race fusion. The fetishism of these people is a kind of religious *cafuso-ism*, outside the mind of the white, in that it results from the mingling of Indian and African religions. That the model for da Cunha's construction of the religious thought of the backlands is developed out of his miscegenetic theory is made explicit. Under the headline "HISTORIC FACTORS IN MESTIZO RELIGION" he simply announces: "It would not be too far amiss to describe them [the historic factors] as miscegenation of beliefs. Here they are, plain to be seen: the anthropomorphism of the savage, the animism of the African, and, what is more worthy of note, the emotional attitude of the superior race itself in the period of discovery and colonisation. This last is a notable instance of historical atavism."[60] It is above all this element of African religion, or African "fetishism" as da Cunha obsessively reiterates it, that is a kind of social time bomb making both the formation and destruction of Canudos inevitable. Da Cunha makes almost no direct comparisons between what he sees as the very different cultures of the black seaboard and the mestizo interior. Yet he is prepared to break down this separation when it comes to hammering home his point about the hold African superstition has on the mind of the backlander. African fetish religion comes to stand as a sign for African influence generally, and consequently for the inheritance of slavery within Brazil:

> The fact of the matter is that even in normal times their religion is a vague and varied one. Just as the Haussá negroes, adapting to the liturgy the whole of the Jorubano ritual, afford the anomalous site, but the common one in the Bahian capital, of worshippers following the solemnities of the Mass in a manner to accord with their own fetishistic practices, so the *sertanejos*, unfortunate heirs to age-old vices, may be seen leaving the holy services for the pagan love-feasts of the African *candomblés*.[61]

Although slavery, slaves, and ex-slaves are hardly mentioned in this text, they are constructed indirectly. Afro-Brazilian influence leaps out here, and syncretism bursts upon the scene. First the Hausa slaves of Bahia are presented absorbing the whole of the Catholic liturgy into their African religious ritual. The process is then compared to the *sertanejos* leaving Catholicism to throw themselves in the erotics of "*candomblés*." In this passage, odd in the context of the race agendas outlined above, da Cunha seems to be tearing down his own separationist categories. Here the dangerous degeneration and credulity of the *sertanejos* is articulated via association with the hybrid Afro-Catholic cults of the seaboard. Yet the sophisticated rituals of *Candomblé* are not taken seriously, but written off as "pagan love-feasts," and again the obsessive reiteration of the charge of fetishism is used as a dismissive *vade mecum*. The extreme care with which da Cunha so delicately penetrates the thought and culture of the backlanders does not extend to the black, or to any area where the culture of the Afro-Brazilian rubs shoulders with the *sertanejo*. Da Cunhas's African reference here occurs as an introductory coda for the ultimate set piece in which African-evolved cults established as the outer limit for the religious depravities underlying the mentality of the backlanders. Describing the unstable religious practices evolved in the backlands in the decades preceding the rise of Canudos, da Cunha states that this is a vast and unresearched field. He then claims to be able to essentialize the situation by looking "at one incident among many, selected at random." Not much method to the madness here, it would seem. Yet the supposed "example" is by no means random, and again crucially involves a *cafuso*, this time a self-proclaimed prophet in Pernambuco in the late 1850s, who has claimed the "Pedra Bonita," or "Wondrous Rock," as a natural pulpit to preach from. The passage merits quoting at length because of the involved European–Africanist inheritance it develops. The site supposedly has a dark history and is saturated in traumatic fetishistic memory and quite literally in African blood, or to be specific Afro-Brazilian Ashanti infant blood:

> In 1837 this site was a theatre where scenes were staged that recall the sinister religious solemnities of the Ashanties. A visionary mamaluko or cafuso here gathered about him the entire population of the neighbouring farms and, climbing up into the rock pulpit, proclaimed in a tone of conviction the near advent of the enchanted kingdom of Dom Sebastião. The rock having been shattered not by the blows of a mallet but by the miraculous blood of infants, spilled upon it as a holocaust, the great king would then burst forth surrounded by his gleaming bodyguard and would visit an inexorable punishment upon an ungrateful humanity, while heaping riches upon those who had contributed to his "disenchantment." A nervous shudder ran though the region.
>
> This unbalanced individual had found a suitable setting for the spread of his insane teachings. Mothers with infants in their arms crowded around the monstrous altar and fought with one another to be the first to offer their young ones as a sacrifice. Blood gushed and spattered over the rock and stood about in pools—in such quantities according to the newspapers of the time, that when the lugubrious farce was at last ended it was impossible for anyone to remain in the vicinity of this infected spot.[62]

This takes us full circle and provides da Cunha's original contextualization for the presence of Ashanti fetishism within backlands culture. But for this extended description no sources are given validating the details of the atrocities described. The edited editions of *Os Sertões* do not give evidence that any of the "newspapers of the time" provided any of this detail. This is because da Cunha is not, in fact, describing Brazilian syncretic religious practice at all, and is not composing a digest "according to the newspapers of the time." What he is actually doing is drafting in some horror stories first popularized in European intellectual circles by Hegel, stories that, while never established as having basis in historical events, nevertheless entered the common store of European intellectual racism. Afro-Brazilian religious culture, in reality so complicated, and so intimate in the way it negotiated and hybridized Catholicism, here manifests itself as something completely other, a violent reinvention, or transplantation, of inhuman African rituals. Where did da Cunha get his facts and details regarding sub-Saharan religious excess? Why the Ashanti altar, and why the focus on infanticidal holocaust? This scene appears to have no relation to the genuine practices of *Candomblé, Macumba*, or any of the major Afro-Brazilian syncretic religions. One searches the pages of the great French anthropologists of Brazilian syncretism Roger Bastide and Pierre Verger in vain to find accounts of mass infant sacrifices at any Afro-Brazilian shrines at any time in any part of Brazil. This is because da Cunha was not drawing upon Brazilian sources for his descriptions but looking to a *locus classicus* and indeed notorious *locus horribilis* within European philosophy and letters.

In choosing Ashanti culture, in dwelling on human sacrifice focused on ritualized mass child murder, and in drawing out the description of the orgiastic sadism of the African mothers as they battle to sacrifice their babies on the fetish altar, da Cunha is tapping into a fabulously rich vein of European Negrophobe mythography. We shall be considering below the centrality of Hegel's *Lectures on the Philosophy of History* to da Cunha's race theory. Here I merely want to note that da Cunha was intimate with this text, and that it provided the detail in this description.

Hegel's *Lectures on the Philosophy of History* sets out a broad plan for categorizing the world populations. He provides a broad-brush survey of the major world populations and of their relative capacities for involvement in the Hegelian scheme of human perfectibility. This capacity is defined by the kind of physical surroundings in which different peoples dwell. Put simply (and Hegel to the consternation of his disciples does put it disconcertingly crudely), we are given a deterministic argument that climate and geography defines culture and mental capacity. Da Cunha, profoundly influenced by this idea, extended it in some strange, un-Hegelian directions. But to return to Hegel's race classification: the Africans are entirely excluded from, and written out of, his plans for human improvement. Africans are quite simply constructed as existing outside humanity, and the central empirical example Hegel sets up in order to jettison blacks from his grand project is the blood sacrifice rituals of the Ashanti.[63] Hegel never visited Africa, but using a meagre set of unreliable sources he spins a lurid, and even for the period madly excessive, fantasy of horror and blood lust. He serves up an adult portion, infants and women pounded to a paste and consumed, by men and other women; mountains of skulls; enormous cannibalistic feasts and ceremonies; orgies, blood lust, mayhem, a subhuman orgiastic, fetishistic chaos. The imagined Ashanti rituals, and the fantasies generated around the kingdom of Dahomey in particular, were popularized in Europe in the propagandas generated during the slavery debates of the 1780s. In England they remained a staple in nineteenth-century missionary propaganda demonizing the heathen, as well as in popular fiction. Yet these horror stories were not culturally restricted, and well into the twentieth century they had a home in the elevated realms of high literary modernism and art. Edith Sitwell for example serves up the feast with some weird Bloomsbury gusto in the 1920s in her long, late, powerful poem "Gold Coast Customs." Her original footnotes reveal that she is again taking her lead directly from the atrocity descriptions in Hegel, which she explicitly cites and parodies.

What is intriguing about da Cunha, and what he does with this cultural inheritance, is again the indirect nature of his approach. He draws, via Hegel's Dahomeyian montage, on an established European anti-Africanist rhetoric located on the slave coast, in order to discredit the religious thought of a half-black, half-Indian religious leader, reportedly operating in 1830s Pernambuco, whose name, fortuitously, he cannot even remember. The African ritual and its mass murder are then linked, via the supposed fantasies of the insane black priest, with Sebastianism—this is the "enchanted kingdom of Dom Sebastião" referred to. Although he has set the scene back in the 1830s, this link is not in fact as arbitrary or eccentric a move on da Cunha's part as it might now appear. The Portuguese religious cult of Sebastianism used interpretations of the Book of Revelation to prophecy that the boy King and Crusader Sebastian I would return and establish a Holy Christian Portuguese Empire. Sebastian had disappeared during the massacre of the Portuguese by the Moroccans at the catastrophic battle of Alcabar Quibir in 1578. His mystical shadow had then hung over Portugal and Brazil during the ensuing centuries. Any significant event or disaster seemed to bring out religious enthusiasts who claimed the second coming of Sebastian was imminent. It is difficult to understand as a non-Luso-Brazilian exactly how inspirational this myth was, and remains. Of course, the traumatic events in Brazil in the 1880s and 1890s surrounding the abolition of slavery, the abolition of the monarchy, and the establishment of the republic had generated mass revivals of Sebastianism in many areas across Brazil. Religious monarchists including Conselheiro and his followers were definitely influenced by the belief that the Sebastianic Second Coming was imminent. It makes sense to see elements of the religious enthusiasm that galvanized Canudos as lying in the sudden rise of Sebastianist cults. The peculiar and ingenious move that da Cunha makes is to link Sebastianism so directly with Ashanti religious mass murder as a way of discrediting the Afro-Brazilian religious element within Canudos.

Having provided this sinister Africanist lineage for the believers of Canudos, da Cunha moves on to describe the customs and ceremonies developed by

Conselheiro through a further set of African-related allusions. Conselheiro himself is presented as a crazed and enfeebled mystic, not really in charge of what he thinks or sees. He is surrounded by a set of military leaders, some of whom are black such as Estevão, a "burly misshapen negro with a body tattooed by bullet and dagger wounds," and all of whom are tragically impressive.[64] Yet Conselheiro's right-hand man, when it comes to the organization of religion, is shown as a devious mulatto:

> Amid these tragic profiles there is the ridiculous figure of Pious Anthony, a lean and seedy-looking mulatto, emaciated from fasting, who is very much in the Counsellor's confidence; half-sacristan, half-soldier, a devotee of the blunderbuss, spying, watching, searching, shrewdly worming his way into the homes and ferreting out every nook of the village he immediately reports all the latest happenings to the supreme leader.[65]

The MC overseeing the religious ceremonies of Canudos is shown to be a cunning half-African, as much political spy and informer as religious devotee. This figure is shown as central to the perversion of Conselheiro's religion. The symbols and ceremonies of the Catholic Church are shown as corrupted by the influence of what again is described as African fetishism. Having exhausted the more ritualized forms of Catholic ceremony, or in da Cunha's words "having run the gamut of litanies, said all the rosaries, and intoned all the rhyming benedicities," the whole community is then called upon for the " 'kissing' of the images."[66] This ceremony is stage-managed by Pious Anthony and involves the physical kissing of all the sacred statues from Christ and Mary down through all the saints and holy relics. The process of multiple kissing is presented as a grossly physical one: "Then came the succession of all the saints, images, veronicas, crosses to be passed along from hand to hand, from mouth to mouth . . . the dull smack of innumerable kisses could be heard."[67] It is this physical engagement with the sacred objects, a cult commodity fetishism with undertones of slobbering eroticism, that finally takes the believers into a world of spirit possession explicitly set out as a "barbarous mysticism," not a Christian or syncretic mysticism:

> Then it was that the intoxication and vertigo of these simple souls would reach a peak. Individual emotions now overflowed, finding themselves suddenly confounded with the general and irrepressible contagion. It was as if the supernatural powers which a naïve animism had conferred on these

images had at last penetrated their consciousness, for they were writhing now in the throws of an irrepressible hallucination . . . clasping to their bosoms the images slavered in saliva, the deluded women would sink down in the violent contortions of hysteria, while the frightened children wailed in chorus. Laid hold of by the same aura of madness, the masculine group of fighters, amid the general uproar and the clash and jingle of their weapons were quivering to the same terrifying rhythmic beat, one that marked the powerful explosion of a barbaric mysticism.[68]

Da Cunha's style here is fascinating—he seems to be forcing the hideous truth out of his narrator, almost it seems against his will. And so the revelation is to explain that the sacred rights at the heart of the Canudos ceremony are anchored not in Catholicism but the *Candomblé*. The animism and spirit possession that can form the climax of some *Candomblé* rituals are transplanted into the congregation of Canudos. The gross and sexualized physicality with which, in this vision, the Catholic icons are treated finally leads into the inevitable process of a "barbaric" possession. A primal percussion takes over the proceedings, as the male fighters clash their weapons to a "terrifying rhythmic beat." This symbolic, intimidating, ritual clashing of weapons echoes through the fictions of slavery, and we are back with a projected terror of the Ashanti ritual. Da Cunha has also entered a symbolic world that calls up Melville's black slave crew, in *Benito Cereno*.[69]

As we have seen, da Cunha will not allow an open discussion of slavery or its inheritance within his text. The subject, and the author's extreme anxieties concerning this repression, lead to a set of codified treatments. The transformation of Conselheiro's religion into a composite fantasy that combines the Ashanti blood sacrifice with Afro-Brazilian ritual hybrid is another example of this silent witnessing.

The contamination of Conselheiro's visionary religion by a devolved African element is essentialized in the figure of the mulatto, already alluded to, Antonio Beato, or "Pious Anthony." When Canudos finally falls, this figure is shown as the only man who wants to play diplomatic games with the victors. He is a sort of corrupted middleman, the fallen mulatto slave who is willing to do deals with the white officers while the real heroes fight to the death. Presenting a façade of opaque resignation to his interrogators, Beato's betrayal of the commune and its leader appears to know no limits. Questioned by the general, Beato manages to write off the achievement of Conselheiro with a single colloquialism. Asked about the fate of the mystic leader, the response is reported as follows:

> [Beato] went on to explain that, weakened by an old wound from the splinter of a grenade which he had received on a certain occasion as he was going from the church to the "Sanctuary" the Counsellor had died on the 22nd September of dysentery, or as he put it "the trots"—an expression so horribly comic as to evoke at once an irrepressible ripple of laughter despite the painful gravity of the occasion. He [Beato] did not notice this, however; or perhaps he was pretending not to notice, as he stood there motionless, his face calm and inscrutable . . .[70]

Conselheiro exits history with a single coprophagic and comic reference: in Brazilian Beato's phrase "uma caminheira" is absurdly comic suggesting a locomotive chugging along. The great Conselheiro is seen shitting himself to death, as far as da Cunha is concerned a metaphor for his religious philosophy no doubt. From da Cunha's official perspective this is an appropriate end for the would-be savior. Conselheiro gets the narrator and witness he deserves, and da Cunha gets his man. Yet the text is uncertain about who is laughing at whom. We are led to question the extent to which Beato is in control of the comedy he evokes—does he not notice what he is doing, or does he pretend not to notice? The whole episode is deliberately shrouded in ambiguity and leads to questions that cannot be answered with certainty. Is he finally a black Iago, or a reincarnated Aaron the Moor, an inscrutable character inhabiting a moral and spiritual dead end whose unreadability is the mask for a grim existential humor? Is this mask finally worn by da Cunha himself? Da Cunha leaves the matter open, up to the reader to decide. Is Beato a conscious ironist who always understood the absurdity inherent in Conselheiro's aspiration to prophetic status, or is he just a credulous mulatto?

"And these things created no impression": Da Cunha's Final Valorization of Africanity and the Moral Superiority of the Slave

In a text that, it must now be apparent, so resolutely refuses to come at slavery and the Afro-Brazilian diaspora directly, the weird swerves away from, and tangential reapproaches towards, blacks and mulattos must hold a special weight. It is the mutability of da Cunha's approach to Brazil's slavery inheritance that makes his text such a crucial window. It is an open text, and includes examples of da Cunha's capacity to transcend race politics, and indeed the white archive, and to provide an inspirational reading of black insurrectionary violence. While so often he rubs our faces in the ordure of white Negrophobe fictions, he also, at points, transmogrifies his black subject into something magnificent. I will give one lengthy and terrific example where da Cunha seems to be writing against the grain of his habitual race agenda:

> Um negro, um dos raros negros puros que ali havia, preso em fins de setembro, foi conduzido à presença do comandante da 1.ª coluna, general João da Silva Barbosa. Chegou arfando, exausto da marcha aos encontrões e do recontro em que fora colhido. Era espigado e seco. Delatava na organização desfibrada os rigores da fome e do combate. A magreza alongara-lhe o porte, ligeiramente curvo. A grenha, demasiadamente crescida, afogava-lhe a fronte estreita e fugitiva; e o rosto, onde o prognatismo se acentuara, desaparecia na lanugem espessa da barba, feito uma máscara amarrotada e imunda. Chegou em cambaleios. O passo claudicante e infirme, a cabeça lanzuda, a cara exígua, um nariz chato sobre lábios grossos, entreabertos pelos dentes oblíquos e saltados, os olhos pequeninos, luzindo vivamente dentro das órbitas profundas, os longos braços desnudos, oscilando—davam-lhe a aparência rebarbativa de um orango valetudinário. Não transpôs a couceira da tenda. Era um animal. Não valia a pena interrogá-lo.
>
> O general de brigada João da Silva Barbosa, da rede em que convalescia de ferimento recente, fez um gesto.
>
> Um cabo de esquadra, empregado na comissão de engenharia e famoso naquelas façanhas, adivinhou-lhe o intento Achegou-se com o braço. Diminuto na altura, entretanto, custou a enleá-lo ao pescoço do condenado. Este, porém, auxiliou-o tranqüilamente; desceu o nó embaralhado; enfiou-o pelas próprias mãos, jugulando-se . . . Perto, um tenente do estado-maior de primeira classe e um quintanista de medicina contemplavam aquela cena. E viram transmudar-se o infeliz, apenas dados os primeiros passos para o suplício. Daquele arcabouço denegrido e repugnante, mal soerguido nas longas pernas murchas, despontaram, repentinamente, linhas admiráveis—terrivelmente esculturais—de uma plástica estupenda.
>
> Um primor de estatuária modelado em lama. Retificara-se de súbito a envergadura abatida do negro aprumando-se, vertical e rígida, numa bela atitude singularmente altiva. A cabeça firmou-se-lhe sobre os ombros, que se retraíram dilatando o peito, alçada num gesto desafiador de sobranceria fidalga, e o olhar, num lampejo varonil, iluminou-lhe a fronte. Seguiu

impassível e firme; mudo, imóvel a musculatura gasta duramente em relevo sobre os ossos, num desempenho impecável, feito uma estátua, uma velha estátua de titã, soterrada havia quatro séculos aflorando, denegrida e mutilada, naquela imensa ruinaria de Canudos. Era uma inversão de papéis. Uma antinomia vergonhosa.

E estas coisas não impressionavam . . .[71]

(A black, one of the few pure blacks who was held there, who had been taken at the end of September, was conducted before the Commander of the first column, General João de Silva Barbosa. He [the black] arrived swaying, exhausted from the march and from the encounters and reencounters in which he had been taken. He was a dried-out nail. His organism was ruined by the rigors of battle and famine. His skinniness drew him out in a gentle curve. His vast mane of hair drowned a straight and fugitive/sloping brow; his face, where prognathous-ness was accentuated, disappeared in the dense fuzz of his beard, the whole thing was a battered and obscene mask. He walked in lurches. His gait was twisted and sick, the head was woolly, the countenance diminutive, the nose flat above thick lips, and between these the teeth were oblique and jutting, the little eyes glittered with life from within the deep sockets, his long, naked dangling arms gave him the rebarbative air of a valetudinarian orangutan.

They wouldn't let him across the threshold. It was an animal. It was pointless to try and question it.

The general of the brigade, João da Silva Barbosa, from the hammock where he lay recovering from a recent wound, made a gesture.

The head of a squadron attached to the engineering commission, who was famous for such doings, understood what was meant and brought out the rope. Of diminutive stature, he found it difficult to adjust the halter about the condemned man's throat; at this, however, the prisoner with tranquility helped him, fastening the noose that would strangle him about his own neck.

Nearby, a headquarters lieutenant and a fifth-year medical student contemplated this scene. They saw a transformation in the unfortunate one as he made his first steps towards his torture. This skeleton degraded and repugnant, badly supported by its long skinny legs, suddenly took on the most admirable lineaments—terrifically sculptural—and of a stupendous plasticity.

> It was a first-rate statue modelled from the mire. He suddenly erected himself and spreading himself the negro raised himself up in a most beautiful and singularly elevated attitude. The head was firm set on the shoulders, which were held back wide with chest out. He had the proud bearing of an ancient Fidalgo, and the eyes, with a limpid virility, illuminated his face. Impassive and firm he followed; mute, immobile, the exhausted but enduring musculature moved above his bones in an impeccable demeanor, he was a statue, an ancient statue of Titan, entombed four centuries earlier, now unearthed and mutilated in this immense ruin of Canudos. Here was a world turned upside down. An Antinomian disaster.
> And these things made no impression . . .)[72]

What are we to make of such writing, and what exactly does that awful last line mean with its hyperbolic denial? If "these things made no impression," where did this passage come from, where did the book come from?

It is a confusing piece of writing. On who or what did "these things" make or not make an "impression"? If they made no impression on the killers, then there were no witnesses, no one who could be bothered to look at an old black and beaten beast done to death. So who really sees "estas coisas" (these matters), and on whom do they make an impression? The two young military witnesses, soldier and doctor, the victim, the audience, the reader, the author, all may or may not be implicated in, or impressed by, this phrase. Da Cunha has placed himself in an unstable fictional space.

This set piece is a rhetorical deconstruction of Western racist discourse at its roots. The essence of negrophobia is conjured up in the first paragraph only to be obliterated in its turn by a transcendent vision of negritude in full-blown anticolonial and "Antinomian" celebration. In terms of relative viewpoints and rhetorical layering, the passage is highly sophisticated. It opens with an excessive, grotesque caricature of a black man. Its very excess demands that the writing function satirically, throwing the lazy hyperbole of negrophobe semiotics back at the reader. Da Cunha is writing here very much in the mold of the caricatures of comically ugly black men meticulously operated by certain negrophobe authors. Perhaps the most precise analogies in popular fiction are to be found in the pages of Thomas Dixon Junior's *The Clansman*. But da Cunha is no Dixon; his method is parodic, his parodies satiric. Da Cunha uses racist excess in much the same way that the masters of Marntiniquean Negritude used it. Frantz Fanon frequently in *Black Skin, White Masks* and Aimé Césaire in *Notebook of a Return to My Native Land* at key points in their respective critiques of race troping are, like da Cunha, not frightened to wallow in the filthy metaphorics of racism in order to throw European classificatory norms back into the eyes of their European readers. When they show us that they are aware of their complicity in these structures, they simultaneously celebrate the fact that they have (in da Cunha's case temporarily) gone beyond such complicity into a new racial space. Césaire explains the confessional processes involved:

> You must know the extent of my cowardice. One evening on the streetcar facing me a nigger.
> A nigger as big as a pongo . . . poverty was working on some hideous cartouche. One could easily see how that industrious and malevolent thumb had kneaded bumps into his brow, bored two bizarre parallel tunnels in his nose, over exaggerated his lips . . . He was a gangly nigger without rhythm or measure. A nigger whose eyes rolled bloodshot weariness. A shameless nigger and his toes sneered in a rather stinking way at the bottom of the yawning lair of his shoes.
> Poverty without any question had knocked itself out to finish him off.
> It had dug the socket, painted it with a rouge of dust mixed with rheum.
> It had stretched an empty space between the solid hinge of the jaw and the bone of an old tarnished cheek. Had planted over it the small shiny stakes of a two—or three day beard. Had panicked his heart, bent his back.
> And the whole thing added up perfectly to a hideous nigger, a grouchy nigger, a melancholy nigger, a slouched nigger, his hands joined in prayer on a knobby stick. A nigger shrouded in an old threadbare coat. A comical and ugly nigger, with some women behind me sneering at him.
> He was COMICAL AND UGLY,
> COMICAL AND UGLY for sure.
> I displayed a big complicitous smile . . .[73]

And so da Cunha begins, as Césaire begins, with a caricature black, with shoddy beard, giant stature, slouching gate, an ape. This initial caricature created by da Cunha is also deliberately "COMICAL AND UGLY." Like Césaire, da Cunha gives the reader a big complicitous smile of encouragement and demands that we face our own cowardice and our own racist corruption. And yet, as also with Césaire, this caricature is at once a confession and a trap. Césaire's comical and ugly black transforms in the course of the poem into many other forms, which include the heroic Toussaint L'Ouverture, the glories of African civilizations, as well as the compromised product of the slave systems. Each of these versions of negritude is shown to be a truth, and it is the final achievement of *Os Sertões* that da Cunha is prepared to get to work on the job of dismantling the complicities and contradictions of the Brazilian construction of blackness.

Da Cunha has reached a point in the text where he is prepared, finally, to creatively embrace contradiction, rather than drown in it. He introduces conflicting techniques that ask similar didactic questions to those of Césaire's *Notebook*. The prose tells us almost from the outset that it is not what it seems, that it sees through its own illusions. We open with a fully realized parody, with a catalogue of signs, and the most extreme of racist animalizations. Blacks look like apes and this one looks like the orangutan (another name for which, as Césaire knew, is pongo). This is the species of large primate so memorably placed at the center of race debate in the late eighteenth century by Lord Monboddo and already the subject of intricate literary parodies by the early nineteenth century.[74] Yet at its very outset the writing is complicated, the passage stating also that what we are being shown is "a filthy mask." In this sense, as whenever a mask is worn, there is a directive to wait and to ask questions: who made the filth, who made the mask, who put them together, who can see beyond the filth, and the mask? Of course, sub-Saharan cultures make some of the most aesthetically refined and artistically complex masks ever created by humans. Yet the mask we are invited to see is a human face beaten, befouled, and abused by Europeans. It is the traces of our violence that make this human face into the beaten ugly thing that da Cunha offers up as a sign of abjection. The mask we must look into is a mirror of the colonizer's abuse, not the beautiful face that finally faces death with such stoic equanimity.

The technique uses space, time, and fragmentation cleverly, and the descriptive methods are almost filmic. First there are, in close-up, a series of typical traits, drawn from a negrophobe matrix, details that combine to make the perfect picture of the ape-like black—narrow forehead, protruding jaw and teeth, thick lips and flat nose, small deep-set eyes, woolly hair. Second, the point of view pulls back from this portrait to present a minidrama in a series of mimed actions, and the mimicry is political and racial. Da Cunha, having presented the black as an animal, takes the analogy further: if he is an animal then he exists outside language, and therefore there is no point introducing words into the equation, and interrogating him before execution. All this is summarized with economy in the lines: "They wouldn't let him across the threshold. It was an animal. It was pointless to try and question it."

The scene is a darkly comic satiric mime. The wounded commander in his hammock makes a sign, indicating the black is to be strung up. The commander's sidekick understands this gesture, which we as readers will never see, and gets a rope. The flunky-executioner is too short to place the rope around the black man's neck. The black man helps him and puts the noose around his own neck. Not a word is exchanged. The whole thing, like a dumb show or pantomime, is enacted through wordless sign and gesture; the space of terror, the space of death, is a silent space. It is our job to read the signs. I take the space of terror and death, and the idea of its silence, from Michael Taussig. His analysis of descriptions of casual murders and torture carried out in the Columbian jungle by Aranjo's men during the Putamayo rubber boom suggest an abject space similar to that of da Cunha. Terror and torture reached a stage where the indigenous Indians would mutilate themselves and carry severed limbs to the tyrant. Was this a satiric gesture, or an act carried through because they thought that was what their torturers wanted? Da Cunha posits a similar dilemma when his black helps to place the rope around his own neck—is this satire or complicity, or complicitous satire?[75]

The passage then moves into its third and strangest phase. The reader is to be shown what lies behind the mask, but is not to be shown this directly, but rather through a new point of view, a new narrational mask. Again, the technique tempts filmic analogies since the whole scene is given from one new camera angle: "P. O. V. Near foreground, young lieutenant and medical student." As so often in this narrative maze da Cunha himself disappears, or rather is here, there, everywhere, and nowhere. This, the key scene of black heroic transformation in Brazil's epic, the visionary creation of a pure black Brazilian rebel as a figure of mythic heroism and beauty, is presented as the vision of two young white men, one an aspiring doctor, one an aspiring soldier, who are silent witnesses on the periphery of the action. Da Cunha initially invites the reader to look through the eyes of these fictive witnesses, as we are encouraged to believe that it is they who see something incredible. They witness the movement of this degraded, filthy, black animal into an ideal of noble human self-sacrifice, Yeats's terrible beauty (words combined in da Cunha's passage) giving birth before our eyes.

Yet the prose is then immediately on the move again, new elements flood in, distantiations, ideological regressions and doubts. What exactly has this statuesque, resolute, glorious black nobility come to signify, where does da Cunha want to take it, and where is he prepared to leave it? Again, the black hero, silent and complete in his gestures, cannot be seen simply for what he is, he must be qualified, explained. He is not only a black revolutionary facing death without fear, but a classical statue. He is a configuration of one of the Titans buried four hundred years ago, before the colonization of Brazil or the African slave trade began, and now exhumed, apparently by an inexplicable chance, in this silent theatre of cruelty. It is possible to provide a reading that sees da Cunha breaking out in the final two lines in an expression of horror and bemusement that represents a confession. If anything in this bewildering book might be said to involve the author's final testimony, maybe this is it: "Era uma inversão de papéis. Uma antinomia vergonhosa."

With that announcement, da Cunha places the interpreter in a strange place. The prose has moved beyond aesthetics or didacticism and into mystery (the capacity to induce such losses in the reader may well be a definition of a great work of art). This writing demands questions and self-questioning in a reader; it does not give answers. What does that massive "Era" (it was) refer back to—the black man, the statue, the vision of the two witnesses, the vision of the author, the whole of the previous scene? What is "antinomy" doing here coupled with shame? "Anti" means against, the "noumos" is the law, but what law is being opposed here—the law that nobility, and beauty, are the preserve of white culture? The aesthetic law that black bodies are filthy, laughable, and reflect an inner moral degradation? "Antinomy" has many meanings: a paradox, a conflict of authority, something that should not be but is. The word gave rise to the Antinomians, maybe the most radical religious rebels of all time, flaunting their excesses on the peripheries of the English Revolution. What roles have been reversed here, and why is the antinomy shameful? Is da Cunha saying that the black is behaving like a beautiful god, upholding human potential, while the white is behaving like a beast? The reader is only allowed to glimpse this possibility, hanging as it does among other equally likely readings. The shameful nature of the antinomy might imply that it is shameful for a black to parody such noble behavior, such appearance, given his true nature, or again the shame might relate to the author himself, or his imagined witnesses, for conjuring up such a vision of black heroism.

The only thing that is certain about this wonderful writing is that the final statement is a deliberate lie. It may be true that the black was executed anyway, that the two white witnesses could not communicate what they had seen and experienced to each other, to the black man, or to us, and that the brutal reductions of late nineteenth-century Brazilian racism remained intact, as they have remained intact across the Americas and Europe. And yet *that* this extraordinary passage was written, and written by a man whose masterpiece in so many ways appears so often to take other paths around issues of race in its earlier pages, means that "these things," whether they happened or not, and whether they were witnessed or not, have created, create now, and will continue to "create an impression." "E estas coisas não impressionavam" (And yet these things did not impress). At one level this statement has the acerbic negativity of the pragmatist. Throughout this sensational and emotional text, da Cunha wants to keep hold of a certain violent cynicism. He likes to keep his distance through a shroud of black comedy, and in this quality frequently mimics the brutal sarcasm of the narrator in Thomas Carlyle's *French Revolution*. In consequence he casts in, as a continual flavoring, the dry bitters of a particular ironic humor around violent excess. He does this in order to make the horror of his story bearable and in order to compromise its rare but extreme sentimentalism (another quality he incidentally shares with Carlyle). Is the final inscrutable statement announced in this tone of bleak humor, or in a voice of unironic lamentation? Is he saying, "Of course these things meant nothing, it was business as usual"? Or is he crying out against the fact that this beautiful miracle, this transmutation, fell upon the stone hearts and blind eyes of the brutalized white militia, and that their indifference is nothing short of a tragedy? The greatness of *Os Sertões* lies in its inclusiveness, and its Whitmanesque empathy with contradiction. Thus the book allows for both suggested readings, and for both readings to be historically a form of "truth," terrible though such honesty might be.

Beyond Hegelian Synthesis: A Racial Theory of Intussusception

The passage describing the killing of the mulatto matters, because it shows *Os Sertões* to have a more multifaceted approach to race than da Cunha tells us it has, or than his critics and defenders have so far allowed his book to have. The vision of this Titanic black man, who can rise above circumstance, and above historical reality, to enter a mythic space of death, a chosen space, is, in a sense, da Cunha's worst nightmare. Da Cunha has the imaginative extremity and temerity to refute his own central argument and to face down his demons.

The bulk of the foregoing analysis has made it clear that if *Os Sertões* has one overriding cultural thesis it might be termed a socio-geographics of race. The argument, and the explanation for the extraordinary opening section, which first-time readers might mistake for a dull lesson in the geography and geology of the backlands, is nicely formulated by Afrânio Peixoto in his passionate preface to *Os Sertões*. For Peixoto part of da Cunha's uniqueness lies in his ability to take natural description into what is almost a new fictional dimension. Putnam describes da Cunha's prose as capturing the "emotional drama of inanimate nature," and in this sense is suggesting that we cast natural description within *Os Sertões* as a form of inspired pathetic fallacy. But what Peixoto sees is something beyond a mere emotional projection of human emotion onto nature. Peixoto outlines an extreme politics of race as the ultimate generative force behind da Cunha's metaphorics of landscape. In this reading humanity becomes the slave of an agonized earth, growing out of it, incapable of growing beyond it, even through the mixing of races. In this sense the soil is thicker than blood or water, and da Cunha is founding a nationalist myth based in the land and not in race.

Very Hegelian, one might think. In this way the threat of slave blood on the populations and myths of Brazil can be silenced, erased, or sidestepped. Put essentially, this thesis states that it is the physical state of the land that dictates the physical state of the population: "The land may be changed and man thereby may become a different being from the one he is." And this ability of the land to form a population is set against the ability of humans to form and reform populations through interbreeding: "Sociology is here made dependent upon an historical moment in which human interconnection through miscegenation is incapable of altering the population of a land—a population that remains a direct expression of the soil."[76]

The silent war da Cunha wages on the memory of slavery, on silencing it and keeping it out, has the effect of saturating his landscape with metaphors of torture and suffering. Again, against his official narrative agenda, the memory of Afro-Brazilian suffering reaches out through a landscape that again and again can only be seen as enslaved, tortured, and finally martyred. "Stunted flora ... which give the landscape here its impinging and tormented aspect." He sees "the almost convulsive appearance of a deciduous flora lost in a maze of undergrowth" which "is in a manner of speaking the martyrdom of the earth, brutally lashed by variable elements which run the gamut of climatic conditions."[77] "The natural life is limited in these parts ... it is crushed to earth"[78]; "vegetation standing rigidly in space or spreading out sinuously along the ground, representing, as it would seem, the agonised struggles of a tortured writhing flora."[79] This is not merely a landscape of torture but an enslaved landscape that, in its terror, tortures itself. The normal source of heat and life is a force of death. Afflicted by the desert sun, the vegetation is seen burying itself alive, the plants become perpetual fugitives hiding from too much light: "The sun is the enemy whom it is urgent to avoid, to elude, or to combat. And avoiding it means, in a manner of speaking ... the inhumation of the moribund flora, the burying of its stalks in the earth."[80] As the descriptions mount, the climate must not only be evaded but, in the form of a cruel tyrant, actively tortures the flora until it must hide to escape: "Lashed by the dog-day heat, fustigated by the sun, gnawed by torrential rain, tortured by the winds, these trees would appear to have been knocked out completely in the struggle with the antagonistic elements, and so have gone underground in this manner, have made themselves invisible."[81] This is an almost perfect articulation for the manner in which the memory of slavery is articulated in this book. The plants themselves are presented at times as an instrument of torture, afflicting the land: "The northeaster roars in the wilderness; and, like a lacerating haircloth, the *caatinga* extends across the earth its thorny branches." So completely is his scientific vision attuned with his historical vision that when, in this extraordinary landscape, something actually flowers, da Cunha cannot see beauty but the presage of the haphazard brutality of massacre: "inelegant and monstrous melocacti, fluted and ellipsoidal in form, with thorny buds that converge above in an apex formed by a single bright-red flower. They make their appearance in an inexplicable manner over the barren rock, really conveying, in their size, their conformations and the manner of their dispersion, the singular impression of bloody, decapitated heads tossed here and there, without rhyme or reason, in a truly tragic disorder."[82] This is the "tragic disorder" inherent in every massacre of the weak by the powerful, from Palmares to Canudos. And of course this tragic floral disorder of decapitated heads stands in rhetorical counterpoint to that ordered floral display of decapitated heads and uniforms created by the rebels when they come to deal out death, and then turn it into a desert installation.[83] Da Cunha is in fact setting and finally springing a brilliant aesthetic trap. His landscape is designed to grow on, or into, the mind; it is no landscape at all but both an explanation and enactment of the population of Canudos, including its blacks.

How da Cunha finally infuses his landscape descriptions into a radical race theory, and into the very memory of slavery, is by no means a straightforward matter. His final solution comes via a clever refutation of Hegel's geographically based theory of race. In many ways the key to da Cunha's method lies in the magical fifth chapter of his first section, entitled "A GEOGRAPHICAL CATEGORY THAT HEGEL DOES NOT MENTION." Hegel is of course these days very much at the center of one area of postcolonial debate because of the absorption of his "master–slave dialectic" into a whole range of discussions on the power relations of slavery. But da Cunha reminds us that when nineteenth-century readers wanted to think about Hegel on race and slavery, they did not, like every self-respecting postcolonial theorist of today, go to the arcane abstractions of the *Phenomenology of Spirit* but via a much more direct route, namely the brutal racial categorizations of the *Lectures on the Philosophy of World History*. In this work, which has proved something of a sorry moral choke pear for Hegel's philosophical disciples,

Hegel produces a crude fantasy of ethnic differentiation based on the physical makeup of the earth—in other words, a geographically and climatically justified map of race. Da Cunha's point is that Hegel sets out three defining categories for forming racial characteristics: firstly the steppe lands and deserts, secondly the fertile irrigated valleys, and finally the coastline and island. Turning to the backland landscape, da Cunha sees it as involving a periodic paradox that refutes the Hegelian divisions. During the winter rains, the backlands are briefly transformed from arid desert to a flowering paradise. In his phrase the backlands are both "barbarously sterile and marvellously exuberant" and this paradox of course will carry through to their populations.[84] What da Cunha goes on to do is to set this population up in a special character of victimhood, and heroic endurance. The landscape and the population it creates have a bizarre capacity to go beyond the Hegelian dialectic through suffering. Sterility is the thesis, exuberance the antithesis, but a synthesis is only possible if a regular alteration occurs. The next stage is to suggest a scenario where the thesis and antithesis cannot exist. Da Cunha describes a natural world with no respect for Hegelian balance, where prolonged drought can throw a mighty spanner into the synthetic works. The idea is disturbing, indeed difficult, but is articulated in the following passage describing the return of drought to the land:

> The days of torture return; the atmosphere is asphyxiating; the soil is hard as rock; the flora is stripped bare, and on those occasions when summer meets summer without the intermittency of rain—the dreadful spasm of the drought. Nature here rejoices in a play of antitheses. And these antitheses accordingly call for a special division in the Hegelian scheme, the most interesting and significant of them all.[85]

What a bizarre thesis: if you live in a place where suffering produces a unique moral landscape, where piling negativity on negativity, or antithesis upon antithesis, creates a positively ludic space where "nature rejoices in a play of antitheses," you have gone beyond Hegelian synthesis, and into a space of unendingly and mutually enriched antithesis. The only development possible in this world occurs mystically, through a suffering beyond logic. In the end da Cunha is saying that the backlanders have a unique capacity to suffer, and to be ecstatic in relation to their suffering, because their landscape has this capacity. Both Hegel's dialectical model and his geographical determinism are taken out of, or beyond, themselves, and reinvented as a uniquely Brazilian earth-martyrology:

> The earth may then be seen engaged in a silent struggle, the effects of which go back for historic cycles—a deeply stirring struggle for one who views it down the ages. Rendered torpid by the adverse agencies with which it has to contend, but holding tenaciously, not to be coerced, it is transmuted like an organism, by intussusception, and remains indifferent to the riotous elements that lash it in the face.[86]

It is not only the riotous elements that lash nature in the face. As the analysis into landscape and its relation to man develops, da Cunha sets up an ambitious parallel between the rape of nature and the processes of colonialism in Brazil. It is at this point that da Cunha turns from the backlands to think about the formation of deserts and the part that humans have played in their creation. Man is seen as "a terrible maker of deserts." This begins with use of fire by "primitive" peoples, to open up land, but is then seen as the principle effect of the early processes of European colonization. In Brazilian colonial mythology the bands of early explorers, setting out inland under the direction of the captaincies in search of mineral wealth and slaves, hold an exalted position under the title of *Bandeirantes*. Here they are described as barbarians, laying nature waste through centuries of conflagration, and creating the very landscape that is to form the Canudos martyrs. The uniquely off-center opening discussion of the land finally makes the bonding of human backlander and of scorched earth, through the martyrdom of colonialism, emphatic: "The martyrdom of man is here reflective of a greater torture, more widespread, one embracing the general economy of life. It arises from the martyrdom of earth."[87]

And so da Cunha is forced to outwit Hegel in order to find no place for the martyrdom of the slaves within "the general economy of life." And yet this is not the whole story. If we return to that climactic description of da Cunha's ideal of a suffering earth, somehow raised to a new level of heroic indifference, another picture comes to mind. The words describing the transmutation of intussusception cause an analogical shock: "Rendered torpid by the adverse agencies with which it has to contend, but holding tenaciously, not to be coerced, it is transmuted like an organism, by intussusception, and remains indifferent to the riotous elements that lash it in the face." Suddenly the text leaps forward to the apparently inexplicable transmutation of defeated black slave rebel, from torpidity to heroic indifference. We have reached the still point of the turning world. Da Cunha's long-delayed, much-disguised equation of slave and earth through their capacity to be indifferent to their suffering is the vital point. *Os Sertões* finally offers a transformative model for thinking about the memory of slavery in Brazil. What you are forced to look into then is a world of unending abuse and denial, the silenced and indescribable world of slavery. This is a world Hegel had absolutely no interest in, and which da Cunha as above all else a Brazilian finally had to confront despite his astonishingly elaborate strategies for its avoidance.

In allowing the slave to colonize his sacred terrain of backlands suffering, albeit at the eleventh hour, da Cunha's work finally looks out and reaches out. Maybe the slave can triumph over the enslaver without entering the violent and self-defeating dynamic of the death struggle at the center of the rather showy Hegelian master–slave dialectic. Maybe you don't need to engage with such a melodramatic model, maybe you can just look away, or even straight through and beyond the terms of this primitive power relation. There are different forms of freedom. One might consist of entering a death struggle with your oppressor, but what if your oppressor denies you that option and has decided to kill you, with no struggle, in cold blood? In fact, what if the oppressor can't be bothered to kill you herself or himself but quietly, cynically, gestures for someone else to do it? In this scenario maybe true freedom lies in quietly taking the instrument of death into your own hand, and in staring down the oppressor's version of death. And while you do this something magical happens; even in the eyes of your oppressors you have suddenly been transformed, into a god, a Titan, a Black Promethean savior modeled out of Brazilian earth. This black savior is not just for "your people" but embodies the very idea of liberty and the fact that every human being must be understood to be born free.

CHAPTER 6

After-Words and After-Worlds: Freyre, Llosa, Slavery, and the Cultural Inheritance of *Os Sertões*

It has recently been intimated that da Cunha might have gone beyond *Os Sertões* in reading Brazilian culture once again through the land. Susanna Hecht gives a wonderful glimpse of where da Cunha might have moved had his abortive project to write an Amazonian epic ever taken form. Of course, given what survived, it will remain a glimpse, and a fantasy, and from the evidence Hecht provides it looks most unlikely that da Cunha could have surpassed, or even provided a valuable variant upon, what he did in *Os Sertões*.[1] What we do have is *Os Sertões*, a new mixing of linguistic registers and the all-encompassing but parodic approach to knowledge systems that came of age during a period when the self-help manual, and the idea that everyone could master all knowledge with a home encyclopedia, were first mass-marketed.

So what is so special about da Cunha? How does this peculiar writer essentialize a Brazilian state of consciousness that works against the grain of the other major diasporic slaving cultures? In order to answer these questions, it is instructive to consider the way da Cunha has been inherited and developed within the Latin American imaginary. That his influence was immediate, remained vast, and goes on developing within Brazil is self-evident. A useful snapshot of how he is now moving into global literary and IT consciousness emerged early in 2017 at the UK Brazilian Embassy's event dedicated to *Os Sertões* as a multilingual and indeed increasingly global text.[2] Yet da Cunha was being adapted, and used, by the European market for travel literature from an early date. Robert Cunninghame Graham shamelessly plagiarized da Cunha's masterpiece in 1920, producing a mediocre crib posing as mystical travel literature under the title *A Brazilian Mystic*.[3] Three decades later in France, Lucien Marchal provided another imitative variant, *Le Mage du Sertão*, a simplified, abbreviated text based on the mystery of Canudos and the Magus, Conselheiro.[4] Da Cunha's epic has since appeared in all sorts of wonderful guises, including an opera. I don't want to end by descending into the critical underworld of a survey of da Cunha's cultural reception, translation, appropriation, or abuse within Europe and North America. I would merely observe that to date he has not been well served by his "adaptors" outside Latin America. I do want to think about how he provided a fertile environment, an amniotic fluid, that allowed both Brazilian and indeed Latin American fiction and cultural history to evolve in its engagement with Atlantic slavery, and all that its inheritance might offer. Da Cunha also shifted the focus away from an exclusive obsession on the coastal regions, and began to ask what slavery, miscegenation, and race relations were doing in the interior, away from the lush sugar plantations of the North East. The analysis will now shift to think about how da Cunha has been reconfigured by two authors, Gilberto Freyre and Mario Vargas Llosa. Both writers are intimately and continually in dialogue with *Os Sertões*, but in very different ways.

The first author I am using, Gilberto Freyre, is arguably Brazil's greatest cultural theorist, some might say cultural provocateur. Freyre was a North East coastal Brazilian, a passionate *Pernambucano* from Recife who thought deeply about da Cunha and his creative process many times and in many different works. Freyre was intensely interested in what da Cunha meant and means to Brazilian racial memory. His writing is invigorated and, in many ways, enabled by the fact the Freyre set himself up in almost compulsive competition with da Cunha. If da Cunha had created the first great epic on Brazilian racial configurations, geographical identity, and the emergence of the republic, Freyre wanted not only to put him in his time and place but to supplant him, to replace him. In this sense there is an intense anxiety of influence, one might even say, if Freudian models are to be trusted, a constant Oedipal pressure, not to say fury, in Freyre's negotiations with da Cunha. The second author who will be analyzed is Mario Vargas Llosa, who wrote a best-selling novel, epic in its ambitions and length, entitled *The War at the End of the World*. This work adapted, fed off, and parodied *Os Sertões* in very direct ways. Now that the dust has settled, it is clear that Llosa did not manage to create a great work of art. He did, however, produce a revealing tool with which to uncover what makes *Os Sertões* inimitable, and which also indicates what da Cunha did do, and what he did not want to do.

Gilberto Freyre's Troubled Debts to Euclides da Cunha

Gilberto Freyre was the most influential cultural historian of Brazil. He is an author who remains, with the possible exception of da Cunha, the only Brazilian historian with a global reputation. Obsessed with *Os Sertões*, Freyre fully recognized da Cunha's importance as a theorist of emergent Brazilian nationhood, and saw into many aspects of his formal and methodological experimentation. He recognized that da Cunha had produced a new sort of writing. Freyre also finally seems to realize that he will never be able to surpass da Cunha's achievement as the voice of the Brazilian North East interior.

Freyre wrote a long discussion of *Os Sertões* considering it as an experimental mode of South American writing. Early in his career Freyre also wrote the introduction to a published edition of da Cunha's diaries written during the Canudos campaign.[5] There has been recent scholarly interest in Brazil concerning the nature of Freyre's creative and methodological debt to da Cunha, although the extent of the debt is not recognized outside Brazil.[6] What Freyre saw in da Cunha in formal terms are techniques and elements that we would now consider in their heterogeneity, and hetero-glossian amplitudes, essentially "postmodern." Freyre detected the synthetic mind of a cultural bricoleur at work, before that term became theoretically fashionable. He demonstrates triumphantly how da Cunha opened a space for, or to use a fashionable phrase "gave permission" for, a new post-historiographical and satiric manner of writing through and within slavery's history. Yet Freyre was also, before everything else, a man of the North Eastern coast, specifically a man from Recife. Freyre consequently places his ultrafertile home territory in competition with da Cunha's mythologization of the North Eastern *sertão*, the burning, infertile, testing, semidesert of the interior. Freyre was a sensualist committed to a mythology of Brazil's miscegenetic fertility. In terms of his aesthetic sensibility, and his supposed anti-erotic agenda, da Cunha is consequently set out by Freyre as anathema to the energy and sexuality of Brazil's black coastal slave populations and the physical geography in which they exist.

One arm of Freyre's critique reached a climax in the discussion of *Os Sertões* in his book *Vida Forma e Côr*. This energized satiric assault includes charges that the geography da Cunha devoted himself to writing about is, in a larger Brazilian context, trivial. He quotes "the geographer John Casper's" harsh dismissal of da Cunha as a minor poet of a minor landscape: "The poet is sovereign in the little kingdom where his fantasy enthrones him." He refers to da Cunha's love of the arid landscape of the North East as "narcissistic," smirking at the picture of an author who "should have chosen to have had himself portrayed bony and Romantic beside the burning sand of the *sertões*." In what devolves into a rather shoddy ad hominem attack, da Cunha emerges as an increasingly absurd self-appointed apostle of aridity: "One might call him a martyr . . . the skinny awkward fellow, who seemed to have a thousand left hands and once bent a sword in a moment of rage." Da Cunha is reduced to a fanatical posing mystic, a sort of desiccated desert father, whose language is brutally stripped of the "qualities of discrimination and Romance" that typify the work of Machado de Assis and Joaquim Nabuco. And Freyre's final conclusion with regard to what he sees as extreme puritanical and mystical sensibility in da Cunha is that he is completely isolated from the sensuality and fertility of the Brazilian North East coast. Freyre concludes by setting up an imprisoning geographic binarism that is intensely gendered and sexualized. He asserts that "Euclides felt a kind of repugnance for what was rounded plenteous and full in the vegetation of the tropics and the landscape dominated by sugar plantations" and conversely was exclusively attracted "by what is angular, bony and rigid in the ascetic dryly masculine contours of the arid *agreste* and *sertões*." The charges extend into the very style as Freyre proclaims da Cunha to write "in words that are unyielding, words that hardly flow at all, words that are almost a-sexual."[7] By this point the charges have become absurdly exaggerated and reflect Freyre's divisive obsessions rather than da Cunha's remarkable prose. In fact, Freyre's continued engagement with da Cunha as stylist and aesthetician is not served well by the critique and went far deeper than this rather daft parody.

Freyre wrote a vast amount, but his reputation rests on the three huge and related studies of the impact of slavery on the development of Brazilian culture during and after slavery. The first volume was *Casa Grande e Senzala* (1933), translated as *The Masters and the Slaves* (1946); the second volume was *Sobrados e Mocambos* (1936), translated as *The Mansions and the Shanties: The Making of Modern Brazil* (1962); and the third volume, *Ordem e Progresso* (1959), translated as *Order and Progress: Brazil from Monarchy to Republic* (1970). The latter two books take the central insights of *Casa Grande* and follow them through Brazil's subsequent development. *Casa Grande* considers slavery most directly in terms that resonate with da Cunha, and indeed with the other authors I discuss within this book, and *Casa Grande* is Freyre's strongest text. The first part of the trilogy has generated by far the greater part of writing about Freyre in Europe and America. Given my focus on Freyre as a satirist and as the inheritor of a literary ambience around slavery that is peculiarly Brazilian, it is also relevant that *Casa Grande* is formally, stylistically, and technically the most experimental of the volumes.

Freyre has remained influential in diaspora studies but has never been easily assimilated within Anglo-American scholarship. Freyre's reputation abroad has steadily declined from the heady days during the middle decades of the twentieth century when he was championed, and indeed translated by Samuel Putnam, and when he became something of the darling of Latin American departments in the United States. Atlantic studies departments in North America and postcolonial departments in Europe have gently let him go. They have also gently mauled his remains in the process, and there is now something of a consensus that Freyre is not only unscholarly, but in terms of his sexual politics, misogynistic and fairly obnoxious. One reason academics have a problem embracing him is that as a deliberate formal disciple of da Cunha, Freyre remains hard to classify, indeed uncategorizable. Like da Cunha, Freyre did not write straightforward history, sociology, anthropology, or fiction, in any academically accepted definition of these fields. Yet I would argue that it is time to reassess his work. Despite his obsession with the sexualized mulatta and the celebration of miscegenation as a sort of unending productive colonial orgy, Freyre was creating something new and unbalanced, work that is not so much interdisciplinary as extra-disciplinary. He is also very funny, a deliberate satirist and ironist who delighted in playing games with his own narrational persona. He has recently fallen foul of North American theoretical responses that see him, understandably, as following unenlightened agendas around race and gender. Freyre's masterpiece *Casa Grande e Senzala* does not flow easily through the current political filters of Euro-American slave historiography or postcolonial theory. If, however, the book is considered as a development of certain tendencies of the Brazilian sensibility and read through the shadows cast by da Cunha, then its essential Brazilian-ness and its relation to slavery and sexual depravity becomes more understandable.

Casa Grande e Senzala is best read as a form of ingenious satire directed at the Brazilian sugar aristocracy and at race theory, a sort of sociological and inspired development of his fictional progenitors. The second of Freyre's big studies, *Order and Progress* in chronological terms covers the period of Brazil's move from monarchy to republic at the end of the nineteenth and beginning of the twentieth centuries. This is of course precisely the period through which da Cunha lived, and it is consequently in this work that Freyre takes da Cunha on in the most concrete ways. It is worth thinking through Freyre's insights because they reveal many of the wellsprings of da Cunha's power.

Brazil emerged into the twentieth century from slavery and the foundation of the New Republic as a divided and increasingly brutally racist nation. The evolution and fate of the Canudos community, so minutely anatomized by da Cunha, articulated with grim acuity this descent into an atavistic system of apartheid. What is not generally recognized outside Brazil is just how bad racism got, within Brazilian politics, in the first half of the twentieth century. Brazilian racism took acrid and vicious forms, and support of extreme negrophobe, eugenicist, and finally Nazi dogma became commonplace among the elite classes and was happily consumed in grotesquely simplified forms. It can be argued that Freyre's entire oeuvre is a hymn of joy in denial of nineteenth-century race dogma and the final excesses of Nazism. He also critiques the frightening directions in which Brazilian race theory veered during the decades immediately following abolition and leading into World War II. In this sense Freyre is a soul mate of the authors at the core of *The Black Butterfly*. He looks back to Alves's, and indeed Joaquim Nabuco's, profound and fervent respect for Afro-Brazilians. He commits to the heroic construction of Afro-Brazilianism that da Cunha finally managed to glance at but never embraced. He also provides a variant upon the intimacy between black and white cultures that, I have argued, Assis saw into and that is a part of slavery's inheritance. Miscegenation within Brazil was a specter that negrophobe race theory in the first half of the twentieth century tried to deny and stamp out. Freyre's race politics are in this sense a radical slap in the face for neo-Nazi race theory in Brazil. Freyre posits slavery as a social experiment, a miscegenetic process on a vast scale and of vast complexity. Such a social construction of slavery was, of course, the worst nightmare of the followers of extreme race theory in Brazil during the first half of the twentieth century.

Freyre's satiric insights are most strongly in evidence when he writes about sexuality within the slave household. There is no equivalent for Freyre's exuberant satiric voice within the historiographies of Anglo-American slavery, and yet there is much that his dark humor has inherited from his creative sources in Assis and da Cunha.

Historiographical Satire: Da Cunha's Formal Legacy for Freyre

Gilberto Freyre provided a panoramic vision of the development of the slave cultures of Brazil, and of their cultural fallout in post-emancipation Brazil. I would argue that it is also the case that Freyre's commitment to inventing energized and creative aspects of Afro-Brazilian culture is generated by a desire to write over da Cunha's profound terror of Africans and Africanism. The scale of his ambition as a surveyor of the evolution of Brazilian thought and culture, and the unpoliced, unpredictable, and playful nature of his thought, come directly out of the dark, skeptical, ludic qualities of da Cunha. Not surprisingly, Freyre's major work remains an ambiguous presence outside Brazil.[8] Yet Freyre's *Casa Grande*, when put in historical perspective, should be seen as a heroic refutation of brutal race dogma. These dogmas obviously found their fullest expression in Germany in the years 1930–1945, but they were also developed by Brazilian race theorists in a Latin American context in the period when Freyre's masterpiece was conceived, researched, written, published, and first widely read.

There is no point rehearsing the reactions of his critics at any length because this has already been done, and more importantly because they are to a large extent irrelevant to what I am trying to draw attention to.[9] I look to Freyre in this conclusion and to his masterpiece *Casa Grande e Senzala* because he operates outside the conventional filters of slave historiography and postcolonial theory as they have evolved in the Euro-American tradition. I look to him because he looks back to what is most confrontational and unusually challenging in the Brazilian creative and literary inheritance of slavery. Freyre is not, in the context of Creolization, what Richard Price satirically alludes to as a "proper historian." If Freyre is considered on his own terms as an artist, an aesthete, and above all a satirist, he emerges as umbilically linked to da Cunha.

The intermittent enthusiasm and exasperation that have greeted *Casa Grande* were inevitable given the ways in which processes of translation, retranslation, distortion, and ludic mayhem were inbuilt into the book from the beginning. Freyre was acutely—indeed, on the evidence of his unending prefaces and introductions to editions of *Casa Grande*, extravagantly—aware of his book as protean text, as paradigm bender, and as theatrical display. He did not see his work as history, sociology, or anthropology, in any academically accepted definition of the fields, and it is wise not to approach his writings as such now. Freyre was making something that, if one has not read *Os Sertões*, appears new, unbalanced, and in many ways inexplicable. If one has read da Cunha, Freyre appears as the inheritor and substantiator of a Brazilian way of composing national history. It is above all in his approaches to the undeniable entanglement of Brazil in the complexity and horror of its slavery inheritance that Freyre looks back to the trinity of authors discussed in the foregoing chapters.

Casa Grande—Academic *lusus naturae* or an *Os Sertões* of the *massapé*?

Let it be freely admitted that Gilberto Freyre appears methodologically bizarre, indeed crazily inappropriate, if set against the norms of contemporary historical slavery scholarship in North America and Europe. Exactly the same has been said of da Cunha's *Os Sertões*. Freyre continues to trouble and annoy those American-based academics who would categorize him. American scholars still tend to view with a certain sniffiness Freyre's patrician background, his private wealth, and his unconcern with academic institutions or their methods. David

Cleary is as bemused as any other commentator on where to place Freyre in terms of the forms and disciplines his work straddles, stating that the major work falls into "the grey area between social history, anthropology and sociology." He also comments on the wildly swinging nature of Freyre's critical reception inside and outside Brazil. Cleary suggests that Freyre is a decayed aristocrat writing unrigorously about the decay of the slave aristocracy: "Freyre's temperament was not suited to the kind of long-term primary research typical of the orthodox academic world he kept at arm's length all his life . . . he wrote about aristocracy, patriarchy and decline from the inside."[10] There is no gainsaying Freyre's flagrant unrespectability; yet the fact that he is not really an historian, in any accepted sense, must surely force us to ask—*what then is he?* The fact that he kept "the orthodox academic world . . . at arm's length" is surely no bad thing. That he could write "from the inside," like da Cunha and Assis, might generate unique strength and complexity.

Freyre is in terms of genre and methodology a satirist and parodist. These elements, almost wholly lacking from analysis of him to date, are as central to his method and his Brazilian cultural context as they are to the writing of da Cunha. When Freyre was maturing as a writer in the 1920s and 1930s, Brazil was developing a celebratory and satiric cultural environment that stood out against extant white elitist traditions of racism. The strong institutional, political, and intellectual traditions of eugenics and scientific racism had generated a counterculture, a celebratory popular culture. Within the flourishing art forms of music, votive art, *capoeira*, football, costume, and cuisine, Afro-Brazilian culture was prioritized in the ways we are now familiar with, globally, as essentially Brazilian. Freyre is to be understood as a satirist of the Brazilian slave patriarchy, who absorbed and contributed to contemporary emergent popular antiauthoritarian forms and who set these off against more elevated literary satire.

Freyre amalgamated these Brazilian contexts with the traditions of Anglo-American satiric literature in which he was deeply versed.[11] Finally, however, it is Freyre's full frontal celebration of Africanism, and his insistence on saturating his text with a weird and wonderful gallimaufry of Afro-Brazilian contributions to the national culture, which set him fundamentally apart from the monuments of European modernism, as well as the Anglo-American historiographies of the slave diaspora. In this sense he is a proto-Negritude intellectual, although he has not been seen as the soul mate of René Depestre and Aimé Césaire, any more than da Cunha has.[12] Freyre's embrace of Luso-Africanist Brazilian culture, so neglected when he wrote, and so patronized when it was not neglected, was finally and admirably motivated by a hatred of German Fascism.

Freyre's passionate concern to take Afro-Brazilianism seriously is, in many ways, motivated by his obsession with, and anger at, the perceived lack of such seriousness in the work of both da Cunha and Assis. Freyre's writing repeats again and again accusations concerning the absence of black Brazil in the imaginative worlds of Assis and da Cunha. I have already discussed Freyre's disapproving take on Assis's construction of his mixed-race background.[13] Freyre was also concerned to highlight da Cunha's negativity over the African presence in Brazil and goes so far as to accuse da Cunha of writing blackness out of *Os Sertões*. Da Cunha is constructed as focusing upon a primitive Brazil of the interior, a sort of dark chaotic space existing in precise contradistinction to the "enlightened" societies of Brazil's North Eastern coast. In *Order and Progress* Freyre summarized his position as follows: "*Os Sertões*, the monumental semi historical work by Euclides da Cunha, aroused both literary admiration for its author and political awareness of the problem it treated, the segregation of rustic populations and archaic structures of the *sertões* from the civilized populations and cultures of the Atlantic coast."[14] Freyre would continue to set the book out as a sort of brutal exotic specimen, which only appealed to Europeans because of the way it broke with the civilized norms of the Brazilian coastal cultures: "*Os Sertões* was probably the first Brazilian book to give Europeans a picture of rural tropical Brazil incorporating (along with virtues that exceed its many defects) a true spirit of the people and the setting which could be understood by Europeans as essentially different, bearing the mark of a culture and a destiny apart from European patterns." He went so far as to hold da Cunha out before his readers as a sort of brutal primeval force of nature, a furious figure who outraged Brazil's literary elite and their Francophile refinement. Da Cunha embodies "a nationalism with a feeling for the tropics which to the Francophiles [within the Brazilian white elite] seemed to connote bad taste, incontinent or inelegant language, primitivism of feeling and thinking, the genuine incapacity for *nuance* in the finer sense of the word—these are the very qualities which they found in abundance in Euclides da Cunha's *Os Sertões*."[15] Under Freyre's rhetorical wand, da Cunha emerges as a sort of defecating bestial literary yahoo, a wild man of the *sertão*.

When it comes to da Cunha's historical narrative, again and again Freyre sees it as a fiction intent on writing out the existence of the Afro-Brazilian. For example, Freyre talks of Canudos and its sizeable black population in the following terms:

> Some of these former slaves became nostalgic for the monarchy and the Princess Isabel, it is quite possible that such mal-adjusted ex-slaves were

among those who joined the rebellious whites and *caboclos* under Antonio Conselheiro in their uprising against the republican Army—an aspect of that struggle between soldiers and backlanders which seems to have escaped the notice of the engineer-sociologist Euclides da Cunha."[16]

Freyre quite simply accuses his great rival of ignoring the blacks, implying that this process of ignorance stems from the man's training and social position, and that he is merely an "engineer-sociologist," not a literary artist.

The Fascist Context for Brazilian Slavery Studies

It is not in the direct assaults on da Cunha, however, but in the more complex processes of Freyre's internalization of his great rival, that da Cunha's true worth to Freyre emerges. One might see the whole project of *Casa Grande e Senzala* as a dialogue with *Os Sertões*, and an attempt to redress da Cunha's perceived racism. *Casa Grande* was published amid fairly general unconcern in Brazil in 1933, the year Hitler came to power as chancellor in Berlin. The book was never, in terms of its interpretation or reception, a stable phenomenon. Its English-language publication in 1946, at almost the precise moment of Hitler's death, saw the book assimilated into a European consciousness forced to fuse trauma and race theory in humbled, raw, and terrified ways. Freyre's book had a unique timeliness that gave it a cultural charge now probably beyond the power of any single reader to recapture, or even comprehend. We now lack that historical memory. What did Auschwitz mean to Brazil, and what did Brazilian slavery and Afro-Brazilianism mean to Europe after the Jewish Holocaust? Was there any meaningful way to relate the disaster of the Jewish Shoah to the Black Holocaust of slavery in Brazil? The recent activities within Nazi Europe, and their global outfall, meant that from 1946 onwards academic historians across Central Europe and America were forced to think about race, and the sexual processes related to imperial formation, by using utterly new approaches. The old rule books of scientific racism, the brutish race tropes that as we have seen resurface frequently in *Os Sertões*, had led directly to the crematoria of the Lagers. Had they also led to the obliteration of Canudos? Was the thoroughness of its obliteration an act of ethnic cleansing? The period 1945–1950 saw intellectuals in Europe shattered, for the most part intellectually destabilized if not paralyzed over the whole miasma of race.

Because of his background and training, because he was a disciple of Franz Boas, but also deeply saturated in the protomodernism of Assis and the eccentric historiographical experiments of da Cunha, Freyre had fascinating, probably unique intellectual credentials when it came to writing about race theory and its relation to Europe, America, and Brazil. While studying at Columbia University where Boas was a visiting teacher, Freyre would have gained an unusual perspective on antiblack and anti-Semitic Anglo-American traditions of racist thought. Boas was a long-term enemy of German racism during, and well before, World War II. Yet Boas was also a committed critic of American racial theory. As early as 1894 Boas spoke out against racial prejudice. He was a personal victim of anti-Semitism, and he thought deeply about the comparative relation of antiblack and anti-Jewish systemic and institutional racisms in America.[17] Yet it was finally Boas's assimilationist arguments regarding, and celebrating, the ex-slave populations of North America that would have the most impact on Freyre's approach to black populations in Brazil, and to the overall strategy of *Casa Grande*. Although there is not space to go through Freyre's methodological debt to Boas in detail here, it might be forcefully argued that Freyre transported the central tenets of Boas's antiracist anthropology, focused upon the achievements of Afro-American cultures, to his study of Brazilian slave societies.[18] Boas might then be seen to inform the attitudes lying behind Freyre's take on da Cunha. Boas provided Freyre with the beginnings of a model for thinking about the cultural construction of the outfall of slavery in ways that valued black culture. Back in Brazil, Freyre was able to look down upon both European and North American racist traditions, and their vulgar but influential manifestations in his homeland. He was able to do this in large part because he could draw on such extraordinarily rich creative traditions as those developed by Assis and da Cunha.

Freyre's reading of slavery was shamelessly amalgamative, and it is above all the intimate social lives of blacks and whites under slavery that constitute a cultural revolution that grows richer over three hundred years. In celebrating the evolutionary positives of miscegenation, Freyre was taking on Hitler and the European racist codes he had fed off that fueled a generation of influential race theorists in Brazil. Hitler's race theory was founded in the false, and jaw-droppingly crude, assumption that nature operates a total ban on sexual miscibility:

> All the innumerable forms in which the life-urge of Nature forms itself are subject to one fundamental law—one may call it an iron law of Nature—which compels the various species to keep within the definite limits of their own life-forms when propagating and multiplying their kind. The titmouse cohabits only with the titmouse . . . the house-mouse with the house-mouse, wolf with the she wolf etc.[19]

From this position Hitler develops his thesis that any form of hybridizing has only one result, namely the sterility and degeneration of the offspring. If they interbreed, the strong and beautiful (Aryans) are always adulterated and ultimately destroyed by the weak and ugly, which in Hitler's analysis of human types are constituted by the Jew and the Black. The conviction that interracial sexual unions were fundamentally unnatural and led to the production of degenerate humans remained at the forefront of European and American, and indeed Brazilian, race theory in the first half of the twentieth century.[20]

Freyre, of course, not only defied the Nazis' obscene dogma of race but he provided a powerful theoretical counter to the orthodoxies of race and eugenic theory in his own country. The most influential figures to write on race in the context of Brazilian nation formation were Nina Rodrigues, *Os Africanos No Brasil* (The Africans of Brazil, 1933); *O animismo fetichista dos negros baianos* (The Animistic Fetishism of Bahian Blacks, 1935), and Oliveira Viana in *As Populações Meridionais do Brasil* (The Southern Populations of Brazil, 1920).[21] Yet it is important to see how far beyond this now relatively familiar Brazilian context, so conditioning in its view of black culture, Freyre was operating. Freyre suggests a Brazilian history of social and cultural formation in fundamental opposition to the inheritance of the entire European tradition of Aryan racism. He storms a phenomenal edifice, finally inhabited by Nazi Germany, but built by French, English, and German intellectuals since the late eighteenth century.[22] Freyre opens *Casa Grande* by celebrating the mingling of black ("Saracen") and Jewish peoples within the ethnographic mix of pre-Imperial Portugal. He continues by celebrating every aspect of interethnic hybridity within Brazil during the period of colonial slavery. According to Freyre, the relations between masters and mistresses; white children and their black slave playmates; white boys and girls and their black wet nurses and maids, who so often took the emotional place of the biological mother; white mistresses and their mulatto or *cafuso* servants; and white males and their varied female slave partners developed bonds of love and trust. Freyre argues that these emotional bonds often went beyond the artificial dynamics of European racist codes— codes that certainly were transplanted to the Brazilian intellectual elite, but according to Freyre never took root. For Freyre the great cities and plantations of the Atlantic seaboard constitute a finally triumphant social experiment that never stopped growing. What should be emphasized at this point is the historical context of *Casa Grande*. Scholars now acknowledge that Freyre was setting his stall out against early twentieth-century race theory in Brazil. What has not been seen is that more importantly his work had a global relevance, in that it was a passionate assault on fascist race theory and its all-too-practical results in Europe.

It is worth emphasizing at this point the extent to which Brazilian culture has elsewhere defined itself through its miscibility as a triumphant refutation of fascist race theory as evolved in Germany and then developed elsewhere in Europe and in North America. Consider for example Pedro Archango, the black autodidact cultural theorist, *capoeirista*, woman chaser, and devotee of *Candomblé* in Jorge Amado's novel *Tent of Miracles*, first published in 1969 as *Tenda dos Milagres*. This tremendous satire is devoted to the ridicule of North American humanities scholarship on slavery, and to the celebration of racial and cultural fusion in Salvador Bahia, for over a century the world's biggest slave port.[23] Yet the book is also a committed assault on institutionalized white Brazilian racism and its explicit links to Nazi race dogma. In 1942 Brazil first became seriously aware of the implications World War II might have for it. Up until this point the dictatorship of Vargas had attempted to remain neutral, despite populist support for the Allies. German U-boats began sinking ships off the Brazilian coast. Vargas gave permission for Allied bases to be built on the Brazilian coast closest to Africa, and German submarines then began serious assaults on Brazilian shipping, killing over six hundred Brazilians. In August 1942 Vargas's government declared war on the Axis powers. It is within this context that Amado's and Freyre's analysis of race theory needs to be read. It is also in this context that Freyre's suspicion of da Cunha's race politics as protofascist needs to be understood. At the opening of *Tent of Miracles*, as Pedro Archanjo collapses, he has one thing on his mind: remembering a statement made that night in a bar by a huge blacksmith, as they listened to American radio give details of the defeat of the Nazis. In this deeply tolerant and inspiringly Brazilian vision of progress, all humans are part of humanity and Brazilian racial miscibility stands up in all its beauty as a triumphant antithesis of the Nazi's dream state. Freyre adapts such an approach wholeheartedly, transplanting it back to the history of the plantations, and his method has great advantages over the Anglo-American interpretive traditions used to remember Atlantic slavery.

Freyre, da Cunha, and Brazilian Landscape as Satiric Continuum

Consideration of Freyre the satirist can take him, and us, into spaces hitherto neglected by Anglo-American scholarship. The dual characteristics of intimacy and satiric exaggeration lie at the heart of Gilberto Freyre's vision, and in methodological terms came straight out of a reaction to *Os Sertões*. He can come at slavery and sexual corruption from a variety of standpoints that are shocking and illuminating. Take for an opening example the following where Freyre seeks to articulate the fertility of the *massapé* of the North East—the earth that generated the first rush of sugar plantations. The effect is that of a caricature seemingly aware of its absurdity—celebratory and simultaneously self-deflating.

Freyre desires to destabilize the clichéd view of the North East backlands of Brazil as an inhospitable and arid desert, the agonized and testing symbolic landscape so typically the creation of Euclides da Cunha, and still a central cultural myth of Bahia. Freyre's first move is to provide a distillation of da Cunha's vision, a parody of the first hundred pages of *Os Sertões*. The summation of da Cunha's landscape aesthetic takes three sentences:

> Droughts and dry sands of the *sertões* crunching beneath one's feet; the harsh landscape of the *sertões* making one's eyes ache; the cactuses, the bony cattle and horses; the tenuous shadows like ghosts from another world fearful of the sun.[24]

Freyre wittily described da Cunha as "The El Greco of Brazilian Prose," a fanatic who transformed landscape into a form of spiritual torture that engulfs the human in infernal pain.[25] If the essential quality of this land is its dryness, its repulsiveness, and its infertility, then Freyre will set his alternative vision of the other North East, the *massapé*, in precise and exaggerated opposition to these terms. He will obliterate one extreme with another, a land saturated with moisture, fertility, a land of sucking uterine longing. "In this North East you can always see a patch of water: an arm of the sea, a river, a stream, a greenish lagoon, in this North East the water does what it will with the soft yielding earth."[26]

Freyre takes a simple cliché, the idea of a "fertile mother earth," and runs with it in weird directions. The descriptive compounds "mother-earth" and "fertile-soil" are exhausted metaphoric currency, yet Freyre brings them violently back to linguistic life via outrageous literalizing. His vision of the earth as black, female, and fertile rapidly becomes sexual: this mother earth is a voracious woman demanding sexual fulfillment and sexual relationships. Freyre's *massapé* becomes an oleaginous and saccharine landscape where plants, people, and earth drip with oil and sugar juices: "This is an oily North East where, on moonlit nights, a rich oil seems to stream from people and things; from the earth, from the black hair of mulattoes and caboclos, from the trees dripping with resin, from the water, from the brown bodies of men who work ... pressing the sugar cane." Colonization, and all that it has created, is presented as involved in a prolonged act of intercourse with the soil it both penetrates and is consumed by: "For four hundred years the *massapé* of the North East has been pulling into itself the sugar cane stalks, men's feet, the hoofs of oxen ... mango and jack-tree roots, the foundations of houses and churches; allowing itself more than any other land in the tropics to be penetrated by the agrarian culture of the Portuguese."[27] In Freyre's intensely eroticized vision, the land is not merely sweet and fertile, it is positively vaginal, and the mere act of walking on the moist black soil of the *massapé* becomes intimately sexual. The soil exists in a state of perpetual excitation and lubrication: "Nothing could be more different from the North East of hard-baked earth and arid sand than the other North East with its *massapé*, its spongy clay, its fatty humus. Here the earth is as sticky as honey, clinging to a man like a woman aroused."[28] How many English or American slavery historians have ever thought or written in such terms about the soil that sustained slavery? Freyre in his passion to create a countermythology to that of da Cunha's *Os Sertões* seems to have moved to a world of shifting realities more akin to Aleijo Carpentier or the tropical visions of Buñuel's *Death in the Garden* than to the canonical works of Anglo-American slavery historiography. This is quintessential Freyre, explosive, almost surreal, in competition with the imagistic and imaginative extremities of da Cunha, combining distortion with a disturbing and explicit naturalism, bringing his argument home through a visual and tactile prose that carries a forthrightly outrageous, even indecently direct, erotic charge.

This strangely intimate and grotesque approach to landscape description, and indeed metaphoric appropriation, is frequently the technique of both da Cunha and Gilberto Freyre when writing in their most extravagant manner of Brazilian racial admixture. This takes us full circle to my opening contention that intimate satire is one quality that lies at the heart of Brazilian cultural fictions of slavery, a quality that does not find powerful analogues in the slavery archives of England and North America.

La Guerra del fin del Mundo: Vargas Llosa's Dickensian Vision of *Os Sertões*

Moving from Freyre's competitive and agonistic engagement with the race agenda of *Os Sertões*, Vargas Llosa's approach to the same theme in *La Guerra del fin del Mundo* constitutes a contrary phenomenon. Jorge Mario Pedro, First

Marquis of Vargas Llosa, is a disciple of da Cunha who attempts to flesh out the lean spaces on race in *Os Sertões*. His fictional take constantly hovers around issues of race and sexuality, and he is concerned to take forward certain tensions, and to give a voice to silences, within da Cunha's text. The cultural mistranslation, misquotation, and deformation of da Cunha within this adaptation are educative because they reveal what is inimitable, valuable, and terrifying in da Cunha's art.

Mario Vargas Llosa's *La Guerra del fin del Mundo* was published in Spain in 1981 (and then under the title *The War at the End of the World* in America and Britain in 1984). It became a global best seller and, forced out through the modern mass marketing machinery of European and North American trade publishers, has sold vastly more copies than its source. Yet it is finally no exaggeration to conclude that this long work is a parody of *Os Sertões* that reinvents the master narrative in the form of historical fiction, or more precisely a grand historical novel in the tradition of Dickens's experiments attempting to reenact great social revolutions, *A Tale of Two Cities* and *Barnaby Rudge*. Indeed, *La Guerra* might be seen to stand in relation to *Os Sertões* in a similar manner in which *A Tale of Two Cities* stands beside an equally overpowering and inimitable model, Carlyle's *French Revolution*. *La Guerra* was Llosa's first, and he believed greatest, attempt at the genre of the grand historical novel. The project began as a commissioned film script for a Brazilian movie produced by Ruis Guerra. The film did not materialize, but Llosa was paid and sponsored to undertake long research trips in the backlands of Brazil before the project fell apart. He subsequently became obsessed with da Cunha's text, and indeed with Canudos as a social experiment. He developed his researches into the long novel, *La Guerra*.[29] The book made quite a splash in the English-speaking world thirty years ago; although now neglected, Llosa's experiment still provides important lessons. Llosa takes the structural bones of da Cunha's account of Canudos and layers onto this narrative skeleton the elements that, in the late twentieth century, were seen to constitute a saleable political fiction with then fashionably utopian socialist leanings. To write the history of the Canudos rebellion from the outside *in*, in Llosa's manner, has the danger of applying a normalizing glaze over all that is trivial and precarious, perverse and difficult, and more crucially a lot that is inimitably Brazilian, about da Cunha's vision.

Da Cunha took a small backlands revolt carried out mysteriously by people who did not fully understand what they were doing, and who were not understood when they did it. He erects a magnificent creative and essentially literary construct around the event, producing, in genre terms, a baffling text that evades labelling. *Os Sertões* is not a novel, or a formal or even chronicle history. Indeed, it is a work that continues to evade the critics, if a definitional label is required then C. S. Lewis's "tertiary epic" may be the most useful.[30] Da Cunha does unprecedented things with narrative and semiotics. He finds a new set of tools for making "history speak," for want of a better concept to indicate our creative consciousness of the past. Certainly he has very definite cultural and political agendas, but the peculiar nature of his professional training and the bitterness of his vision mean that art finally triumphs over politics and the narration of historical facts. Llosa takes *Os Sertões*, an innovative creation, something paradoxically tough yet all too fragile, and mutates it into a text that is reassuring. Canudos suddenly becomes familiarized, and is narrated with all the elements of clichéd romanticism and heroism necessary for a good page-turner. Llosa finally writes for, and under the shadow of, an Anglo-North American novelistic tradition, and the novel's spectacular success in translation in Europe and America would suggest that he has successfully written for a Euro-American readership. *La Guerra* finally emerges as, and indeed reads like, a standard North American historical novel with slavery and revolt as its central theme. William Styron's *Confessions of Nat Turner* would be a fitting analogue. Llosa provides a tamed and pleasing version of da Cunha, a big, safe novelistic creature that reassuringly wags its tail at a readership wanting to immerse themselves in a soggy, late-Romantic blockbuster with Latin American overlays of magic realism.

Llosa's work is concerned with containing and drawing the teeth of da Cunha. Canudos emerges within a recognizable narrative framework and language that is not finally all that Brazilian or even Latin American. Reading *La Guerra* is not difficult or in any way unsettling for an audience brought up on the tradition of the mainstream nineteenth-century novels of Europe and North America. *Os Sertões* has never enjoyed an equivalent readership outside Brazil, and this is because in so many ways it is linguistically and culturally untranslatable. Whereas Llosa is reassuringly Dickensian, or even Disraelian, to read da Cunha, according to the conventions of the novels of Dickens, Disraeli, Balzac, or even Dostoevsky, would result in the reader's complete dislocation. Under Llosa's imaginative control Canudos becomes a backdrop that enables a set of invented but formally over-familiar fictional personae to play out their life dramas. A cast of characters is developed out of the lurid outlines da Cunha indicated but never developed as conventional characters. *La Guerra* provides a set of people with recognizable, indeed predictable, appearances, speech patterns, thought processes, behavioral traits, psychological needs, and motivations. Nothing about their psychological makeup surprises; they operate within the sentimental narrative confines of the post-Dickensian novel. Like the characters in *Uncle Tom's Cabin* or *Gone with the Wind*, they are people who need to be cared about, looked after when they suffer, imaginatively nurtured when they feel insecure, imaginatively mourned when they die, above all empathetically projected onto and lived out by the reader. It is a perfect novel to turn into a Hollywood movie, and as noted it is important to remember that the whole project started out as a commercial film script. The disquieting mercurial prose of da Cunha, sometimes disembodied, sometimes overblown and baroque, sometimes forensic, sometimes scientific, sometimes quite simply and gloriously mad, is swept away and replaced by emotive dialogue, emotional relationships, logical motivations, and sentimentally charged interior monologues. Llosa's world is finally as much that of the soap opera script as of the novel. Llosa did a tremendous amount of commercially successful and astute writing for film and television, and this expertise shows at every turn of *La Guerra*. The text invites the reader in, it encourages, and works through, an easy variation on the willing suspension of disbelief. Integrity is consequently an issue with Llosa. Da Cunha writes the way he does because it is for him the only way of finally unearthing the mystery of Canudos. Along the way he gives an account of slavery's memory, showing how through paradox and indirection this dark shadow contaminates the continuing present of Brazilian national life. Da Cunha creates a world that constantly demands exclusion, objectivity, bewilderment, and cruelty. His imagination is capable of a proto-Borgesian imaginative fusion of forensic coldness and epiphanic vision, a fusion that, in its economy and intelligence, is alien to Llosa's way of thinking and writing.

As I have argued above, da Cunha creatively embraces the processes of his own bewilderment, and finally asserts that humans and their humanity are ridiculous and peripheral. Da Cunha has a Shakespearian capacity to communicate the sad truth that humans are perhaps most ridiculous and peripheral at their moments of greatest tragic intensity. He teaches the grim lesson that the only constants lie in the irrefutable cycles of nature, over time, for all time. Llosa offers us a very different artistic solution to Canudos; it becomes a conventionally scripted, failed, idealistic adventure.

Detailed critical comparisons of *Os Sertões* and *La Guerra* have been undertaken by several academics. These readings invariably construct the close relation between the two books as a serious case of "intertextuality," and as a dialogue revealing deep links within Latin American fiction. Some comparative interpretations devolve into a veritable literary love-in. Analysis can descend into the platitude of presenting an extended fictional family of Latino authors: "the two books create an inter-American inter-textuality and affirm a kinship among American nations based on the recognition of shared problems."[31] In fact these analyses reveal a lot about how Brazil was able to see itself and yet remains unseen in the wider contexts of Latin America. I don't, however, want to descend into discussions of the limitations of literary pan-Americanism if set against the exceptionality of Brazilian fiction here.[32] I want to focus on a single issue that criticism has so far not dealt with, namely that the essential formal and stylistic differences between Llosa and his source are at their most marked with regard to the representation of slavery.

Llosa uses Canudos as a grand setting for what is essentially historical romance. The whole work is built on the premise that there is a cast of characters the author and the reader identify with, believe in, as fully fleshed out psychological phenomena. The work also injects an element alien to da Cunha, namely romance, in the sense of sexual relationships, between the main characters. *La Guerra* revolves around a consistent fixation that is both *macho* and romantically sentimental, the sexuality of a mulatta *femme fatale*. His single significant female character, Jurema, is an object of obsession for four of the main male characters, and she is sexually involved with three of them. It is not enough to tell us what these people did, but we must be led into the minds of the protagonists. The reader is given detailed instructions as to why they do what they do sexually, and inevitably what they do in bed.

There is a constant pressure to involve the reader in the mimicry of the feeling of characters, to make us love, hate, laugh, and cry, in accordance with certain ready emotional prompts. Canudos as a historical phenomenon provides a ready-made landscape, and Llosa's job as storyteller is to people it with the old mannequins of Revolutionary theatre albeit transposed to the borrowed political theatre of a Brave New World. Llosa consequently creates a cast of characters familiar from the Conrad of *Nostromo* but not from the Canudos of da Cunha. And so Canudos becomes a sort of São Tome, with the spiritual silver mine of Antonio Conselheiro at its center, rather than the mineral silver of Charles Gould. Under Llosa's literary wand, the familiar cast of characters emerge. He "rounds up the usual suspects": a political idealist from Europe; a political journalist from Europe; an erotically magnetic, sexually voracious, and physically enduring, dusky "woman of the people"; a homegrown cynical, aristocratic political operator, complete with minions including a noble peasant doomed to follow the code of the backlands *sertanejo*; and a beautiful but mentally fragile wife. There is also a concomitant set of dodgy Latino military figures who might have come straight out of one of Sam Peckinpah's fruity Mexican extravaganzas. Indeed, as the novel moves to its conclusion there is more than a hint of *The Wild Bunch* about its violent pyrotechnics. The cast of Latino military males range from the good old pro, through the career opportunist, to the young innocent. At the heart of the plot lurks Conselheiro, a religious fanatic and spiritual guru with a host of weird and wonderful disciples. *Déjà vu* descends, a secondhand sense of the uncanny fogs things up, a feeling descends of having met all these characters before, many times, in many ways, maybe in more than one television miniseries.

The cast is strangely timeless; they could be acting out their agonies and ecstasies in Renaissance Florence under the aegis of Irving Stone, or in Ancient Egypt under the aegis of Norman Mailer, or early Christian Rome under the aegis of Gore Vidal. All their little souls could be shown rising in Revolutionary Haiti under the aegis of Madison Smartt Bell, or in the British slave trade under the direction of Barry Unsworth, or, as hinted above, in rural Virginia under the control of William Styron and his oddly queer slave rapist Nat Turner. Brazil provides an exotic location, a set of local colors and flavors that provide the latest costume for a theatrical company, which has been touring the literary imagination of Europe and North America for two hundred years with its version of slavery. What has gone is the unsettling essence of da Cunha, the contradictions, the emotional opacity, the utter weirdness. There is none of da Cunha's coldness about things that should be emotionally charged, or sustained passion about things that are normally ignored and even dead—the color and constitution of soil, a cactus, a dried dead horse.

Because da Cunha did not write a sentimental novel, there are huge and inevitable parts of the machinery of historical fiction that Llosa must import to make his soap opera operate. Foremost among them, as indicated, is love interest. Da Cunha isn't much concerned with romantic love, let alone explicit sex. In fact, he doesn't care a fig for the tender human emotions, which as we have seen infuriated the sensualist imagination of Gilberto Freyre. Because the core of Llosa's narrative is given over to the effects his backlands mixed-race beauty Jurema has on the lives of a series of men, he writes utterly outside the emotional theatre of his original. The motley crew of lechers includes the character referred to as the "near sighted journalist," a thinly disguised and increasingly ludicrous representation of da Cunha himself (Llosa's revenge on da Cunha no doubt for being so unsexual and intellectually ambiguous, not to mention a far greater writer). Every major male character either rapes Jurema or would like to rape her—there is a lot of enthusiastic rape in this book. There is not a single description of rape, graphic or otherwise, in *Os Sertões*. Da Cunha has much more disconcerting and ambitious ways of coming at the articulation of extreme abuse.

So what of slavery in *La Guerra*? The opening chapters of Llosa's novel seem, on the face of it, committed to doing what the critics say da Cunha does not do, namely to tackling the issue of slavery and Canudos head on. Llosa's primary technique for the transformation of the Canudos narrative into a novel lies in the creation of a series of central stock characters, one of whom is a black slave. The first hundred pages of the book incorporate a series of mini personal narratives introducing the central protagonists, the majority of whom will develop into the key disciples of Conselheiro. This is one of the few areas where Llosa is on his own, without the guiding hand of da Cunha. Da Cunha spends a lengthy section of his narrative analyzing the character, life, and mythology surrounding Conselheiro. His primary motivation is to write the man off as an eccentric and fanatic, who happened to provide a focus for a set, or rather series of subsets, of aggrieved people. Outside this debunking of the myth of Conselheiro, da Cunha has very limited interest in the construction of character, literary or historical, when it comes to Conselheiro's disciples. As the earlier analysis reveals, there are some exceptions, most notably the figure of the messianic mulatto Antonio Beato, or Pious Anthony. In an important sense, however, this figure is merely an adjunct to, or avatar of, Conselheiro. Beato is a mixed-race extension of the aberrant religious fetishism of his leader. Otherwise the interest that da Cunha has in the creation of characters is limited to the military leaders of the various official expeditions sent out against Canudos. So while da Cunha provides a detailed blueprint for various soldiers, most notably the charismatic, brutal, and finally ineffective Colonel Moreira (blueprints that Llosa shrewdly grasps and expands), da Cunha does not provide an equivalent for the military leaders of Canudos.

Llosa's solution is to seize upon the fragmentary references to notable characters that do emerge, and to use these as seeds out of which to cultivate his major cast. The construction of Conselheiro is buttressed by five primary disciples, a pentagon of characters who hold the novel's plot together. The first is a female ascetic and religious fanatic who finds no analogue in da Cunha. The second is a figure called "the little blessed one," loosely based on the Antonio Beato of *Os Sertões*. Yet because Llosa does not make him a mulatto, an element crucial to da Cunha's construction of the figure, he is consequently shut out from the slave and Africanist debates so central to *Os Sertões*. The third is a nod to magic realism and the grotesque, a deformed dwarf with leonine head who walks on all fours and says and does strange things. This freak comes out of the blue, as if he is an extra drafted in from the pro-colonial excesses of Werner Herzog's *Cobra Verde*. The other two figures, João Grande and Pajehú, are two of the most important military leaders within Canudos and are both developed out of set-piece vignettes in *Os Sertões*, vignettes I have already discussed in detail above because of their relation to da Cunha's slavery and race agendas. In Llosa's narrative only the figure he terms "Big João" is seen as relating directly to Brazilian slavery. Pajehú is not presented as a *cafuso* and so his particularly charged racial characteristics are not carried through from the source. When it comes to João Grande/Big Joe, da Cunha's figure suddenly appears, carries out a brief and deadly attack, and disappears, apparently obliterated, literally blown to pieces. He might be read as an incarnation of guerrilla warfare as a literary tactic. Llosa's development of this figure is far more elaborate, and in many ways defines the gulf of understanding and of method that separates da Cunha and Llosa over the memory of slavery.

Where da Cunha is explicit about writing the slaves, as literary characters, out of his narrative, Llosa, with his metropolitan, liberal, global political agenda, is vague and confused, but he really feels obliged to create empathetic big black slaves. There are fragmentary references to the presence of ex-slaves among Conselheiro's followers. The only major full-frontal engagement with this aspect of Brazilian history is the figure of João Grande. Where da Cunha gives a strangely opaque vignette, glazed with a thick rhetoric of racism, but saturated at its core with an inexplicable terror and incomprehension of the black slave, Llosa creates something altogether more familiar and reassuring. The transformation is worth considering in more detail for it places Llosa's imaginative take on the revolutionary slave consciousness alongside other normalizing, and in race terms deeply compromised, North American interpretations.

The Fleshing out of João Grande: A Test Case for Llosaian Re-familiarity

João Grande, one of the close followers of Conselheiro, is a figure granted an individual minibiography at the opening of Llosa's text. Big João is introduced as the product of an inspirational protoeugenic breeding experiment conducted by Sir Adalberto de Gumúcio, a slave-owning patriarch. The slave owner prides himself on being able to breed black slaves with the same precision with which he hybridizes horses. In the account of Jorge Mario Pedro, First Marquis of Vargas Llosa, the voice of a disembodied narrator elides uneasily into that of the slave-owning breeder. Big João, and indeed his nameless mother, are described by this unreliable omniscient narrator in racist and knowingly nasty terms: "The product born of the mating was undeniably magnificent. The boy had very bright, sparkling eyes and teeth that when he laughed filled his round blue-black face with light. He was plump, vivacious, playful and his mother—a beautiful woman who gave birth every nine months—suspected that he would have an exceptional future."[33] The infant Big João is brought into the *casa grande* from the sugar fields and reared as a pet by the patriarch's unmarried sister Adelinha. The boy, having grown up mollycoddled by the doting spinster, but cut off from all meaningful contact with his mother, is trainable only up to a point, and shows wild and violent behavior. His refusal to become a cultured pet is catastrophically celebrated when the physically advanced boy, having been entrusted to drive Adelinha to a convent, brutally murders her. The account strives for the narrative power of da Cunha's curt sarcasm when dealing with the atrocious things that humans can do to one another, apparently for no clear reason. Yet again, however, there is narrational confusion as to the controlling voice. Llosa gives the narration purportedly through the eyes of the only surviving witness, a small, black slave boy named with a painful, indeed risible, attempt at symmetry, Little João:

> Big João had subjected Adelinha to a thousand evil acts. He had stripped her naked, and laughed at her as she covered her breasts with one trembling hand and her privates with the other, and had made her run all about, trying to dodge the stones he threw at her as he heaped upon her the most abominable insults that the younger boy had ever heard. Then he suddenly plunged his dagger into her belly and once she was dead vented his fury on her by lopping off her breasts and her head. Then, panting, drenched with sweat, he fell asleep alongside the bloody corpse. Little João was so terrified that his legs buckled beneath him when he tried to run away . . .[34]

The last line suggests that Llosa wants us to read this as the terrified testimony of a slave boy, who knows as a witness to a crime he is inevitably to be executed. Yet in the rest of the passage when it comes to describing the violence the language is tired, the excessive use of useless adjectives is melodramatic and lacks a power to shock. Llosa has no language for the description of intimate violence, only the language of sham—tired adjectival compounds and the clichéd verbs of bad journalism predominate: "a thousand evil acts," "one trembling hand," "the most abominable insults," "plunged his dagger," "vented his fury," "drenched with sweat," "bloody corpse."

When Llosa attempts to enter the mind of his slave-murderer, the results are equally shallow. The psychological explanation of Big João's activity is banal, boiling down to stereotypical defensive platitudes invariably wheeled out by the masters, namely, extreme religious mania. Here Big João's action is explained specifically in terms of demonic possession. When Little João finally asks Big João what motivated him to carry through the atrocity, the following dialogue results: " 'Why did you kill the mistress?' 'Because I've got the Dog in me,' Big João answered immediately. 'Don't talk to me about that any more.' The Kid thought that his companion had told him the truth."[35] Does Llosa think that he has told us the truth as well? The revelation that Big João has made a pact with the devil is again narrated ambiguously, supposedly through the eyes of Little João as he travels on with the murderer, but the uncertain voice of a less-than-omniscient narrator hovers yet again in the wings:

> He [Little João] was growing more and more afraid of this companion of his since childhood, for after the murder of their mistress, Big João became less and less like his former self. He scarcely said a word to him, and, on the other hand, he continually surprised him by talking to himself in a low voice, his eyes blood shot. One night he heard him call the Devil "Father," and ask him to come to his aid. "Haven't I done enough already Father?" He stammered, his body writhing. "What more do you want me to do?" The Kid became convinced that Big João had made a pact with the Evil One and feared that in order to continue accumulating merit, he would sacrifice him as he had their mistress.[36]

Llosa gives no evidence throughout the novel that he has any knowledge of cultural forms of resistance and rebellion, which were developed within the variegated slave cultures of Brazil. The explanation here is a sociological dead end: Big João murders because he is a very predictable Catholic Satanic servant. The development of the complex hybrid Afro-Christian religions of the slaves offered variegated and ingenious methods of contaminating and defusing white power structures, but in the later nineteenth-century seaboard these did not generally consist of confrontation and atrocity. The random murder of a white woman closely related to a slave owner by a personal slave in mid-adolescence would have been an act with massive repercussions within the slave community. It would have been unlikely, indeed virtually impossible, for an unbalanced juvenile with violent propensities to have got as far as Big João. He would have been taken in hand by the other house slaves and brought into line, evicted and returned to the sugar fields, or indeed executed, long before he hacked up the spinster. The fallout from Big João's murder of a white woman would have been colossal; the owner of the plantation would have used torture and extreme retribution in response to the murder. It was the knowledge of the consequences of slave rebellion, and the innate complicity within the privileged community of the house slaves, that prevented such things as Big João's murder happening. Slaves, male and female, did indeed murder white women within the plantation household, but carried out the actions slowly, cleverly, undetectably, using poison and magic.

But even passing over the unfeasible nature of the crime, Llosa seems determined to refuse Big João volition or agency. The murder is not presented as an act of rebellion or even revenge, but as an act of madness. Big João acts under the delusion that he is possessed by the Evil One. With his bloodshot eyes, crazy monologues, and blood lust, he is closer to the mechanics of a Hammer horror film, or *Candyman*, than to the forces that led to the formation of the Canudos rebellion. It is at the point, the single point, where Llosa attempts to introduce the subject of slavery that, paradoxically, we are taken the furthest from it. Big João, wandering undetected for years in the backlands, chances to hear Conselheiro speak. Bang! He is immediately converted from good to evil. His discipleship is presented as founded in the ecstatic mists of a Constantinian-style Christian conversion, the sinner saved in a shattering experience combining joy and remorse. The idea that Big João might have carried out the murder as an act of calculated rebellion, as the first blow in a war of liberation, is never presented as a fictional option. Indeed, through the rest of the text Big João is presented as the broken and faithful dog, who feels perpetually unworthy to be in the presence of Conselheiro and who must find a way to redeem himself from his sin of carving up a white woman. The writing presenting this relationship is sentimental in the extreme, and stylistically overblown:

> The Counselor took Big João's two hands and obliged him to lift his head. The saint's incandescent pupils stared into the depths of the ex-slave's tear filled eyes. "You are still suffering Big João," he said softly. "I'm not worthy to watch over you," the black sobbed.[37]

"One must have a heart of stone to read the death of *little Nell* without laughing," quipped Oscar Wilde, and you need a heart of stone not to laugh at the conversion of Big João. Amazingly there is no evidence of comic irony here, the exaggerated emotionalism again marked by excessive adjectival compounds ("incandescent pupils," "tear filled eyes"). The ex-slave, it seems, has moved from one form of earthly bondage to a new form of neo-spiritual bondage. In finding Conselheiro, he has found his new master, he has entered a voluntary servitude, and he has fallen back in line; there will be no random murder of female authority figures this time round. When the final battle in Canudos arrives, Big João is presented as a central figure organizing defensive skirmishes. Llosa's farewell articulation of the ex-slave's state of mind shows him slipping in and out of different states of consciousness (these flashbacks are an essentially filmic device). Big João attempts to escape the horrors of war via pastoral fantasy, rather in the manner of Russell Crowe and his manly fingertips caressing rippling wheat at the start of Ridley Scott's *Gladiator*. The fantasy he is given does, however, possess a certain charge for Big João does not recess into a vision of ecstatic and escapist freedom, but into a landscape that expresses the desire to reenter the slave culture. Staring at the vast canon that incessantly bombards Canudos, Big João is shown falling into the following dream vision: "And all of a sudden Big João sees before him in a peaceful dream . . . the white sea foam. The scent of cane fields, of fresh molasses, of crushed cane, perfume the air."[38] In this extraordinary lacunae Llosa presents the ex-slave's ideal fantasy as a return to the slave crop ("cane fields"), and indeed the processes of the sugar factory ("fresh molasses," "crushed cane"). This flight of fancy exposes a suppressed agenda behind Llosa's text, for when it dares to introduce the theme of slavery it unknowingly enforces traditional master–slave relationships. What is perhaps even more interesting is the manner in which the text operates a cultural apartheid with regard to blacks and the memory of slavery, which is far more persistent than that of da Cunha. There are very few places in the text where Llosa deals with the presence of slave rebels and fugitives within the social makeup of Canudos. It is highly significant that when the presence of mulattoes and of *Candomblé* ritual does register in the discussion of the evolution of Canudos, Llosa introduces a theory of voluntary segregation on the part of the blacks that curiously mimics apartheid:

> As they came into being each narrow winding street was given the name of a saint, in a procession . . . Many of the newcomers took new names, thereby symbolizing that a new life was beginning for them. But sometimes dubious customs were grafted upon Catholic practices, like parasitic plants. Thus, certain mulattoes began to dance as they prayed, and it was said that they believed that by stamping their feet on the ground in a frenzy they were flushing out sins from their bodies with their sweat. The blacks gradually grouped together in the northern section of Canudos, a block of mud and straw huts that later became known as the *Mocambo*—the Slave Refuge.[39]

There is no account of such a separate *mocambo*, or slave refuge, within Canudos in da Cunha's or any other account. Why the black ghetto, a sort of proto-*favela* of "mud and straw huts" within but also without Canudos, should be named the *mocambo* only "later," presumably after the downfall of Canudos, is not explained and makes no sense. My earlier close readings reveal da Cunha has a complex set of conflicting agendas around Africanist syncretic religion. Given that Canudos was a protosocialist agrarian commune, and that the inhabitants shared not only the religious vision of Conselheiro, but a fundamental camaraderie based in the need to survive through sharing, internal factionalization was anathema to the entire social structure of Canudos. Llosa appears as a good old South American white Catholic boy, and seems to consider blacks and their *Candomblé* ritual and beliefs as an invasive, indeed culturally destructive element. Slave religion is curiously assessed as "dubious" when set against the purity of Catholicism. Conselheiro's Catholicism was, in the vision of da Cunha, itself hybrid, and extremely politicized, if indeed it constituted a form of Catholicism at all. Da Cunha outlines the extent to which Afro-Brazilian cult religion could be easily, and indeed centrally, absorbed into the commune. Da Cunha goes so far as to detail the extent to which what he sees as African fetish religion fuses into, and even eroticizes, the ceremony of Cunudos's religious ritual in ways embraced by all. Llosa's take on religion is, in comparison, completely orthodox and conservative. The African cult element is metaphorically constructed as a "parasite" feeding on the apparently healthy body of the host, the true faith, Catholicism. Such religious revisionism based in the maintenance of a strict sectarian approach to the religion of the slaves and of the masters underlines the profound fear present in Llosa when it comes to Africanity. He separates out and marginalizes black slave religion within Canudos, physically isolates the slave presence within a fanciful *mocambo*, and presents slave-evolved fetish religion as a corrupting and apparently fatal parasite greedily sucking up the Catholic Church. Llosa's take on the religion of the rebels here is a retrograde approach to racial categorization rooted in an inability to question the basic structures evolved by whites to contain their fear of blackness. It is precisely in the interrogation and finally destabilizing of such basic structures that *Os Sertões* is rooted.

Conclusion

The Black Butterfly thinks through how three great Brazilian literary artists explored the effects of Atlantic slavery—a crime against humanity and a gargantuan moral evil—that existed legally for four hundred years. Alves, Assis, and da Cunha in their starkly different ways all wrote against the grain of extant Euro-American antislavery propagandas. All three authors envisioned slavery (in Alves's case prophetically) as a process that in its social and economic operations did not end when Princess Isabel picked up her jewel-encrusted quill in 1888 and signed some renowned paperwork. All three writers ingested the bitter truth that slavery remained in the blood and being of Brazil and Brazilians, and that its cultural aftermath lived on throughout the Atlantic diaspora. All three saw that slavery constituted an agonized living inheritance, and this inner vision makes them very modern and creatively vivacious when they might so easily have been belated and flogging a politically, morally, traumatically, and aesthetically dead horse.

Alves, Assis, and da Cunha emerge as writers who take on slavery and moral paralysis, slavery and bourgeois disillusion, and slavery and fictional mendacity. They saw in their diseased and dying subject creative openings that the cultural resources of other major slaving nations had avoided. Castro Alves has a capacity for illogical incandescence and for inhabiting suffering that finally puts him close to Rimbaud, if European analogies are to be sought. How often does he undercut his own indignation with something completely off-whack that takes us to that *Bateau Ivre* of the young French lyrical genius and creative misfit? With Assis we get a Brazilian developing, in the context of urban slavery in fin de siècle Rio de Janeiro, unexpected critiques of exhausted and corrupted white bourgeois civilizations that run in parallel with those developed by Joyce in *Dubliners* and large parts of *Ulysses*, and in Flaubert's *Madame Bovary*. But Assis also has an emotional mainline into the ultimate sufferings of those who are outside power and beneath recognition by those with power. In this sense he is closer to the Russian sensibility working through the coruscation of *serfdom*. Assis writes of the slave with a combination of distance, infinite subtlety, and sudden jabs of candor that suggest Chekhov's technique when it comes to explaining, in psychological terms, what slavery does to humans, both slaves and slave owners. In da Cunha we get a version of the Brazilian hyperintellectual generated by nineteenth-century industrialization, science, and literary art. It is as if nothing is beyond the man. He embraces popular fictions, folklore, engineering, natural history in all its branches, geology, theology, syncretic religion, and as Borges pointed out so skillfully in a footnote to his story "Three Versions of Judas," maybe above all heresy, and not just of a theological brand.[1]

The aftermath of Brazil's saturation in the slave trade, plantation slavery, and the slave systems within urban centers has persisted, and still persists, in unacknowledged ways. The same conclusion could be drawn in relation to the inheritance of Atlantic slavery in North America and the major European slaving nations. Slavery's social and cultural legacy has been deeply internalized as a living emotional nexus, and is profoundly disguised or camouflaged as a parasitic or symbiotic phenomenon. The majority of literary art generated in Europe and North America during the last phases of slavery and the first phases of its abolition are crudely drawn, sentimental, or empathetic projections generated by a desire or pressure to assuage white guilt over slavery and to superscribe an optimistic philosophy of ignorance. This is a generalization but I think it holds up, for we are dealing with a creative legacy sunk in a persuasive, maybe immovable, fiction. This fiction insists that not only slavery but the memory of slavery died at the moment of legally tendered emancipation. I have tried to expose the terrifying pervasiveness of this fiction at great length, from many angles, through many books, over many decades. It took a long time for American writers to realize that slavery's memory was vivacious and indestructible and that the legacies of slavery were dark and parasitic constructs, still very much alive beyond the myth of the Emancipation Moment. William Faulkner's *Absalom, Absalom!*, Toni Morrison's *Beloved*, and maybe even some parts of Eldridge Cleaver's *Soul on Ice* and Gayle Jones's *Corregidora* (I am thinking particularly of the Brazilian flashbacks) aesthetically reopened slavery's most perverse wounds and the intimate ambiguities its history and memory twisted around. One thing *The Black Butterfly* demonstrates is that Brazilian literary art had moved into similar although distinct memorial terrain much earlier. Indeed, Brazilian writers operating before the abolition moment of May 1888 elaborately and precisely instruct how slavery must and will live on as a cultural legacy.

The works that form the focus for *The Black Butterfly* may contain elements of melodrama and sentiment that glance back at earlier Anglo-American abolition literatures of slavery. For the most part, however, they are based in subtle and powerful strategies for interrogating, destabilizing, deconstructing, and finally overturning the sentimental tradition of abolition propaganda to which Brazil's literate population was exposed and that in much of its popular abolition publication it internalized. A viewing of Steve McQueen's crowd-pleasing *Twelve Years a Slave*, strutting its stuff with its alpha male cast list, demonstrates triumphantly and with a sort of watertight and immense precision how stable and immovable the ideological juggernaut of the myth of the Emancipation Moment remains. Why this stuff has a global profile as a useful analysis of "the horrors of slavery," while the cinematic genius of Aleia's *Ultima Cena* (*Last Supper*) or Gilo Pontecorvo's equally challenging *Queimada* (*Burn*) do not, is equally educative and bewildering. Both of these works of cinematic genius were produced by Marxists who worked with the diasporic populations of the Caribbean. Both films focused upon slave insurrection, and indeed upon doomed slave heroism in the face of abortive slave insurrection. These facts might have something to do with the way Europe and America have refused to take these difficult masterpieces into the memorial mainstream while the irrepressibly "feel-good" and sentimentally celebratory *Amistad* and *Twelve Years a Slave*—and come to that Quentin Tarantino's *Django Unchained* for all its gloss of revolutionary violence—are so heartily embraced.

This book ends by maintaining its focus on Brazilian cultural *difference* over slavery's memory. I realize that the way this book is structured raises the constant dangers of cherry-picking and star-gazing. The Brazilian literary choice-fruit that lie at the stellar core of *The Black Butterfly* could be seen as merely exceptional. The unique elements in the work of my Brazilian authorial trinity are at risk of being artificially isolated or overemphasized. Yet Alves, Assis, and da Cunha, while each remains quite unique in their creative takes on slavery, were not completely detached from the rest of Brazilian culture. These writers can be considered as a magnificent tripartite keystone at the apex of a wider Brazilian slavery literary *zeitgeist*.

The Black Butterfly is dedicated to explaining that what was unique about my three exceptional Brazilian writers was the subtlety, thoroughness, and originality with which they came at the ironizing of slavery and the parody of the Anglo-American abolition tradition. The power of their achievement is, however, part of a bigger creative experiment that happened in Brazil during the final decades of legal slavery, and that can be better understood by setting these individual achievements against other illuminating texts predating them. There is not space for a full contextualizing discussion here—that would take another book. It is fitting to end this study by gesturing towards two remarkable figures at the heart of Brazilian antislavery thought, agitation, and literary art—Joaquim Nabuco and Luís Gama. Both men are remembered in Brazil primarily for their long-term, hands-on, and terrific activism and agitation during the height of the abolition struggle. I want to end by arguing that both figures also deserve recognition both inside and outside Brazil purely for their quality as literary writers. I also want to stress that their literary achievements, and particularly the work of Gama, were carried through in the context of a slave and abolition culture that produced absolutely no autobiographical slave narrative, as defined by the North American tradition and models. I consequently devote a portion of the discussion to thinking about why this extraordinary aporia exists. This part of the discussion necessitates a detailed treatment of the misreading of the only text claimed to constitute a Brazilian slave narrative, namely the *Biography of Mahommah G. Baquaqua*.

Gama and Nabuco could not have come from more diametrically opposed backgrounds. Nabuco was a very white Pernambucan aristocrat of Luso-Brazilian lineage whose family were plantation owners and part of the slaveholding elite. Gama was an Afro-Brazilian mulatto from Bahia, who was, at the age of ten, cynically sold into slavery as part of a debt-clearing operation by his white father, as a result of which he was torn from his adored black mother. Both men threw up quite new formal and aesthetic ways of thinking slavery through in written words. Nabuco was an antislavery polemicist and biographical mythographer of genius; Gama was a poet and satirist of genius. Both of them wrote in ways suggesting that Alves, da Cunha, and Assis, even at what might seem to a European or American reader their most extraordinary and experimental, were very much of their time and place. It is also worth adding that both Nabuco and Gama, while revered as political activists, remain almost unknown outside Brazilian literary and historical studies as literary figures and as vital creative precursors to the authors focused on in *The Black Butterfly*. My final act in this book is consequently to put on display a sample of Gama's and Nabuco's beautiful and horrifying writing on slavery with the hope that they may gain some recognition, and indeed familiarity, in the English-speaking world. Both authors demand more serious treatment as creative forerunners who essentially laid down many of the key aesthetic criteria that future writers would creatively negotiate when confronting the terrifying terrain of Brazil's slavery inheritance.

Nabuco, Assis, Wordsworth, and Slavery's Transmogrifying Paternalisms

Brazil's greatest, most idolized, and internationally best-known antislavery polemicist was Joaquim Nabuco. Nabuco was an old-school Brazilian noble, a privileged product of a slave-owning elite, brought up on a plantation in

Pernambuco. Yet as a young man he traveled to Europe, living mainly in London but spending significant periods in Paris and also living briefly in Rome. He also lived in North America, and thought deeply about its responses and activities around slavery and the Civil War and how these might relate to Brazil. He was fascinated as to why Brazil had never come close to descending into Civil War over the resolution of the slavery issue. He internalized Europe's cultures and its political philosophies at a profound level. He also thought deeply about Brazil's position within a much greater Pan-American historical experiment. He returned to Brazil a passionate, articulate, and ingenious propagandist determined to fight to end Brazilian slavery. In many ways he has been reduced, in the popular historiography of Brazilian abolition, to the equivalent of William Wilberforce in Britain, William Lloyd Garrison or even Abraham Lincoln in North America, or Victor Schoelcher in France. The huge difference, of course, the one thing that makes his core relationship to human bondage quite distinct, is that Nabuco was brought up as an infant by slaves. Nabuco suckled from a black wet nurse, his blood was quite literally formed out of the transformed blood of black, female slaves. He was intimately enmeshed in the process of slavery in ways the white American and European abolition luminaries were not.

Nabuco, as his fame and career both as a writer and politician evolved, was steadily internalized by the Brazilian elite. He increasingly brooded over Brazilian slavery as a vast paternal benevolent national conscience. He was projected as "a friend of the black," a lover of the slave, a father of abolition, a symbol of progressive enlightenment, a passionate Pan-American, a man of letters, a public intellectual, and quite literally a global ambassador for the new Brazilian Republic. Unlike many North American and European abolitionist celebrities, Nabuco thrived after the end of slavery. Becoming Brazil's most globally celebrated statesman, he died as Brazilian Ambassador to the United States in 1910. After a funerary procession in Washington, his body was brought back to Rio, where a vast crowd of tens of thousands followed his coffin's passage through the streets, and he was then given a state funeral in his hometown of Recife. The photographs in the Nabuco family collection recording the enormous crowds and processions at these events give some sense of the great public love for him.[2] He was famous enough to be merchandised: cigar brands, beer cans, and a host of other consumables were emblazoned with his magnificent mustachioed countenance. He became a popular myth, larger than life, a hero to worship, to market, and to consume. Gliberto Freyre, so often so profoundly in tune with the cultural heartstrings that make Brazilian reactions special, observed that the "extension of literary ideas to non literary or even illiterate Brazilians, is not rare in Brazilian history." He pursued this insight by seeing Nabuco as a perfect exemplar of the process: "For example, Joaquim Nabuco, as an abolition writer became so popular as to be considered almost a folk hero."[3] This public Nabuco-ian chimera, benign, reassuring, white, male, safely dead, does not seem engaged with the terror and horror of slavery; indeed the creation seems to shut this terrifying area of history down, to stitch it up.

Yet there is another Nabuco within the writing, an agonized yet ludic imaginary encased in his written work. His writings, even his most famous book *A Abolição*, reveal a mind imbued with many of the deeply skeptical and profoundly realistic insights into the continued life of slavery within the soul of the Brazilian nation that permeate the works of Alves, Assis, and da Cunha. Late in life Nabuco, like many political celebrities, wrote an autobiography, *Minha formação* (recently translated as *My Formative Years*, but more accurately rendered as "My Formation," "My Becoming," or "My Evolution"). Yet unlike the vast majority of autobiographies by celebrities, this is a most sensitive and coruscatingly honest work. In many ways it is an antibiography or deconstructed autobiography. It is, much like the writings of Assis and da Cunha, both a structurally and linguistically destabilizing text, and reading it is a confusing experience. The book generates a sense of literary vertigo. Nabuco knowingly created a wolf in sheep's clothing. Initially he seems to set out a narrative upholding the popular myths generated around him as public figure, as Pan-American theorist, and as Europhile intellectual. Yet the book is not chronologically arranged, and this is done in order to spring a profound creative trap that suddenly brings slavery alive with a juddering intimacy. *Minha formação* opens *in medias res* with Nabuco's college days and moves through his various residencies abroad, his significant new friendships, and his discovery of key authors (perhaps the most fascinating major influence is the now largely forgotten Walter Bagehot). But as the book develops, Nabuco dismantles his own myth in increasingly dark, mystical, and outrageous terms. He only gets directly engaged with his thought and work around slavery very late in the volume in chapters 21 and 22, entitled respectively "Massangana" and "Abolition." "Massangana" constitutes one of the most remarkable pieces of prose to be generated by the printed archive of Atlantic slavery. The short chapter confronts the impact of slavery upon the imagination of a privileged child, and then considers the continuing development of that impact on the adult. In this sense it approaches analogous territory to Assis's *Brás Cubas*. This chapter is an unsettling mediation and meditation that I want to use to frame Assis's slavery writing, and to provide a final context for *The Black Butterfly*.

Conclusion

My earlier analysis dealt at some length with the ironic games that Assis plays with Wordsworth, and with how frightening the notion that "The child is father to the man" might become when the abuses of slavery are its focus. Nabuco, a literary Anglophile of passion, provides his own riff on the same theme, and again draws the reader into some dark shadows of a most un-Wordsworthian nature. Nabuco begins with these terrific words:

> The whole design of life is above all a child's drawing later forgotten by the man but it is this which surrounds him for ever without his knowing it . . . For my part I believe I have never been transported beyond the limit of my first four or five impressions . . . For the first eight years of life I know for certain were those that definitively formed my instinctive and moral development. I passed this initial period, so remote and yet so present, on a sugar plantation in Pernambuco, my birth state . . . The population of this little dominion, completely shut off to foreign influences, like all the other feudal settlements, was composed of slaves, distributed throughout the different parts of the slave quarters, the vast black dovecote existing at the side of the plantation house, and the tenants, tied to the landowner by the beneficence of the wattle and daub shacks that sheltered them and the little crops that he allowed them to grow on his land. In the center of the little canton of the slaves the residence of the master rose up, staring out over the buildings of the cane mills, and in the background upon an undulation in the land, was a chapel dedicated to St. Mathew . . . Of all these impressions not one will ever die. The sons of fishermen will always feel the rasp of the grit of the beach between their feet and hear the sound of the waves. For myself I feel that I am standing on that thick carpet of crushed cane which surrounds the plantation and hear the drawn out squeaking of the huge wooden ox carts . . .[4]

What is important here is not merely that Nabuco claims he will never get outside or beyond this remembered vision of slavery, but that he sees into the ways its larger religious and social structures encase his memory and mind. He remembers not merely the plantation but the symbiotic relation between the poor white trash tenants and the slaves who exist side by side upon the plantation, all overseen by the house of the master. He calls up the policing role of Christianity, the chapel of Saint Mathew also raised as an architectural and spiritual overseer. He ironizes religious imagery at its very base, the symbol of the Holy Spirit, the white dove blackened and multiplied in that extraordinary poetic and metaphoric leap whereby the slave bodies are transformed into black doves. The ironies mount, mythic images are upended. In the final sentences Nabuco calls up the maritime imagery so beloved of Cariocas and Bahianas—the beach, the sand, the fisherman, the sound of the tides—and recasts them hideously in his own memorial monument. The sand on the beach is transformed into a carpet of crushed sugarcane trash. Cane trash, the fragments spewed out by the crushing mills, are a hitherto invisible monument, the mountain of refuse unknowingly created by the generations of slaves undertaking the exhausting and perilous job of feeding sugarcanes into the lethal machinery. The child of the slave masters stands on a carpet of refuse that embodies the labor, suffering, death, and exploitation of generations of Afro-Brazilian slaves. The sound of the waves on the beach is ousted by the squeak of the ox carts. They squeak because they are laden with heavy, ripe sugarcane, cane that the slaves must put through the mills to make more trash. The sights and sounds of natural freedom and beauty are supplanted in the child's, and child-father's, mind by the sights and sounds of sugar production and slave suffering in the burning fields of Pernambuco. The writing is dangerous because it is both lyrical and hideous, both committedly nostalgic and profoundly bitter, celebratory and simultaneously agonized. It is writing designed to make the reader uneasy. Nabuco is in love with these irrepressible memories but at the same time knows that they enshrine horror and the full weight of slavery's evil.

For Wordsworth, the child has access to a visionary and privileged world that the adult must spend their time trying imaginatively to repossess, although the attempt is doomed. This central thesis is most powerfully articulated in Wordsworth's *Ode: Intimations of Immortality from Recollections of Early Childhood*. Nabuco in revisiting the operations of his infant imagination follows this Wordsworthian theoretical path, but throws an aesthetic spanner in the works. What if the imaginative world imprinted with visionary splendor upon the child's inner eye is not simply glorious but both beautiful and horrible, namely the world of slavery?

Nabuco, profoundly enamored of the English Romantics, and specifically the nature poetry of Wordsworth, continues his analysis of how slavery's memories are implanted in the infant Nabuco's mind by carefully revisiting and reexamining Wordsworth's theory of childhood imagination in the context of "The Rainbow" lyric. This literary site is then ironized when Nabuco recasts it through the vision of the great British aesthetic theorist (but ironically negrophobe, racist, and pro-slavery political philosopher) John Ruskin.[5] As the chapter progresses, Nabuco returns to the image of the small chapel on the plantation and talks of being "enchained" to an unbroken and long-inherited tradition of Brazilian Catholicism that is both benevolent and irresistible. He concludes that it was "In the little chapel of Massangena that I was united with my chain" and then immediately continues:

> The impressions which conserve this idea demonstrate well in what profundity our first foundations are hurled down. Ruskin wrote this variant on the thought of Christ concerning infancy: "The child very often holds in its fragile fingers a truth which the mature intellect with all its strength is not able to cling on to and which old age has the privilege to discover afresh."[6]

Nabuco then goes on to talk of traveling to Europe, and of seeing in Rome the Sistine Chapel, the great religious works of Raphael, and of hearing the Angelus. He then swerves dramatically from Christianity and talks of how he finds the "lost notes of the Angelus" in the chapel of his childhood, and of how this discovery involves hearing what he terms his "inner *muezzin,* the peals that echoes in my ears at prayer time, is that of the little bells of the slaves at prayer time murmuring 'Praise be to Our Lord Jesus Christ'."[7] And so what he hears is not a Christian message but somehow the African-Muslim voice of the slaves ringing through the mask of Christianity. It is also significant that the passage of Ruskin that Nabuco quotes as a development of Christ's thought is in point of fact a precise development of Wordsworth's "The Rainbow" lyric, and of the very lines that so obsessed Machado de Assis. The original Ruskin text runs: "There is a singular sense in which the child may peculiarly be said to be the father of the man. Childhood often holds a truth with its feeble fingers, which the grasp of manhood cannot retain, which it is the pride of utmost age to recover."[8] And so we are back with the forceful paradox in which Wordsworth framed the capacity of the child's imagination to come back and infantilize and simultaneously transmogrify the stunted and bound adult imaginary: "The child is father to the man." Yet we return to this Wordsworthian aesthetic, as with Assis and his ghastly parable of Procópio, under the shadow of slavery and its capacity to ruin the mind of the slaveholder while still a child.[9]

Nabuco may be exposed to the most glorious art and music the Italian Renaissance can muster, but such work is powerless to challenge the religious truth that Nabuco hears as he is repossessed by the voice of Afro-Brazilian Muslim Slaves. What flashes upon his inward eye, whether he wants it to or not, is the vision of the slaves in his childhood singing out their version of the Angelus, their Africanity and their pain ringing through the façade of Christianity. Where this impression stands in moral terms and where it leaves Nabuco around slavery and memory are not easy questions to answer.

As this passage develops, it is the very benevolent aspect of the slavery Nabuco witnessed, or claims to remember, in his childhood, and the unquestioning passivity of the slaves, that causes him the most extreme pain:

> It is not possible to think back to the slavery of my infancy without an involuntary sorrow. As I felt it move within me, so it is conserved in the same way in my memory now like a gentle yoke/bondage ["jugo" is literarily a yoke for oxen, but also extends to mean bondage], the outward vanity/haughtiness of the master but also the intimate pride of the slave, something equivalent to the subservience of an animal which nothing can alter because the ferment of a sense of inequality can never penetrate it.[10]

This is haunting, peculiar writing, articulating a belief that the pall of slavery still hangs over the mentality of Brazil, and within the body and soul of Nabuco. As if he is, in a ghastly paradox, evolved with an almost surreal perversity out of Wordsworth's "child father" image, a pregnant child, Nabuco feels the body of slavery "move within me." Nabuco is haunted by a vast, soft sorrow, which forces him to combine both the arrogance *in* ownership of the slave master and the impenetrable passivity and moral docility of the slave. We do not now find it easy to think about the slave as a tamed and patient animal that has lost the capacity to rebel. What is Nabuco saying in those difficult final words? Maybe he is suggesting that the impenetrability of the mind of the slave, specifically in terms of the master's ability/inability to understand that mind, provides the slave with a unique *otherness* or *difference*, a self-sufficiency beyond the ken of white ownership and privilege. Those peculiar final words are constructed with a deliberate generosity and ambiguity. Nabuco indicates that slavery has created vast and powerful emotional worlds within the slave's imaginary, worlds that the masters and their descendants will not have access to without serious reconfiguration. If they wish to enter the imagination of slaves, the masters and their descendants need to cast aside preconceptions and to work in a spirit of constant humility.

Literary Slaves of Brazil: Slave Narrative Aporia and the Transmogrificatory Example of Luís Gonzaga Pinto da Gama

There is a case to be made, and I try to make it in *The Black Butterfly*, that in many key respects the Brazilian literary response to slavery, in its entirety, stands quite apart from the rest of the Atlantic slave diaspora. One question that must be asked is: "Did such exceptionalism come at the price of the silenced or absent creative voices of the slaves themselves?" To which I would reply: "Yes in the main, but no, not entirely; there is always Luís Gama." Gama is the point of origin, the black catalyst, the literary black gold or *ouro preto* who enabled, who in Cageian parlance "gave permission to," what followed. In this sense he is one point of inception into what is strange, strong, and different in the Brazilian imagining of slavery.

There are no great slave poets outside Brazil. When Anglo-American slaves were hypothetically allowed a creative space to inhabit on their own terms, it was a prosaic box, a policed box, called "The Slave Narrative." So here is an intriguing fact to throw into the mix. I take a deep breath and pronounce the truth that, despite the fact that each Brazilian slave lived their own unique life story, there are no published Brazilian slave narratives. To put it another way, it would not be possible to make a Brazilian version of *Twelve Years a Slave*, for the simple reason no source text exists to adapt. Brazil, the nation that imported more slaves from Africa than any other, which had the largest African evolved slave population in the Americas, produced absolutely no slave narratives as such.[11] There is only one surviving text that has a claim, and a very thin claim, to be considered a Brazilian slave narrative. The *Biography of Mahommah G. Baquaqua, a Native of Zoogoo, in the Interior of Africa* was ghostwritten, maybe wholly written, in English by an Anglo-Canadian missionary who supposedly "interviewed" Baquaqua. The resultant tract was printed in English in Detroit, Michigan in 1854. A small portion of this text purports to describe Baquaqua's experiences under Brazilian slavery.

Mahommah Baquaqua: An Unconvincing Plug with Which to Fill the Unbelievable Black Hole of Brazilian Slave Narrative

Baquaqua's *Biography* is an extreme example of clichéd and compromised Anglo-American missionary propaganda. What is surprising is that it is still posted within certain areas of Atlantic studies as an authentic, indeed unique and uniquely valuable, piece of Brazilian slave testimony. Baquaqua's *Biography* has no such status, and I wish to place it in relation to Gama, and Gama in relation to Alves, Assis, and da Cunha, in order to explain why this text is not just misleading but dangerously obfuscatory. Luís Gonzaga Pinto da Gama was, by any standards, not just an abolitionist activist of unique force, but a phenomenal poet who had mastered many registers and styles. Gama is an authentic creative essence, one of the only Brazilians, white, black, or any shade in between, who was born into slavery yet who creatively, lovingly, ferociously, confrontationally, inhabited his subsequent freedom and forced his readers to inhabit what he had learned.

It is important to scrutinize any claims that Baquaqua's *Biography* has to constitute an authentic Brazilian slave narrative, because of the excessive claims now made for this text. The work is a frightening example of how closed down and ruthlessly effective an account of slave experience in Africa, Brazil, North America, and the Caribbean could be, once policed by the full powers of the Anglo-Canadian missionary societies. The full, one might say excessive, title of the *Biography* is worth quoting in its somewhat absurd entirety because it lays out exactly how this text defines itself. It also uncovers many of the essential problems that arise in claiming this text as the first pure example of Brazilian slave narrative:

> *Biography of Mahommah G. Baquaqua, a Native of Zoogoo, in the Interior of Africa. (A Convert to Christianity,) With a Description of That Part of the World; Including the Manners and Customs of the Inhabitants, Their Religious Notions, Form of Government, Laws, Appearance of the Country, Buildings, Agriculture, Manufactures, Shepherds and Herdsmen, Domestic Animals, Marriage Ceremonials, Funeral Services, Styles of Dress, Trade and Commerce, Modes of Warfare, System of Slavery, &c., &c. Mahommah's Early Life, His Education, His Capture and Slavery in Western Africa and Brazil, His Escape to the United States, from Thence to Hayti, (the City of Port Au Prince,) His Reception by the Baptist Missionary There, The Rev. W. L. Judd; His Conversion to Christianity, Baptism, and Return to This Country, His Views, Objects and Aim. Written and Revised from His Own Words, by Samuel Moore, Esq., Late Publisher of the "North of England Shipping Gazette," Author of Several Popular Works, and Editor of Sundry Reform Papers*[12]

On and on the title page goes, spectacularly verbose and prolix even by the standards of the day. The first thing that jumps out is how little of the work concerns Brazil. The second thing that jumps out is how little authority or control Baquaqua had over this creation generated under the watchful eye of the late publisher of the *North of England Shipping Gazette*. The *Biography* is a grotesquely sentimental, brutal, and misleading work. The self-publicizing missionary zeal of Samuel Moore effectively colonized and inhabited the short text and erased any authentic manifestation of Baquaqua. The title makes it all too clear that what is being described is a text that is, or claims to be, far too many things: a spiritual autobiography, a conversion narrative, an ethnography of Zoogoo, a missionary tract, a piece of British antislavery and anti-American propaganda, a text of British colonial expansionism, an anti-Papist rant, a temperance lecture and by a very long stretch, the only extant text that has been designated a Brazilian slave narrative proper.

The jury may be out on the status of this text and its value as testimony, but surely any verdict on the *Biography* as an exclusive Brazilian slave narrative cannot seriously be in doubt. It is an astonishing fact that out of the more than four million Africans shipped to Brazil, and the enormous volume of their slave descendants, apparently not one ever wrote, or was in a position to write, or even dictate, an expanded account of their life in a form that might equate to the conventions of the classic North American slave narratives. This genuinely weird fact is, however, no reason to cling with desperation to Baquaqua as a magical way of filling such a testimonial vacuum. The *Biography of Mahommah G. Baquaqua* was not produced in order to inaugurate a nonexistent canon of Brazilian slave narratives; this Protestant tract was produced because Baquaqua had been appropriated by the Anglo-Canadian missionary abolitionists. The *Biography* is consequently a profoundly compromised text, as the prefatory apparatus to the first edition makes all too clear.

We are told that Baquaqua begins in the interior of Africa as a Muslim and then goes through several stages of captivity. First he is enslaved in Africa, then he endures the Middle Passage and is briefly enslaved in Brazil, sold through a series of small holdings into commercial shipping. Then he escapes from maritime trading and moves precariously through North America and Haiti, where he is converted to Christianity, to emerge in Canada, as a subject of her Britannic majesty. He is finally inspired with a burning desire to return to Africa, a driven man bringing his "countrymen" Evangelical Christianity. The text enacts a well-rehearsed redemptive Evangelical British narrative, and in this sense is linear, but the text also enacts, in its anticipated return of Baquaqua as a missionary to Africa, a deferred cyclical movement, beginning and ending in the continental homeland.

The Reverend Moore—editor/arranger/rearranger/interpolator/user/fictionalizer/censor/utilizer/reinscriber, and finally eraser—of Baquaqua, produced a hefty preface that sets out with confidence the filters and the agendas operating in his reconstruction of the narrative relayed to him in what he describes as "the imperfect English spoken by Mahommah." His stylistic agenda prioritizes a propagandistic clarity, and he aims at a style of universal accessibility, wanting "to render the work as readable and clear as possible to the capacities of all classes of readers." Moore reiterates that he has attempted to transpose Baquaqua, "without any figured speech, but in the plainest style possible; all the phrases used are 'familiar as household words.'" If one turns to the text, this claim is clearly self-serving nonsense.

Moore decided to present Baquaqua's narrative not as first-person narrative but with a third-person omniscient and omnipresent narrator. The massive gap between this text and what might be termed "classic" African slave narrative comes out in the opening words. Baquaqua is not allowed to say: "I was born . . .", the celebrated statement of origination, the three words that establish a slave narrative as an individual's testimony. Instead he is mired within the narrative limbo of Moore's ever-present interpolation. Moore as editor stands apart to inform us: "The subject of this memoir was born in the city of Zoogoo. . . ." It is only in the second chapter that the style uneasily slips into first-person narrative, inevitably and repeatedly distanced or alienated for the reader by the bracketed announcement: "(Mahommah says)."

Moore's thematic aim as it emerges in his preface is also far from transparent. He claims that he sets out to describe trauma, and he emphasizes he wants the potential readers of his rendition to "see throughout its pages, the horrible sufferings and tortures inflicted upon that portion of God's creatures, merely because 'their skin is of a darker hue.'" But the real driving force behind the book is to promote British imperial expansion in Africa through the Livingstonian activities of antislavery agitation and missionary activity on an explicitly global scale:

> Mahommah has desired for a long time past, indeed ever since his conversion to Christianity whilst at Hayti, to be enabled to return again to his native land, to instruct his own people in the ways of the gospel of Christ, and to be the means of their salvation, which it is to be hoped he will be able to accomplish ere long; in the meantime he has become a subject of the Queen of England, and is at present living under her benign laws and influence in Canada. Stirring up the colored population and agitating for the abolition of slavery all over the world, a cause which ought to occupy the hearts and feelings of every benevolent and charitable man and woman throughout the world.[13]

Moore's propagandistic and nationalistic agendas are crudely, almost grotesquely, paraded. Baquaqua's narrative is, then, framed as a text that contributes to the celebration of British philanthropy, abolition, and morally elevated imperial expansion. The first chapter opens with an account of "Mohammedism" in Baquaqua's part of Africa. This chapter ends with a description of the annual fast, and the only phrase presented in inverted commas as Baquaqua's own is the statement that: "Occasionally the chief priest will 'squat like a toad.'"[14]

The narrative is in fact *anything* but a simple transcription of an interview. Moore constantly slips abolition verse and canonic poetic quotations from esoteric sources into Baquaqua's mouth. His experience in Africa is set up with the words: "Up to the time that Mahommah was 'forced from home and all its pleasures,' the foot of the white man had not made its first impress upon the soil." Here the "simple slave" articulates his experience not in "simple household words" but through a quotation from one of the most celebrated English abolition poems of the first phase of antislave trade agitation. Cowper's *The Negro's Lament* opens with the words "Forced from home and all its pleasures" and presents a passive and pleading image of a sentimental victimized enslaved Africanism. So although the claim at one level is that Baquaqua lives in a land unknown to whites, he is already proleptically jettisoned into a universal experience of diasporic slavery where all African slaves share a tearful victimhood as innocent black lambs, and where all Atlantic slaves endure the same processes of forced migration and cultural evacuation.

Cowper was Britain's primary abolition poet, and his verse is insinuated into Baquaqua's mouth on numerous occasions and at key moments. For example, once in Brazil Baquaqua's suicide attempt is described in the following terms:

> I at last made up my mind to drown myself; I would rather die than live to be a slave. I then ran down to the river and threw myself in, but being seen by some persons who were in a boat, I was rescued from drowning. The tide was low at the time, or their efforts would most likely have been unavailing, and notwithstanding my predetermination, I thanked God that my life had been preserved, and that so wicked a deed had not been consummated. It led me seriously to reflect that "God moves in a mysterious way," and that all his acts are acts of kindness and mercy."[15]

The phrase "God moves in a mysterious way" is the first line of one of Cowper's most celebrated and traumatized hymns of prayer. Yet Moore's crass adoption of the line, thrust into Baquaqua's mouth as an expression of God's unending benevolence and care for mankind, fails to comprehend the darkness lurking in the original. Cowper was periodically afflicted with a ghastly mental illness, and believed himself to have been personally damned by God. His faith was a traumatized affair, and the statement "God moves in a mysterious way, His wonders to behold" can be read as a bitter and ironic lament on Cowper's anguished spiritual state. It is of course a double irony that this disturbing construction of the lines would work perfectly in the context of Baquaqua's attempted suicide, but Moore is closed to the darker implications of his own gaudy literary pastiche.

Frequently, when the narrative approaches the subjects of physical and spiritual agony, Moore drowns out Baquaqua's narrative with inappropriate quotations from English poetic giants including Shakespeare, Milton, and Pope. Take for example the following elaborate refusal to give details of the narrator's physical torments as a slave in Brazil:

> The limits of the present work will not allow more than a hasty glance at the different scenes which took place in my brief career. I could tell more than would be pleasant for "ears polite," and could not possibly do any good. I could relate occurrences which would "freeze thy young blood, harrow up thy soul, and make each particular hair to stand on end like quills upon the fretful porcupine;" and yet it would be but a repetition of the thousand and one oft told tales of the horrors of the cruel system of slavery.[16]

"The limits of the present work" are of course entirely decided and circumscribed by Moore. Imagined terror is set out via a long quotation from *Hamlet*, namely the famous oration by the ghost of Hamlet's father warning of the horrors he has been through and how they would be too much for the imagination of his son to bear. This is powerful stuff, yet when Moore then states that it is apparently beyond the bounds of good taste to mention scenes that would not be "pleasant for 'ears polite,'" he again seems blind to the doubly ironic context of the phrase he quotes. The phrase "ears polite" is taken from a notorious assault by Pope on both the false sensibilities of the gentry and the corrupt nature of the clergy who serve them. In a celebrated passage excoriating bad modern taste in the form of "Timon's Villa," in the *Epistle to Lord Burlington*, Pope observes: "To rest the cushion and soft dean invite, Who never mentions Hell to ears polite" (lines 149–50). In other words, Pope insinuates that superficial aristocrats committed to conspicuous consumption do not take kindly to the thought that they may suffer eternal damnation for their lives of venal superficiality. Consequently, the clergy who service the aristocracy excise "Hell" as concept and word from their theological vocabulary. In attempting to draw a veil over the gross realities of slave suffering, and to retreat into a world of literary doublespeak, Moore is again blind to the meaning of his own quotation.

The voice that takes us through Baquaqua's experience as a Brazilian slave is that of a full-fledged, utterly evangelized, and completely unbelievable Uncle Tom. We get a moralizing running commentary on the misbehavior of the other slaves, given over to the demon drink or to slothfulness and of how they drag Baquaqua into sin. The text also contains attacks on Catholicism and idol worship. The *Biography* is a crudely written Protestant propaganda tract that makes the most extreme of the censorious "editors" of the North American slave narratives look positively liberal. If one follows the dismal extant trail of the slave narrative in Brazil, it seems that the voice of the slave is, in literary terms, walled up. On the single occasion when a Brazilian slave is supposed to be given a space in which to speak, he is buried alive and overwritten by a particularly grotesque form of Anglo-American sadistic puritanism.

Luís Gama, the Missing Link—Slave Poet, Love Poet, Satiric Poet

If Brazil had no slave narratives as such, it did have some literary slaves who gave the world something quite incandescent within the nineteenth-century slavery marketplace. Luís Gama appeared in the literary and political firmament of São Paulo, in the middle decades of the nineteenth century. An ex-slave poet of exceptional originality, quality, experimental ambition, and satiric ferocity, Gama remains unjustly unknown outside a tiny coterie of Brazilian admirers today. Gama could operate as a creative free agent in ways that were not open to American ex-slaves, not even to Frederick Douglass. He certainly lived a life under and through slavery that, had he decided to write it, could have generated the most sensational and heartwrenching of narratives. Indeed, had there been a big market for slave autobiography, Gama, like a Brazilian Frederick Douglass, could have launched a personal industry around his life story.

By his own account he was born in 1830, the son of a ruined Luso-Brazilian nobleman who lost his fortune gambling, and of a first-generation Afro-Brazilian mother, Luísa Mahin. Luísa was from the Mina region of Africa and was idolized by Gama, who remembered her not only as a great beauty but as a fierce political radical. He claimed that she was part of the core of black revolutionaries who organized the great slave revolt of the Mâles, or black Muslims, in Bahia in 1835. Gama's father secretly sold Luís (who was technically a free black) back into slavery. Gama was shipped down south as part of the slave "migration" that resulted from the coffee boom and ended on a coffee farm near São Paulo. He was taught to read and write by a sympathetic law student who took him under his wing. When Gama found out his true status as free, he fled to São Paulo and began studying law. Although unable to graduate, he still practiced as an autodidact lawyer and became legendary as an orator, fighting court cases for freed slaves. He purportedly managed to win several hundred slaves their freedom in a vast series of court battles, and he used the court as a publicity hub for his abolitionist activities. Gama also threw himself into the literary and journalistic debates of the time, getting to know leading liberal intellectuals and abolitionists.[17] In the 1860s and 1870s, Gama wrote polemical journalism, collaborating with Angelo Agostini, a visual satirist of genius, on several satiric journals.[18] Gama also, and in terms of his literary reputation most crucially, created a book of verse *Primeiras Trovas Burlescas de Getulino* (The First Satiric Ballads of Getulino), which appeared in December 1859 and was Gama's only published volume.[19] The poems are by turns elegiac, lyric, romantic, erotic, and fiercely satiric. It is a book the like of which the world of slavery studies has not seen before or since, and is one of the very best first volumes written by any poet in the nineteenth century. The book caused a sensation and was republished in several revised and expanded editions. If it is true to say Brazil generated no great slave narratives, it is also true to say that North America generated no great antislavery satire in verse.[20] Brazil did, however, for Gama's work stands on its own in upending the myths and pretentions that underlay the assumed superiority of the slaveholding elite. The book had a wide aesthetic range: as well as its scathing political satiric polemic, it also contained intense and erotic responses to the emotional agonies generated upon the male and female imagination by the pressures of slavery. As an anatomist of tragic love and loss, Gama stands in intensity beside Alves, but the one human Gama loves beyond all others, and the woman who inspired his greatest love poem, is his African mother. As a satirist of social pretensions, Gama stands alongside Machado de Assis. He blew open the taboos, the mysteries and hypocrisies surrounding race and sex in Brazilian urban society. Brazil's interracial Pandora's box was opened up by Gama and tossed as a fertile box of tricks not only to the ironies of Machado de Assis but to the disapproving acerbity of Euclides da Cunha. In his visionary intensity, bold explorations of sexuality, unorthodox and inclusive manipulations of rhetorical registers and linguistic resources, and above all his furious excoriation of the racism and sexism generated by slavery, Gama also existed as an important touchstone for Cruz e Souza. I would argue that without Gama's poetic example, Brazil's great symbolic and mystical black

Conclusion

8. Angelo Coutinho, illustration "Bodarrada" for Gama's poem *Quem Sou Eu* in the journal *Alvorada*, wood engraving, December 1953.

poet Cruz e Souza, who wrote just after Gama and died tragically young, would not have written the way he did.

Several of the poems in Gama's *Primeiras Trovas Burlescas de Getulino* deal, in a sensationally confrontational manner, with the effects of racial intermixture in Brazil, poking fun at the pretensions of Brazil's minor aristocracy to possess pure blood. Questions of identity and the confusion of identity that result from hybridity are examined from several directions. Other poems move into thinking about the emotional trauma of slavery and consider both the Middle Passage and forced migration within Brazil. The work is mercurial and paradoxical, combining lyrical fury, celebratory sadness, and intense eroticism. It can also assume a casual and whimsical tone, an urbane, gently mocking satire. I will end by indicating a couple of the still untapped and hidden poetic resources Gama gave us, and by insisting that the wider world of global slavery studies wake up, and catch up with this wonder. Gama's best slavery poetry should be required and familiar reading on every course syllabus dealing with Atlantic slavery.

Brazilian Slavery and Traumatic Motherhood: Gama's *Minha Mae*

Minha Mae, "My Mother," articulates both the intense love between slave mother and son and the agony caused by the female slave's vulnerability. There is nothing quite like this poem within slavery's cultural canon in the Americas. The poem is almost emotionally unhinged, a lyric firework display flaring out with confusions and vibrant chaos. It links with the wilder lamentatory passages of Alves's *Paulo Afonso Falls*, but also, as intimated above, with Cruz e Souza's most visionary celebrations of black female sexuality. The erotic lyrics *Rosa Negra* (Black Rose), *Boca* (Mouth), and *Aspiração* (Aspiration) demonstrate how deeply Cruz e Sousa had internalized the erotics of Gama.[21] Yet Gama's uniqueness and daring lie in making the core of his lyric outburst not a young lover but his mother. Gama contemplates the sexual exploitation of black women, his intense relationship with his mother, and the negotiation of the memory of that shattered relationship. The verse finally moves into profound elegy and almost unbearably intimate confrontation with what has been corrupted, messed up, scrambled, hurt, and then left within the poet to deal with. This brilliant love poem lyrically recreates the Virgin of the Sorrows as a black virgin of martyred motherhood, of stolen black infancy. She emerges as a tragic figure who must disguise and parody her own emotional torment because of the system of surveillance in which she exists. Told from the perspective of the adult male Gama, looking back at his infant relationship with his mother, the poem articulates a slave mother's loss and the fluidities of childhood states of consciousness confronted with the mother's compromised state. The poem is sexually charged and full of hurt, a desperate statement of the emotional damage slavery inflicted.

Gama sees not only into his own childhood but that of his mother, transforming the black adult female into a girl, a female child who is both creatively mother and strangely also father/mother to the man and a victim of horror. It is a poem that does strange synesthetic things with suffering; it latches onto the "seeing tears" of Andrew Marvell, which so fascinated Jacques Derrida, as an ultimate articulation of suffering, and takes them into a rich sentient terrain.[22] I quote the poem with a prose paraphrase/commentary of my own, which tries to get over some of the layered meaning of the original. The poem opens with a simple statement of the mother's beauty and of her enforced transplantation from Africa to Brazil:

> Minha Mãe
> (*My Mother* [source, origin])
>
> Era mui bela e formosa,
> (*She was most beautiful and handsome*)
> Era a mais linda pretinha,
> (*She was the most beautiful little black girl*
> or
> *She was the most lovely little black thing*)

["Lindha pretinha" is a powerful descriptive compound: it could be innocent but also erotically emotional; it might describe a lovely child or an infantilized ideal female lover.]

> Da adusta Líbia rainha,
> (*Little queen from the deserts of Libia*
> or
> *A little queen from scorched Libia*)

[Again, "rainha" is a word that you might apply to a little girl, but which men use in the North East to describe adult females they worship in erotic terms, or merely wish to flirt with.]

E no Brasil pobre escrava!
   (*And in Brazil a poor slave!*)

Oh, que saudades que eu tenho
   (*O, the longing which possesses me.*)

["Saudade" in its evocation of terrible loss and yearning doesn't really have any equivalent in English; "longing" doesn't come close to the total sense of absence evoked by this word in Brazilian Portuguese. "Saudaaajeeeeeee" is how it is pronounced; there is an infinite sorrow in this sound.]

Dos seus mimosos carinhos,
   (*For her delicate caresses*)
Quando c'os tenros filhinhos
   (*When with her tender children*)
Ela sorrindo brincava.
   (*She played smiling.*)

Éramos dois—seus cuidados,
   (*We were two—her responsibilities/vulnerable wards/cares.*)

["Cuidados" carries a lower meaning of something in intense danger, or threat, of something that must be guarded against violent attack or abuse. If a criminal is on the loose, then the public warnings always begin "Cuidado!" (Look out, Warning, or Beware!)]

Sonhos de sua alma bela;
   (*The dreams of her beautiful soul*)
Ela a palmeira singela,
   (*She was the simple/plain/supreme palm tree*)
Na fulva areia nascida
   (*Born in the tawny sand*)
Nos roliços braços de ébano,
   (*In her rotund/roly-poly/rounded ebony arms*)
De amor o fruto apertava,
   (*The fruit of love clutched/opened, squeezed*)

E a nossa boca juntava
  (*And joined/coupled/fused at our mouth/opening*)
Um beijo seu, que era vida.
  (*A kiss existed, which was life/the life force*)

Quando o prazer entreabria
  (*When the joy/pleasure opened slightly*)

[Again, "entreabria" is untranslatable into English in any single verb. It calls up a series of meanings to do with an entry into interior space becoming visible; it can mean "half-opened" (as the eyes), "was set ajar" (as a door), or "opening out, blooming, blowing" (as a flower).]

Seus lábios de roixo lírio,
  (*Her lips like the purple lily* [of the Madonna])
Ela fingia o martírio
  (*She mimicked/feigned the martyr*)
Nas trevas da solidão.
  (*In the darkness/shadows of solitude*)
Os alvos dentes nevados
  (*The white* [white of the eye] *snow-capped white teeth*)
Da liberdade eram mito,
  (*Were a myth of liberty*)
No rosto a dor do aflito,
  (*In the countenance the agony of the afflicted*)
Negra a cor da escravidão.
  (*Blackness the tint/pigment/ heart/complexion of slavery.*)

Os olhos negros, altivos,
  (*The black haughty/supercilious eyes*)
Dois astros eram luzentes;
  (*They were two lucent stars*)
Eram estrelas cadentes
  (*They were falling stars*)
Por corpo humano sustidas.
  (*Held back, enfolded, by the human body*)
Foram espelhos brilhantes
  (*They were sparkling mirrors*)

Da nossa vida primeira,
   (*Reflecting our first life*)
Foram a luz derradeira
   (*They were the after-birth of light*)

[In colloquial Brazilian "derradeira" is the placenta from a womb.]

Das nossas crenças perdidas.
   (*Of our lost/fallen beliefs*)

Tão terna como a saudade
   (*They were as tender/vulnerable as the longing*)
No frio chão das campinas,
   (*For the fresh and flat grasslands*)
Tão meiga como as boninas
   (*As sweet as the daisies*)
Aos raios do sol de Abril.
   (*In the rays of the April sun.*)
No gesto grave e sombria,
   (*In a grave and sombre gesture*)
Como a vaga que flutua,
   (*Like an emptiness that floats*)
Plácida a mente—era a Lua
   (*Peaceful in mind—it was the moon*)
Refletindo em Céus de anil . . .
   (*Reflected in the indigo sky*)
. . . Se junto à Cruz penitente,
   (*If fastened to the penitent's cross*)
A Deus orava contrita,
   (*She prayed contritely to God*)
Tinha uma prece infinita
   (*She recited an infinite prayer*)
Como o dobrar do sineiro;
   (*Like the tolling of bells*)
As lágrimas que brotavam
   (*The tears which rolled down*)
Eram pérolas sentidas,
   (*Were feeling/hearing/smelling/perceiving/sentient pearls*)

> Dos lindos olhos vertidas
> (*Poured out from the lovely eyes*)
> Na terra do cativeiro
> (*In the land of the captive*)

There have been attempts to enter into the suffering of the slave mother given no rights over either the procreation of her children or their experience growing up. The powerlessness of the slave infant under the impact of an all-consuming maternal passion is not a space that art can easily enter. Toni Morrison went there with her indomitable courage in *Beloved*, and this is also a space that Gama explores in this poem. What is truly extraordinary is the charged sexuality that saturates the descriptions of the physical exchanges between mother and male child. Within the European aesthetic, a distinct eroticism is encrusted onto the figure of the Virgin Mary and her ecstatic relation with the divine baby, her doomed, adored, sexualized, infant boy-God. The sexuality of the child Christ, and the Virgin's energized fixation with this aspect of her child, is blatantly celebrated in Renaissance visual art, and has been daringly and irrefutably set out by Leo Steinberg.[23] The latent and tactile eroticism in Gentile Bellini's multiple depictions of the Madonna and the naked Christ child has been exquisitely uncovered by Julia Kristeva in her meditation "Motherhood according to Bellini." The sexual element in the Madonna and Child relationship also sometimes bursts out in violent and masochistic Luso-Brazilian art depicting the Virgin of the sorrows. In Gama's verse the black mother is cleverly moved into the iconographic realm of the eroticized Madonna. From being the little black girl in Libya, and then the majestic royal palm, the black woman assumes the role of mother, but her grasp from the start is not merely sensual but sexual and spiritual; she is both mother and idealized lover. In the space of five lines the figure moves from a very flesh and blood black woman, with round plump arms, to a mystical martyr whose love for her children is both ecstatic and agonized. The squeezing arms morph into the pressing lips that join mother and infant at the mouth. The lips themselves described as the petals of a specific plant, the "Lily of the Madonna," are outrageously open, deep purple labia that are both oral and genital. The kiss, "which is life," then affects the eyes of the mother/Virgin, transforming the expression into something that is described in language as not only ecstatic but masochistically orgasmic, the joy of martyrdom: "Quando o prazer entreabria / Seus lábios de roixo lírio, / Ela fingia o martírio." The verb "entreabrir" is intensely intimate, undeniably sensual, referring to something open a little bit, and encouraging penetration, the eyelids half open, half closed, the crack of an opening door, a flower bud about to break out into its fertile state and bloom. And why is this expression/ experience described as false, as a feigning, a shamming, a performance (the verb "fingir" means all of these with a feeling that the performer is hypocritical or manipulative)? Why can the pain of martyrdom not be real for the mother? Gama, with his terrible honesty, intimates that as a female slave the woman can never let her honest emotions take over. Gama knows that the mother knows that in the world of slavery she is always watched and manipulated, used and abused, and so she must watch and manipulate herself, even at her moments of utmost intimacy with her children.

In this obscene world of false shows and real suffering, it is only the tears, not the eyes, that can hold and express emotion. This comes out in the astonishing descriptive compound "Eram pérolas sentidas" used to describe the mother's tears. Tears as pearls is a similitude that hovers around cliché, but tears as pearls that are sentient, living, feeling things suddenly breathes a new and terrible life into that cliché. We are transported to that magical world isolated by Derrida as he reads Marvell's lines "Those weeping eyes, Those seeing tears" and marvels: "Tears that see, do you believe? I don't know one has to believe."[24] Here Gama gives us, at a moment of supreme, maybe inexpressible suffering, tears that are synesthetic: they feel, they smell, they see, they have sense. Confronted by eyes that will not show the truth, eyes in which the light we see is only the rejected afterbirth of light, we must see into and through the tears themselves. This is Gama at his most outrageously protosurreal, fighting through to the emotional depths generated by slavery's abuse in a language at the very limits of communicability. This is Gama setting out the path Alves will follow in the final sections of *Paulo Afonso Falls*.

"Porque tudo é Bodarrada!": Slavery and Hybrid Goatishness

The varieties of Gama's poetic diction and his formal range are enormous. *Quem sou eu?* (Who Am I?) is, in terms of a poetic approach to slavery, diametrically opposed to *Minha Mae*. Here Gama is the contemptuous, playful, celebratory, raunchy, empowered satirist, sending up the racial pretentions of the white slaveholders, the aspiring mulatto and mulatta, and indeed anyone who clings to an idea of racial purity.

Gama, when assuming this narrational persona, delights in embracing the unrespectability of racial admixture, trumpeting Brazil's endless bastardization through slavery with a hearty but embittered gusto. This delight in Brazil's miscegenetic tsunami will, as has been noticed in the context of da Cunha, be taken up by Gilberto Freyre and Jorge Amado, and will be the defiant strain with which Brazilian artists put down racist dogma.[25] Yet Gama's bouncy, irreverent octosyllabic couplets are not only prophetic but also intensely contemporary. Gama's poem should also be linked to popular nineteenth-century bawdy narrative in the ballads of *cordel* literature, and to comic pornography in particular.[26]

There were a lot of eighteenth- and nineteenth-century poems, often written by quite elevated literary figures, that write punningly and quite frankly about sexual unions between blacks and whites. Much of this verse is focused upon the white male's obsession with black female and mulatta sexuality, and with venereal disease. As early as the mid-seventeenth century, the great satiric master of the Brazilian baroque Gregório da Mattas was not only excoriating the corruption of Catholic priests, but was writing complex, ironic, scathing verse about black prostitutes and their bodies. By the mid-nineteenth century there was a lot of openly pornographic verse, some popular, some esoteric, that confronted and celebrated interracial sexuality. Francisco Moniz Barreto, an ingenious late Romantic Brazilian poet who was not frightened to experiment with the erotic, is frequently reminiscent of Gama in tone and style. He wrote a very funny, hyperbolic paean in celebration of the mixed-race bodies available to the white man that climaxes frankly with a poetic recasting of a clichéd take on female mixed-race sexuality: "Convem, pois, brancas mulattas, / Crioulas todos foder; / Brancas paras poetar-se; / Mulatas para gozar-se; / Crioulas para viver"[27] (Whites, mulattos, creoles it's fitting for all to fuck—Whites poetically—Mulattas for pleasure—Creoles for life). In his worldliness and his combination of irony and positive energy, Barreto is often close to Gama. It is only the use of obscenities that really separates the miscegenetic triumphalism of *Aos Negreiros* (To the Blacks) from *Quem sou eu*. This is, however, an important divide, for although he does not shy away from sex, Gama is not a comic pornographer, and his enthusiasm about Brazil's sexual intermixture stems from a profound hatred of color-encoded prejudice.

It is then right and proper that *The Black Butterfly*, after all the chasing of shadows, all the unravelling of the chicanery, subtlety, and charged ambiguities of Assis and da Cunha, ends with an outrageous, priapic, goatish hymn of praise written by an Afro-Brazilian in praise of rampant Brazilian sexual coupling. Gama butts into white fictions of respectability and race purity head on, clashes horns with prudish lies and hypocrisy which turn a blind eye to miscegenation. He gives us sex as a force that the proudly mulatto Gama sees very clearly will finally render any attempt to set up racial categorizations, or a Brazilian caste system, both impotent and risible. His hatred of racial hypocrisy and belief in the positive aspects of miscibility may not come to fruition in Brazil yet, but when it comes to sex the country is still arguably the most liberated and tolerant in the ex-slave diaspora. Gama opens with an epigraph from his exact contemporary, the strange abolitionist priest Junqueira Freire. Freire was born two years after Gama in 1832 and died very young at twenty-three, having renounced the priesthood just before his death. He had produced a small body of high quality and highly varied poetry that was by turns mystical, morbid, ironic, Byronic, philosophical, whimsical, and often satiric, voicing abolitionist and anti-Catholic views. The quotation from Friere chosen by Gama is a self-dramatizing and proto-existential passage quizzing the meaning of life and identity:

> Quem sou eu?
>   (*Who am I?*)
> Que importa quem?
>   (*What does it matter who?*)
> Sou um trovador proscrito,
>   (*I am a tabooed troubadour*)
> Que trago na fronte escrito
>   (*Who bears, inscribed on the forehead*)
> Esta palavra—Ninguém!
>   (*This word—No-one!*)

Gama reads this as a meditation on Brazilian race and sees it as a warning shot across colonialism's albinistic obsessional bows. It is a statement that you are not what you appear, that it doesn't matter how you appear, that skin color signifies nothing. Gama creates a fictional antithesis to the thesis of the black butterfly put forward by Brás Cubas and borrowed by me for my title. In Gama's *Quem sou eu?* there is no black and white but brindled and shaded vistas, beauty in confusion, positivity in mixing things up, impurity as pure energy. I don't want to end this book with yet another attempt to explain the unexplainable and self-explanatory. So I will let Gama take us out. As he tosses down his forthright answer to the question we all ask and can never answer, *Quem sou eu?* (Who am I?), he proclaims his very Brazilian variant on the theme. I will try to let the words speak for themselves and give the crudest, most literal of paraphrases, while hoping to catch at something of Gama's priapic energization. Just enjoy the ride as Gama's boisterous, vivacious, preposterous, outrageous, delicious paean to human admixture and Brazilian interracial sexuality predicts, and indeed goes beyond, what Gilberto Freyre and Jorge Amado would have to say about the Brazilian enthusiasm for miscibility:

> Se negro sou, ou sou bode
>> (*If I am a nigger or a goat*)
>
> Pouco importa. O que isto pode?
>> (*It doesn't matter much. Who is to know?*)
>
> Bodes há de toda a casta
>> (*There are goats of all breeds*)
>
> Pois que a espécie é muito vasta...
>> (*For this species is absolutely vast*)
>
> Há cinzentos, há rajados,
>> (*There are ash greys and stripes*)
>
> Baios, pambas, malhadas,
>> (*Arse colours, white faces, piebald/brindled*)
>
> Bodes negros, bodes brancos
>> (*Black goats, white goats*)
>
> E, sejamos todos francos,
>> (*And, let us all be completely frank*)
>
> Uns plebeus e outros nobres,
>> (*Some plebs and a load of nobles*)
>
> Bodes ricos, bodes pobres,
>> (*Rich goats, poor goats*)
>
> Bodes sábios importantes
>> (*Goats who know their importance*)
>
> E também alguns tratantes...
>> (*And several scallywags*)
>
> Aqui, nesta boa terra,
>> (*Here in this lovely land*)
>
> Marram todos, tudo berra;
>> (*All of them butt, all of them bleat*)
>
> Nobres, condes e duquesas,
>> (*Nobles, counts, duchesses*)
>
> Ricas damas e marquesas
>> (*Rich noble ladies and Marquises*)
>
> Deputados, senadores,
>> (*Deputies, senators*)

Gentis-homens, vedores,
  (*Gentlemen, aldermen*)
Belas damas emproadas
  (*Beautiful proud ladies*)
De nobreza empantufadas;
  (*Puffed up with nobility*)
Repimpados principotes
  (*Little princes brimful with conceit*)
Orgulhosos fidalgotes
  (*Vainglorious Lordlings*)
Frades, bispos, cardeiais,
  (*Friars, bishops, cardinals*)
Fanfarrões imperiais,
  (*Imperial boasters*)
Gentes pobres, nobres gentes
  (*Poor people, noble people*)
Em todos há meus parentes.
  (*And my parents are all of them*)

Nos domínios de Plutão,
  (*In the domains of Pluto*)
Guarda um bode o Alcorão;
  (*A goat stands guard over the Quaran*)
Nos lundus e nas modinhas
  (*In the performing of the lundus[28] and mondinhas*)
São cantadas as bodinhas:
  (*The goats are singing*)
Pois se todos têm rabicho,
  (*For if everyone possesses a rump/hairy-appendage/dag*)
Para que tanto capricho?
  (*Why is there such caprice/playfulness*)
Haja paz, haja alegria,
  (*Let there be peace, let there be ecstasy*)
Folgue e brinque a bodaria;
  (*Loosen up/let it all out and play/romp about with goatishness*)

Cesse, pois, a matinada,
  (*Stop, then, at break of day*)
Porque tudo é *bodarrada*!
  (*Because everything is essence of goat*)

Anyone who wants to comprehend the anarchic and explosively comic takes on slavery and sex that the Afro-Brazilian imagination can encompass should read the whole of Gama's experimental masterpiece. This book, at points sublime, trivial, experimental, cheeky, mischievous, heartrendingly beautiful, and saturated in *saudade*, still awaits its first translation into English or indeed any language outside Portuguese. When it comes to Brazil, slavery, and the literary imagination, Gama's *Primeiras Trovas Burlescas* is the silver lining to slavery's storm cloud.

NOTES

Introduction

1. Terry Caesar, " 'So That's the Flag': The Representation of Brazil and the Politics of Nation in American Literature," *Criticism*, Vol. 41, No. 3 (Summer 1999), p. 365.
2. For the limited reception of Assis in America in the 1950s, 1960s, and 1970s, and for his patronization as a "black author" by Harold Bloom and others, see Earl Fitz, "The Reception of Machado de Assis in the United States during the 1950s and 1960s," *Luso-Brazilian Review*, Vol. 46, No. 1, "Edição Comemorativa do Centenário da Morte de Machado de Assis" (2009), pp. 16–35.
3. Amado recently entered the *Guinness Book of Records* as the most translated author on the planet. See Marly D'Amaro Blasques Toog, *Traduzindo o Brazil : o país mestiço de Jorge Amado*; https://amerika.revues.org/5008?lang=en: "Jorge Amado, who entered the *Guinness Book of Records* as 'the world's most translated author' in 1996, was also the first Brazilian to have his/her name in *The New York Times* best seller list."
4. See my analysis of Amado and Freyre in the forthcoming *Exploding Archives*.
5. See for example the brutal Janer Cristaldo, *Brazil's Dr. Faustus*: http://www.brazzil.com/p26apr98.htm; for Freyre and race politics, see Marcus Wood, "Slavery, History and Satire: the legacy of Gilberto Freyre," in *Recharting the Black Atlantic Modern Cultures, Local Communities, Global Connections*, ed. Analisa Oboe and Anna Scacchi (London, Routledge, 2008), pp. 128–47.
6. For the ingenuity and ferocity of the disguised satire on racism in *Tent of Miracles* see Marilyn Grace Miller, *Rise and Fall of the Cosmic Race: The Cult of Mestizaje in Latin America* (Austin, University of Texas Press, 2004), pp. 100–110.
7. See Marcus Wood, *The Horrible Gift of Freedom* (Athens, University of Georgia Press, 2010).
8. "The Dark Night of the Soul" is now a secular cliché but I refer back to its terrific source, "La noche oscura del alma," the Carmelite mystic St. John of The Cross's great lyric poem on spiritual annihilation and rebirth through personal moral struggle and meditation.
9. For a detailed comparative analysis setting the myths of the Emancipation Moment in Brazil against those of North America, see Marcus Wood, *Black Milk* (Oxford, Oxford University Press), pp. 399–470.
10. Wood, *Black Milk*, pp. 399–470.
11. See chapter 4 of this book.
12. In the definitions from two specialist Brazilian Portuguese dictionaries—Taylor, *A Portuguese English Dictionary*, and the standard scholarly dictionary, *Novo Michaelis*—the definitions are as follows. **Preto/Preta**: *n.* The colour black, black, dark, forbidding, somber, dismal. "Preto" means a male black, "Preta" a female black; in

Michaelis: *n.* (1) "Preto/Preta" means a Black-a-moor (2) black colour (3); *adj.* (1) negro (2) black, jet, sooty (3) somber sad mournful. **Negro/Negra** *m. n.*, Taylor: Negro man, slave, *f. n.* Negro female, slave, *adj.* black, gloomy. *Michaelis*, **Negro/ Negra**: *n.* (1) negro, black person, nigger, African; slang: blacky, darky, blackamor (2) black slave; *adj.* (1) black, dark, dark skinned, ebony (2) sullen, gloomy (3) African.

13. Aimé Césaire, *Cahier d'un Retour au Pays Natal, Notebook of a Return to my Native Land* (Newcastle, Bloodaxe Books, 1995), p. 85.

Chapter 1

1. For Castro Alves within Brazilian culture, see his portal in the Brazilian Academy website: http://www.academia.org.br/academicos/castro-alves. See also the lavishly illustrated pdf devoted to the Alves myth: http://www.outorga.com.br/pdf/Artigo%20 317%20-%20Castro%20Alves.pdf.

    Major works based on the biography are Jamil Almansur Haddad, *Revisão de Castro Alves* (São Paulo: Editora Saraiva, 1953), 3 vols.; Xavier Marques, *Vida de Castro Alves* (Salvador: Tipografia Bahiana de Cincinnato, 1911); A. Waldemar de Mattos, *Bahia de Castro Alves* (São Paulo: Instituto Progresso Editorial, 1948); Afrânio Peixoto, *Castro Alves: o poeta e o poema* (Paris: Ailland & Bertrand, 1922); H. Ferreira Lopes Rodrigues, *Castro Alves* (Editora Pongetti, Rio de Janeiro, n.d.), 3 vols.; Alberto da Costa e. Silva, *Castro Alves* (São Paulo: Companhia das Letras, 2006). For an excessively fetishistic text devoted to the minutiae of the poet's life and reproducing everything from images of all his mistresses, to popular songs devoted to the Alvesian cult and even cups and teaspoons he may or may not have used, see Norlandio Meirelles de Almeida, *Cronologia de Castro Alves* (Editora di Pedro, São Paulo, 1960).

2. Textual Note. When Castro Alves died he had published only one small book of poems and none of the great abolition poems, all of which obviously appeared posthumously. These exceptional works were, however, published before the abolition of slavery in 1888 and enjoyed vast popularity in the years directly leading up to the abolition bill. *A Cachoeira de Paulo Afonso* was published separately in 1876; *Vozes de Africa, O Navio Negreiro*, and *A Cachoeira de Paulo Afonso* then appeared, together with other minor abolition verse, in the volume *Os Escravos* (The Slaves) in 1883. Until the appearance of Castro Alves, *The Major Abolitionist Poems: World Literature in Translation*, ed. int. and transl. Amy A. Peterson (New York and London, Garland Publishing, 1990), there was no published translation of the major slavery poetry in English. Peterson's dual-language volume is invaluable and the Portuguese texts are excellently edited. Peterson based her texts on a collation of the definitive scholarly editions of Afranio Peixoto, ed. *Obras Completas de Castro Alves* (Rio de Janeiro, Companha Editora Nacional, 1922) and Homero Pirez, *Castro Alves Poesias escolhidas* (Rio da Janeiro, Imprensa Nacional, 1947) using Alves's indications of his preferred copy text as her guide. Peterson also rightly stated that when her edition came out there existed no definitive scholarly edition of *A Cachoeira de Paulo Afonso*. Alves is, as the following analysis indicates, impossible to translate. Peterson is fully aware of this impossibility and of Alves's often bizarre adaptations of Portuguese. She emphasizes that her translations are "a very extended annotation or commentary" and that she is "sceptical of any claims for absolute translation." I have

therefore not used Peterson's attempts at English translations but have quoted all passages analyzed in Portuguese and then provided my own prose renditions. These are ugly and literal but at least accurate. They are not translations exactly and are deliberately unpoetic but precise, and similar in form and function to the ungainly but strictly literal prose transliterations of Vladimir Nabokov's "translation" of *Eugene Onegin*. Frequently within my discussions I then offer two or three possible options of what Alves's protean words might extend to.

3. For the complicated publishing and performance history of *O Navio Negreiro*, see the precise notes to the poem in *Castro Alves Obra Completa* (Rio de Janeiro, Eitora Nova Aguilar, 1997), pp. 819–20, 829.

4. No part of *O Navio Negreiro* was published during Alves's short lifetime. Although he had performed it to mass theatre audiences several times in Rio in 1868, its first appearance in print was 1886.

5. Arguments have been made to support a reading of Coleridge's *Rime of the Ancient Mariner* as a poem concerning the Atlantic slave trade and the guilt of the Middle Passage. For a listing of these theoretical readings and analysis of their extreme limitations, see Marcus Wood, *Slavery Empathy and Pornography* (Oxford, Oxford University Press, 2004), pp. 218–19. English Romanticism did generate some inferior verse on the Middle Passage, such as Cowper's "Sweet meat hath sour sauce or the Slave Trader in the Dumps," and Robert Southey's "A Sailor Who Served in the Slave Trade," a ridiculous, melodramatic parody of the *Rime of the Ancient Mariner*. See Marcus Wood, *The Poetry of Slavery: An Anthology* (Oxford, Oxford University Press, 2004), pp. 88–90; 219–22.

6. Evidence for the probable date of composition as May 1854 is circumstantial; see Jeffrey L. Salmons, *Heinrich Heine* (Princeton, Princeton University Press, 1979), p. 332. For Heine's position on slavery during the last years of his life and the impact of Stowe, see Marian Musgrave, "Heinrich Heine's Anti-Slavery Thought," *Negro American Literature Forum*, Vol. 6, No. 3 (Autumn, 1972), pp. 91–94. For Heine's ability to get outside historical specificities and narrow propaganda agendas in the late poems, see Robert C. Holeb, "Heinrich Heine on the Slave Trade: Cultural Repression and the Persistence of History," *The German Quarterly*, Vol. 65, No. 3/4, 1492-1992: Five Centuries of German-American Interrelations (Summer–Autumn, 1992), pp. 328–39. For a discussion of the impact of *Das Sklavenschiff* in Brazil and Machado de Assis's imaginative use of the poem in his own writing on slavery and abolition, see chapter 3 of this book.

7. The first and still the most detailed attempt to take Branagan seriously as an American Romantic is Lewis Leary, "Thomas Branagan: Republican Rhetoric and Romanticism in America," *The Pennsylvania Magazine of History and Biography*, Vol. 77, No. 3 (July 1953), pp. 332-52. http://www.jstor.org/stable/20088486.

8. For an ambitious but doomed attempt to construct Branagan as a deliberately bad poet who manipulates "his seeming ineptitude as a performance" and who writes in a mode of "inarticulate innocence," a literary strategy that it is ambitiously argued he shares with none other than Whitman and Melville, see Christopher N. Phillips, "Epic, Anti-Eloquence, and Abolitionism: Thomas Branagan's 'Avenia' and 'The Penitential Tyrant,'" *Early American Literature*, Vol. 44, No. 3 (2009), pp. 605-37. http://www.jstor.org/stable/27750151.

9. Thomas Branagan, *Avenia or a Tragical Lament on the Oppression of the Human Species* (1805) book v, reproduced in Wood, *Poetry of Slavery*, pp. 423–45.
10. Wood, *Poetry of Slavery*, p. 456.
11. Whittier, *The Slave Ships*, in Wood, *Poetry of Slavery*, p. 501.
12. Quoted in Wood, *Poetry of Slavery*, pp. 496–97.
13. For American verse treating the Middle Passage and its rarity within American abolition literature, see Wood, *Poetry of Slavery*, pp. xxv–li, 426–42, 473–77; for Whittier "The Slave Ships," pp. 499–503; Longfellow "The Witnesses," p. 531. The only attempt to think about the impact of North American abolition verse on Brazil and to introduce a comparative take on Alves, Whittier, and Longfellow remains Thomas Braga, "Castro Alves and the New England Abolitionist Poets," *Hispania*, Vol. 67, No. 4 (December 1984), pp. 585–93; http://www.jstor.org/stable/341913. This does not however address the issue of the slave trade or discuss Alves's *Navio Negreiro* in the context of Whittier and Longfellow's Middle Passage poems.
14. For a meticulous account of the evidence relating to whether Castro Alves ever saw Heine's *Slave Ship* in its French translation and for a thorough rundown of the heated denials by Brazilian Critics that this could have happened, see David T. Haberly, "Heine and Castro Alves, a Question of Influence," *Romanische Forshungen* no. 97 (1985), pp. 239–48; http://www.jstor.org/stable/27939428. Haberly's attempts to prove through comparative close reading that Alves's masterpiece is an expanded take on the final stanzas of Heine's *Slave Ship* are inconclusive, and in parts a case of special pleading. For a modern illustrated Brazilian edition of Alves and Heine's slave ship poems, see Priscilla Figueiredo ed., *Navios Negreiros Castro Alves Heinrich Heine* (Rio de Janeiro, S. M. Paradidátio, 2016).
15. For the final stages of the collapse of the slave systems in Brazil, see Robert Conrad, *The Destruction of Brazilian Slavery* (Berkeley, University of California Press, 1972), pp. 199–230.
16. For an ironic literary treatment of these late smuggled slave cargoes, see the discussion of Assis in chapter 4 of this book.
17. For the Brazilian social and economic context for this line of argument, see Haberly, pp. 242, 245–46.
18. For accounts of this celebratory visual art and its imperialist agendas, see Marcus Wood, *Blind Memory* (Manchester, Manchester University Press, 2000), pp. 23–27; Wood, *The Horrible Gift of Freedom*, pp. 71–73.
19. Longfellow, *The Witnesses*, reproduced in Wood, *Poetry of Slavery*, p. 53.
20. For the Zong case and its subsequent cultural construction, see Jeremy Krikler, "The Zong and the Lord Chief Justice," *History Workshop Journal*, Vol. 64, No. 1 (2007), pp. 29–47; Jeremy Krikler, "A Chain of Murder in the Slave Trade: A Wider Context of the Zong Massacre," *International Review of Social History*, Vol. 57, No. 3 (2012), pp. 393–415; Anita Rupprecht, " 'A Very Uncommon Case': Representations of the Zong and the British Campaign to Abolish the Slave Trade," *Journal of Legal History*, Vol. 28, No. 3 (2007), pp. 329–46; Anita Rupprecht, "Excessive Memories: Slavery, Insurance and Resistance," *History Workshop Journal*, Vol. 64, No. 1 (2007), pp. 6–28; and Anita Rupprecht, "A Limited Sort of Property: History, Memory and the Slave Ship Zong," *Slavery & Abolition*, Vol. 29, No. 2 (2008), pp. 265–77.

21. For analyses of Brookes and its creative legacy in the visual arts, see Wood, *Blind Memory*, pp. 16–21; *Horrible Gift of Freedom*, pp. 263–84.
22. In 1959 the poem formed the focus for a dedicatory volume, *Navio Negreiro* (São Paulo, Aguiar e Souza), with text and translations in Portuguese, French, German, and English and a series of essays and commentaries by leading international scholars and poets including the great cultural theorist and folklorist Edison Carneiro. This volume also made available publicly for the first time the suite of twenty large woodcuts by Hansen. These constitute a powerful visual narrative on the horror of the Middle Passage in their own right, and provide a visceral post-expressionist visual dialogue with Alves's masterpiece. Of the several musical settings the most influential interpretation of the poem is that of Caetano Veloso, on the 1997 LP album *Livro*, track "O Navio Negreiro," with vocals by Veloso, Mariah Bethânia, and Carlinos Brown, a mesmeric interpretation that combines a sort of rap delivery voice overlay by Veloso with powerful traditional Bahian percussion and backing vocals. This interpretation was, and remains, hugely popular in Brazil. See YouTube: https://www.youtube.com/watch?v=9v1hZE8fbDM; for a recent film version: https://www.youtube.com/watch?v=SuR1vWgddy4.
23. The hallucinogenic address to a personified ship, which accretes profound experiences to itself, uncannily anticipates *Le Bateau Ivre*, a work that metaphorically engages with the dark inheritance of French colonialism.
24. See Schneider, *Dictionary of African Borrowings*, pp. 34–35.
25. I refer to William Empson's commitment to the idea that great intellectual verse embodied multiple meanings that may often creatively contradict one another but run simultaneously in parallel. The concern with prolix ambiguity saturates all Empson's close reading but the most sustained elaboration of his ideas in this area is to be found in *Seven Types of Ambiguity*.
26. The translation of this crucial line is by Aquiles Alencar Brayner. I originally preferred the translation "We exist on the open sea," but had it pointed out to me by Aquiles that "The difference between the verbs 'Ser' and 'Estar'—both meaning 'to be'—is quite clear in which 'estar' means a temporary situation which might change while 'ser' embodies characteristics of being which are immutable."
27. For the lack of literary or propagandistic representations of the subject of slave "dancing" within the Atlantic slavery archive, see Rediker, *The Slave Ship*, pp. 19, 61, 164, 237–38, 260, 267; Wood, *Horrible Gift of Freedom*, pp. 172–74.
28. For popular millennialism and slavery, see J. F. C. Harrison, *The Second Coming: Popular Millenarianism 1780–1850* (London and Henley, Routledge and Kegan Paul, 1979), pp. 65, 68, 84. For the treatment of the destructive tempest in popular abolition verse, and for Fuseli's possible use of Thomas Day's *The Dying Negro*, see Honour, *Image of the Black*, 4:1, pp. 93–94; see also Wood, *Blind Memory*, pp. 39–40, 52–54.
29. For a sensitive and detailed analysis of why Veloso was drawn to *O Navio Negreiro* and how he was creatively attuned to Alves's vision, see Mario Catelli, "Caetano Veloso o el arte de la relectura: sobre *O Navio Negreiro*, de Antonio de Castro Alves," *Guaraguao*, Año 13, No. 31/32 (Invierno 2009), pp. 137–42.
30. For Alves and the possible influence of Victor Hugo, see Hans Jürgen Horsch,

Antônio de Castro Alves (1847–1871): Seine Sklavendichtung Und Ihre Beziehungen Zur Abolition in Brasilien (Hamburg, Cram de Gruyter & Co., 1958), pp. 79–86.
31. Alves, *Abolitionist Poems*, p. 10.
32. See my reading of Machado de Assis's remarkable metaphoric games with "borboleta negra" (black butterfly) which are explored below and which provide the image and metaphor for the title of this book.
33. Alves, *Abolitionist Poems*, p. 10.
34. These meanings are all incorporated in the range that "acender" covers in Brazilian Portuguese: *PDLP* gives "fazer arder, atear, entusiasmar, animar, transportar, enlevar, provocar, irritar."
35. *The Complete Works of John Ruskin*, ed. Cook and Wedderburn (London, George Allen, 1904), vol. 5, p. 205.
36. Ruskin, *Works*, vol. 5, p. 209.
37. See Wood, *The Horrible Gift of Freedom*, pp. 170–81.
38. Alves, *Abolitionist Poems*, p. 14.
39. All meanings given in *Novo Michaelis*, under "brilhar."
40. Alves, *Abolitionist Poems*, pp. 14–15.
41. Wood, *Black Milk*, pp. 1–4, 438–41.
42. José Verissimo, *A Educação Nacional* (Rio, 1906), translated and quoted Robert Conrad, *Children of God's Fire* (Princeton, Princeton University Press, 1983), p. 223.
43. For the *mãe praeta* in the visual arts, see Marcus Wood, *Black Milk*, pp. 1–2, 137–38, 194, 416, 439–42.
44. See my discussion "Black Milk, White Greed, White Milk Black Memory, the Virgin Mary as *Mãe Preta*" in *Black Milk*, pp. 438–41.
45. All meanings given under the verb "regar" in *Novo Michaelis*.
46. For the "bath of Christ's blood," see Catherine Innes-Parker ed., *The Wooing of Our Lord and The Wooing Group Prayers* (London, Broadview Press, 2015), p. 195 note 35: "the idea of Christ's blood as a bath that makes souls clean from sin, or heals the sickness of sin is common." The most spectacular fantasies on this subject are in the anchoress treatise *Ancrene Wisse*, 6: 8–9.
47. Alves, *Abolitionist Poems*, p. 16.
48. Henrich Heine, *Selected Verse*, ed. transl. Peter Bascombe (London, Penguin, 1968), p. 216, my prose translation.
49. See the accounts and relevant footnotes in Wood, *Horrible Gift of Freedom*, pp. 170–77; Rediker, *Slave Ship*, 19, 61, 164, 170, 237–38, 260, 267, 325, 332.
50. H. B. de Groot, "The Ouroboros and the Romantic Poets: A Renaissance Emblem in Blake, Coleridge and Shelley," *English Studies*, 50 (1969), pp. 553–64.
51. Alves, *Abolitionist Poems*, p. 16.
52. Alves, *Abolitionist Poems*, p. 16.
53. Alves, *Abolitionist Poems*, p. 16.
54. Lydia Maria Child, "The Devil's Walk in Washington," reprinted in Wood, *Poetry of Slavery*, pp. 480–82. This poem is in turn a parody of Samuel Taylor Coleridge's satiric squib, "The Devil's Thoughts."
55. Alves, *Abolitionist Poems*, p. 18.

Chapter 2

1. For an overview of the rhetorical stereotypes covering English and North American poetry of the eighteenth and nineteenth centuries describing Africa, see Wood, *The Poetry of Slavery*, pp. xxvi–xl. For an overview of the wider cultural context, see Philip D. Curtain, *The Image of Africa: British Ideas and Action, 1780–1850* (Madison, University of Wisconsin Press, 1964); Robin Law, *Barbot on Guinea: The Writings of Jean Barbot on West Africa, 1678–1712*, ed. P. E. H. Hair, Adam Jones, and Robin Law (London, The Hakluyt Society, 1992); William B. Cohen, *The French Encounter with Africans: White Response to Blacks, 1530–1880* (Bloomington, Indiana University Press, 1980); Mary Louise Pratt, *Imperial Eyes: Travel Writing and Transculturation* (London, Routledge, 1992).
2. Luis de Camões, *The Lusiads, in Sir Richard Fanshawe's Translation*, ed. Geoffrey Bullough (Carbondale, Southern Illinois University Press, 1963), p. 183.
3. *La Lettre de Pero Vaz de Caminha* (Paris, Editions Chandeigne, [1500] 2011), pp. 25–37. Dual language edition Portuguese and French.
4. Fanshawe, *Lusiads*, p. 186.
5. For the literary constructions of Adamastor up to 1988, see M. van Wyk Smith comp. and intro., *Shades of Adamastor: Africa and the Portuguese Connection, an Anthology of Poetry* (Grahamstown, South Africa, Institute for the Study of English in Africa, 1988).
6. *Novo Michaelis*: voz: voice; a sound uttered by man or animals; faculty of speaking; ability to sing, to cry, to call; suffrage, right to speak; loud complaint or clamour; order given in a loud voice.
7. *The Cambridge Bible, The Book of Psalms* (Cambridge, Cambridge University Press, 1952), Psalm 22, 1–2.
8. For the vast ambiguities of this text and its ability to make the speaker both individual, proto-Christological martyr, and "the mouthpiece of a nation," see the superb commentary of A. F. Kirkpatrick, *The Cambridge Psalms*, pp. 112–24.
9. Alfredo Bosi, "Under the Sign of Ham," in *Brazil and the Dialectic of Colonization* (Urbana, University of Illinois Press, 2015), p. 217: "the combination of an arcane Africa ('For two thousand years') with Africa-as-subject ('I cried forth') is the poem's first novel element."
10. Alves, *Abolitionist Poems*, p. 2.
11. For Prometheus in other verse by Alves, see "Tragédia do lar" and "Prometeu," both published in *Os Escravos*.
12. For the centrality of the Promethean myth to Western creative thought, and German Romantic thought in particular, see the magnificent but now sadly forgotten C. Kerényi, *Prometheus, Archetypal Image of Human Existence*, transl. Ralph Manheim (Princeton, Bollingen Series LXV, Princeton University Press, 1963). For the engagement of the major Romantics with the Promethean myth in the context of Atlantic slavery, see Wood, *Slavery, Empathy and Pornography*, pp. 246–50; for other abolition verse drawing on Prometheus, see Wood, *The Poetry of Slavery*, pp. 368–72. Alves himself returns to the figure frequently in his poetry and wrote his own verse treatment of the myth *Prometeu*.
13. Alves, *Abolitionist Poems*, p. 2.

14. Camoes, *Lusíadas*, canto x, stanzas 121–22.
15. Vozes de Africa, ll. 37–38.
16. For the complex development of the *Phrygian cap* from classical times into the Atlantic slave diaspora, see Wood, *Horrible Gift of Freedom*, pp. 44–58.
17. David M. Goldenberg, *The Curse of Ham: Race and Slavery in Early Judaism, Christianity, and Islam* (Princeton, Princeton University Press, 2005); David M. Whitford, *The Curse of Ham in the Early Modern Era: The Bible and the Justifications for Slavery* (Burlington, VT, Ashgate Publishing, 2009).
18. Lucretia S. Gruber, "Alfred de Vigny's 'Eloa': A Modern Myth," *Modern Language Studies*, Vol. 6, No. 1 (Spring, 1976), pp. 74–82.
19. Alves, *Abolitionist Poems*, p. 6.
20. For the identification of Blackness with the devil, see Jean Devisse, *The Image of the Black in Western Art* (Lausanne, Menil Foundation, 1979), part 2, vol. 1, pp. 70–80. For the later development of these associations, see Jean Devisse and Michel Mollat, *The Image of the Black in Western Art* (Lausanne, Menil Foundation, 1979), part 2, vol. 2, pp. 59–78, 229–32; and Wood, *Blind Memory*, pp. 158–59, 168.
21. Alves, *Abolitionist Poems*, p. 6.
22. For Gama, see the conclusion.
23. Alves, *Abolitionist Poems*, p. 4.
24. Paulo de Vivemus Afonso came across the falls in the late seventeenth century. For their centrality to Brazilian visual iconography in the nineteenth and twentieth centuries, see Kátia M. de Queiros Mattóso, *Iconografia Baiana do Século XIX*, pp. 120–24; Wood, *Black Milk*, pp. 254–57; for Marc Ferrez photographs, see the Yield Magazine website: http://003.yieldmagazine.org/yield3curatorialstatementonmarcferrez; for Lydia Pape's use of the blood waterfall as metaphor for black suffering, see Cyriaco Lopes, "The "Cão Mulato in Context: Concept and Presence of the Mulato in Brazilian Art," *Notes in the History of Art*, Vol. 31, No. 3, Special Issue: Cross Cultural Issues in Art from the Nineteenth Century to the Present (Spring 2012), pp. 50–51.
25. For an uplifting account of what the falls meant, see Sarah Hopkins Bradford, *Scenes in the Life of Harriet Tubman* (Auburn, New York, 1869), pp. 33–35; for Niagara falls freedom photographs and their relation to the iconographic inheritance of the Paulo Afonso falls, see Wood, *Black Milk*, pp. 254–57.
26. For the fusion of tourism with the imagery of liberation, see the discussion of the Niagara freedom photographs in Wood, *Black Milk*, pp. 250–53.
27. Alves, *Abolitionist Poems*, p. 131.
28. All meanings of "rolar" as given in *Novo Michaelis*.
29. All meanings of "abrir" as given in *Novo Michaelis*.
30. Alves, *Abolitionist Poems*, p. 32.
31. William Blake, *William Blake's Writings, Volume II: Writings in Conventional Typography and Manuscript*, ed. G. E. Bentley (Oxford, Oxford University Press, 1978), pp. 1287–88.
32. Piero di Cosimo, "A Forrest Fire," tempera on wooden panel, Ashmolean Museum, Oxford.
33. Alves, *Abolitionist Poems*, p. 38.
34. Alves, *Abolitionist Poems*, p. 42.
35. Alves, *Abolitionist Poems*, p. 42.

36. Alves, *Abolitionist Poems*, p. 80.
37. Alves, *Abolitionist Poems*, pp. 43–44.
38. Alves, *Abolitionist Poems*, p. 86.
39. Alves, *Abolitionist Poems*, p. 86.
40. Alves, *Abolitionist Poems*, p. 52.
41. Alves, *Abolitionist Poems*, p. 54.
42. For representations of the slave power as slave dog, see Wood, *Blind Memory*, pp. 95–98.
43. For images of slaves captured by dogs, which set up tense dialogues between slave and animal, see Wood, *Blind Memory*, pp. 95–99.
44. Walt Whitman, *Leaves of Grass* (London, Penguin Modern Classic), p. 121.

Chapter 3

Epigraph. M. I. Finley, *Ancient Slavery and Modern Ideology* (London, Chatto and Windus, 1980), p. 116.

1. Obviously the crucial intervention of Roberto Schwarz has made it extremely hard to argue that Assis was not engaged in a sophisticated social and societal critique, but there remains the conundrum of slavery. For my takes on Schwarz, see chapter 3 of this book.
2. Eduardo de Assis Duarte, "Machado de Assis's African Descent," *Research in African Literatures*, Vol. 38, No. 1, *Lusophone African and Afro-Brazilian Literatures* (Spring 2007), pp. 134–51; for a competent assessment of critical responses to Assis prioritizing race, see Paul Dixon, "Machado de Assis's Early 'Mulato' Narratives," *Afro-Hispanic Review*, Vol. 29, No. 2, *The African Diaspora in Brazil* (Fall 2010), pp. 39–54. http://www.jstor.org/stable/41349339.
3. The text is rearranged from the screenplay in Portuguese, Spanish, English, and French: Roteiro de Sylvia Back, *Crus e Souza O Poeta Desterro* (Rio de Janeiro, 7 Letras, 2000), pp. 27–28. I am grateful to Cristian José Oliveira Santos Brayner for the translations of Brazilian idioms here.
4. For Querino's rediscovery and his absorption into the Afro-Brazilian literary heritage via the character of Pedro Archanjo in Jorge Amado's *Tenda dos Milagres*, see Marilyn Grace Miller, *Rise and Fall of the Cosmic Race: The Cult of Mestizaje in Latin America* (Austin, University of Texas Press, 2004), pp. 1–2, 4, 115–16, and also my chapter on *Tenda dos Milagres* in my forthcoming monograph *Exploding Archives*.
5. The first serious accounts of the treatment of the slaves and slavery in Assis outside Brazil were Helen Caldwell, *Machado de Assis: The Brazilian Master and His Novels* (Berkeley, University of California Press, 1970). For Assis's black characters in relation to the nineteenth-century Brazilian novel generally, see Giorgio Marotti, *Black Characters in the Brazilian Novel* (Los Angeles, University of California Press, 1987). For the most recent analysis of Assis's mixed-race status and its impact on his fictional characters, see G. Reginald Daniel, *Machado de Assis: Multiracial Identity and the Brazilian Novelist* (University Park, Penn State University Press, 2012).
6. Silvio Romero, *Historia da literatura Brasileira*, 5 vols. (Rio de Janeiro: José Olympio, 1953). For a detailed reassessment of Romero on Assis, see Alberto Schneider, transl. Richard Correll, "The Brazil of Sílvio Romero and Machado de Assis: History of a

'Polemic,' or the Writer as Critic of the Critic," *Portuguese Studies*, Vol. 26, No. 2 (2010), pp. 205–23.
7. Schneider, "Romero," p. 206. This careful piece explains why Romero's nationalistic approach to the construction of Brazilian literature was highly influential, and also explains why Assis was not going to fare well within Romero's sociopolitical agenda. It also, however, brings out how Romero's very hostility to Assis made him the most aesthetically refined early reader of Assis.
8. For Brazilian race theorists in the first half of the twentieth century, see Florestan Fernandes, *The Negro in Brazilian Society* (New York, Columbia University Press, 1969); Jeffrey D. Needell, "History, Race, and the State in the Thought of Oliveira Viana," *The Hispanic American Historical Review*, Vol. 75, No. 1 (February 1995), pp. 51–77; Thomas Skidmore, *Black into White: Race and Nationality in Brazilian Thought* (New York, Oxford Press, 1974); T. Skidmore, "Biracial USA vs. Multiracial Brazil: Is the Contrast Still Valid?" *Journal of Latin American Studies*, 25/2 (1993), pp. 373–86; F. W. Twine, *Racism in a Racial Democracy: The Maintenance of White Supremacy in Brazil* (New Brunswick, Rutgers University Press, 1998); Lilia Moritz Schwarcz, *O espetáculo das raças: dentistas, instituições e questão racial no Brasil, 1870–1930* (São Paulo, Companhia da Letras, 1993).
9. For Freyre's race agendas and regionalism, see Marcus Wood, "Slavery, History and Satire: The Legacy of Gilberto Freyre," in *Recharting the Black Atlantic Modern Cultures, Local Communities, Global Connections*, ed. Analisa Oboe and Anna Scacchi (London, Routledge, 2008), pp. 128–32.
10. Gilberto Freyre, *Order and Progress*, p. 165.
11. A powerful and witty reading that sees Assis as a sort of Cervantes *redivivus* is Carlos Fuentes, *Machado de la Mancha* (Mexico, Fondo de Cultura Econòmica, 2001). For Assis and Sterne, see Nícea Helena Nogueira "A forma livre de Laurence Sterne e o romance de ruptura de Machado de Assis"; Luana Ferreira de Freitas, *Sterne em Memórias Póstumas de Brás Cubas e Dom Casmurro* (Universidade Federal do Ceará Fortaleza, Ceará, Brasil); Schwarz, *A Master*, pp. 134, 144, 156–57.
12. The most recent analysis to comment in detail upon Assis and the issue of race is Renata R. Mautner Wasserman, "Race, Nation, Representation: Machado de Assis and Lima Barreto," *Luso-Brazilian Review*, Vol. 45, No. 2 (2008), pp. 84–106. This piece is structured around a parallel reading of Assis and Barreto, who was in terms of sociopolitical engagement in his work the opposite of Assis. The excellent extended notes to the article provide a series of précis that accurately outline the main authors and schools of thought that have developed around Assis and the themes of race and slavery during the course of the twentieth century.
13. For readings of *Pai contra Mãe* as a hands-on slavery tale confronting enslavement as a moral dilemma, see Wasserman, p. 93; K. David Jackson, *Machado de Assis: A Literary Life* (New Haven, Yale University Press, 2015), pp. 147–48; Duarte, "Assis's African Descent," p. 143. For my own reading of this story in the context of trauma literature, see chapter 4 in this book.
14. See Wasserman, "Race, Nation, Representation," pp. 84–106, for a detailed comparative take on Assis and Barreto.
15. According to Assis scholars, the mature period is commonly taken to be made up of

those works published after *Iaiá Garcia*. For Assis on the Golden Law of 1888, see the discussion of *Counselor Ayres' Memorial* in chapter 3 of this book.

16. For a patient uncovering of Assis's own assessments of his experimental technique as revealed in auto-critiques within his own fictions, see María Luisa Nunes, "Machado de Assis," Theory of the Novel, *Latin American Literary Review*, Vol. 4, No. 7 (Fall–Winter 1975), pp. 57–66; for Assis as "Modernist," see Jackson, *Literary Life*, pp. 52–58; Estela Vieira, *Interiors and Narrative: The Spatial Poetics of Machado de Assis, Eça de Queirós, and Leopoldo Alas* (Lewisburg, PA, Bucknell University Press, 2013); José Guilherme Merquior, "Género e estilo das 'Memórias Póstumas de Brás Cubas,'" *Colóquio/Letras* 8 (July 1972), pp. 12–20; Alfred J. MacAdam, "Rereading Ressùrreição," *Luso-Brazilian Review*, Vol. IX, No. 2 (Winter 1972); Jackson, *Literary Life*, pp. 52–58.
17. See Duarte, "Assis's African Descent," pp. 134–35.
18. Paul Dixon, "Machado de Assis, the 'Defunto Autor' and the Death of the Author," *Luso-Brazilian Review*, Vol. 46, No. 1, Edição Comemorativa do Centenário da Mortede Machado de Assis (2009), pp. 45–56; for "removability," p. 48. This article contains a valuable and focused assessment of how Brazilian critical responses to Assis during the last thirty years have continued to prioritize issues of national identity, pp. 52–54.
19. Roberto Schwarz, *Ao Vencedor as Batatas: Forma literária e processo social nos inícios do romance Brasileiro* (São Paulo, Duas Cidades, 1977); *Um Mestre na Periferia do Capitalismo: Machado de Assis* (São Paulo, Duas Cidades, 1990).
20. Machado de Assis, trans. intro. John Gledson, *A Master on the Periphery of Capitalism: Machado de Assis* (Durham, NC, Duke University Press, 2000).
21. Schwarz, *A Master*, p. 103; Gledson, intr. p. xxvi, points out Schwarz's coupling of "caprice and volubility" but intriguingly neither author sees this coupling as a unique demonstration of the depravity of slavery.
22. Roberto Schwarz, "Beware Alien Ideologies," quoted in *Misplaced Ideas*, John Gledson, ed. transl. (London, Verso, 1992), p. 40.
23. Schwarz, *A Master*, p. 1.
24. See Schwarz, *A Master*, p. 1; Gledson, intr. p. xvi, and the discussion of Assis's "Instinto de nacionalizade."
25. Schwarz, *A Master*, Gledson, intr. p. xv.
26. Schwarz, *A Master*, is predominantly focused on Assis's *Posthumous Memoirs of Brás Cubas*, and his specific takes on slavery are consequently considered in chapter 3.
27. Heloisa Toller Gomes, *As marcas da escravidão: o negro e o discurso oitocentista no Brasil e nos Estados Unidos* (Rio de Janeiro: Ed. UFRJ/EDUERJ, 1994), p. 211, intriguingly suggests *en passant* that Assis reads slavery backwards or as if in a mirror. This approach might also relate to the famed concept of "misplaced ideas"; see Schwarz, *A Master*, pp. xvi–xviii.
28. See Earl Fitz, "The Reception of Machado de Assis in the United States during the 1950s and 1960s," *Luso-Brazilian Review*, Vol. 46, No. 1, "Edição Comemorativa do Centenário da Morte de Machado de Assis" (2009), pp. 16–35. Fitz asks a good question: "Why . . . was Machado not read in the United States as a writer who had something important to say about race relations?" (p. 27).

29. James Baldwin, "Everybody's Protest Novel," *James Baldwin: Collected Essays* (New York, Library of America, 1998), pp. 11-19.
30. *Obras Completas de Machado de Assis, Reliquas de Casa Velha* (São Paulo, Editora Globo, [1906] 1997), "Pai contra Mãe," p. 3, my translation.
31. Machado Assis, transl. John Gledson, *A Chapter on Hats and Other Stories* (London, Bloomsbury, 2008), p. 230.
32. I am grateful to Aquiles Alencar Brayner for bringing to my attention this secondary meaning of "varo."
33. Duarte, "Assis's African Descent," pp. 140-43, discusses the centrality of slave abuse to the stories "Virginius—Narrativa de um advogado" (Virginius—A Lawyer's Narrative, 1863) and "Mariana" (1871), and in the narrative poem "Sabina" (published in *Americanas*, 1875). See also Dixon, "Early Mulatto Narratives," pp. 42-52.
34. *Obras Completes de Machado de Assis, Reliquas de Casa Velha* (São Paulo, Editora Globo, [1906] 1997), "Pai contra Mãe," p. 3, my translation.
35. Wasserman, "Race, Nation, Identity," p. 92; there is a similar assumption of monolithic directness and moral clarity in Assis's treatment of slavery in *Pai contra Mãe* in Jackson, "Assis," pp. 147-48. These readings are not open to the way Assis plays with and ironizes the different linguistic registers, legal, scientific, colloquial, and proverbial, that had been evolved in Brazil to disguise and fictionalize the slavery business.
36. The line has proved a bit tricky for translators. Gledson translates in Assis, *A Chapter of Hats*, p. 255, "but let's not think about masks"; Caldwell translates in Machado de Assis, William L. Grossman and Helen Caldwell trans., *The Psychiatrist and Other Stories* (Los Angeles, University of California Press, 1963), p. 101, "but let us not concern ourselves with masks."
37. Again the translators have been bamboozled by these words and have come up with various solutions to this insoluble conundrum: Gledson, p. 255, "it was less a punishment than a sign"; Caldwell, p. 101, "it was less a punishment than an identification"; Marotti and Lawton, "the punishment was less serious than the sign."
38. See for example the fantastic martyrological carnivals of Antonio Bento focused on the martyred slave body, Wood, *Black Milk*, pp. 4-8.
39. Assis, *Chapter of Hats*, p. 256.
40. For *Uncle Tom's Cabin* in Brazil and Assis, see Daniel, *Machado de Assis*, pp. 166-69.
41. Assis, *Chapter of Hats*, p. 267.
42. Assis, *Pai contra Mãe*, p. 7, my translation.
43. All quotations from "The Companion" are from Machado de Assis, *The Devil's Church and Other Stories*, transl. Jack Schmitt and Lorie Ishimatsu (Manchester, Carcanet, 1985), pp. 89-97.
44. The story is subtly translated by John Gledson under the title "The Mirror: A Sketch for a New Theory of the Human Soul," in Assis, *A Chapter on Hats*, pp. 27-41. The disguised analysis of slavery in this story was pointed out in a fine analysis by Duarte, "Assis's African Descent," pp. 142-43.
45. Assis's long-term engagement with "clientilism" throughout his oeuvre is superbly analyzed by Schwarz, although he does not consider "The Companion"; see *A Master*, pp. 25, 45, 92, 128, 159, 160.
46. Assis, "The Companion," transl. Schmitt and Ishimatsu, pp. 89-90.

47. For the Brazilian slave narratives, or rather their absence, see Michael A. Gomez, *Black Crescent: The Experience and Legacy of African Muslims in the Americas* (Cambridge, Cambridge University Press, 2005), p. 92. Claims have been made for Baquaqua, but this is not really a Brazilian slave narrative; see my discussion in the conclusion of this book.
48. Indeed, the Valongo market remains a charged political space in Brazil and became part of a passionate and ongoing debate on how Rio's visual inheritance of slavery should be manifested. Excavations around the Rio Olympics in 2016 unearthed valuable material relating to what had been the world's greatest slave market. For an account around the politics of displaying the slave market prior to 2016, see http://web.stanford.edu/group/spatialhistory/media/images/publication/Slave_Transactions_article2.pdf; for the debates thrown up by the 2016 unearthing of the slave market, see https://www.theguardian.com/world/2011/mar/04/archaeologists-find-slave-port; http://www.afroriowalkingtour.com/the-valongo.html.
49. Assis, "The Companion," transl. Schmitt and Ishimatsu, p. 96.
50. See chapter 4.
51. Assis, "The Companion," transl. Schmitt and Ishimatsu, p. 91.
52. See Bryan Edwards, "Inscription at the Entrance to a Burial Ground for Negro Slaves" (1776), reprinted in Marcus Wood, *The Poetry of Slavery*, p. 72.
53. Assis, "The Companion," transl. Schmitt and Ishimatsu, p. 94.
54. Assis, "The Companion," transl. Schmitt and Ishimatsu, pp. 96–97.
55. All quotations from "Dona Paula" are from Machado de Assis, *The Devil's Church and Other Stories*, transl. Jack Schmitt and Lorie Ishimatsu (Manchester, Carcanet, 1985), pp. 68–77.
56. Assis, "Dona Paula," transl. Schmitt and Ishimatsu, p. 68.
57. Assis, "Dona Paula," transl. Schmitt and Ishimatsu, p. 69.
58. Assis, "Dona Paula," transl. Schmitt and Ishimatsu, p. 76.
59. Assis, "Dona Paula," transl. Schmitt and Ishimatsu, p. 77.
60. All quotations from "Eternal" are from Machado de Assis, *The Devil's Church and Other Stories*, transl. Jack Schmitt and Lorie Ishimatsu (Manchester, Carcanet, 1985), pp. 111–21. Quotations from the original Brazilian are from Machado de Assis, *Obra Completa* (Rio, Editôra José, 1962).
61. Assis, "Eternal," transl. Schmitt and Ishimatsu, p. 119.
62. Assis, "Eternal," transl. Schmitt and Ishimatsu, p. 119. Portuguese text, Assis, *Obras*, 2, p. 604.
63. Assis, "Eternal," transl. Schmitt and Ishimatsu, p. 121.
64. The Bom Fim constitutes a sort of demi-peninsula within the bay of Salvador Bahia; it is known throughout Brazil as the area where the most sacred of all the black slave churches is located, the church of O Senhor do Bom Fim, the Lord of the Good End. Brazilian blacks to this day travel on pilgrimage to this church, as to a Brazilian Lourdes, to ask the Senhor to perform miracles. For a discussion of the Church's importance within Afro-Brazilian syncretic cultures, see Wood, *Black Milk*, pp. 427–30.
65. *Pequeno Dicionário Brasileiro da Língua Portuguesa*: Iaiá: Tratamento dado familiarmente às meninas e às moças. Muito usado no tempo da escravidão, e hoje quase abolido (Title colloquially, or intimately given to young women or girls/maids/

servants/slaves/concubines/prostitutes ["moa" could mean any of these] commonly used in the time of slavery and today as good as abolished).
66. For a detailed analysis of the law and its passage, see Conrad, *Destruction of Brazilian Slavery*, pp. 90–98; for the "Law of the Free Womb" and its treatment in print satire, see Wood, *Black Milk*, pp. 141–44.
67. Quoted in Giorgio Marotti, *Black Characters in the Brazilian Novel* (Centre for Afro American Studies, University of California Los Angeles, 1987), pp. 124–25. See also Duarte, "Assis's African Descent," p. 139, where he quotes the opening lines of this outburst as an "openly abolitionist declaration."
68. Quoted in Marotti, *Black Characters*, p. 127.
69. The passage, which introduced "le pauvre homme" into French as sarcastic shorthand for one who massively indulges the pleasures of the flesh while a fellow human suffers, consists of a dialogue between Organ and Dorine upon the relative health of the confidence trickster Tartuffe and Madame Pernelle (the mistress of the house, who has been genuinely ill):

> "Tartuffe? Il se porte à merveille,
> Gros, et gras, le teint frais, et la bouche vermeille.
> – Le pauvre homme!
> [. . .]–Il soupa, lui tout seul, devant elle,
> Et fort dévotement il mangea deux perdrix,
> Avec une moitié de gigot en hachis.
> – Le pauvre homme!
> [. . .] Pressé d'un sommeil agréable,
> Il passa dans sa chambre, au sortir de la table;
> Et dans son lit bien chaud, il se mit tout soudain,
> Où sans trouble il dormit jusques au lendemain.
> – Le pauvre homme!
> [. . .] Il reprit courage comme il faut;
> Et contre tous les maux fortifiant son âme,
> Pour réparer le sang qu'avait perdu Madame,
> But à son déjeuner, quatre grands coups de vin.
> – Le pauvre homme !"
> *Le Tartuffe*, I, 4 (v. 238–40)

70. Jackson, *Assis*, pp. 142–45.
71. All quotations from "A Celebrity" are from Machado de Assis, *The Devil's Church and Other Stories*, transl. Jack Schmitt and Lorie Ishimatsu (Manchester, Carcanet, 1985), pp. 122–31.
72. Assis, "A Celebrity," transl. Schmitt and Ishimatsu, p. 126.
73. The print is available at http://www.wikiwand.com/pt/Lundu.
74. For the passage and ineffectiveness of the law, see Conrad, *Destruction of Brazilian Slavery*, pp. 90–98; for the series of bitter satiric attacks on the law in popular print, see Wood, *Black Milk*, pp. 144–52.
75. For Agostini and other print satirists' take on the law, see Wood, *Black Milk*, pp. 144–50.
76. *Esau and Jacob*, p. 92. Quotations are from the following edition: Machado de Assis, tranl. intr. Helen Caldwell, *Esau and Jacob* (London, Peter Owen, 1966).

77. *Esau and Jacob*, pp. 92–93.
78. Machado de Asis, "A nova geração" (the new generation), in *Obras Completa*, 3: 183.
79. For a detailed analysis of Assis's development of the "theory of misplaced ideas" and its development, see Gledson, in Schwarz, *A Master*, pp. xvi–xix.
80. Quotations are from the following editions: Portuguese, Machado de Assis, *Obras Completas, Memorial de Ayres* (Rio, Editora Globo, 1977); English, Machado de Assis, *Counselor Ayres' Memorial*, transl. Helen Caldwell (Los Angeles, University of California Press, 1972).
81. Assis, *Ayres' Memorial*, p. 19. The line is the focus for a series of discussions of Ayres's inability to emote and failure to show his passion, which run through the novel as the elderly gentleman reveals his frigid character; see *Ayre's Memorial*, pp. 16, 19, 21, 39. The line comes from a lyric fragment of Shelley composed in 1821 and published posthumously under the title *To* —. The line is the first one of the second stanza. The lines are a lament in which the poet self-consciously figures himself as a moth, the night, and a space of absolute sorrow: "I can give not what men call love, / But wilt thou accept not / The worship the heart lifts above / And the Heavens reject not,— / The desire of the moth for the star, / Of the night for the morrow / The devotion of something afar / From the sphere of our sorrow?" *The Complete Poetical Works of Shelley* (Oxford, Clarendon Press, 1904), p. 720.
82. Assis, *Counselor Ayres' Memorial*, p. 31.
83. For a survey of critical reactions and the tendency of modern criticism to read the novel as a political allegory for Brazil and its emergence as a republic, see Wasserman, "Race, Nation, Representation," pp. 89–90.
84. Assis, *Counselor Ayres' Memorial*, p. 41.
85. Assis, *Counselor Ayres' Memorial*, p. 41.
86. Assis, *Counselor Ayres' Memorial*, p. 43.
87. Assis, *Counselor Ayres' Memorial*, p. 43.
88. See Wood, *Black Milk*, pp. 257–61.
89. Quoted in Marotti, *Black Characters*, p. 123.
90. Assis, *Counselor Ayres' Memorial*, p. 44.
91. This object still exists as the star exhibit in the emancipation display in Petropolis; see emancipation publicity of Isabel's signing of the law in Wood, *Black Milk*, pp. 244–45, 257–60, 451–53.
92. Assis, *Counselor Ayres' Memorial*, p. 44.
93. Assis, *Memorias de Ayres*, pp. 31–32, my translation.
94. Sybille Fischer, *Modernity Disavowed: Haiti and the Cultures of Slavery in the Age of Revolution* (Durham, NC, Duke University Press, 2004), pp. 18–19.
95. Marotti, *Black Characters*, p. 123.
96. For Heine and Alves, see the analysis of *O Navio Negreiro* in chapter 1.
97. Henrich Heine, *Selected Verse*, ed. transl. Peter Bascombe (London, Penguin, 1968), p. 212. My prose translation.
98. Assis, *Counselor Ayres' Memorial*, p. 67.
99. Assis, *Counselor Ayres' Memorial*, p. 82.
100. James Boswell, *The Universal Empire of Love*, quoted in Wood, *Poetry of Slavery*, p. 194.
101. Assis, *Counselor Ayres' Memorial*, p. 181.

Chapter 4

1. For presentations of the monstrous planter and slave owner in print satires and graphic art, see Marcus Wood, *Blind Memory*, pp. 154–55, 161–63, 172, 184, 224, 238–39, 261–63; and for Brazilian prints, see *The Horrible Gift of Freedom*, pp. 123–25; and *Black Milk*, pp. 144–47, 176–78, 182–84.
2. For *Uncle Tom's Cabin* in Brazil and Assis, and for the impact of Stowe on race stereotypes in Brazilian abolition fiction in the 1860–1888 period, see G. Reginald Daniel, *Machado de Assis: Multiracial Identity and the Brazilian Novelist* (University Park, Penn State University Press, 2012), pp. 166–69.
3. For a discussion and reproduction of the board game, see Wood, *Horrible Gift of Freedom*, pp. 35–37.
4. Baldwin, "Everybody's Protest Novel," *Collected Essays*, pp. 11–18.
5. Stowe, *A Key to Uncle Tom's Cabin* (Boston, John P. Jewett, 1858), p. 61.
6. For the distance of Assis from Stowe's abolition polemics, see Machado de Assis, John Charles Chasteen transl. intr., *The Alienist and Other Stories of Nineteenth-Century Brazil* (Indianapolis, Hackett Publishing, 2013), pp. vii–viii.
7. All subsequent references to the Brazilian text are to Machado de Assis, *Memórias Póstumas de Brás Cubas* (Sao Paulo, Ediouro, 2004). Unless otherwise stated all English translations are from Machado de Assis, Helen Caldwell transl., *Posthumous Memoirs of Brás Cubas* (Oxford, Oxford University Press, 1997).
8. Assis, *Posthumous Memoirs*, p. 3.
9. Assis, *Memórias Póstumas*, p. 16.
10. Assis, *Memórias Póstumas*, p. 17.
11. Assis, *Posthumous Memoirs*, p. 8.
12. Assis, *Memórias Póstumas*, p. 21.
13. For colloquial extensions of "amolar," see Taylor, *A Portuguese Brazilian Dictionary*, and idioms in *Pequeno Dicionário Brasileira*.
14. For Debret's depictions of knife grinders, see *Debret O Brasil*, G 61; A 97; for illustrations in the illustrated souvenir pamphlet of "Street Trades," see Marcus Wood, *Black Milk*, pp. 305–11.
15. Assis, *Posthumous Memoirs*, p. 23.
16. Pasceola is referred to as coming from Minho, a region in Portugal, and so might be a white midwife. I am grateful to Aquiles Alencar Brayner for this insight.
17. Assis, *Posthumous Memoirs*, p. 23.
18. For a detailed account of the evolving iconography of the sedan chair and the slave carriers, see Marcus Wood, *Black Milk*, pp. 307–10.
19. In this context, "moleque" is a rich and very ambiguous term. A word of African origin, originally Bantu, it carries a whole variety of meanings ranging from "young black boy" or "a very small boy" to "a shameless malicious rascal, a scoundrel," and even "the devil, Satan." For the full range of meanings, see Schneider, *Dictionary of African Borrowings*, pp. 215–16.
20. Assis, *Memórias Póstumas*, pp. 46–47, my translation.
21. For a detailed analysis of this image and other images involving abuse of Brazilian slaves by the children of slave owners and adults, see Wood, *Black Milk*, pp. 324–29.
22. Assis, *Posthumous Memoirs*, p. 25.

23. Assis, *Memórias Póstumas*, p. 49, my translation.
24. Wordsworth, "My Heart Leaps Up," *Poems in Two Volumes* (London, 1807) 2, p. 9.
25. Assis, *Posthumous Memoirs*, p. 108.
26. Assis, *Memórias Póstumas*, pp. 171–72, my translation.
27. *Pequeno Dicionário Brasileira*, "Prudência (o) Virtude que leva o homem a conhecer e a practicar o que lhe convém."
28. See Marcus Wood, *Slavery, Empathy and Pornography*, for an extended discussion of linguistic moral and economic conflations, and particularly the malleability of the term "improvement" in *Mansfield Park*.
29. Assis, *Posthumous Memoirs*, pp. 52–53.
30. Assis, *Memórias Póstumas*, pp. 127–28, my translation.
31. Assis, *Memórias Póstumas*, pp. 128–29, my translation.
32. Assis, *Memórias Póstumas*, p. 267, my translation.
33. Assis, *Posthumous Memoirs*, p. 29.
34. All quotations from "Ideas of a Canary" are from Machado de Assis, *The Devil's Church and Other Stories*, transl. Jack Schmitt and Lorie Ishimatsu (Manchester, Carcanet, 1985), pp. 142–46.
35. For the development of the literary fable in adult literature in eighteenth- and nineteenth-century European literatures, see Kirsten Hoving Powell, "The Art of Making Animals Talk: Constructions of Nature and Culture in Illustrations of the Fables of La Fontaine," *Word and Image* 12.3 (1996), pp. 251–73; Thomas Noel, *Theories of the Fable in the Eighteenth Century* (New York, Columbia University Press, 1975).
36. Assis, "Ideas of a Canary," transl. Schmitt and Ishimatsu, p. 142.
37. For a detailed analysis of Sterne's caged starling in the context of Atlantic slavery, see Marcus Wood, *Slavery, Empathy and Pornography*, pp. 13–18.
38. For an extended account of the formal relations between Assis and *Tristram Shandy*, see Sergio Paulo Rouanet, *Tempo e espaço na forma shandiana: Sterne e Machado de Assis*, http://www.scielo.br/scielo.php?script=sci_arttext&pid =S0103-40142004000200021; and Nícea Helena Nogueira, "A forma livre de Laurence Sterne e o romance de ruptura de Machado de Assis," https://www.filologia .org.br/machado_de_assis/A%20forma%20livre%20de%20Laurence%20Sterne%20e %20o%20romance%20de%20ruptura%20de%20Machado%20de%20Assis.pdf; Marta de Sennas, "Fielding, Sterne and Machado de Assis: A Genealogy," *Portuguese Studies*, Vol. 9 (1993), pp. 176–82.
39. Assis, *Esau and Jacob*, p. 102. There is a short article that examines some parallels between *Brás Cubas* and *A Sentimental Journey*: Luana Ferreira de Freitas, *Sterne em Memórias Póstumas de Brás Cubas e Dom Casmurro*: http://machadodeassis.net /revista/numero14/rev_num14_artigo11.pdf
40. Laurence Sterne, *A Sentimental Journey through France and Italy* (London, Penguin [1768] 1979), p. 96.
41. Assis, "Ideas of a Canary," transl. Schmitt and Ishimatsu, pp. 142–43.
42. See G. R. Mellor, *British Imperial Trusteeship* (London, Faber and Faber, 1951).
43. Assis, "Ideas of a Canary," transl. Schmitt and Ishimatsu, p. 144.
44. For a brilliant creative digression on this theme, see the account of the conception of *Lolita*, and the anecdote of the ape in the *Jardin des Plantes*: Vladimir Nabokov, *Lolita*

(London, Weidenfeld and Nicholson, 1959), pp. 301-2. For Nabokov on Sterne's Starling, and Lolita's sexual slavery, and Humbert's slavery to sexual depravity, see the bleak satiric ballad *Lolita*, pp. 249-50: "Where are you hiding, Dolores Haze, / Why are you hiding darling? / (I walk in a daze, I talk in a daze, / I cannot escape said the starling.)"
45. Assis, "Ideas of a Canary," transl. Schmitt and Ishimatsu, p. 146.
46. Gustave Flaubert, *Madame Bovary: Moeurs de Province* (Paris, Edition Definitive, Paris Bibliothèque-Charpentier, 1926), p. 74.
47. Assis, *Memórias Póstumas*, pp. 100-101.
48. See Laura de Mello e Souza, *The Devil and the Land of the Holy Cross Witchcraft, Slavery and Popular Religion in Colonial Brazil* (Austin, University of Texas Press, 2003), pp. 156-58, for a series of identifications of the butterfly as transformed witch or satanic familiar.
49. Assis, *Memórias Póstumas*, p. 101, my translations.
50. Assis, *Memórias Póstumas*, p. 102, my translation.
51. Angus Fletcher, *Allegory, the Theory of a Symbolic Mode* (Ithaca, NY, Cornell University Press, 1964), p. 2.
52. Assis, *Memórias Póstumas*, p. 102, my translation.
53. For the treatment of slaves and animals as a marker of the moral development of adults and children during the period Sterne was writing, see Markman Ellis, "Suffering Things: Lapdogs, Slaves and Counter-Sensibility," and Lynn Festa, "The Moral Ends of Eighteenth- and Nineteenth-Century Object Narratives" in *The Secret Life of Things, Animals, Objects and It-Narratives in Eighteenth-Century England*, ed. Mark Blackwell (Lewisburg, PA, Bucknell University Press, 2007), pp. 92-117, 309-20.
54. For the slave animal cruelty equation, see Elizabeth Heyrick, *Cursory Remarks on the Evil Tendency of Unrestrained Cruelty, Particularly on that Practiced in Smithfield Market* (London, 1823), and Wood, *Slavery, Empathy, Pornography*, pp. 369-70.
55. Laurence Sterne, *Tristram Shandy* (London, Penguin Classic, 2003), p. 100.
56. Assis, *Memórias Póstumas*, pp. 102-3, my translation.
57. Assis, *Memórias Póstumas*, p. 102, my translation.
58. Sterne, *Tristram Shandy*, p. 100.
59. Lynn Festa, *Sentimental Figures of Empire in Eighteenth-Century Britain and France* (Baltimore: Johns Hopkins University Press, 2006), p. 73.
60. Festa, *Sentimental Figures*, p. 212.
61. Assis, *Memórias Póstumas*, p. 48, my translation.
62. Shakespeare, *King Lear*, 4.1, ll. 38-39.

Chapter 5

1. Vicente Dobroruka, *Antônio Conselheiro, o beato endiabrado de Canudos* (Rio de Janeiro, Diadorim, 1977); for an account of Conselheiro that lodges him firmly within the political minutiae of his day see R. M. Levine, *Vale of Tears: Revisiting the Canudos Massacre in Northeastern Brazil, 1893-1897* (Berkeley, University of California Press, 1995), which has a superb bibliography on Canudos; for a fine account disentangling the provable facts and unknown elements of Conselheiro's life

and legend, see Adriana Michèle Santos Johnson, *Sentencing Canudos: Subalternity in the Backlands of Brazil* (Pittsburgh, University of Pittsburgh Press, 2010), pp. 45–50; http://www.jstor.org/stable/j.ctt9qh5sj.8.
2. João Arruda, *Canudos: Messianismo e conflito social* (Fortaleza, Brazil: Edições Universidade Federal do Ceará / Secult, 1993); Edivaldo Boaventura, *O arque stadual de Canudos* (Salvador, Brazil: Secretaria da Cultura e Turismo da Bahia, 1997); Boaventura, "Parque estadual de Canudos: Criação e evolução," *Revista Canudos* 1.1 (1997), pp. 65–80.
3. For the claim that Canudos might be seen as the last great slave quilombo, see "Canudos: The Last Quilombo" in Dale Thurston Graden, *From Slavery to Freedom in Brazil Bahia 1830–1900* (Albuquerque, University of New Mexico Press, 2006), pp. 216–22. Graden states he got the concept from a newspaper article by José Calasans, "Antônio Conselheiro e os Escravos," *A Tarde*, Bahia, October 5, 1988, p. 6.
4. Textual note. The first edition of *Os Sertões* appeared in Rio in 1902. My quotations and translations from the Portuguese text are from Euclides da Cunha, *Os Sertões* (Rio da Janeiro, Prestígio Editoral, 2006). For over half a century the only English translation was Samuel Putnam tranl., *Rebellion in the Backlands [Os Sertões]* (Chicago, University of Chicago Press, 1945); in 2010 a new Penguin Classics edition appeared, Elizabeth Lowe transl., *Backlands: The Canudos Campaign* (London, Penguin, 2010). Much is to be said for both translations, given how difficult, indeed impossible, it is to convey da Cunha's stylistic games and rhetorical tricks. When I have quoted from a translation and not produced my own translation, I have decided to stick with the Putnam edition. Poor Putnam was brutally lambasted for his many mistakes by no lesser a figure than Claude Lévi-Strauss in an excoriating review ("Rebellion in the Backlands by Euclides da Cunha," review by Claude Lévi-Strauss, *American Anthropologist*, New Series, Vol. 46, No. 3 (July–September 1944), pp. 394–96; http://www.jstor.org/stable/663441). Putnam's translation does, however, have a certain combination of gravitas and black humor that is often close to the original, and also tries to follow the baroque chicaneries of da Cunha's style. Lowe's translation is certainly more readable for a contemporary audience, and technically more accurate, but loses a lot of the overelaborations and willful flamboyance of da Cunha. I have used the following updated edition: Euclides da Cunha, Samuel Putnam tranl., *Rebellion in the Backlands (Os Sertões)* (London, Picador, 1995), referenced as "Putnam." For a penetrating close analysis of the impossibility of translating da Cunha, see John Robert Schmitz, "Translation and Retranslation of Euclides da Cunha's *Os Sertões*: An Analysis of Two Translations in English," http://dx.doi.org/10.11606/issn.2317-9511.v26i0p121-146.
5. For Conselheiro's extant writings, see António Vicente Mendes Maciel, *António Conselheiro e Canudos (revisão histórica): A obra manuscrita de António Conselheiro e que pertenceu a Euclides da Cunha*, ed. Ataliba Nogueira, *Brasiliana*, vol. 355. São Paulo: Companhia Editora Nacional, 1974.
6. For the revival of the Sebastianic cult in Brazil in the 1880s and 1890s, see the discussion in chapter 5.
7. Lizir Arcanjo Alves, *Humor e sátira na guerra de Canudos* (Salvador, Brazil: Empresa Gráfica da Bahia, 1997).
8. Graden, *From Slavery to Freedom in Brazil*, pp. 217–20, quotes several Brazilian

historians and gives various contemporary accounts of the significant size of Conselheiro's slave following.

9. Da Cunha, *Os Sertões*, pp. 204–6.
10. Robert M. Levine, "The Singular Brazilian City of Salvador," *Luso-Brazilian Review*, Vol. 30, No. 2, Special Issue: The World out of Which Canudos Came (Winter 1993), pp. 68–69; http://www.jstor.org/stable/3513954; for Assis and the popular dissemination of the Canudos myth, see Campos Johnson, *Sentencing Canudos*, pp. 67–71.
11. Candace Slater, *Stories on a String: The Brazilian Literatura de Cordel* (Berkeley, University of California Press, 1989); see also: https://www.significados.com.br/literatura-de-cordel/
12. Machado de Assis. "Crônica: 14 de fevereiro de 1897." *A Semana. Obras Completas de Machado de Assis*, 31 vols. (Rio de Janeiro, W. M. Jackson, 1937) vol. 3, pp. 413–18.
13. For the backlands contexts for *Cordel*, see Arnaldo Xavier and M. Christina Guidorizzi, *The Greatest Poet That God Creole*; Callaloo, Vol. 18, No. 4, *African Brazilian Literature: A Special Issue* (Autumn 1995), pp. 777–95.
14. For Che's death photograph, see Alex Selwyn-Holmes, "The Death of Che Guevara," *Iconic Photos*, July 30, 2009, https://iconicphotos.wordpress.com/2009/07/30/the-death-of-che-guevara/; and Nick Kirkpatrick, "New (and Disturbing) Pictures of Che Guevara Right after Death Resurface," *Washington Post*, November 17, 2014, https://www.washingtonpost.com/news/morning-mix/wp/2014/11/17/new-and-disturbing-pictures-of-che-guevara-right-after-death-resurface/.
15. For a fine analysis of the remarkable use of documentary war photography and reproductions of several of the images, see Natalia Brizuela, "Curiosity! Wonder!! Horror!!! Misery!!!!" The Campanha de Canudos, or the Photography of History," *Qui Parle*, Vol. 15, No. 2 (2005), pp. 139–69. http://www.jstor.org/stable/20685695.
16. For published responses to Canudos in the context of the chronology of the military expeditions sent against it, see the Chronology of da Cunha and the "Timetable: The Canudos Campaign" in Euclides da Cunha, Elizabeth Lowe, trans. *Backlands: The Canudos Campaign* (London, Penguin Classics, 2010), pp. xxvii–xxxv. See also the critical apparatus to Euclides da Cunha, *Os Sertões: Campanha de Canudos* (Sao Paulo, Editora Martin Claret, 2007), pp. 607–9.
17. See the extended discussion of Llosa's novel in the second half of chapter 6.
18. For a representative and superbly illustrated survey of the great topographical and natural history studies of the region see Erivaldo Fagundes Neves, Heloisa Mereles Gesteira, *Sertões adentro Viagens nas Caatingas Séculos XVI a XIX* (Rio de Janeiro, Andrea Jakobsson Estúdio, 2012).
19. For the etymological obscurity and continual instability, in terms of meaning, of the words "sertões" and "sertão" in Brazilian Portuguese, see Gustavo Barroso, *Vida e História da palavra Sertão* (Salvador, UFBA, Centro de estudos Baianos, 1983), and Neves, *Sertões Adentro*, pp. 21–43, and the English version of his text "Sertão, backlands, unknown polysemic and controversial," pp. 306–10. The most extreme fictional take on the spiritual centrality of the backlands is *Grande Sertão: Veredas* (1956), translated into English as *The Devil to Pay in the Backlands*. In this vast and finally untranslatable work that mythologizes the existence of the nomadic banditry of the backlands, the *sertão* comes to stand for the entire world.
20. This is not the place to give an account of this hugely influential body of literary and

filmic works. One of the best recent overviews is to be found in Ismail Xavier, "Campo de migrações: Fabiano, Manuel, Ranulfo e os anônimos do sertão." *Significação*, 26: 27–41; also Ismail Xavier, "The Brazilian Backlands as a Site of Migration: From Cinema Novo to Contemporary Cinema," in Pascal Gin and Walter Moser eds., *Mobilités culturelles—Cultural Mobilities* (Ottawa, University of Ottawa Press, 2011), pp. 41–59; http://www.jstor.org/stable/j.ctt5vkc22.6. The most inventive and refreshingly undidactic account of the problems confronting any attempt to locate *Os Sertões* within Brazilian cultural imaginaries is Campos Johnson, *Sentencing Canudos*.

21. Robson Potier, *O sertão virou verso, o verso virou sertão: Sertão e sertanejos representados pela literatura de cordel* (Rio de Janeiro, Novas Edições Acadêmicas, 2016); Gilson Lutosa de Lira, *Lampião O Rei do Cangaço: o Cangaceiro mais temido do Brasil* (Gilson Lira, 2016).
22. Berthold Zilly, "Canudos telegrafado. A guerra do fim do mundo como evento de mídia na Europa de 1897," *Ibero-amerikanisches Archiv, Neue Folge*, Vol. 26, No. 1/2 (2000), pp. 59–96. http://www.jstor.org/stable/43392817.
23. Brizuela, "PHOTOGRAPHY OF HISTORY," *Qui Parle*, Vol. 15, No. 2 (2005), pp. 139–69.
24. These included Afonso Arinos's *Os jagunços*, Dantas Barreto's *Ultima expedição a Canudos*, Manoel Benício's *O rei dos jagunços*, Alvim Martins Horcades's *Descrição de uma viagem a Canudos*, and César Zama's *Libelo republican*; see Leopoldo Bernucci, *A imitação dos sentidos: Prógonos, contemporâneos e epígonos de Euclides da Cunha* (São Paulo, Editora da Universidade de São Paulo, 1995), p. 41.
25. For the shifting historiographies of Canudos, see the painstaking work of Lori Madden, "The Canudos War in History," *Luso-Brazilian Review* 30.2 (1993), pp. 5–22; also "The Canudos War in Marxist Discourse," in *Toward Socio-Criticism: "Luso-Brazilian Literatures,"* ed. Roberto Reis (Tempe, Center for Latin American Studies, Arizona State University, 1991), pp. 189–96; also "Evolution in the Interpretations of the Canudos Movement: An Evaluation of the Social Sciences," *Luso-Brazilian Review* 28.1 (1991), pp. 59–75.
26. Regina Abreu, *O enigma de "Os sertões"* (Rio de Janeiro, Funarte / Rocco, 1998).
27. Putnam, pp. v–vi.
28. There is debate over the number of ex-slaves making up Canudos, but they certainly were substantial, probably between 30 and 50 percent. See Graden, *From Slavery to Freedom in Brazil*, pp. 217–25, and footnotes pp. 286–87.
29. For a discussion of literary works generated by the slavery debates and for Luís Gama's and Joaquim Nabuco's work in particular, see the Conclusion.
30. Manoel Neto, "Canudos na boca do povo," *Revista Canudos* 2.2 (1997), pp. 56–67; for a solid overview of da Cunha and contemporary race/racist theory, see Mónica Ayala-Martínez, "Euclides Da Cunha and the Trap of the Republican Dream," *Chasqui: revista de literatura latinoamericana*, Vol. 34, Special Issue No. 1: *Brazilian and Spanish American Literary and Cultural Encounters* (2005), pp. 57–64; http://www.jstor.org/stable/29742029; for "indians" and Canudos, see Maria Lúcia F. Mascarenhas, "Toda nação em Canudos, 1893–1897: Índios em Canudos (memória e tradição oral da participação dos Kiriri e Kaimbes naguerra de Canudos)," *Revista Canudos* 2.2 (1997), pp. 68–84; Edwin Reesink, "A tomada do coração da aldeia: A

participação dos índios de Massacará na Guerra de Canudos," in *Canudos (Cadernos do CEAS)*, ed. Alfredo Souza Dórea (Salvador, Brazil, Centro de Estudos e Ação Social, 1997), pp. 73–95.
31. A perfect example of such division is Glaucia Villas Bôas, "Casa grande e terra grande, sertões e senzala: duas interpretações do Brasil," *Iberoamericana* (2001–), Nueva época, Año 4, No. 13 (Marzo de 2004), pp. 23–37; http://www.jstor.org /stable/41675388.
32. See Frederic Amory, "Historical Source and Biographical Context in the Interpretation of Euclides da Cunha's Os Sertões," *Journal of Latin American Studies*, Vol. 28, No. 3, Brazil: History and Society (October 1996), pp. 667–85; http://www.jstor.org /stable/157698.
33. Campos Johnson, *Sentencing Canudos*, pp. 9, 138–62. Johnson's work opens up new ways for isolating and understanding da Cunha's exceptionalism, and for evaluating the relative distortions of fiction posing as historiography, or historiographies that mimic fiction. Campos Johnson gives us two now forgotten mythographers of Canudos who narrativized the social experiment in terms that emphasized its unexceptionality or what she terms an "ordinary," or strategically formalized, unexceptional Canudos.
34. Putnam, p. 230.
35. Putnam, p. 230.
36. Graden, "Canudos: The Last Quilombo," in *From Slavery to Freedom in Brazil*, pp. 216–23.
37. For the Palmares connection, see Graden, *From Slavery to Freedom in Brazil*, p. 221.
38. For the manner in which da Cunha skirts around the history of the *quilombos*, and of *Palmares* in particular, see the discussion in chapter 5.
39. For da Cunha's shifting fictionalizations of Canudos prior to *Os Sertões*, see Santos Johnson, *Sentencing* Canudos, p, 106; http://www.jstor.org/stable/j.ctt9qh5sj.8.
40. Johnson, *Sentencing Canudos*, pp. 105–9.
41. For Turner's apocalyptic demonization in the Southern press, see Henry Irving Tragle, *The Southhampton Slave Revolt of 1831: A Compilation of Source Material* (Amherst, University of Massachusetts Press, 1971), pp. 27–171.
42. Putnam, p. 232.
43. da Cunha's excision of black ex-slaves from his narrative has drawn scholarly attention. The great cultural historian of the Brazilian diaspora Gilberto Freyre stated explicitly with regard to black participation in Canudos: "Some of those former slaves became nostalgic for the monarchy and Princess Isabel; it is quite possible that such maladjusted ex-slaves were among those who joined the rebellious whites and *caboclos* under Antônio Conselheiro in their uprising against the Republican Army—an aspect of that struggle between soldiers and backlanders which seems to have escaped the notice of the engineer-sociologist Euclides da Cunha," *Order and Progress: Brazil from Monarchy to Empire* (New York, Knopf, 1970 [1939]), p. 273. For a detailed analysis of the implications of this insight and for the undisputed input of blacks to Canudos, see José Calazans, "Antônio Conselheiro e os "Treze de Maio," in Vincente Barretto ed., *Cadernos Brasileiros 80 Anos de Abolição* 47 (May 1968), pp. 91–95. See also my discussion of Freyre in relation to da Cunha in chapter 6.

44. For a detailed and nuanced account of the origins of da Cunha's racist theory as lying within European texts, and for the significant impact of previously unconsidered French scientific and anthropological texts on race, see Frederic Amory, "Historical Source and Biographical Context in the Interpretation of Euclides da Cunha's *Os Sertoes*," *Journal of Latin American Studies*, Vol. 28, No. 3, Brazil: History and Society (October 1996), pp. 667–85; http://www.jstor.org/stable/157698.
45. Putnam, p. 101.
46. Putnam, p. 475.
47. Putnam, p. 102.
48. Putnam, p. 103. In the Putnam, University of Chicago 1944 edition, p. 71, Putnam appends an extended footnote citing Arthur Ramos, Ronald Pierson, and other scholars who countered da Cunhas's assessment of Afro-Brazilians.
49. For the early narratives of Palmares and its centrality to Southey's *History of Brazil*, see Wood, *Slavery, Empathy and Pornography*, pp. 214–17.
50. Putnam, p. 281.
51. Putnam, p. 103.
52. Gilberto Freyre, *Casa Grande e Senzala*.
53. Jorge Luis Borges, "The Cruel Redeemer Lazarus Morel," in *Collected Fictions* (London, Penguin, 1998), p. 6.
54. See Catherine Hall, "Imperial Man: Edward Eyre in Australasia and the West Indies 1833–66," in Bill Schwarz ed., *The Expansion of England, Race, Ethnicity and Cultural History* (London and New York, Routledge, 1996); and Marcus Wood, *Slavery, Empathy and Pornography*, pp. 395–97.
55. Putnam, p. 72.
56. Putnam, p. xxxix.
57. Putnam, pp. 318–19.
58. Putnam, p. 328.
59. Putnam, pp. 409–10.
60. Putnam, p. 156.
61. Putnam, p. 159.
62. Putnam, p. 161.
63. For the impact of Hegel's construction of Ashanti ritual in monstrist terms, and for the impact of this writing on European literary modernism, see Wood, *Horrible Gift of Freedom*, pp. 22–29.
64. Putnam, p. 226.
65. Putnam, p. 227.
66. Putnam, p. 228.
67. Putnam, p. 228.
68. Putnam, pp. 228–29.
69. Herman Melville, "Benito Cereno," in *The Piazza Tales and Other Prose Pieces, 1839–1860* (Evanston, IL, Northwestern University Press, 1987), p. 224. The murderous power of the rebellious slaves is manifest in the figures of the six Ashanti leaders: "the six hatchet polishers ... sat intent upon their task, except at intervals, when, with the peculiar love in negroes of uniting industry with pastime, two and two they sideways clashed their hatchets together like symbols, with a barbarous din. All six, unlike the generality, had the raw aspect of unsophisticated Negroes."

70. Putnam, p. 702.
71. Da Cunha, *Os Sertões*, pp. 700–702.
72. My translation.
73. Césaire, *Notebook of a Return to My Native Land* (Newcastle, Bloodaxe, 1995), p. 63.
74. For the construction of the orangutan as a separate form of human being closer to the black than the white and a very funny parodic approach to this theory, see Thomas Love Peacock's 1817 novel *Melincourt*. He sends up Lord Monboddo's proto-Darwinian theories of evolution and constructs a plot in which an orangutan named Sir Oran Haut-Ton is a candidate for member of parliament.
75. Michael Taussig, "Culture of Terror—Space of Death. Roger Casement's Putumayo Report and the Explanation," *Comparative Studies in Society and History*, Vol. 26, No. 3 (July 1984), pp. 467–97. The insights into a Space of Death within a Culture of Terror are then developed brilliantly in Taussig, *Shamanism, Colonialism, and the Wild Man: A Study in Terror and Healing* (Chicago, University of Chicago Press, 1991).
76. Putnam, p. xxx.
77. Putnam, p. 17.
78. Putnam, p. 26.
79. Putnam, p. 41.
80. Putnam, p. 42.
81. Putnam, p. 44.
82. Putnam, p. 48.
83. See the discussion of the treatment of the soldiers' bodies and uniforms in chapter 5 above.
84. Putnam, p. 55.
85. Putnam, p. 56.
86. Putnam, p. 57.
87. Putnam, p. 67.

Chapter 6

1. Susanna Hecht, *The Scramble for the Amazon and the Lost Paradise of Euclides da Cunha* (Chicago, University of Chicago Press, 2013).
2. See Courtney Campbell and Nadia Kerecuk, "Special Edition of the Brazilian Bilingual Book Club of the Embassy of Brazil in London," https://sistemas.mre.gov.br/kitweb/datafiles/Londres/en-us/file/cul-bookclub-15-ossertoes.pdf.
3. Robert Bontine Cunninghame Graham, *A Brazilian Mystic: Being the Life & Miracles of Antonio Conselheiro* (London, Heinemann, 1920).
4. Lucien Marchal, *Le Mage du Sertão* (Paris: Librairie Plon, 1952); translated by Charles Duff into English as *The Sage of Canudos* in 1954.
5. *Canudos: diário de uma expedição*, intr. de Gilberto Freyre (Rio de Janeiro, José Olympio, 1939), p. xxv, 186 p.
6. See Fernando Nicolazzi, *À sombra de um mestre. Gilberto Freyre leitor de Euclides da Cunha* (*In the shade of a master. Gilberto Freyre reader of Euclides da Cunha*), http://www.scielo.br/pdf/his/v29n1/15.pdf.
7. All quotations relating to da Cunha's asceticism are from Freyre, *Vida Form e Côr*,

translated as "Euclides da Cunha and the Sertão," in *The Gilberto Freyre Reader*, pp. 200-201.
8. David Cleary, "Race, Nationalism and Social Theory in Brazil: Rethinking Gilberto Freyre," http://www.transcomm.ox.ac.uk/working%20papers/cleary.pdf.
9. Andrews, *Blacks and Whites*; Fernandes, *Negro in Brazilian Society*; Needell, "History, Race, and the State in the Thought of Oliveira Viana"; Needell, "Identity, Race, Gender, and Modernity in the Origins of Gilberto Freyre's Oeuvre"; Degler, *Neither White nor Black*, pp. 110-73; Skidmore, *Black into White*; "Brazil and Race, a Bibliographical Essay," http://www.clas.ufl.edu/users/louthan/Historiography-2/bib-essay.htm.
10. Cleary, "Race, Nationalism and Social Theory in Brazil."
11. Freyre, *Masters and Slaves*, xxi-iii, xliii-iv.
12. For da Cunha and negritude satire, see the comparison with Aimé Césaire in chapter 5.
13. See the opening discussion in chapter 3.
14. Freyre, *Order and Progress*, p. xviii.
15. Freyre, *Order and Progress*, p. 356.
16. Freyre, *Order and Progress*, p. 273.
17. Marshall Hyatt, *Franz Boas, Social Activist: The Dynamics of Ethnicity* (Westport CT, Greenwood Press, 1990), pp. 90-130.
18. Hyatt, *Boas*, pp. viii-x, xli, 87-138; George W. Stocking Jr., *Franz Boas and the Culture Concept in Historical Perspective* (Oxford, Blackwell, 1966), pp. 6-12, 310-30.
19. Hitler, *Mein Kampf*, "XI Nation and Race," pp. 281-325. http://childrenofyhwh.com/multimedia/library/Hitler/mein-kampf.pdf
20. For a balanced account of the relation of Rodrigues's work on African fetishism to the development of racially inflected eugenicist theory, and to wider questions of the shifting discourses of Africanism in Brazilian culture and theory from Machado de Assis to Gilberto Freyre, see Dain Borges, "The Recognition of Afro-Brazilian Symbols and Ideas, 1890-1940," *Luso-Brazilian Review*, Vol. 32, No. 2, Culture and Ideology in the Americas: Essays in Honor of Richard M. Morse (Winter 1995), pp. 59-78; Stefan Kuhl, *The Nazi Connection: Eugenics, American Racism and German National Socialism* (Oxford, Oxford University Press, 2002); and "Eugenics in Brazil, 1917-1940," in Mark B. Adams, ed., *The Wellborn Science: Eugenics in Germany, France, Brazil and Russia* (Oxford, Oxford University Press, 1990), pp. 110-52.
21. For a spirited discussion that passionately argues for the racist limitations of Rodrigues's work together with that of other white Brazilian race theorists, see Ari Lima, "Blacks as Study Objects and Intellectuals in Brazilian Academia," in *Latin American Perspectives* Vol. 33, No. 4, Race and Equality in Brazil: Cultural and Political Dimensions (July 2006), pp. 87-89.
22. Dain Borges, " 'Puffy, Ugly, Slothful, Inert': Degeneration in Brazilian Social Thought, 1880-1940," *Journal of Latin American Studies* 25, 2 (1993), pp. 235-56; J. Edward Chamberlain and Sander L. Gilman, eds., *Degeneration: The Dark Side of Progress* (New York, Columbia University Press, 1985); Daniel Pick, *Faces of Degeneration: A European Disorder, c.1848-c.1918* (Cambridge, Cambridge University Press, 1989); Ann Laura Stoler, "Making Empires Respectable: The Politics of Race and Sexual

Morality in 20th-Century Colonial Cultures," *American Ethnologist* 16, 4 (1989), pp. 634–60.
23. For Freyre and Amado's celebration of the cult of *mestizaje* and for a contextualizing study of the race politics of *Tenda das Milagres*, see Marilyn Grace Miller, *The Rise and Fall of the Cosmic Race* (Austin, University of Texas Press, 2007).
24. Freyre, *Reader*, p. 16.
25. Freyre, *Vida, Forma*, p. 62.
26. Freyre, *Reader*, p. 17.
27. Freyre, *Nordeste* (Rio, 1967), quoted in *Gilberto Freyre Reader*, p. 17.
28. Freyre, *Reader*, p. 18.
29. Celso de Oliveira, "History into Fiction: Euclides da Cunha and Mario Vargas Llosa," *Mediterranean Studies*, Vol. 6 (1996), pp. 158–61. http://www.jstor.org/stable/41166854.
30. The term "tertiary epic" is taken from C. S. Lewis's study of *Paradise Lost*, still a most lucid meditation on the evolution of European epic form and its modern devolutions. In the process of explaining formal aspects of Milton's poem, Lewis sets up a classificatory system for the analysis of epic, which still holds good for novelistic experiment in the New World. In simple summary, Lewis establishes three stages of epic: the primary epic constituted by bedrock classical epic poetry (Homer, Virgil), the secondary epic, which constitutes Renaissance variations on the primary (Spenser, *Faery Queen*; Ariosto, *Orlando Furioso*; Tasso, *Jerusalem Liberata*; Camoes, *Lusíadas*), and the tertiary epic. The tertiary epic keeps certain overriding qualities of the earlier epic form but goes into new, eclectic territories and is concerned with the elaboration of an essentially Romantic approach to probing the consciousness of the individual (Wordsworth, *Prelude*; Byron, *Don Juan*; Ruskin, *Modern Painters*; Carlyle, *French Revolution*; Joyce, *Ulysses*). All these works are quite distinct in formal terms from the novel, and also provide a way of coming at long literary texts that avoids the leveling tendency and confusion of "postmodernism" as a mode of classificatory thought.
31. Renata R. Mautner Wasserman, "Mario Vargas Llosa, Euclides da Cunha, and the Strategy of Intertextuality," *PMLA*, Vol. 108, No. 3 (May 1993), p. 469. http://www.jstor.org/stable/462615.
32. See Wasserman, "Strategy of Intertextuality," pp. 460–73; Celso de Oliveira, "History into Fiction," pp. 157–64. The best consideration of the relationship between da Cunha's and Llosa's texts, which also introduces Cunningham Graham's *Brazilian Mystic* as a plagiaristic stepping stone between the two texts, is Sandra S. Fernandes Erickson and Glenn W. Erickson, "Cunningham Graham's Plagiarism of da Cunha's 'Os sertões' and Its Role in Vargas Llosa's 'La guerra del fin del mundo,'" *Luso-Brazilian Review*, Vol. 29, No. 2 (Winter 1992), pp. 67–85; http://www.jstor.org/stable/3513516. This article also concludes with a useful digest of the major critical comparisons of Llosa and da Cunha.
33. Mario Vargas Llosa, *The War at the End of the World* (London, Faber and Faber, 1984), p. 122.
34. Llosa, *The War*, p. 153–54.
35. Llosa, *The War*, p. 158.
36. Llosa, *The War*, p. 159.

37. Llosa, *The War*, p. 340.
38. Llosa, *The War*, p. 432.
39. Lllosa, *The War*, p. 87.

Conclusion

1. Jorge Luis Borges, "Three Versions of Judas," in *Collected Fictions of Jorge Luis Borges*, transl. Andrew Hurley (London, Penguin, 1998), p. 165 f.n. 3 " . . . Euclides da Cunha notes that in the view of the Canudos heresiarch Antonio Conselheiro 'virtue' is a near 'impiety.'"
2. Some of these photographs are reproduced in Joaquim Nabuco, *My Formative Years*, transl. Christopher Peterson, int. Leslie Bethell (London, Signal Books, and Rio, Bem-te-vi Porduçãos Literarias, 2010), plates section, viii, opposite p. 99.
3. Gilberto Freyre, *Order and Progress: Brazil from Monarchy to Republic* (New York, Alfred Knopf, 1970), p. xvii.
4. The Brazilian text is "O traço todo da vida é para muitos um desenho da criança esquecido pelo homem, e ao qual este terá sempre que se cingir sem o saber . . . Pela minha parte acredito não ter nunca transposto o limite das minhas quatro ou cinco primeiras impressões . . . Os primeiros oito anos da vida foram assim, com certo sentido, os de minha formação instintiva, ou moral, definitiva . . . Passei esse período inicial, tão remoto e tão presente, em um engenho de Pernambuco, minha Província natal. A população do pequeno domínio, inteiramente fechado a qualquer ingerência de fora, como todos os outros feudos da escravidão, compunha-se de escravos, distribuídos pelos compartimentos da senzala, o grande pombal negro ao lado da casa de morada, e de rendeiros, ligados ao proprietário pelo benefício da casa de barro que os agasalhava ou da pequena cultura que ele lhes consentia em suas terras. No centro do pequeno cantão de escravos levantava-se a residência do senhor, olhando para os edifícios da moagem, e tendo por trás, em uma ondulação do terreno, a capela sob a invocação de S. Mateus . . . De todas essas impressões nenhuma morrerá em mim. Os filhos de pescadores sentirão sempre debaixo dos pés o roçar das areias da praia e ouvirão o ruído da vaga. Eu por vezes acredito pisar a espessa camada de canas que cercava o engenho e escuto o rangido longínquo dos grandes carros de bois . . ." Nabuco, *Minha Formação* cap. xx. Electronic text: http://www.iphi.org.br /sites/filosofia_brasil/Joaquim_Nabuco_Minha_Forma%C3%A7ao .pdf. My translation.
5. For an in-depth analysis of the conflict between Ruskin's wonderful aesthetic writing and his abhorrent racist and pro-slavery theory, see Marcus Wood, *Slavery, Empathy and Pornography* pp. 379–96.
6. The Brazilian texts runs "As impressões que conservo dessa idade mostram bem em que profundezas os nossos primeiros alicerces são lançados. Ruskin escreveu esta variante do pensamento de Cristo sobre a infância: 'A criança sustenta muitas vezes entre os seus fracos dedos uma verdade que a idade madura com toda sua fortaleza não poderia suspender e que só a velhice terá novamente o privilégio de carregar.'" Nabuco, *Minha Formação*, electronic text, my translation.
7. I quote here from the excellent translation of Christopher Peterson, in Nabuco, *My Formative Years*, p. 127.

8. John Ruskin, preface to second edition of *Modern Painters*, 1844; Library Edition of the Works of John Ruskin, ed. Cook and Wedderburn, 1906, vol. 3, pp. 30–31.
9. For Assis's bleak recolonization of "the child is father to the man" in the context of unending cycles of slave abuse, see my discussion near the opening of chapter 4.
10. The Brazilian text runs "Nessa escravidão da infância não posso pensar sem um pesar involuntário . . . Tal qual o pressenti em torno de mim, ela conserva-se em minha recordação como um jugo suave, orgulho exterior do senhor, mas também orgulho íntimo do escravo, alguma coisa parecida com a dedicação do animal que nunca se altera, porque o fermento da desigualdade não pode penetrar nela." My translation.
11. See Marcus Wood, "Brazilian and North American Slavery Propagandas: Some Thoughts on Difference," *The Oxford Handbook to Propaganda Studies*, ed. Russ Castronovo (Oxford, Oxford University Press, 2014), pp. 28–49. Here I point out that attempts to elevate Baquaqua's narrative into a position where it can be constructed as a distinct form of Brazilian slave narrative are absurd.
12. *Biography of Mahommah G. Baquaqua* (Detroit, 1854).
13. Baquaqua, pp. 6–7.
14. Baquaqua, p. 10.
15. Baquaqua, pp. 46–47.
16. Baquaqua, p. 47.
17. For Gama's spectacular biography, see Sud. Menucci, *O precursor do abolicionismo no Brasil* (Luiz Gama) (São Paulo, Companhia Editora Nacional, 1937); and Heitor Martins, *Luiz Gama e a consciência negra na literatura Brasileira* (Salvador, Revista Afro-Ásia—Centro de Estudos Afro-Orientais da Universidade Federal da Bahia, no. 17, 1996).
18. For Gama's satiric journalism and collaboration with Agostini, see *Diabo Coxo* (São Paulo, 1864–1865. Redigido por Luiz Gama; ilustrado por Angelo Agostini. Ed. São Paulo, Edusp, 2005). For Agostini's astonishing visual satires on racial abuse and slavery, see Marcus Wood, *Black Milk*, pp. 134–88.
19. Luís Gama, *Primeiras Trovas Burlescas de Getulino* (São Paulo, Tipografia, 1859); second edition, "correct and expanded" (Rio de Janeiro, Tipografia de Pinheiro & Cia., 1861). For an analysis of Gama's formal range and an excellent scholarly edition of all Gama's poetical output, see Lígia F. Ferreira, *Primeiras Trovas Burlescas e outros poemas* (São Paulo, Martins Fontes, 2000); and for the full range of Gama's output, see Ferreira's equally impressive *Com a Palavra Luiz Gama: poemas, artigos, cartas, máximas* (São Paulo, Imprensa Oficial do Estado de São Paulo, 2011).
20. See Marcus Wood, *The Poetry of Slavery*.
21. Cruz e Souza remains scandalously unknown outside Brazil and still awaits an English translator of his major work. For an ambitious if sentimental take on Sousa's life, art, and racial persecution see the multilingual screenplay by Roteiro do Sylvio Back, *Cruz e Sousa O Poeto do Desterro* (Rio de Janeiro, 7Letras, 2000); this includes pp. 121–22 snippets, in English translations by Steven S. White, of the love poems "Black Rose," "Mouth," and "Aspirations," referred to above.
22. Jacques Derrida, *Memoirs of the Blind* (Chicago, University of Chicago Press, 1993), p. 109.
23. Leo Steinberg, *The Sexuality of the Infant Christ in Renaissance Art and Modern Oblivion* (London, Faber and Faber, 1984).

24. For Derrida's discussion of Marvell and its applicability to slavery and memory in the context of J. M. Coetzee and *Foe*, see Wood, *Blind Memory*, pp. 304–5.
25. For the discussion of Freyre's approach to da Cunha on race, see the discussion in the first part of chapter 6.
26. There is a fine anthology of this early Brazilian pornographic verse, Alexei Bueno, *Antologia Pornográfica de Gregório de Mattos a Glauco Mattoso* (Rio, Editora Nova Fronteira, 2004).
27. https://www.literaturabrasileira.ufsc.br/documentos/?action=download&id=37667 #AOSNEGREIROS.
28. "Lundu" is an Angolan word describing both an intensely erotic Afro-Brazilian dance and song. Schneider, *Dictionary of African Borrowings in Brazilian Portuguese*, pp. 173–74: "Lundu: (1) A dance brought to Brazil by Angolan slaves. A single couple enact a passionate love scene by means of the dance, ending with the woman falling into the man's arms in ecstacy . . . The dance also brought to Portugal was banned there by King Manuel I (2) Erotic songs to accompany the *lundu* dance."

Index

Page numbers in italics refer to figures.

abolition, 164
  Anglo-American, 6, 21, 128, 136
  Brazilian slave trade and, 20
  British slave trade and, 22
  North American, 90, 128
abolition in literature, 44
  American poetry, 17
  Anglo-American fiction, 96–97, 246–47
  Luís Gama and, 255
  O Navio Negreiro Tragédia do Mar (The Slave Ship) (Alves), 26
  Os Sertões (The Backlands) (da Cunha), 181–85, 201
  Vozes de África (Voices from Africa) (Alves), 49
Adamastor
  in *Os Lusíadas* (Camões), 49–51
  in *Vozes de África* (Voices from Africa) (Alves), 47–63
Afonso, Paulo de Vivemus, 284n24
Africa, personification of
  Os Escravos (poetry anthology on Brazilian slavery), 58
  Prometeu (Alves), 53
  Vozes de África (Voices from Africa) (Alves), 48–49, 52
Africans, 25
  culture of, 191
  popular portrayals of, 48
Afro-Brazilian culture, 2, 4, 6, 38–39
  Amado and, 3
  in da Cunha's *Os Sertões* (The Backlands), 179, 186
  Freyre and, 226
  religion, 199–200
Afro-Brazilians, 65, 85, 213, 227
  in *Os Sertões* (The Backlands) (da Cunha), 171–218
Afro-Catholic cults, 198
Age of Sentiment, 168
Agostini, Angelo, 262
Alea, Tomas Gutierrez, *Ultima Cena* (Last Supper) (film), 247
Alves, Castro, 1–2, 5–9, 263
  ambiguity and, 23–46
  "O poeta dos Escravos" (the poet of the slaves), 14
  slavery and, 9, 13, 245, 254–55
  translation of, 278n2
Alves, Castro, works by
  A Cachoeira de Paulo Afonso (The Paulo Afonso Waterfall), 14, 47–57, 63–81, 264
  Os Escravos (poetry anthology on Brazilian slavery), 47, 53
  Gonzaga, 13
  O Navio Negreiro Tragédia do Mar (The Slave Ship), 9, 13–47, 63, 65, 68–69, 129–30, 279n4
  Prometeu, 53
  Vendavel Maravilhoso (Most Marvelous Tempest), 13
  Vozes de África (Voices from Africa), 47–63, 65, 67, 69
Amado, Jorge, 13, 85, 191, 270–71, 273
  books burned by Vargas dictatorship, 3
  Brazilian culture memory, 3–6
  colonization, 3–6
  early political work, 3–5
  exile from Brazil, 3
  translation of, 277n3
Amado, Jorge, works by
  ABC of Castro Alves, The, 13

Amado, Jorge, works by *(continued)*
  Donna Flor e seus dois maridos (Dona Flor and Her Two Husbands), 4
  Gabriela, Cravo e Canela (Gabriella, Clove and Cinnamon), 4–5
  Jubaiabá, 3
  O Sumiço da Santa (The War of the Saints), 4
  Tenda dos Milagres (Tent of Miracles), 4–5, 230, 277n6
  Terras do sem fin (The Violent Land), 3
American Civil War, 17, 135, 249
Amistad, 247
animal fables, 177
  "Ideas of a Canary" ("Idéias do Canário") (Assis), 157–62
  "Incident of the Donkey" in *Esau and Jacob* (Assis), 157–62
  in Sub-Saharan Africa, 158
  Tales of the Old Plantation (Harris), 158
animalization, 195
anti-Semitism, 228
antislavery legislation
  Assis and, 115–20
  satire of, 115–20
Antonio Beato ("Pious Anthony"), 203–4
Arionos, Afonso, *Os jagunços*, 180
Ashanti culture, 199–200
Assis, Machado de, 1–2, 5–7, 11–12, 15, 221, 227, 263, 271
  criticism of, 85–86
  emancipation in a global marketplace, 122–34
  Freyre's critique of, 226
  Heinrich Heine and, 122–34
  Laurence Sterne and, 138, 157–62
  Law of the Free Womb (Law of 28 September) and, 116–17
  Marxist analysis of, 87
  mature period, 286n15
  as mixed-race author, 82–90
  Nabuco and, 248–54
  parody and, 87–88
  race and, 82–83
  reception in US, 277n2
  Rio de Janeiro, 9
  slavery and, 9, 11, 86–90, 109–15, 132, 153, 157–62, 245, 248–55
  social criticism and, 87–88, 120

Assis, Machado de, works by
  "Among Saints," 118, 120
  O Caso da Vara (The Case of the Stick), 90–104
  Counselor Ayres' Memorial (Memorial de Ayres), 1, 82, 120, 122–34
  O Enfermero ("The Companion"), 104–9
  Esaú e Jacób (Esau and Jacob), 1, 82, 120–21, 157, 159
  "O Espelho, Esboço de uma teoria da Alma Humana" ("The Mirror, Outline of a New Theory of the Human Soul"), 104
  "Eterno" (Eternal), 112–15
  "Ideas of a Canary" ("Idéias do Canário"), 157–62
  Memórias Póstumas de Brás Cubas (The Posthumous Memoirs of Brás Cubas), 1, 10, 82–134, 135–70, 250
  Pai contra Mãe (Father against Mother), 85–87, 92–104, 288n35
  "Um homem célebre" ("A Celebrity"), 117–18
Auschwitz, 36, 227
Austen, Jane, 9, 153
Azevedo, A. J. W., *Polka-Lundu*, 119

Baldwin, James, 90
Balzac, Honoré de, *Sarrasine*, 27
Baquaqua, Mahommah G., 1, 255–61
Barreto, Francisco Moniz, 271
Barreto, Lima, 86
Barreto, Tobias, 84
Barthes, Roland, *S/Z*, 27
Bastide, Roger, 200
Beckett, Samuel, *The Unnameable*, 40
Behn, Aphra, 18
  Oroonoko, 48, 63, 66
Benício, Manoel, *O rei dos jagunços*, 180
Bernardin de Saint-Pierre, Jacques-Henri, *Paul et Virginie* (Paul and Virginia), 49, 63–64
Bibliothèque Opthalmologique, 18
Biography of Mahommah G. Baquaqua, 248, 255, 257–59
Blake, William, 2, 14, 53
  The Four Zoas (Blake), 71–72
Bloom, Harold, 49, 277n2
Boas, Franz, 227–28

Index

Bom Fim, 289n64
Bom Jesus Conselheiro. *See* Conselheiro, Antônio
Bonita, Maria, 178
Borges, Jorge Luis, 8, 192, 245
   "Three Versions of Judas," 246
Bosch, Hieronymus, *Temptation of St. Anthony*, 10
Boswell, James, *No Abolition of Slavery, or the Universal Empire of Love*, 133–34
Branagan, Thomas, 279n7, 279n8
   Avenia or a Tragical Lament on the Oppression of the Human Species, 16–17
Brás Cubas (character), in *Memórias Póstumas de Brás Cubas* (*The Posthumous Memoirs of Brás Cubas*) (Assis), 138–57, 162, 165, 168–70
Brayner, Aquiles Alencar, 281n25
Brazil (Updike), 5
Brazilian Academy of Letters, 84
Brazilian colonial mythology, 216
Brazilian cultural memory, 3–6, 188
   Amado and, 3–6
   colonization and, 3–6
Brazilian culture, 230
   indigenous, 191
   Luso-Africanist, 225
Brazilian Geographical and Historical Institute, 172
Brazilian Mystic, A (Cunninghame Graham), 218
Brazilian slavery studies, 2, 227–30
Brazil's Academy of Letters, 172
Browning, Robert, *Andrea del Sarto*, 117
Buñuel, Luis, *Death in the Garden*, 232
Burke, Edmund, 11
Byron, Lord, 13

Caesar, Terry, 2
de Camões, Luis Vaz, *Os Lusíadas*, 24, 49–50, 56
Candomblé ceremonies, 5, 65, 198, 200, 243
Canudos rebellion, 2, 10, 183
   da Cunha and, 181, 184, 233–34
   Llosa and, 233–34
Canudos settlement, 193, 216, 227, 244
   Assis and, 174

Afro-Brazilians and, 184
   da Cunha and, 182–84, 201
   former slaves in, 181, 184, 297n28
   Freyre and, 298n43
   Llosa's *La Guerra del fin del Mundo* (*The War at the End of the World*), 237–38
   Luís Gama and, 254–55
   massacre of, 174, 178
   in popular fictions before da Cunha, 172–76
   Os Sertões (The Backlands) (da Cunha) and, 172, 176–81
Carlyle, Thomas, 2
French Revolution, 50, 212, 233
Carneiro, Edison, 281n22
Castro Alves Retrato Falado do Poeta (Castro Alves Picturing the Fame of the Poet) (docudrama), 13
Catholic Church, 202–3
   Brazilian, 173
Cervantes, 85
   Don Quixote, 53
Césaire, Aimé, 225, 235–36
   Notebook of a Return to My Native Land, 9, 12, 207–9
Chagas, Xavier, 42
Chants de Maldoror, Les (Comte de Lautreamont—Isidore Lucien Ducasse), 197
Chekhov, Anton, 87, 245
Chesnutt, Charles, 158
Child, Lydia Maria, "The Devil's Walk in Washington," 44
Cleary, David, 224–25
Cleaver, Eldridge, 246
Coleridge, Samuel Taylor, 11
   Rime of the Ancient Mariner, 15, 23–24, 42, 279n5
Columbus, Christopher, 3, 26, 46
Conrad, Joseph, *Heart of Darkness*, 25
Conselheiro, Antônio, 10, 171, 183, 201, 204, 227, 236–38, 298n43
   da Cunha and, 172–76
   sermons of, 184
   Os Sertões (The Backlands) (da Cunha) and, 184, 197, 238
Cordel literature, 174–75
Corpse of Antonio Conselheiro (Anon.), *174*
Cosimo, Piero di, 72
Coutinho, "Bodarrada," *263*

Cowper, William
  Negro's Lament, The, 259
  "Sweet meat hath sour sauce or the Slave Trader in the Dumps," 279n5
Crowe, Russell, 243
Cruikshank, George, 135
da Cruz e Souza, João, 83–84, 263
  Aspiração (Aspiration), 264
  Boca (Mouth), 264
  Rosa Negra (Black Rose), 264
Cruz e Souza o Poeta do Desterro (Cruz e Souza the Banished Poet) (film), 83–84
da Cunha, Euclides, 1–2, 5–8, 184, 203, 227, 263, 271
  Afro-Brazilianism, 10
  Amazonian epic, 218
  Antônio Conselheiro and, 176, 181, 202
  Assis and, 248–54
  Brazilian landscape and, 230–32
  Freyre and, 219–24
  Hegel and, 212–17
  Latin American fiction, 219
  Llosa and, 234–36
  popular fiction, 172–76
  as postmodern, 220
  race and, 180–81, 200–201, 204–6, 208
  Os Sertões (The Backlands), 1, 10, 171–217, 218–44, 295n4
  slavery and, 10, 182, 204–13, 219, 245, 298n43
Curse of Ham, 59–60

de Sade, Marquis, 9–10, 97
  One Hundred and Twenty Days of Sodom, 152
Debret, Jean Baptiste, 142, 191
Depestre, René, 9, 225
Derrida, Jacques, 264–65
Dias, Bartholomeo, 50
Dickens, Charles, *A Tale of Two Cities*, 233
Diegues, Carlos, *Quilombo* (film), 189–90
Dixon, Thomas, 207
Douglass, Frederick, 261
Duarte, Eduardo de Assis, 93–94

Eliot, T. S., *Four Quartets*, 67
Emancipation Moment, 6–8, 246–47

empathetic theory, 162–70
Empson, William, *Seven Types of Ambiguity*, 281n25

Fanon, Frantz, *Black Skin, White Masks*, 207
Fanshawe, Richard, 50
fascism, 227–30
Faulkner, William, *Absalom, Absalom!*, 89–90, 246
Festa, Lynn, 168
Finley, M. I., *Ancient Slavery and Modern Ideology*, 82
Flaubert, Gustave, 86
  Madame Bovary, 162, 245
de la Fontaine, Jean, 157
Frankfurt school, 88
Freyre, Gilberto, 1, 4–5, 85, 116, 249, 270–71, 273
  gender and, 222
  Hitler and, 225, 228
  landscape and, 230–32
  Llosa and, 218–45
  race and, 222–23, 227, 230
  responses to, 222, 225
  Os Sertões (The Backlands) (da Cunha), 220–21, 231–32
  slavery, 221, 223, 228
Freyre, Gilberto, works by
  Casa Grande e Senzala (The Masters and the Slaves), 222–28
  Ordem e Progresso (Order and Progress: Brazil from Monarchy to Republic), 221–22, 226
  Sobrados e Mocambos (The Mansions and the Shanties: The Making of Modern Brazil), 221
  Vida Forma e Côr, 220–21
Friere, Junqueira, 272

Gama, Luís Gonzaga Pinto da, 1, 61, 247–48
  black women and, 264–65
  da Cunha and, 262
  returned to slavery by his father, 261–62
  sexuality as a theme in, 270–75
  slavery and, 254–55, 261–64, 270–75
Gama, Luís Gonzaga Pinto da, works by
  Minha Mae ("My Mother"), 264–70

Primeiras Trovas Burlescas de Getulino (The First Satiric Ballads of Getulino), 262–64, 275
Quem sou eu? (Who Am I?), 270–72
da Gama, Vasco, 49, 50, 56
Garrison, William Lloyd, 249
Gay, John, 157
Gillray, James, 135
Gledson, John, 87–88
Golden Law (Lei Áurea), Brazilian emancipation law of 1888, 1, 6–7, 82, 86, 88, 180
  Assis and, 120–74
  Counselor Ayres' Memorial (*Memorial de Ayres*) (Assis), 122–34
  Esaú e Jacób (*Esau and Jacob*) (Assis), 120, 122
Governor Eyre of Jamaica, 192
Graham, Robert Cunninghame, 218
Grieco, Agripino, 84
Guevera, Che, 88, 175

Harris, Joel Chandler, *Tales of the Old Plantation*, 158
Hecht, Susanna, 218
Hegel, Georg Wilhelm Friedrich, 48, 199
  da Cunha and, 201, 212–17
  Lectures on the Philosophy of History, 200, 214
  Phenomenology of Spirit, 214
  Philosophy of World History, 48
Heine, Heinrich, 14–16, 29, 40–41
  Assis and, 122–34
  Das Sklavenschiff (The Slave Ship), 15–16, 25, 29, 40–41, 122
Herzog, Werner, *Cobra Verde*, 238
Hitler, Adolf, 225, 227–29
Holocaust, 227
Homer, 24, 35
Hugo, Victor, 2

Iemanjá (Candomblé diety), 65

Jackson, David, *Machado de Assis: A Literary Life*, 85
James, Henry, 86

João Grande (character), in *La Guerra del fin del Mundo* (*The War at the End of the World*) (Llosa), 239–44
John of the Cross, Saint, 26–27
  "La noche oscura del alma," 277n8
Johnson, Campos, 180
Jones, Gayle, Corregidora, 246
Joyce, James, 2, 142, 187
  "The Dead," 87
  Dubliners, 245
  Ulysses, 245

Kafka, Franz, 158
Kingsley, Charles, "Alton Locke," 34
Kipling, Rudyard, 158
Klimov, Elem, *Come and See* (film), 46
Kristeva, Julia, "Motherhood according to Bellini," 269

Law of the Free Womb (Law of 28 September), Assis and, 115–17
Law of the Sixty Year Olds (Saraiva Bill), 116, *121*
  "Among Saints" (Assis) and, 118, 120
Le Négriere (French translation of Heine's *Das Sklavenschiff*), 16
Levi, Primo, 36, 169
Lewis, C. S., 234, 302n30
Leyenda Negra (Black Legend), 192
Lincoln, Abraham, 249
Lispector, Clarice, 158
Llosa, Vargas, 219, 234–36
  da Cunha's *Os Sertões* (The Backlands) and, 233–34
  Freyre and, 218–45
  La Guerra del fin del Mundo (*The War at the End of the World*), 177, 219, 235, 238–44
  João Grande (character), 239–44
  slavery, 237–39, 244
Longfellow, Henry Wadsworth, 16, 19, 22
  Witnesses, The, 18
Lowe, Elizabeth, 176
Lyotard, François, 13

Index

Maciel, Antônio Vicente Mendes. *See* Conselheiro, Antônio
Macumba, 200
mãe-preta (slave wet-nurse), 38–39
Mage du Sertão, Le (Marcal), 218
Mahin, Luísa, 261
Major Abolitionist Poems, The (Alves), 14
Mâles (black Muslims) in Bahia, revolt of, 261–62
Marchal, Lucien, 218
Marvell, Andrew, 264–65
Marx, Karl, 4
Mattas, Gregório da, 271
Maupassant, Guy de, 70, 101
Melville, Herman
  Benito Cereno, 203
  Moby Dick, 21–22, 177
Mengele, 152
Middle Passage, 63, 69, 130, 279n5
  African slaves drowning in, 23, 33
  O Navio Negreiro Tragédia do Mar (The Slave Ship) (Alves) and, 13–46
Milton, John, *Paradise Lost*, 302n30
Miranda, Carmen, 5
Mitchell, Margaret, *Gone with the Wind*, 235
Molière (Jean-Baptiste Poquelin), *Tartuffe*, 116, 290n69
Morrison, Toni, *Beloved*, 152, 246, 269
Morton, Sarah Wentworth, *The African Slave*, 17–18

Nabuco, Joaquim, 1, 221, 247
  A Abolição, 250
  Minha formação (My Formative Years), 250
  slavery and, 248–54
Napoleon, 57, 156
Nazis, 36, 46, 223, 227, 230
Neruda, Pablo, *Canto General*, 67
Newberry, John, *The Life and Adventures of a Fly*, 167
Newton, Richard, 135
Northrup, Solomon, *Twelve Years a Slave*, 135, 246–47
Noyse, Humphrey, 183–84

Oneida Perfectionists, 183–84
Oxum (Candomblé diety), 65

Paff, J. H., "Slave Performing as Carrier for Child," 147
Palmares, 183, 189
parody
  Alves and, 247
  of Anglo-American abolition tradition, 247
  Assis and, 247
  da Cunha and, 247
  Freyre and, 225
  Nazi Germany, 279n5
  of *Rime of the Ancient Mariner* (Coleridge), 279n5
Patterson, Orlando, *Slavery and Social Death: A Comparative Study*, 77
Paulo Afonso Falls, 64, 65
Peckinpah, Sam, *The Wild Bunch*, 116, 236–37
"Pedra Bonita" ("Wondrous Rock"), 198–99
Pedro II, 180
Peixoto, Afrânio, 212–13
Peterson, Amy A., 278n2
Plan of the Slave Ship Brookes, 22
"Polka-Lundus," 118
Pontecorvo, Gilo, *Queimada (Burn)*, 247
Pope, Alexander, *Epistle to Lord Burlington*, 259
Pound, Ezra, *Cantos*, 67
Price, Richard, 224
Princess Isabel, 122–25
Proust, Marcel, 2
Pushkin, Alexander, 13
Putnam, Samuel, 176, 179, 212–13, 221–22

Querino, Manuel, 84

race
  Anglo-American missionary propaganda, 255–56, 261
  da Cunha's *Os Sertões* (The Backlands), 172, 185–96, 209–17, 227
  Nazi Germany and, 223, 230

post World War II, 227
stereotypes, 191–96
racial league tables, 191–96
racial theories
  Amado and, 230
  American, 228
  Brazilian, 223–24, 230
  fascist, 223, 228–30
  Os Sertões (The Backlands) (da Cunha) and, 212–17
racism, 195
  in America, 228
  Aryan, 229
  in Brazil, 222–23, 230
  Conrad and, 185–86
  da Cunha and, 195
  eugenics and, 225
  German, 228
  in Hollywood films, 48
  Tenda dos Milagres (*Tent of Miracles*) (Amado), 277n6
"Regionalist" movement, 3
religions, African
  in Canudo, 196–204
  Os Sertões (The Backlands) (da Cunha), 197–98
religions, Afro-Christian, 241, 244
religions, Canudos, 183, 196–204
Revista Illustrada, 118
Rimbaud, Arthur, *Le Bateau Ivre* (Drunken Boat), 23, 245, 281n23
Rio Olympics of 2016, 289n48
Rocha, Gluber, 178
  Antônio das Mortes (film), 178
  Deus e o Diabo na Terra do Sol (film), 178
  Terra em Transe (film), 178
Rodeur (French slave ship), 18
Rodrigues, Nina
  Os Africanos No Brasil (The Africans of Brazil), 229
  O animismo fetichista dos negros baianos (The Animistic Fetishism of Bahian Black), 229
Romantic poetry, 14, 192
Romanticism, 13, 67
  Brazilian, 16, 22–23
  English, 53, 252

European, 15
French, 26, 58, 63
Romero, Silvero, 84
Rousseau, Jean-Jacques, 25
Ruskin, John, 34–35, 252

Santo Antônio Aparecido. *See* Conselheiro, Antônio
Santos, Hemetério dos, 83
satire
  Amado and, 277n6
  Assis and, 115–22, 131
  Brazilian, 222–25
  da Cunha and, 223–24, 261–64
  empathetic theory and, 162–70
  Freyre and, 222, 230–31
  of racism, 222, 277n6
Schoelcher, Victor, 249
Schwarz, Roberto, 285n1
  A Master on the Periphery of Capitalism: Machado de Assis (Schwarz, trans Gledson), 87–88
  Um Mestre na Periferia do Capitalismo: Machado de Assis (Schwarz), 87
Scorsese, Martin, 178
Scott, Ridley, *Gladiator*, 243
Sebastianic Second Coming, 201
O Senhor do Bom Fim (Black slave church), 289n64
Shakespeare, William, 169
  Hamlet, 27, 259
  King Lear, 169
Sharpe, Granville, 22
Shelley, Percy Bysshe, *Prometheus Unbound*, 14, 70
Sitwell, Edith, "Gold Coast Customs," 201
Slave Coast in Recife, 4
slave diaspora, 22–23, 47, 254
slave narratives, 1, 200, 248
  Anglo-American fiction and, 86, 254
  North America and, 106, 135
slave owners
  Alves and, 11
  Assis and, 90–91, 137, 152
slave poetry, of Luís Gama, 261–64
slave power nations, 2, 22
slave revolt, Virginia, 184
Slave Ships, The (Whittier), 18–19

slave trade, 15-16
  Alves and, 21-22, 278n2
  American poets and, 17
  Atlantic, 1-2, 6-7, 13, 88, 245
  Brazil and, 20-21
  England and, 15
  France, 15
  Freyre, 13
  Holland and, 15
  Portugal and, 15
  Os Sertões (The Backlands) (da Cunha), 186-87
slave women, rape and, 66
slave-riding scene, in *Memórias Póstumas de Brás Cubas* (*The Posthumous Memoirs of Brás Cubas*) (Assis), 146
slavery, 6
  Afro-Brazilians and, 171-218
  American poetry, 17
  Brazil and, 2, 6-7, 14, 61, 82, 87, 227, 246, 255
  A Cachoeira de Paulo Afonso (The Paulo Afonso Waterfall) (Alves), 63-64, 66, 80
  Casa Grande e Senzala (*The Masters and the Slaves*) (Freyre), 221
  O Caso da Vara (The Case of the Stick) (Assis), 91-104
  horrors of, on public display, 91-104
  "Ideas of a Canary" ("Idéias do Canário") (Assis), 162
  La Guerra del fin del Mundo (*The War at the End of the World*) (Llosa), 237-39
  Laurence Sterne and, 162-70
  Memórias Póstumas de Brás Cubas (*The Posthumous Memoirs of Brás Cubas*) (Assis), 1, 140-42, 144-45, 151-52, 156, 162-70
  Minha Mae ("My Mother") (Gama), 264-70
  O Navio Negreiro Tragédia do Mar (The Slave Ship) (Alves), 13-46
  North America and, 65, 90, 106, 128, 135, 228
  Pai contra Mãe (Father against Mother) (Assis) and, 91-104
  paternalism and, 248-54
  Portuguese, 58
  Os Sertões (The Backlands) (da Cunha) and, 171-245
  translation of English poetry about, 278n2
  Vozes de Africa (Voices from Africa) (Alves) and, 62
slavery, memories of, 8-10, 171-72
  Os Sertões (The Backlands) (da Cunha), 216-17
slavery, urban
  Assis, Machado and, 82, 87
  Tristram Shandy, 139
slaves, 73-74, 107, 109-15
  in "Dona Paula" (Assis), 110-12
  forced to dance on ship's deck, 36
  suicides on the Middle Passage, 68-69
slaves, former, in North America, 228
slaves, torture of, in *Pai contra Mãe* (Father against Mother) (Assis), 93, 95-96
Smart, Christopher, *Jubilato Agno*, 71
Soul on Ice (Cleaver), 246
Southerne, Thomas, 48
Southey, Robert, 190
"Sailor Who Served in the Slave Trade, A" 279n5
Stahl, Augusto, photo of Paulo Afonso Falls, 64, 65
Steinberg, Leo, 269
Sterne, Laurence, 9, 85-86
  animal vignettes, 164
  Assis and, 138, 157-62
  Memórias Póstumas de Brás Cubas (*The Posthumous Memoirs of Brás Cubas*) (Assis), 159, 162-70
  Slave Ship (*Slavers Throwing Overboard the Dead and Dying, Typhoon Coming On*), 162-70
  theory of sentiment, 164
Sterne, Laurence, works by
  A Sentimental Journey through France and Italy, 139, 159-61, 164
  Tristram Shandy, 143, 159, 164-65, 167-68
Stowe, Harriet Beecher, 16
  Key to Uncle Tom's Cabin, A, 137
  Uncle Tom's Cabin, 16, 63, 90, 98, 101, 136-37, 235

Styron, William, 237
  Confessions of Nat Turner, 234
"Subaltern Studies," 181
Surviving Prisoners at Canudos (Anon.), 175

Tarantino, Quentin, *Django Unchained*, 136, 247
Tartar Stundists, 183
Taussig, Michael, 210
Teixeira, Múcio, 84
Tennyson, Alfred Lord, *Maud*, 66–67
Turner, J. M. W., 20–22, 25, 29
  Slave Ship (Slavers Throwing Overboard the Dead and Dying, Typhoon Coming On), 21, 25, *31*
Turner, Nat, 184

Ulysses, 24
Underground Railroad, 65
Updike, John, 5

Valongo slave market, Rio, 151, 289n48
Veloso, Caetano, 23, 26
  "O Navio Negreiro" on album *Livro*, 281n22
Verger, Pierre, 200
Verissimo, José, 38

Viana, Oliveira, *As Populações Meridionais do Brasil* (The Southern Populations of Brazil), 229
Vigny, Alfred de, *Eloa*, 58
Virgin of the Sorrows, 269–70

Wagner, *Tristan und Isolde*, 70
Whitman, Walt, 78
  Leaves of Grass, 80–81
Whittier, John Greenleaf, 15–16, 18–19
Wilberforce, William, 249
Wilde, Oscar, 242
Woolf, Virginia, 86
Wordsworth, William, 68, 135
  Assis and, 144, 148–49, 248–54
  Nabuco and, 248–54
  Ode: Intimations of Immortality from Recollections of Early Childhood, 252

Xavier, Ismail, 178

Yeats, William Butler, 8
Young Gentleman and Lady's Magazine, 168

Zahler, Craig C., *Bone Tomahawk* (film), 196
Zong (slave ship), 18, 21–22, 29–30
Zumbi, Ganga, 189–90

www.ingramcontent.com/pod-product-compliance
Lightning Source LLC
Chambersburg PA
CBHW051536230426
43669CB00015B/2616